Law and Veganism

Law and Veganism

International Perspectives on the Human Right to Freedom of Conscience

Edited by
Jeanette Rowley and Carlo Prisco

LEXINGTON BOOKS
Lanham • Boulder • New York • London

Published by Lexington Books
An imprint of The Rowman & Littlefield Publishing Group, Inc.
4501 Forbes Boulevard, Suite 200, Lanham, Maryland 20706
www.rowman.com

6 Tinworth Street, London SE11 5AL, United Kingdom

British Library Cataloguing in Publication Information Available

Library of Congress Cataloging-in-Publication Data

Names: Rowley, Jeanette, editor. | Prisco, Carlo, editor.
Title: Law and veganism : international perspectives on the human right to freedom of conscience / edited by Jeanette Rowley, Carlo Prisco.
Description: Lanham : Lexington Books, [2021] | Summary: "Law and Veganism explores the rights of vegans and how vegans can be protected from discrimination. Framed in a legal and socio-political context, this book will appeal to the broadest range of legal practitioners and legal and critical scholars alike"—Provided by publisher.
Identifiers: LCCN 2021020448 (print) | LCCN 2021020449 (ebook) | ISBN 9781793622617 (cloth) | ISBN 9781793622624 (epub)
Subjects: LCSH: Vegans—Legal status, laws, etc. | Veganism—Political aspects. | Food law and legislation—Philosophy.
Classification: LCC K3253 . L39 2021 (print) | LCC K3253 (ebook) | DDC 344.04/23—dc23
LC record available at https://lccn.loc.gov/2021020448
LC ebook record available at https://lccn.loc.gov/2021020449

Disclaimer: The information in this book for discussion only and does not constitute legal advice. If you are concerned about discrimination or human rights violations, you should seek advice from a lawyer who will discuss with you the merits of your case. The editors and chapter authors accept no liability for losses incurred as a result of acting on information given in this book. The editors and contributors to this volume do not necessarily agree with the legal provisions discussed, or with each other regarding enacted law and social and political issues related to veganism and anti-speciesist activities.

Contents

Foreword

Richard Twine

As more academic reflections on the rise of veganism emerge, coalescing around 'vegan studies,'[1] a further strand of critical animal work reaches into food studies, examinations of sustainable transitions and so much more. This time, though, the focus seems inescapably to be upon the human, and is therefore potentially suspicious. However, the creation of vegan culture, rather than being an anthropocentric distraction from hands-on work for the benefit of nonhuman animals, is the very contestation of the human required for human/animal relations to fundamentally shift. It is surely a measure of the potency of anthropocentrism as an intransigent social norm that the identity and practice of veganism itself may require legal protections.

What of this anthropocentrism? Calarco defines it as "the view that human beings (in opposition to animals and other nonhuman beings) are of supreme importance in ethical, political, legal, and existential matters . . .[2] Among the primary characteristics of anthropocentrism are: (1) a narcissistic focus on human exceptionalism; (2) a binary account of human–animal differences; (3) a strong moral hierarchy that ranks human beings over animals and other nonhuman beings; (4) a tendency to de- and subhumanise certain populations; and (5) institutions that aim to protect and give privilege to beings deemed fully human." This is an important definition, because it further embeds anthropocentrism within other forms of power, and signals just why it may be such a pivotal part of the social order. Researchers of vegan jurisprudence[3] are at the forefront of understanding challenges to that social order. The same might be said of linguists, or social scientists listening to vegan narratives of successful, yet fraught, transition. Therein lies one reason why vegan research is important: it is sociologically intriguing.

Vegans are space invaders,[4] pivoting between stridency and hiding in plain sight—networking food fairs and potlucks, promoting the gradual creep of 'vegan capitalism' (a transitionary phase, one hopes), embedding themselves in local, regional, national, and transnational registers, having everyday conversations, and contesting institutions and their omnivorous normativity. None of these activities are yet nearly enough, but they are a beginning. This makes it an especially interesting time to examine whether anthropocentric cultures are making or restricting space for vegan practice. This should pique the interest of social scientists and legal scholars, irrespective of any direct concern with veganism.

Vegans are killjoys,[5] reweaving dominant meanings of happiness itself. How could an entire ideology of mass violence have convinced so many of happy meat, of happy cows, of happy birthday parties in fast food 'restaurants' serving up high-fat, high-salt misery? The appeal of consuming less violently should not be underestimated. If an omnivore could choose to be seated for two hours in the company of vegans, or on the killing floor of a slaughterhouse, which would they choose? Ultimately, which would they really find more intelligible? How does one make sense of the chasm between 'normal,' assumedly happy, consumption and the mass violence inherent in it? Odd perhaps to pair 'vegan' with 'kill,' but killjoy-ing is a bloodless, creative practice, foregrounding the joy of emancipation from constraining ideology. That might be feminist or queer camaraderie in its original theorization,[6] or the sharing of empathy for, and with, nonhuman animals in the *vegan* re-making of joy.

But it is not exactly a shared vision yet. Discrimination against vegans? Marginalizing vegans? Outrage at vegan parenting? Veganism as pathological? Legal attempts to prevent plant-food companies using the signifiers 'milk,' 'meat' and 'cheese'? No surprise *at all* at the defense of the social norms that are deeply constitutive of the social order. Such practices and discourses are human exceptionalism protecting itself. Employment and social rights extend the practice of veganism, further embedding societal change. For example, protections to ensure access to vegan food in institutions such as schools, universities, hospitals, and prisons, leveraged justly via equality laws and codes of practice, can embed food-related vegan practices widely in the social milieu. Although the struggle for eating 'options' may be deferential to an omnivorous core and is enabled within a context of neoliberal individual consumer choice, it does at least achieve nascent normalization. Ultimately, veganism as a secular belief system (or one that individuals tether to their religiosity) has as much right to protection as is typically accorded to religious belief in cosmopolitan liberal 'democracies.'

Critical animal studies has interrogated some of the foundational concepts of law in such societies—reason, autonomy, individual rights,[7] and so it is entirely correct that a vegan jurisprudence would critically examine notions of 'belief,' 'rights' and the 'individual.' A focus on practice at larger scales, in institutions, and across social systems, also assuages any lingering doubts over the human vegan focus, returning us to questions around the legality and justness of the machinery of the animal-industrial complex.

This complex is a key player in climate, biodiversity, and human health crises, and multitudes of studies and reports argue for the co-benefits of meat and dairy reduction—yet the complex refuses to budge. Questions related to the legality of our dominant political economy, therefore, need to be asked. What can be concluded when international climate emissions agreements remain silent on the food system? Or when national dietary guidelines continue to naturalise animal consumption as necessary? Or, when countries introduce so-called ag-gag laws, hoping to conceal the violence of the animal-industrial complex? Here, we see anthropocentrism protecting itself at grander scales—but we begin to understand that 'human-centredness,' far from benefitting a falsely homogenised human, is of *detriment to the many* and of short-term benefit only to the already rich few.

We then find ourselves in vital debates around the need for a plant-based food system[8] wondering how to birth the new when the old refuses to die. We need to expose the ways in which governments and transnational players like the FAO intervene (contra neoliberalism) to favour the animal-industrial complex, and what legal avenues may be open to civil society to exert political pressure for plant-based food systems. The Stop Ecocide campaign and child-led, James Hansen–inspired lawsuits against aged, white, male governments may point the way. It seems fair that a capitalist pre-occupation with the profitability of the animal-industrial complex does not somehow matter more than the right to life, matter more than a viable environment for future generations of human children and other species.

When thought is directed at these grander scales, the vitality, urgency, and intersections of veganism become clearer. Since anthropocentrism is enfolded into the histories and presents of capitalism, colonialism, and male domination, to contest really 'presses a button'; it 'touches a nerve'—because veganism questions the underlying taken-for-granted model of the human which has been crucial to these projects. The chapters in this volume speak to many of the topics I have mentioned and there are several illuminating country reports. Books like this are themselves important historical markers of the early and fraught normalization of veganism. We might say that Vegan Jurisprudence is to Animal Law as Vegan Studies is to Critical Animal Studies, but these demarcations matter less than a further reason why vegan research is important: it is wholly imperative to the crises of our time.

NOTES

1. Jodey Castricano, and Rasmus Simonsen, eds. *Critical Perspectives on Veganism* (London: Palgrave MacMillan, 2016); Laura Wright, ed. *The Routledge Handbook of Vegan Studies* (London: Routledge, 2021).

2. Matthew Calarco, *Animal Studies—The Key Concepts* (London: Routledge, 2021), 18.
3. Jeanette Rowley, *Towards a Vegan Jurisprudence: The Need for a Reorientation of Human Rights* (New York: Lexington Books, 2020).
4. Nirmal Puwar, *Space Invaders: Race, Gender and Bodies Out of Place* (Oxford: Berg, 2004).
5. Sara Ahmed, *The Promise of Happiness* (Durham: Duke University Press, 2010); Richard Twine, "Vegan Killjoys at the Table—Contesting Happiness and Negotiating Relationships with Food Practices," *Societies* 4, no. 4 (2014): 623-639.
6. Sara Ahmed, *The Promise of Happiness* (Durham: Duke University Press, 2010).
7. Maneesha Deckha, "Critical Animal Studies and Animal Law," *Animal Law* 18 (2012): 207-236.
8. Morris, C., Kaljonen, M., Aavik, K., et al. "Priorities for social science and humanities research on the challenges of moving beyond animal-based food systems." *Humanities and Social Sciences Communication* 8, 38 (2021).

BIBLIOGRAPHY

Ahmed, S. *The Promise of Happiness* Durham: Duke University Press, 2010.

Calarco, M. *Animal Studies—The Key Concepts*. London: Routledge, 2021.

Castricano, J. and Rasmus Simonsen. eds. *Critical Perspectives on Veganism*. London: Palgrave MacMillan, 2016.

Deckha, M. (2012) "Critical Animal Studies and Animal Law," *Animal Law* 18: 207-236.

Morris, C., Kaljonen, M., Aavik, K. et al. "Priorities for social science and humanities research on the challenges of moving beyond animal-based food systems." *Humanities and Social Sciences Communication* 8, 38 (2021).

Puwar, N. *Space Invaders: Race, Gender and Bodies Out of Place*. Oxford: Berg, 2004.

Rowley, J. *Towards a Vegan Jurisprudence: The Need for a Reorientation of Human Rights*. New York: Lexington Books, 2020.

Twine, R. (2014) "Vegan Killjoys at the Table—Contesting Happiness and Negotiating Relationships with Food Practices." *Societies* 4, no. 4 (2014): 623–639.

Wright, L. ed. *The Routledge Handbook of Vegan Studies*. London: Routledge, 2021.

Acknowledgments

This important book would not have been possible without the support and enthusiasm of the individual contributors, who have given their time and energy so generously. We are proud of our collaboration and privileged to have worked with you all; especially given that a few months after we all started this project, the world was struck by a pandemic!

We would especially like to thank Lexington Books for giving us the opportunity to publish this volume, and Becca for her help and support throughout the drafting and publication processes.

We owe a huge debt of gratitude to all the vegans who have contacted us over the years. Our thinking around vegans' rights and equality issues, and the support we are able to offer vegans in difficult circumstances, have become more finely tuned as a result of listening and working with you.

Several people have gone the extra mile to support this volume. Nicolas Feil's help with German translation was invaluable. Nicolas is a final-year undergraduate student at the London School of Economics and currently leads Food4Thought, a plant-based university campaign in the United Kingdom. He has previously interned with Animal Ethics and ProVeg International. Karen Atkinson's faultless professionalism, enthusiasm, positive energy and 'fresh pair of eyes' on redrafts were very helpful during the final stages of revision. Mary Ann Cameron's interest in the volume and support for the French translation was invaluable. Her knowledge of the French language is as interesting and insightful as it was helpful. Richard Twine's excellent insights on the context for the volume succinctly offer the reader various points of entry to wider stands of critical thinking in vegan studies.

We would also like to extend our thanks to Carolina Academic Press for giving us permission to reproduce content in Adam Karp's contribution to this volume, some of which is taken from a chapter in his publication *Understanding Animal Law* (2016).

The contributors to this volume would also like to thank everyone who supported them throughout the development of their drafts: Camille Labchuk is grateful to Benjamin Oliphant for his invaluable comments on the ideas presented in Camille's and Krystal-Anne's chapter; to participants in various international symposia on vegan rights hosted by the International Vegan Rights Alliance, and later the International Rights Network; and above all, to Adam Knauff for his courage and tenacity. Krystal-Anne Roussel would like to thank her co-author, Camille Labchuk, for her unwavering support, knowledge and mentorship, and Adam Knauff for his outstanding bravery and commitment to advancing vegan rights.

Thank you also to Alyssa Berris for her support, and to another enthusiastic supporter (who wishes to remain anonymous) for so generously lending us a computer to complete this publication project following a catastrophic motherboard failure.

We are grateful to all the vegans and non-vegans alike who have shown their interest in this project and made time to think through and discuss with us some of the issues presented. Last but by no means least thank you, our readers, for your interest in this book.

Introduction

Should we consider veganism as a right? Should we consider it as a duty? Answering these questions raises complex issues, and opinions given in response are likely to be fundamentally divided between vegan and non-vegan people.

Many vegans, if not all of them, will state that their refusal to eat animals and derivatives is not an option, but must be considered mandatory, since human beings do not own neither animals nor nature. Probably, such a perspective will not be shared by non-vegans, who commonly refer to the so called 'law of nature' to enforce their right to eat or exploit any nonhuman animals.

In complex, consumerist, societies, the degree and complexity of interactions and the number of goods and products available often prevents us from acquiring direct knowledge of what lies 'behind' behaviors, product ingredients and their origins. Of course, most of us can say that we are not directly exploiting, killing or participating in the use of animals when we think about our personal actions. On the other hand, how much do we know about the shampoo that we purchase at the supermarket, about the origins of fibers and the processes used to make our clothes, or about the ingredients in the food or medications administered to us when we are in hospital? How is veganism perceived in different countries, and how do different governments, public and private bodies, and individual people relate to and deal with instances of veganism? These are some of the questions raised in this book for discussion and debate, and insights and answers are given by authors from around the world, all experienced in some way in veganism, law and rights.

Veganism is not new; there is a plethora of historical literature evidencing the human desire and practice to live with compassion and care for other animals. But being vegan in 2021 can still present challenges. In fact, sometimes, it will imply that you must be ready to fight for your right to practice your moral convictions, perhaps even file a lawsuit on the grounds of unlawful discrimination or unlawful interference with the right to be vegan; to protect other animals, the environment, for world food security and for good health.

It is our opinion that supporting veganism is the best way to support animal rights because the general rule of law still does not recognize animals as rightholders: they are still considered 'things,' and, therefore, their interests are not taken adequately taken into account by law as a matter of justice. This is the issue with so-called 'animal protection laws' that are actually written to protect the interest of human beings rather than to liberate nonhuman animals from human domination and exploitation.

Although supporting human rights to support animal rights may, at first, appear meaningless, or even wrong, we believe that it remains the most effective way to protect the animals against exploitation and killing: at least, as long as our laws fail to recognize other animals as rightholders. On this view, we see no differences between claims for animal rights and those for the human rights of vegans: this leads us to the conclusion that the positive development of veganism in law deals with both issues.

Considering that almost every country on Earth, if not all of them, rejects the same idea of ownership of rights by animals, it should not be surprising that animal 'protection' laws around the world are very similar, and that, in Western countries, they are almost identical. Things are different when we compare how instances of veganism are treated in different countries, and this comparison is very helpful, not only to take a picture of the present, but also to learn from each other and find inspiration for a more optimistic future.

The contributors to this book rightly identify that the daily practices of vegans are strictly connected with one of the most fundamental and important human rights: the right to freedom of belief, and this explains why the countries more orientated to recognizing freedom as a commonly shared value are also more likely to be open to recognizing and supporting veganism and the practices of vegans.

Many authors of this book are lawyers, others are scholars, some are both, while others are vegans who have been involved with the law and legal reform in important ways. Through their knowledge and experiences, they reveal how complicated it can be to be a vegan in modern societies, discuss the legal, social, and political issues involved, and offer legal and personal insights on facing the challenges observed.

Case by case, the reader will be guided into what we could describe as 'the struggle for veganism': some vegans will experience favorable outcomes, while others will experience defeat. The hope is that the chapters in this book will inspire further interdisciplinary discussion and motivate urgent action now and in the future.

We hope that this volume and future works like this will give confidence to vegan people, and we hope that their freedom to live with compassion and care for others will be actively supported by those who have legal, political or social power to influence and to help bring about real change. We hope that through this new movement of vegan validation, vegans will no longer experience discrimination or interference with their moral practice, not because we merely become more able to remove obstacles, but because we encourage a paradigm shift in social policies and practices so that they offer tangible alternatives for the development of a mainstream practice of veganism that supports animal liberation and the additional, related, urgencies of our time.

As noted above, our societies are very complex, and many aspects of our lives are, if not controlled, at least intertwined with consumer conglomerates, government entities and powerful corporations through our interactions with them: this fact of our lives is complicated, and it is difficult to be fully aware of the potential indirect impact of our choices. For example, in some countries, just being able to receive a non-dairy food option could be considered a success, but we cannot forget that, as taxpayers, we are likely to still be involved in animal exploitation, for example in circumstances where governments finance dairy industries with tax revenues.

Ultimately, the next step in actively promoting vegan people's rights will be no longer limited to single actions taken by individuals but is likely to include class/collective actions. Currently, in most countries being vegan means to be a pioneer, and being a vegan legal scholar or lawyer is even more pioneering—but once this situation changes, hopefully through books such as this, even influencing the use of public funds will become possible.

Of course, some changes to the status quo require political intervention rather than court action, but these two avenues for change are intertwined: laws are the result of politics, as well as common values: the entire system of rights and duties cannot be separated from society's opinions and the politics that reflects them.

The reader could consider this book as advocating another step toward animal rights and human rights, as well as a tool for vegans to better understand, determine and defend their rights and claims, while even non-vegans should recognize in it a 'brick in the wall' against discrimination.

Over the last decade or so, scholars, lawyers and engaged lay vegans have had many discussions about vegan rights and discrimination as issues intrinsic to animal rights, but the final frontier remains intact: the one that concerns more directly the status of other animals. Before passing that frontier, we will need to defeat discrimination against vegans: it is not merely fanciful and engaging—it is a necessary step to go further and beyond. To give effect to the rights of animals, we must recognize and defend the human right to care about them.

I [Carlo] can still remember the day when the Italian court ruled that my client's son should eat a vegan diet, rather than omnivorous diet, despite his father opposing the idea. It was the first time a ruling such as this had been made: in my country, the outcome of all other similar cases was the opposite. One thing made this victory even more remarkable: it was the fact that the judge, during the first hearing, had stated that making a child eat a vegan diet would have been a wrongful imposition. In the end, even after medical trials, tests, and by presenting lots of supporting evidence, the same judge had to change her mind and rule in our favor. That case proved how a well-argued and sustained defense can make the truth so clear that even well-ingrained prejudices cannot prevail.

Our wish is that this book can contribute to the truth at any level, to create more awareness and to help fight against prejudices that perpetuate injustice.

THE STRUCTURE OF THE BOOK

Following the foreword from Richard Twine, which explains the context for the study of vegan law, the chapters have been arranged in the following order: First are those that discuss veganism in the context of country-specific constitutional arrangements, and vegan litigation. In this section, there are contributions from Angela Radich (Australia), Camille Labchuk and Krystal-Anne Roussel (Canada), Adam Karp (USA), Ralf Müller-Amenitsch (Germany), and Carlo Prisco (Italy).

The second theme concerns the provision of vegan food. In the section covering this theme, Nuno Alvim (Portugal) discusses Portuguese legislation for the provision of vegan food, and Joe Wills (UK) offers a critical examination of animal agriculture in the context of the international right to food.

The third section introduces discussions on specific issues relating to the legal protection of vegans and the growth of veganism. In this section, Marie Laffineur-Pauchet (France) highlights the cultural and socio-political complexities for the growth of veganism and the legal protection of vegans. Matthew Overton discusses the legal meaning of 'belief' and the potential insecurity of protection for vegans in the UK. Jeanette Rowley and Edie Bowles discuss the law applicable to the protection of vegans in education in the UK, and Jade Elliott-Archer explains the law applicable to the treatment and protection of vegans with eating disorders in the UK. Also, in this section, Jordi Casamitjana discusses his recent court action against his employer for discrimination against him as a vegan and explains why, in his view, it is important that vegans have the protection of law.

The book ends with a cautionary afterword from Sorin Ionescu (Canada), who discusses the utility of law to protect vegans and advance veganism. Sorin explains failed attempts to bring about legislation for the provision of vegan food in public refectories and highlights the complex socio-political challenges for the anti-speciesist journey ahead.

The chapters in this book will be of interest to a wide range of readers, including practicing lawyers, academics working in law, critical legal studies, vegan and critical animal studies, lay readers, and anti-speciesist activists. To cater to all, references in individual chapters that point to the same formative articles in international treaties or elements of human rights and equality law are repeated and remain in place to offer the reader a full understanding of each individual chapter without the need to read the book cover to cover or to search the pages for relevant legal context or additional information. This is particularly helpful for those who have specific interests, for example, in the law applicable to protection for 'belief,' treatment of vegans with eating disorders in the UK, or vegan legal issues in education.

Chapter One

Veganism and the Law in Australia

Is Discrimination against Ethical Vegans Unlawful?

Angela Radich

1. INTRODUCTION

In Australia, interest in veganism has surged over recent years. This has led to an increase in the availability of vegan products as well as the mainstream acceptance of veganism. It seems that almost every week a new vegan product becomes available in supermarkets, and fast-food restaurants like Hungry Jack's, Domino's and Pizza Hut now have a variety of vegan options. The mainstream acceptance of veganism can also be seen in developments such as the recent vegan certification of Australia's iconic spread, Vegemite, and the extensive vegan cookbook range now being published by *Australian Women's Weekly* magazine (one of Australia's most widely read magazines) including the titles "Vegan in 30 Minutes," "# Vegan Life," and "Super Vegan." These are but a handful of the positive changes in Australia in recent years.

Despite these advances, it appears that still more needs to be done to protect and support the growing number of ethical vegans in Australia. For example, many hospitals, schools and nursing homes continue to provide inadequate meals for vegans, and recently vegan activist James Warden was forced to go hungry while in jail when his request for vegan food was refused.[1] On social media, ethical vegans also report a range of poor treatment, such as negative comments by co-workers and requirements to attend work functions at places of animal exploitation like racetracks. Unsurprisingly, these kinds of issues present obstacles to people both becoming vegan and staying vegan.

In the United Kingdom, in the recent case of *Casamitjana v. The League Against Cruel Sports*,[2] an Employment Tribunal found that ethical veganism is a philosophical belief and therefore a protected characteristic under the *Equality Act 2010* (UK). As a result, discrimination on this basis, including in areas other than employment, is unlawful. This chapter will examine the question of whether ethical vegans are similarly protected from discrimination in Australia. In doing so, consideration will be given to the protections contained in the Australian Constitution, in international human rights treaties, and in Australian anti-discrimination and human rights legislation. Through a consideration of this patchwork of laws, it will become apparent that the protections afforded to ethical vegans in Australia are currently very limited. Nevertheless, there are still opportunities vegans can pursue in seeking both protection and societal change.

2. OVERVIEW OF THE AUSTRALIAN LEGAL SYSTEM

Those unfamiliar with the Australian legal system should note two matters by way of background. First, Australia is a federation of six states (New South Wales, Victoria, Queensland, Western Australia, South Australia and Tasmania) and two main Commonwealth territories (the Australian Capital Territory and the Northern Territory).[3] There are therefore two tiers of legislation relevant to the question of whether discrimination against ethical vegans is unlawful: federal (or Commonwealth) and state/territory. Second, Australia is a common law country, so it is necessary to consider the case law concerning the interpretation of the relevant legislation. In this regard, the highest court is the High Court of Australia, which hears appeals from both federal and state/territory courts. Naturally, courts lower in the Australia court hierarchy are bound to follow the judgments of the High Court. In this chapter, we will consider a number of significant High Court cases.

3. THE AUSTRALIAN CONSTITUTION

In many countries, individual rights are protected in foundational documents such as constitutions or bills of rights. However, the framers of the Australian Constitution rejected a proposal to include an express guarantee of individual rights such as that found in the United States Constitution.[4] They thought that individual rights were best protected by the common law and the legislature.[5] Therefore, the Australian Constitution deals almost exclusively with "the structure and relationship of government rather than with individual rights."[6] For example, it defines the law-making power of the Commonwealth Parliament and enshrines the concept of the separation of powers (i.e.

separation of the legislative, judicial and administrative arms of government).

The Australian Constitution does contain limited protections in relation to religion.[7] Relevantly, section 116 of the Constitution states that "the Commonwealth shall not make any law . . . prohibiting the free exercise of any religion." It is important to note, however, that section 116 merely operates as a fetter on the law-making power of the Commonwealth Parliament, with offending legislation liable to be struck down as unconstitutional.[8] It does not apply to state legislation (but it may apply to territory legislation[9]), nor does it impliedly confer "an independent or free-standing right which, if breached, sounds in damages at the suit of the individual."[10] It therefore provides very little protection against discrimination, even if ethical veganism is found to constitute a "religion" for the purposes of section 116 (which presents its own difficulties—see the further discussion below).

4. INTERNATIONAL HUMAN RIGHTS TREATIES

In *Casamitjana v. The League Against Cruel Sports*,[11] the UK Employment Tribunal considered the scope of section 10 of the *Equality Act 2010* (UK). Section 10 mirrors article 9 of the *European Convention on Human Rights*[12] ("ECHR"), which contains the "right to freedom of thought, conscience and religion."[13] This is the right that appears to have the greatest potential to protect ethical vegans from discrimination.

While Australia is not a party to the ECHR, the right to freedom of thought, conscience and religion has been enshrined in a number of other international human rights treaties ratified by Australia. Of principal importance is the *International Bill of Human Rights*, which includes the *International Covenant on Civil and Political Rights* ("ICCPR").[14] Article 18(1) of the ICCPR provides:

> Everyone shall have the right to freedom of thought, conscience, and religion. This right shall include freedom to have or to adopt a religion or belief of his [or her] choice, and freedom, either individually or in community with others and in public or private, to manifest his [or her] religion or belief in worship, observance, practice and teaching.[15]

In *General Comment No. 22: The Right to Freedom of Thought, Conscience and Religion (Art. 18)* ("General Comment No. 22"), the United Nations Human Rights Committee made clear that the words "religion" and "belief" in article 18 of the ICCPR are to be broadly construed and are not limited to traditional religions.[16] It said:

> The right to freedom of thought, conscience and religion (which includes the freedom to hold beliefs) in article 18.1 is far-reaching and profound; it encompasses freedom of thought on all matters, personal conviction and the commitment to religion or belief, whether manifested individually or in community with others. The Committee draws the attention of States parties to the fact that the freedom of thought and the freedom of conscience are protected equally with the freedom of religion and belief. . . . Article 18 is not limited in its application to traditional religions or to religions and beliefs with institutional characteristics or practices analogous to those of traditional religions.[17]

Unsurprisingly, the United Nations Human Rights Committee also said that the observance and practice of religion or belief may include the observance of dietary regulations.[18]

There are a number of other international treaties that seek to protect the right to freedom of thought, conscience and religion (as well as the right to hold opinions) and to prevent discrimination on those grounds.[19] However, the focus of this chapter will be article 18 of the ICCPR, as it provides the greatest scope for the protection of ethical vegans in Australia. So, what is the legal effect of the ratification of treaties by Australia, and what avenues of redress may they provide to individuals?

4.1 Status of Treaties in Australian Law

While Australia is a party to a range of international human rights treaties, those treaties only have legal force in Australia if validly incorporated into Australian law by statute. The High Court has explained the basis of the rule as follows:

> This principle has its foundation in the proposition that in our constitutional system the making and ratification of treaties fall within the province of the Executive in the exercise of its prerogative power whereas the making and the alteration of the law fall within the province of Parliament, not the Executive. So, a treaty which has not been incorporated into our municipal law cannot operate as a direct source of individual rights and obligations under that law.[20]

The extent to which relevant international treaties have been incorporated into Australian anti-discrimination and human rights legislation is discussed further below.[21] It can be noted at this point, however, that it has been said the level of protection afforded to the right to freedom of religion and belief in Australia is "relatively weak compared to a number of other comparable countries"[22] and that "Australia does not fully satisfy its international human rights obligations relating to freedom of religion and belief as set out in the ICCPR."[23] Significantly, Australia remains the only democracy in the world that has not passed federal legislation directly implementing the ICCPR.[24]

However, even where international treaties have not been incorporated into Australian law by statute, they may still be used by the courts when interpreting legislation[25] and they can also play a part in developing the common law.[26] Additionally, the High Court has held that the ratification of treaties can give rise to "a legitimate expectation" that executive decision-makers will act in accordance with the treaties.[27] That protection is not absolute, however, as the legitimate expectation can be displaced if there is a statutory or executive indication to the contrary.[28] Further, the decision-maker may act contrary to the relevant treaty so long as the affected person is given notice and an opportunity to present their case against such a course being taken.[29]

4.2 Complaints to the United Nations Human Rights Committee

In circumstances where the ICCPR has not been incorporated into Australian law, individuals can still take action based on the right to freedom of thought, conscience and religion contained in article 18. This is because Australia has agreed to be bound by the First Optional Protocol to the ICCPR, which allows the United Nations Human Rights Committee to receive and consider communications from individuals who claim that their rights under the ICCPR have been violated.[30] The Human Rights Committee then hears from the relevant State Party and provides its views regarding the complaint.[31]

There are a number of limitations to this complaint mechanism. First, it is not available where the violation is alleged to have been committed by an individual or a private company (it only applies to the Commonwealth, states and territories).[32] Second, findings made by the Human Rights Committee are not enforceable, although they may prompt positive legislative or other government action.[33] Third, it is necessary for the complainant to have exhausted all available domestic remedies before approaching the Human Rights Committee.[34] Finally, a complaint cannot be made anonymously, and the making of a complaint has previously led to negative repercussions for an Australian complainant.[35] Despite these limitations, a complaint to the Human Rights Committee has the potential to raise awareness of the issues faced by ethical vegans and may be a catalyst for systemic change.

Of critical importance in determining whether this mechanism is available is the question of whether ethical veganism constitutes a "belief" for the purposes of article 18 of the ICCPR. In this regard, the matter of *Alger v. Australia*[36] may provide guidance. Mr Christopher Alger made a complaint to the Human Rights Committee that compulsory voting in Australian elections violated his rights under article 18 of the ICCPR. He argued that his reasons for not voting were other "beliefs" protected by that article.[37] Those beliefs were essentially that he did not have sufficient information to make a meaningful decision on who to vote for as he was unable to differentiate between what was true and what was false in statements made by politicians during an election campaign.[38] Mr Alger said that his reasons for not voting were "predominantly a manifestation of his belief driven by long-term non-religious convictions related to values such as honesty, accountability, legitimacy, decency and mutual obligations between electors and politicians."[39] He said that as a consequence of his beliefs, he was duty-bound not to vote.[40]

In response to the complaint, the Australian Government said that Mr Alger's views did not constitute a "belief" for the purposes of article 18 as:

> The preparatory work of the Covenant suggests that the term "belief" refers to belief systems, ideologies and philosophies of life, such as pacifism and atheism, rather than the limitless individual viewpoints on ideas and issues that could be reached for a variety of reasons. The terms "religion" and "belief" are described in the preparatory work as including, in addition to various theistic creeds, such other beliefs as agnosticism, free thought, atheism and rationalism. In the present case, the author's views in relation to compulsory voting are not a belief for the purpose of article 18 of the Covenant. His alleged belief is merely a viewpoint that he should not have to attend a polling place on election day and submit a ballot, and is not analogous to a belief system, such as pacifism or atheism.[41]

The Human Rights Committee agreed, finding that Mr Alger's claims based on article 18 had not been sufficiently substantiated and were inadmissible. It said (echoing its comments in General Comment No. 22):

> The Committee recalls that article 18 protects theistic, non-theistic and atheistic beliefs, and the right not to profess any religion or belief. The terms "belief" and "religion" are to be broadly construed. Article 18 is not limited in its application to traditional religions or to religions and beliefs with institutional characteristics or practices analogous to those of traditional religions. Although the contents of a religion or belief should be defined by the worshippers themselves, in general, beliefs are formed by a system of principles or philosophical consideration of life. . . . In the present case, the author has failed to submit convincing arguments to show that his wish not to vote at the 2010 federal election was based on a belief in the sense of article 18 of the Covenant.[42]

In light of the above statements of principle, it appears that ethical veganism would constitute a "belief" for the purposes of article 18, being a non-religious belief system analogous to pacifism or atheism. Ethical veganism is described as a "philosophy and way of living which seeks to exclude—as far as is possible and practicable—all forms of exploitation of, and cruelty to, animals for food, clothing or any other purpose."[43] It is a matter of personal conviction and consists of a system of principles based on a philosophical consideration of life. Therefore, where the act in question is that of an Australian government entity, it would appear to be open to an ethical vegan to make a complaint to the United Nations Human Rights Committee that their rights under article 18 have been violated. But are there other avenues available that may provide more concrete outcomes—for example, under the Australian anti-discrimination and human rights legislation?

5. Anti-Discrimination Legislation

Australia's anti-discrimination laws have been described as having a "maze-like complexity."[44] Legislation exists at both the federal and state/territory level, and the various acts differ in terms of scope and precise wording. Importantly, unlike the *Equality Act 2010* (UK), none of the acts prohibit discrimination based on a person's "belief" *per se*.[45] The two attributes with the greatest potential to apply to ethical vegans are "religious belief or activity"[46] and "political belief or activity."[47] In this section we will therefore focus on the meaning of the terms "religious" and "political" and whether they could encompass ethical veganism.

It should be noted that while anti-discrimination legislation exists at the federal level, none of those pieces of legislation make discrimination on the basis of "religious" or "political" belief or activity unlawful.[48] As at the time of writing, the Federal Parliament is considering passing three bills known collectively as the "Religious Freedom Bills," however the scope of the protections contained in the bills is controversial and they face considerable public opposition. This is primarily due to the proposed protection of statements of religious belief (e.g., a student with disability may be told by their teacher their disability is a trial imposed by God).[49] Those bills are still under consideration by the Federal Cabinet, and it may be some time until such legislation is passed.

However, anti-discrimination legislation has been passed in every Australian state[50] and territory.[51] Those pieces of legislation provide protection from both direct and indirect discrimination[52] on the basis of particular grounds or attributes, in areas such as work, education, accommodation and the provision of goods and services.[53] The relevant attributes include race, sex, age, gender identity, parental status, disability and, as noted above, religious belief or activity and political belief or activity.[54] Unfortunately, there are some geographic limitations in that the attributes of "religious belief or activity" and "political belief or activity" are not protected by the New South Wales legislation,[55] and the South Australian legislation only prohibits discrimination on the basis of "religious appearance or dress" in the areas of work and study[56] (there are limited protections in those jurisdictions under the *Australian Human Rights Commission Act 1986* (Cth), which is discussed further below).

If able to be utilised, such legislation could provide ethical vegans with valuable protection as discrimination complaints can be taken before courts and tribunals, and a range of orders can be made (including for the payment of damages).[57] For example, the Queensland Anti-Discrimination Tribunal has previously found that a Muslim prisoner suffered direct and indirect discrimination when prison authorities refused his request to be provided with fresh halal meat, and he was awarded compensation.[58] The key question is whether ethical vegans are protected by the legislation. As none of the relevant acts contain substantive definitions of the words "religious" and "political,"[59] it is necessary to turn to the case law to determine their scope and meaning.

5.1 What Does "Religious" Mean?

Australian courts have said that defining "religion" is "difficult, if not impossible."[60] The leading authority is the High Court's judgment in *Church of the New Faith v. Commissioner of Pay-Roll Tax (Vic) ("Scientology case")*.[61] At the time of that decision, it was said that there was "paucity of Australian authority"[62] and a "need for an authoritative Australian exposition of the concept of religion."[63] In those circumstances, the Court said that it may be aided by judgments of courts outside the Australian hierarchy in clarifying the concept.[64]

In their joint judgment, Acting Chief Justice Mason and Justice Brennan noted that courts in the United Kingdom had taken a narrow view of what constitutes a "religion."[65] Their Honours referred to *In re South Place Ethical Society; Barralet v. Attorney-General* where Dillon J in the Chancery Division of the High Court of Justice had limited the concept to theistic religions, stating "[i]t seems to me that two of the essential attributes of religion are faith and worship; faith in a god and worship of that god."[66] Their Honours rejected Dillon J's test as too narrow, as it excluded acknowledged religions that did not involve a belief in God or a supernatural Being, such as Theravada Buddhism.[67]

Acting Chief Justice Mason and Justice Brennan also considered the more expansive definition of "religion" adopted by courts in the United States. In *United States v. Seeger*,[68] the U.S. Supreme Court had considered legislation containing an exemption from armed combat for persons conscientiously opposed by reason of their "religious training and belief." That expression was defined in the relevant legislation as meaning "an individual's belief in a relation to a Supreme Being involving duties superior to those arising from any human relation, but [not including] essentially political, sociological, or philosophical views or a merely personal moral code."[69]

The U.S. Supreme Court said that the requirement for "belief in a relation to a Supreme Being" extended to include "a sincere and meaningful belief which occupies in the life of its possessor a place parallel to that filled by the God of those admittedly qualifying for the exemption."[70] Therefore the exemption applied to those who objected to war on grounds that were not traditionally religious.

Seeger was followed in *Welsh v. United States*,[71] which concerned the same legislation. In that case, the United States Supreme Court said that the exemption

> is not limited to those whose opposition to war is prompted by orthodox or parochial religious beliefs. A registrant's conscientious objection to all war is "religious" within the meaning of [the exemption] if this opposition stems from the registrant's moral, ethical, or religious beliefs about what is right and wrong and these beliefs are held with the strength of traditional religious convictions. In view of the broad scope of the word "religious," a registrant's characterization of his beliefs as "nonreligious" is not a reliable guide to those administering the exemption.[72]

Subsequently, Judge Adams in the United States Court of Appeals for the Third Circuit in *Malnak v. Yogi*[73] identified three useful, though not essential, indicia of a religion:

> The first and most important of these indicia [is] "the nature of the ideas in question," whether they reflect those ultimate concerns which embody the fundamental problems of human existence. The second indicium is the element of comprehensiveness by which a set of ideas forms an integrated belief-system as distinct from a treatment of one or a number of isolated questions. The third indicium relates to forms and ceremonies which are comparable to those adopted by accepted religions.[74]

In doing so, Judge Adams said that one's views on the deeper and more imponderable questions, such as the proper moral code of right and wrong, are those likely to be the most "intensely personal" and important to the believer, and as such are to be carefully guarded from government interference.[75]

However, Acting Chief Justice Mason and Justice Brennan also rejected the approach taken by the United States courts as being too broad.[76] Their Honours specifically rejected the view that purely ethical beliefs fall within the definition of "religion," saying:

> To attribute a religious character to one's views by reference to the *questions* which those views address rather than by reference to the *answers* which they propound is to expand the concept of religion beyond its true domain. As the decision in *Welsh* illustrates, such an approach sweeps into the category of religious beliefs philosophies that reject the label of a religion and that deny or are silent as to the existence of any supernatural Being, Thing or Principle.[77]

Their Honours said:

> In all societies and in all ages man has pondered upon the explanation of the existence of the phenomenological universe, the meaning of his existence and his destiny. ... For some, the natural order, known or knowable by use of man's senses and his natural reason, provides a sufficient and exhaustive solution to these great problems; for others, an adequate solution can be found only in the supernatural order, in which man may believe as a matter of faith, but which he cannot know by his senses and the reality of which he cannot demonstrate to others who do not share his faith. ... Faith in the supernatural, transcending reasoning about the natural order, is the stuff of religious belief.[78]

On this basis, Acting Chief Justice Mason and Justice Brennan said that the criteria of religion are twofold: belief in a supernatural Being, Thing or Principle and acceptance of canons of conduct in order to give effect to that belief.[79] Their Honours also emphasised that there must be a real connection between the person's belief in the supernatural and the conduct they engage in, in the sense that the belief is the motivation for the conduct.[80]

Justices Wilson and Deane, in their separate joint judgment, identified five of the more important indicia of "a religion" noting that it is "unlikely that a collection of ideas and/or practices would properly be characterized as a religion if it lacked all or most of them."[81] One of the more important indicia was said to be a belief in the supernatural,[82] therefore again excluding purely ethical beliefs from the ambit of "religion." In addition, their Honours thought it important that the adherents themselves see the collection of ideas and/or practices as constituting a religion (observing that this was "perhaps more controversial").[83] This is also likely to be problematic as most ethical vegans do not see veganism as a religion.

Not long after the *Scientology case*, the New South Wales Anti-Discrimination Board recommended that the New South Wales anti-discrimination legislation be amended to make discrimination based on "religious belief" unlawful, and that this term be defined to include "a comparable deeply held belief that can broadly be conceived of as religious."[84] In this regard, the Board said:

> Deeply held moral objections, such as objections to contraception or abortion, may be maintained by individuals with the strength of traditional religious views. It would be unjust to exclude complaints from people with such convictions solely because the religious group from which their views may originally have derived no longer publicly maintained those views, or because the person holding those objections had an individual belief and did not belong to any religious group.[85]

However, as noted above, the New South Wales legislation was not amended to include discrimination on the basis of religious belief (and this definition was therefore not included in the legislation). The Australian Human Rights

Commission has made similar recommendations at the federal level, which are also yet to be adopted.[86] Therefore, regardless of the strength with which the particular beliefs are maintained, or the importance of those beliefs to the individual, in Australia a belief will not be a "religious belief" unless it includes a belief in the supernatural.

So, could ethical veganism fall within the meaning of "religion" as described by the High Court? In *Casamitjana v. The League Against Cruel Sports*, Employment Judge Postle said that "[p]hilosophically, the concept of veganism is rooted in the ancient concept of Ahimsa," meaning "to cause no injury and to do no harm."[87] The basis for this belief is the idea that "all living beings have the spark of the divine spiritual energy and therefore to hurt another being is to hurt oneself."[88] Therefore members of the Hindu, Buddhist and Jain religions (of which ahimsa is a cornerstone[89]) who practise veganism would likely be protected from discrimination on that basis. This may also be the case for members of other religions, such as Relonism, which is described as "the world's first official Vegan religion."[90] Note that it would likely be necessary to establish that veganism is a characteristic appertaining generally to persons of the relevant religion (or is an attribute generally imputed to persons of that religion).[91]

What about ethical vegans who don't hold such religious beliefs? Ethical vegans whose beliefs are based, for example, on scientific evidence as to the sentience or self-awareness of non-human animals—that which the High Court referred to as known by the "use of man's senses and his natural reason."[92] Unfortunately, it appears that such persons would not be protected from discrimination on the basis of religion, as their ethical veganism is not grounded in a belief in the supernatural. So, could such ethical vegans be protected from discrimination on the basis that their beliefs constitute "political" beliefs or opinions? Again, it is necessary to consider the meaning given to that word by the courts.

5.2 What Does "Political" Mean?

Defining "political" has been viewed by the courts as just as difficult as defining "religion." In *Nestle Australia Ltd v. Equal Opportunity Board*, Vincent J in the Supreme Court of Victoria said:

> Personally rewarding and satisfying as it undoubtably would be for me to resolve for philosophers and political scientists alike the problem of defining the nature and ambit of politics in present day society, it is not by reason of a thoroughly justified sense of humility that I do not propose to embark upon such an enterprise. The question before the court raises a problem of statutory interpretation and must be approached from that perspective.[93]

Australian courts agree that "political" is to be given the meaning ascribed by ordinary or common usage,[94] and it has been held that an activity or belief that relates to the processes of government is in a broad sense "political."[95] In *Ralph M Lee (WA) Pty Ltd v. Fort*, Anderson J in the Western Australian Supreme Court further explained that for a conviction to be political, it must have

> to do with government—the policies of government, the structure, composition, role, obligations, purposes or activities of government. Convictions about these things and other things of that kind relating to government or the relationship between citizens and government may be properly characterised as political convictions.[96]

Some activities will be clearly of a political nature, such as membership of or affiliation with a political party.[97] However, "there are many cases in which the line of demarcation between political and non-political activities will be difficult to draw and will depend on the facts of the particular case."[98] Importantly, the courts have been careful not to give the legislation too wide an application.[99] It should also be borne in mind that it is the activity in question that must possess a political character.[100] It is not enough that an activity was undertaken "for a political object or with a political motive or for the furtherance of some political cause or campaign."[101]

What is political must be determined objectively, taking into account the nature of the activity or belief.[102] It is not to be determined by the characterisation given by the complainant, and in most cases the perceptions of the parties will be irrelevant.[103] However, what is regarded as political activity or belief will to some extent depend on "the mores and attitudes and state of the particular society at the particular time."[104] Therefore, where a person considers that a belief is political because society in general (and all other people who hold the relevant belief) also consider it to be political, this "may well be evidence that the belief is in fact political."[105]

In the cases, a distinction is drawn between activities undertaken within existing government frameworks and those that seek to alter those frameworks.[106] For example, in *Nevil Abolish Child Support v. Telstra Corporation Limited*, the act of changing the complainant's surname to "Abolish Child Support and Family Court" was found to be an indication or manifestation of his political belief as it advocated the abolition of a major arm of the judiciary (being part of the system of government) and a major initiative of government policy.[107] The former Anti-Discrimination Tribunal of Victoria said that this involved major legislative change, or some more violent action for change, and went beyond the mere suggestion for administrative reform falling within the framework of government.[108]

On the other hand, in *CPS Management Pty Ltd v. Equal Opportunity Board*, Marks J in the Supreme Court of Victoria found that a belief in the principle that the administration and application of public monies ought to be ethically and responsibly regulated with full public accountability was not a political belief for the purpose of the relevant anti-discrimination legislation.[109] His Honour said "[a]lthough it is not necessary to find a category for the beliefs articulated in the complaints here, the description 'ethical' readily comes to mind as appropriate."[110] Beliefs of a political nature were said to differ in kind from beliefs such as a belief in honesty, which underpin the existing social structures including government.[111] Further, merely discussing the issue with a politician did not make it political.[112]

In light of the above cases, it appears that merely living as an ethical vegan (in the sense of avoiding, as far as is possible and practicable, the consumption of animal products as food, clothing and for any other purpose[113]) would be unlikely to constitute a political belief or activity for the purposes of the anti-discrimination legislation. It is more likely that it would be viewed as a personal philosophical belief or ethical choice. This is despite some vegans seeing veganism as a political act signalling their refusal to participate in the oppression and exploitation of non-human animals. It seems that more would be required in order for an individual's ethical veganism to be categorised as "political."

Activities directed at changing the law and the practices of the executive arm of government have been found to be "political."[114] Therefore, campaigning and participating in protests may take ethical veganism from the realm of the personal to the political. However, activities directed to private enterprises, such as employers, manufacturers and restaurants, would be unlikely to have a sufficient connection to government to be characterised as a political activity.[115] It appears the relevant activities would need to be directed to government and seek, for example, a change in the law (such as the law regarding the labelling of vegan products) or to government policy (for example, regarding the availability of vegan food in public hospitals). It is important to note, however, that submissions to parliamentary and other inquiries have been held not to be political activities as they take place within, and not outside, the framework of government.[116]

In some situations, an individual's ethical veganism may be linked to their membership of, or affiliation with, a political party. In *Hein v. Jacques* the Victorian Equal Opportunity Board, in considering whether the complainant had suffered discrimination based on his refusal to join a trade union, said that while not all trade unions were involved in political activities, the trade union in question was so involved by virtue of its affiliation to the Australian Labor Party.[117] Therefore, if an ethical vegan is a member of the Animal Justice Party (which advocates a plant-based diet free of all products derived from animals[118]) and suffers discrimination on the basis of that membership, that may constitute unlawful discrimination. There is also the potential for veganism to be found to be a characteristic appertaining generally to members of the Animal Justice Party (although that does not seem likely, given the diversity of the Party's membership), or an attribute generally imputed to members of that political party,[119] making discrimination on the basis of veganism itself unlawful.

Given the judicial interpretation of the terms "religious" and "political," would it be more fruitful for ethical vegans to pursue their rights under the Australian human rights legislation?

6. HUMAN RIGHTS LEGISLATION

Australia has a number of pieces of human rights legislation, both at the federal and state/territory level. These pieces of legislation provide a much greater scope for the protection of ethical vegans from discrimination than the Australian Constitution and the anti-discrimination legislation. However, there are still some significant limitations, including the redress available to individuals who establish that their human rights have been violated.

At the federal level, the *Australian Human Rights Commission Act 1986* (Cth) was passed to establish the Australian Human Rights Commission ("the Commission") in response to the ratification of the ICCPR in 1980.[120] The Commission has two relevant functions. The first is to inquire into any act or practice (including any systemic practice) that may constitute discrimination in employment or occupation on the basis of religion or political opinion.[121] This may to some extent fill the gaps in the New South Wales and South Australian anti-discrimination legislation referred to above. While the Commission has the power to attempt to conciliate complaints of discrimination, it cannot make enforceable findings.[122] It merely serves notice of its findings and recommendations,[123] and may report its findings to the Minister.[124] There are, of course, also the difficulties flowing from the requirement for the discrimination in question to be based on "religion" or "political opinion."

The Commission's second relevant function is to inquire into any act or practice that may be inconsistent with or contrary to any human right.[125] "Human right" is broadly defined in the legislation to include the rights and freedoms recognised in the ICCPR.[126] It is therefore likely that an ethical vegan would be able to make a complaint to the Commission that their rights under article 18 of the ICCPR have been violated. There is an important limitation, however, in that the relevant act or practice must have been engaged in by or on behalf of the Commonwealth (or an authority of the Commonwealth), in a territory, or under a Commonwealth or territory enactment.[127] Further, as with complaints of discrimination, the Commission only has power to attempt to conciliate, make findings and recommendations, and report to the Minister.[128] While it is not possible to obtain enforceable orders, a complaint may still lead to positive practical outcomes, such as greater exposure of the issues facing ethical vegans and the potential for change in policies and practices.[129]

At the state and territory level, only three jurisdictions have passed statutory bills of rights: the Australian Capital Territory (*Human Rights Act 2004* (ACT)), Victoria (*Charter of Human Rights and Responsibilities Act 2006* (Vic)) and, most recently, Queensland (*Human Rights Act 2019* (Qld)).[130] These pieces of legislation also mirror article 18 of the ICCPR in that they protect an individual's right to freedom of thought, conscience, religion and belief, including their right to manifest their beliefs.[131] Significantly, the legislation does not limit their protection of "beliefs" to beliefs of a political or religious nature.[132] It has also been held that each right in the statutory bills of rights is to be construed in "the broadest possible way."[133] So what beliefs do the statutory bills of rights protect?

"Belief" is not defined in the acts, however each provides that relevant international law and judgments of foreign and international courts and tribunals may be considered when interpreting that word.[134] Therefore the broad interpretation of article 18 expressed by the United Nations Human Rights Committee in General Comment No. 22 and set out in *Algers* may be taken into account by a court when considering the meaning of that word.[135] Similarly, the decision in *Casamitjana v. The League Against Cruel Sports*,[136] that ethical veganism is a philosophical belief protected under the *Equality Act 2010* (UK), would likely be of relevance if a court was called on to determine whether ethical veganism constitutes a "belief" protected by the statutory bills of rights.[137]

While the protection afforded by these acts is likely to encompass ethical veganism, the acts "do not establish individual rights in the sense that an individual is able to invoke protective relief against the world."[138] The acts primarily make it unlawful for "public authorities" or "public entities" to act in a way that is incompatible with a human right or to fail to give proper consideration to a relevant human right when making a decision.[139] Nevertheless, the acts would apply to public hospitals, prisons and schools, amongst other public entities, and could therefore be of great value to ethical vegans. Additionally, in the Australian Capital Territory and Queensland, private entities are able to "opt in" to the legislation,[140] which can extend their scope of operation. To date, seven private entities have done so in the Australian Capital Territory.[141]

So, what action can be taken under the statutory bills of rights? In Queensland, a complaint can be made to the Queensland Human Rights Commission ("QHRC"), which will attempt to conciliate the complaint.[142] If the complaint cannot be resolved, the QHRC must prepare a report, which may include details of any action the respondent should take to ensure its acts and decisions are compatible with human rights.[143] In Victoria, complaints are made to the Victorian Ombudsman,[144] who may conduct an enquiry to see if the matter can be resolved informally, mediate or conciliate, or conduct an investigation.[145] Following an investigation, the Victorian Ombudsman may prepare a report including its opinion and recommendations.[146] In the Australian Capital Territory, there is no complaint mechanism as the ACT Human Rights Commission does not investigate individual complaints of breaches of human rights.[147]

In both Victoria and Queensland, a person may only commence legal proceedings alleging a violation of their human rights if they already have another cause of action available to them (such as for discrimination).[148] This will present a challenge for most ethical vegans for the reasons discussed above. Further, damages cannot be awarded for any violations of human rights found in those proceedings.[149] In the Australian Capital Territory, complainants are able to commence proceedings against the relevant public authority in the ACT Supreme Court on the basis of a breach of the statutory bill of rights alone.[150] However, as in Victoria and Queensland, the court is unable to award damages if it finds a human right has been violated.[151]

Nevertheless, other useful orders can be sought. As the statutory bills of rights are directed to protecting human rights, where there has been an infringement of those rights the court's concern will usually be to bring the infringement to an end (even in jurisdictions where damages are available).[152] Naturally, this can have wider benefits than just for the particular individual. In this regard, the ACT Supreme Court has said:

> The determination of appropriate relief requires a balancing process guided by four objectives: first, addressing the wrong occasioned by the contravention of the Act; second, deterring future violations; third, making an order that can be complied with; and fourth, ensuring fairness to all those who might be affected by the relief.[153]

The Court also noted that the finding of a violation in itself is often an important part of the remedy, by way of vindication, in the sense of defending against encroachment or interference with rights.[154]

The mere making of a complaint or commencement of proceedings may also lead to positive changes. For example, in *Weaven v. The Secretary, Department of Justice*,[155] a prisoner commenced proceedings seeking orders to compel prison authorities to provide him with yeast-free food, which was necessary for medical reasons, as required under the *Corrections Act 1986* (Vic). The proceedings were unsuccessful because by the time they were heard, the prisoner had begun receiving adequate meals. In this regard, Macaulay J observed "I can well understand Mr Weaven's suspicion that the improvement in the prisons' treatment of him … *appears* to have coincided with the instigation of his proceeding."[156] In a similar way, action under the statutory bills of rights may be effective in raising awareness and may also lead to policy changes by public (and in some case private) entities to better accommodate ethical vegans.

7. CONCLUDING THOUGHTS

As can be seen from the above discussion, Australia has a complex patchwork of laws, some of which may protect ethical vegans in certain circumstances. The strongest and most comprehensive protections are provided by the state and territory anti-discrimination legislation. However, to avail themselves of those protections, ethical vegans must establish that the relevant discrimination is based on their "religious" or "political" belief or activity. While not impossible, in most cases this will be challenging given the judicial interpretation of those words. The protections will therefore most likely apply only to certain subsets of ethical vegans, being those whose beliefs are grounded in a belief in the supernatural and those who are politically active.

Section 116 of the Australian Constitution can largely be placed to one side given that it is only applicable to legislation prohibiting the free exercise of religion and provides only limited protection even in that regard. Article 18 of the ICCPR and the Australian human rights legislation are likely to encompass a wider range of "beliefs," including ethical veganism. However, the entities bound are primarily public entities and the redress available to successful complainants is much more limited. Nevertheless, these complaint mechanisms may provide fertile ground on which ethical vegans can seek societal change, including greater support and protection of vegans. If this can be achieved, barriers to becoming and remaining vegan may be removed.

8. NOTES

1. Elle Georgiou, "Vegan Activist James Warden 'Forced to go Hungry' in Hakea Prison," *The West Australian*, April 19, 2019, https://thewest.com.au/news/wa/vegan-activist-james-warden-forced-to-go-hungry-in-hakea-prison-ng-b881174255z.

2. *Casamitjana v. The League Against Cruel Sports*, ET 3331129/2018, Preliminary Hearing Judgment, January 21, 2020 (Employment Judge Postle).

3. There are a number of other Commonwealth territories, including Jervis Bay Territory, Australian Antarctic Territory, Norfolk Island, and Christmas Island. "Territories of Australia" Department of Infrastructure, Transport, Regional Development and Communications, last modified May 12, 2020, https://www.regional.gov.au/territories/.

4. *Kruger v. Commonwealth ("Stolen Generations case")* (1997) 190 CLR 1, 61 (Dawson J).

5. *Stolen Generations case*, 190 CLR 1 at 61 (Dawson J). The right to freedom of thought, conscience and religion is recognized by the common law in the negative sense that it is assumed to exist if there are no legislative limitations imposed on it. LexisNexis, *Halsbury's Laws of Australia* (last updated 7 March 2018) 80 Civil and Political Rights, '10 Freedom of

Thought, Conscience and Religion' [80-1445] citing *Nationwide News Pty Ltd v. Wills* (1992) 177 CLR 1, 48 (Brennan J) and *Australian Capital Television Pty Ltd v. Commonwealth* (1992) 177 CLR 106, 182 (Dawson J).

6. *Stolen Generations case*, 190 CLR 1 at 61 (Dawson J).

7. Limited protection of freedom of conscience and religion is also provided in section 46 of the *Constitution Act 1934* (Tas). The High Court has also held that the Australian Constitution contains an implied freedom of political communication, however it is beyond the scope of this chapter to consider its potential application to ethical vegans.

8. Even in this respect a narrow approach has been taken by the High Court and no law has ever been found to violate section 116 of the Australian Constitution.

9. Judicial opinion appears divided on the question. See *Stolen Generations case*, 190 CLR 1 at 85-86 (Toohey J), 122-23 (Gaudron J), and 160-61 (Gummow J).

10. *Stolen Generations case*, 190 CLR 1 at 125 (Gaudron J).

11. *Casamitjana*, Case No. 3331129/2018.

12. Council of Europe, Convention for the Protection of Human Rights and Fundamental Freedoms (ECHR), November 4, 1950, 213 U.N.T.S. 221, https://www.echr.coe.int/Documents/Convention_ENG.pdf.

13. Council of Europe, ECHR, article 9.

14. UN General Assembly, International Covenant on Civil and Political Rights (ICCPR), December 16, 1966, 999 U.N.T.S 171, https://undocs.org/en/A/RES/2200(XXI).

15. UN General Assembly, ICCPR, article 18(1). See also articles 19 and 26.

16. UN Human Rights Committee, General Comment No. 22: The Right to Freedom of Thought, Conscience and Religion (Art. 18), CCPR/C/21/Rev.1/Add.4, para 2 (July 30, 1993).

17. UN Human Rights Committee, General Comment No. 22, paras 1–2.

18. UN Human Rights Committee, General Comment No. 22, para 4.

19. See, for example, UN General Assembly, Declaration on the Elimination of All Forms of Intolerance and of Discrimination Based on Religion or Belief, A/RES/36/55 (November 25, 1981), https://undocs.org/en/A/RES/36/55 and UN General Assembly, Convention on the Rights of the Child A/RES/44/25, article 14 (November 20, 1989), https://undocs.org/en/A/RES/44/25.

20. *Minister of State for Immigration & Ethnic Affairs v. Ah Hin Teoh ("Teoh's case")* (1995) 183 CLR 273, 287 (Mason CJ and Deane J). See also *Dietrich v. The Queen* (1992) 177 CLR 292, 305-306 (Mason CJ and McHugh J), 321 (Brennan J), 348-349 (Dawson J), 359-360 (Toohey J) in relation to the ICCPR.

21. Note that on 6 November 1984 Australia made the following declaration in relation to the ICCPR: "Australia has a federal constitutional system in which legislative, executive and judicial powers are shared or distributed between the Commonwealth and the constituent States. The implementation of the treaty throughout Australia will be effected by the Commonwealth, State and Territory authorities having regard to their respective constitutional powers and arrangements concerning their exercise." "Legislative and Other Measures for Implementation," Rights and Freedoms, Australian Human Rights Commission, published May 1, 2013, https://humanrights.gov.au/our-work/rights-and-freedoms/legislative-and-other-measures-implementation.

22. Human Rights and Equal Opportunity Commission (HREOC), *Article 18: Freedom of Religion and Belief* (Sydney: Human Rights and Equal Opportunity Commission, 1998), 23, https://humanrights.gov.au/sites/default/files/content/pdf/human_rights/religion/article_18_religious_freedom.pdf.

23. HREOC, *Freedom of Religion and Belief* at 24.

24. Jane Stratton, *Hot Topics: Human Rights: Chapter 4C: Implementing Treaties in Australian Law* (Sydney: Library Council of New South Wales, 2013), https://legalanswers.sl.nsw.gov.au/human-rights-australia/implementing-treaties-australian-law.

25. Where the language of the statute is ambiguous. *Teoh's case*, 183 CLR 273 at 287 (Mason CJ and Deane J); *Applicant A v. Minister for Immigration and Ethnic Affairs* (1997) 190 CLR 225, 230-31 (Brennan CJ), 239-40 (Dawson J), 251–53 (McHugh J), 272–73 (Gummow J), 294 (Kirby J); *Chiropedic Bedding Pty Ltd v. Radburg Pty Ltd* (2008) 170 FCR 560,

paras 33–37 (French, Rares and Besanko JJ); *Cheedy v. Western Australia* (2011) 194 FCR 562, paras 106-8 (North, Mansfield and Gilmour JJ).

26. *Mabo v. Queensland [No. 2]* (1992) 175 CLR 1, 42 (Brennan J, with whom Mason CJ and McHugh J agreed); *Teoh's case*, 183 CLR 273 at 288 (Mason CJ and Deane J).

27. *Teoh's case*, 183 CLR 273 at 291 (Mason CJ and Deane J). However, reservations were expressed regarding this principle in *Re Minister for Immigration and Multicultural and Indigenous Affairs; Ex parte Lam* (2003) 214 CLR 1, from para 81 (McHugh and Gummow JJ), para 120 (Hayne J), para 139 (Callinan J).

28. *Teoh's case*, 183 CLR 273 at 291 (Mason CJ and Deane J).

29. *Teoh's case*, 183 CLR 273 at 291–92 (Mason CJ and Deane J).

30. UN General Assembly, [First] Optional Protocol to the International Covenant on Civil and Political Rights, A/RES/2200 A (XXI), article 1 (December 16, 1966), https://undocs.org/en/A/RES/2200(XXI).

31. UN General Assembly, First Optional Protocol, articles 4 and 5.

32. UN General Assembly, First Optional Protocol, articles 1 and 10.

33. For example, the United Nations Human Rights Committee found that Tasmanian legislation criminalizing homosexual sex violated the right to privacy in article 17 of the ICCPR and said that an effective remedy would be the repeal of the offending law. *Toonen v. Australia*, Communication 488/1992, United Nations Human Rights Committee (March 31, 1994). In response (and following the Tasmanian Parliament's refusal to repeal the law) the Commonwealth Parliament passed overriding legislation. "Human Rights Explained: Case Studies: Complaints About Australia to the Human Rights Committee," Education, Australian Human Rights Commission, published December 14, 2012, https://humanrights.gov.au/our-work/education/human-rights-explained-case-studies-complaints-about-australia-human-rights. See also *Croome v. Tasmania* (1997) 191 CLR 119.

34. UN General Assembly, First Optional Protocol, articles 2 and 5(2)(b). For example, by making a discrimination complaint.

35. After making a complaint to the United Nations Human Rights Committee regarding Tasmanian legislation criminalizing homosexual sex, Mr Nicholas Toonen lost his job as General Manager of the Tasmanian AIDS Council because the Tasmanian Government threatened to withdraw the Council's funding unless his employment was terminated. "Human Rights Explained," Australian Human Rights Commission, 2012.

36. *Alger v. Australia*, Communication 2237/2013, UN Human Rights Committee (July 13, 2017).

37. *Alger*, 2237/2013 at para 2.7.

38. *Alger*, 2237/2013 at para 2.2.

39. *Alger*, 2237/2013 at para 3.3.

40. *Alger*, 2237/2013 at para 2.11.

41. *Alger*, 2237/2013 at para 4.8.

42. *Alger*, 2237/2013 at para 6.5.

43. "Definition of Veganism," The Vegan Society, accessed August 2, 2020 https://www.vegansociety.com/go-vegan/definition-veganism. The author is aware that there are other ways to define veganism. See for example Karp and Roussel and Labchuk in this volume.

44. Anne Hewitt, "Navigating the Maze of Australia's Complex Discrimination Legislation: A Case Study of Belief Discrimination" (2011) 24 *Australian Journal of Labour Law* 24, 43.

45. Hewitt, "Navigating the Maze" at 27.

46. These words are used in the Queensland, Northern Territory and Victorian legislation. *Anti-Discrimination Act 1991* (Qld), section 7(i); *Anti-Discrimination Act 1992* (NT), section 19(1)(m); *Equal Opportunity Act 2010* (Vic), section 6(n). The words "religious conviction" are used in the Western Australian and Australian Capital Territory legislation. *Equal Opportunity Act 1984* (WA), section 53; *Discrimination Act 1991* (ACT), section 7(1)(u). The words "religious belief or affiliation" and "religious activity" are used in the Tasmanian legislation. *Anti-Discrimination Act 1998* (Tas), section 16(m) and (n).

47. These words are used in the Queensland and Victorian legislation. *Anti-Discrimination Act 1991* (Qld), section 7(j); *Equal Opportunity Act 2010* (Vic), section 6(k). The words "political conviction" are used in the Western Australian and Australian Capital Territory

legislation. *Equal Opportunity Act 1984* (WA), section 53; *Discrimination Act 1991* (ACT), section 7(1)(o). The words "political opinion, affiliation or activity" are used in the Northern Territory legislation. *Anti-Discrimination Act 1992* (NT), section 19(1)(n). The words "political belief or affiliation" and "political activity" are used in the Tasmanian legislation. *Anti-Discrimination Act 1998* (Tas), section 16(o) and (p).

48. *Racial Discrimination Act 1975* (Cth); *Sex Discrimination Act 1984* (Cth); *Disability Discrimination Act 1992* (Cth); *Age Discrimination Act 2004* (Cth). See also Hewitt, "Navigating the Maze" at 29.

49. Paul Karp, "Religious Discrimination Bill: What Will Australians Be Allowed to Say and Do if It Passes?" *The Guardian*, December 14, 2019, https://www.theguardian.com/world/2019/dec/14/religious-discrimination-bill-what-will-australians-be-allowed-to-say-and-do-if-it-passes.

50. *Anti-Discrimination Act 1977* (NSW); *Equal Opportunity Act 1984* (SA); *Equal Opportunity Act 1984* (WA); *Anti-Discrimination Act 1991* (Qld); *Anti-Discrimination Act 1998* (Tas); *Equal Opportunity Act 2010* (Vic).

51. *Discrimination Act 1991* (ACT); *Anti-Discrimination Act 1992* (NT).

52. See, for example: *Anti-Discrimination Act 1991* (Qld), sections 10 and 11; *Anti-Discrimination Act 1998* (Tas), sections 14 and 15; *Equal Opportunity Act 2010* (Vic), sections 8 and 9.

53. See, for example: *Anti-Discrimination Act 1991* (Qld), Part 4; *Anti-Discrimination Act 1992* (NT), Part 4; *Anti-Discrimination Act 1998* (Tas), section 22.

54. See for example: *Anti-Discrimination Act 1991* (Qld), section 7; *Discrimination Act 1991* (ACT), section 7(1); *Anti-Discrimination Act 1992* (NT), section 19(1); *Anti-Discrimination Act 1998* (Tas), section 16. In some jurisdictions religious vilification is also unlawful. See, for example, the *Racial and Religious Tolerance Act 2001* (Vic), section 8.

55. The definition of "race" in section 4 of the *Anti-Discrimination Act 1977* (NSW) includes "ethno-religious" origin, however in *A v. Dept. of School Education* (2000) EOC 93-039 the New South Wales Administrative Decisions Tribunal found that this did not operate to extend the scope of the legislation to discrimination on the ground of religion. In its 2018-19 Annual Report the Anti-Discrimination Board of NSW reported that approximately one-third of the discrimination enquiries it received in the relevant period were not covered by the legislation, and that this included enquiries concerning religious discrimination. Anti-Discrimination Board of NSW, *Annual Report 2018-19*, 9, https://www.antidiscrimination.justice.nsw.gov.au/about-us/annual-reports. The Board is, however, empowered to "carry out investigations, research and inquiries relating to discrimination and in particular discrimination against a person or persons on the ground of . . . religious or political conviction." *Anti-Discrimination Act 1977* (NSW), section 119(1)(a)(iv).

56. *Equal Opportunity Act 1984* (SA), sections 85T(1)(f), 85U and 85ZD.

57. See, for example, *Anti-Discrimination Act 1991* (Qld), section 209; *Anti-Discrimination Act 1977* (NSW), section 108; *Equal Opportunity Act 1984* (SA), section 96.

58. *Mahommed v. State of Queensland* [2006] QADT 21, upheld on appeal in *State of Queensland v. Mahommed* [2007] QSC 018. It is perhaps unsurprising that the complainant said the vegetarian meals provided to him were unacceptable as they were "just salad" and the portions were "too small." He also said they "frequently contained meat or items which he could not identify."

59. The definitions largely relate to the scope of these terms, for example to include both having and not having such beliefs, and engaging and not engaging in such activities. See *Equal Opportunity Act 1984* (WA), section 4(3); *Anti-Discrimination Act 1991* (Qld), schedule 1; *Discrimination Act 1991* (ACT), dictionary; *Anti-Discrimination Act 1992* (NT), section 4(5); *Anti-Discrimination Act 1998* (Tas), section 3; *Equal Opportunity Act 2010* (Vic), section 4(1). Note that Aboriginal and Torres Strait Islander spiritual beliefs and practices are expressly recognised in some acts. *Discrimination Act 1991* (ACT), dictionary; *Anti-Discrimination Act 1992* (NT), section 4(4).

60. *Adelaide Company of Jehovah's Witnesses Inc. v. Commonwealth* (1943) 67 CLR 116, 123 (Latham CJ). See also *Church of the New Faith v. Commissioner of Pay-Roll Tax (Vic) ("Scientology case")* (1983) 154 CLR 120, 131 (Mason ACJ and Brennan J) and 173 (Wilson and Deane JJ).

61. (1983) 154 CLR 120.
62. *Scientology case*, 154 CLR 120 at 130 (Mason ACJ and Brennan J).
63. *Scientology case*, 154 CLR 120 at 131 (Mason ACJ and Brennan J).
64. *Scientology case*, 154 CLR 120 at 131 (Mason ACJ and Brennan J).
65. *Scientology case*, 154 CLR 120 at 131 (Mason ACJ and Brennan J).
66. *In re South Place Ethical Society; Barralet v. Attorney-General* [1980] 3 All ER 918, 924 as cited in *Scientology case*, 154 CLR 120 at 140 (Mason ACJ and Brennan J).
67. *Scientology case*, 154 CLR 120 at 140. Note in Theravada Buddhism there is no omnipotent creator God of the sort found in Judaism, Islam and Christianity. Each being has to make their own way to enlightenment without the help of God or gods. "Theravada Buddhism," Religions, BBC, last modified October 2, 2002, http://www.bbc.co.uk/religion/religions/buddhism/subdivisions/theravada_1.shtml.
68. 380 U.S. 163 (1965).
69. Universal Military Training and Service Act of 1948, 50 U.S.C. § 6(j) (1958).
70. *United States v. Seeger*, 380 U.S. 163 (1965), 176.
71. 398 U.S. 333 (1970).
72. *Welsh v. United States*, 398 U.S. 333 (1970), 333–34 and 335–44.
73. 592 F.2d 197 (1979).
74. *Scientology case*, 154 CLR 120 at 175 (Wilson and Deane JJ). See *Malnak v. Yogi*, 592 F.2d 197 (1979), 207–10.
75. *Malnak*, 592 F.2d 197 at 208.
76. *Scientology case*, 154 CLR 120 at 139–40 (Mason ACJ and Brennan J).
77. *Scientology case*, 154 CLR 120 at 139 (Mason ACJ and Brennan J) (my emphasis).
78. *Scientology case*, 154 CLR 120 at 133–34 (Mason ACJ and Brennan J).
79. *Scientology case*, 154 CLR 120 at 136 (Mason ACJ and Brennan J).
80. *Scientology case*, 154 CLR 120 at 135 (Mason ACJ and Brennan J).
81. *Scientology case*, 154 CLR 120 at 174 (Wilson and Deane JJ).
82. *Scientology case*, 154 CLR 120 at 174 (Wilson and Deane JJ).
83. *Scientology case*, 154 CLR 120 at 174 (Wilson and Deane JJ).
84. Anti-Discrimination Board of NSW, "Discrimination and Religious Conviction: A Report of the Anti-Discrimination Board in Accordance with Section 119(a) of the Anti-Discrimination Act 1977" [1984] *IndigLRes* 4, paras 1.54 and 1.64.
85. "Discrimination and Religious Conviction," [1984] *IndigLRes* 4 at para 1.63.
86. HREOC, *Freedom of Religion and Belief* at v–vi. See also Professor Gary Bouma, Professor Desmond Cahill, Dr Hass Dellal, and Athalia Zwartz, *2011: Freedom of Religion and Belief in 21st Century Australia* (Sydney: Australian Human Rights Commission, 2011), 8, https://humanrights.gov.au/sites/default/files/content/frb/Report_2011.pdf.
87. *Casamitjana*, Case No. 3331129/2018 at para 11.
88. *Casamitjana*, Case No. 3331129/2018 at para 11.
89. *Casamitjana*, Case No. 3331129/2018 at para 11.
90. The website for the Church of Veganism; www.churchofveganism.org, accessed November 28, 2020. In *In the matter of Eric R Burns*, Initial Order, Washington State Office of Administrative Hearings, Docket No. 094464, April 10, 2020 at para 16 Administrative Law Judge Lockwood said that "Relonism contains a belief or philosophical system that includes the relationship between beings and deities, and a code or guide of proper conduct for believers" and concluded that "Relonism is a 'religion' within the broad meaning of the law, and within general human acceptance of what constitutes a religion."
91. LexisNexis, *Halsbury's Laws of Australia* (last updated 7 March 2018) 80 Civil and Political Rights, '1 Equality and Discrimination' [80–260].
92. *Scientology case*, 154 CLR 120 at 134 (Mason ACJ and Brennan J).
93. [1990] VR 805, 814.
94. *Nestle Australia Ltd v. Equal Opportunity Board* [1990] VR 805, 816 and 819 (Vincent J); *CPS Management Pty Ltd v. Equal Opportunity Board* [1991] 2 VR 107, 110 (Marks J); *Ralph M Lee (WA) Pty Ltd v. Fort* [1991] 4 WAR 176, 183 (Anderson J); *Nevil Abolish Child Support v. Telstra Corporation Limited* [1997] VADT 44, 10.
95. *Nestle*, [1990] VR 805 at 819 (Vincent J).

96. *Ralph M Lee*, [1991] 4 WAR 176 at 183 (Anderson J). See also *CPS Management*, [1991] 2 VR 107 at 111–12 (Marks J); *Nevil Abolish Child Support* [1997], VADT 44 at 12.

97. *Nevil Abolish Child Support* [1997], VADT 44 at 12 citing *Evershed v. City of Geraldton* [1995] EOC 92–745.

98. *Nevil Abolish Child Support* [1997], VADT 44 at 12.

99. *CPS Management* [1991], 2 VR 107 at 115 (Marks J); *Ralph M Lee*, [1991] 4 WAR 176 at 184-85 (Anderson J).

100. *Nestle* [1990], VR 805 at 817 (Vincent J).

101. *Nestle* [1990], VR 805 at 817 (Vincent J).

102. *Nevil Abolish Child Support* [1997], VADT 44 at 12.

103. *CPS Management* [1991], 2 VR 107 at 110 (Marks J); *Nevil Abolish Child Support* [1997], VADT 44 at 12 citing *Duggan v. South Yarra Constructions Pty Ltd* [1987] EOC 92-220.

104. *Nevil Abolish Child Support* [1997], VADT 44 at 12.

105. *Nevil Abolish Child Support* [1997], VADT 44 at 12.

106. See, for example, *Nestle* [1990], VR 805 at 815 and 816 (Vincent J) (in the context of trade union activities).

107. *Nevil Abolish Child Support* [1997], VADT 44 at 15-16.

108. *Nevil Abolish Child Support* [1997], VADT 44 at 15.

109. [1991] 2 VR 107 at 111–12 (Marks J).

110. *CPS Management* [1991], 2 VR 107 at 112 (Marks J).

111. *CPS Management* [1991], 2 VR 107 at 112 (Marks J).

112. *CPS Management* [1991], 2 VR 107 at 112 (Marks J).

113. "Definition of Veganism," The Vegan Society.

114. See *Thorne v. R* [1986] EOC 92-182 and *Oldham v. Women's Information and Referral Exchange* [1986] EOC 92–158, referred to in *Nestle* [1990], VR 805 at 816 (Vincent J) and *Nevil Abolish Child Support* [1997], VADT 44 at 13.

115. In *Jones v. Jacobs & Clark* [2004], QADT 34 the complainant's involvement in student politics was not political as it did not bear on government. See also Hewitt, "Navigating the Maze" at 29.

116. *Nevil Abolish Child Support* [1997], VADT 44 at 13.

117. *Hein v. Jacques* (1989) EOC 91–188, referred to in *Nestle* [1990], VR 805 at 815–16 (Vincent J).

118. "Human Diet and Animals," Humans, Animal Justice Party, accessed August 2, 2020 https://animaljusticeparty.org/policieslist/humans/human-diet-and-animals/.

119. LexisNexis, *Halsbury's Laws of Australia* (last updated 7 March 2018) 80 Civil and Political Rights, '1 Equality and Discrimination' [80–260].

120. Stratton, *Hot Topics: Chapter 4C*.

121. *Australian Human Rights Commission Act 1986* (Cth), section 3 definition of "discrimination," sections 3(8) and 31(b)(i), and Schedule 1. This function is given to the Commission in pursuance of Australia's international obligations under International Labour Organization General Conference, Discrimination (Employment and Occupation) Convention (No. 111), (June 4, 1958), https://www.ilo.org/dyn/normlex/en/f?p=NORMLEXPUB:12100:0::NO::P12100_ILO_CODE:C111. Complaints can also be made to the Fair Work Commission in relation to discrimination on the basis of religion or political opinion in the context of employment. *Fair Work Act 2009* (Cth), section 351.

122. *Australian Human Rights Commission Act 1986* (Cth), sections 31(b)(ii) and 34.

123. *Australian Human Rights Commission Act 1986* (Cth), sections 35(2)(a), 35(2)(b), 35(2)(c) and 35(3).

124. *Australian Human Rights Commission Act 1986* (Cth), sections 32A and 35(2)(d).

125. *Australian Human Rights Commission Act 1986* (Cth), section 11(1)(f)(i).

126. *Australian Human Rights Commission Act 1986* (Cth), section 3 definition of "human rights." In *Hanes v. Human Rights and Equal Opportunity Commission* [2007] FCA 751, para 28 it was not in dispute that the "Nature Philosophy" practiced by the applicant could be considered a belief for the purposes of article 18(1) of the ICCPR.

127. *Australian Human Rights Commission Act 1986* (Cth), section 3 definitions of "act," "practice" and "enactment."

128. *Australian Human Rights Commission Act 1986* (Cth), sections 11(1)(f)(ii), 20A, 28, 29(2)(a), 29(2)(b), 29(2)(c), 29(2)(d) and 29(3).

129. Note the Commission's functions also include undertaking educational programs to promote human rights and publishing guidelines for the avoidance of acts or practices inconsistent with or contrary to human rights. *Australian Human Rights Commission Act 1986* (Cth), sections 11(h) and (n).

130. There are some wording differences between the acts, but for the purpose of this chapter these differences have been put to one side.

131. *Human Rights Act 2004* (ACT), section 14; *Charter of Human Rights and Responsibilities Act 2006* (Vic), section 14; *Human Rights Act 2019* (Qld), section 20.

132. Hewitt, "Navigating the Maze" at 33 (in relation to the ACT and Victorian legislation, the Queensland Act not yet having been passed).

133. *Certain Children (by their Litigation Guardian, Sister Marie Brigid Arthur) v. Minister for Families and Children* [2016] VSC 796, para 143 (Garde J); *Islam v. Director-General of the Department of Justice and Community Safety Directorate* [2018] ACTSC 322, para 39 (McWilliam AsJ).

134. *Human Rights Act 2004* (ACT), section 31(1); *Charter of Human Rights and Responsibilities Act 2006* (Vic), section 32(2); *Human Rights Act 2019* (Qld), section 48(3). But note the words of caution in *Momcilovic v. R* (2011) 245 CLR 1, paras 18–19 (French CJ) and paras 146–161 (Gummow J).

135. Such material has been referred to by courts in interpreting the rights contained in the statutory bills of rights. See, for example, *Certain Children*, [2016] VSC 796 at para 160 (Garde J); *Islam v. Director-General Justice and Community Safety Directorate (No. 3)* [2016] ACTSC 27, para 153 (Mossop AsJ). See also *PJB v. Melbourne Health* (2011) 39 VR 373 at paras 64–73 (Bell J) regarding Australian courts' reference to and reliance on the findings and general comments of the UN Human Rights Committee when interpreting relevant legislation; Hewitt, "Navigating the Maze" at 33.

136. *Casamitjana*, Case No. 3331129/2018.

137. See, for example, *Islam*, [2018] ACTSC 322 at para 67 where McWilliam AsJ referred to a United Kingdom case considering the scope of a right protected under the European Convention on Human Rights. See also Hewitt, "Navigating the Maze" at 33.

138. Hewitt, "Navigating the Maze" at 33 (in relation to the ACT and Victorian legislation, the Queensland Act not yet having been passed).

139. *Human Rights Act 2004* (ACT), section 40B(1); *Charter of Human Rights and Responsibilities Act 2006* (Vic), section 38(1); *Human Rights Act 2019* (Qld), section 58(1).

140. *Human Rights Act 2004* (ACT), section 40D; *Human Rights Act 2019* (Qld), section 60.

141. Companion House Inc., Centre for Australian Ethical Research, Women's Legal Centre (ACT and Region) Incorporated, Relationships Australia Canberra and Region, Amnesty International Australia, ACT Disability, Aged and Carer Advocacy Service, and Advocacy for Inclusion Incorporated. No entities have opted in to the Queensland legislation as at the time of writing.

142. *Human Rights Act 2019* (Qld), part 4, division 2, sub-divisions 2 and 4.

143. *Human Rights Act 2019* (Qld), section 88(4).

144. *Ombudsman Act 1973* (Vic), section 13(2). Complaints concerning police conduct are made to the Independent Broad-based Anti-corruption Commission. *Ombudsman Act 1973* (Vic), section 15(1); *Independent Broad-Based Anti-Corruption Commission Act 2011* (Vic), section 15(3)(b)(iii).

145. *Ombudsman Act 1973* (Vic), sections 13A, 13G and 15B.

146. *Ombudsman Act 1973* (Vic), section 23.

147. The ACT Human Rights Commission can only investigate individual complaints about unlawful discrimination, health services, services for older people, disability services and services for children and young people. "Enforcing Human Rights," Human Rights, ACT Human Rights Commission, accessed August 22, 2020, https://hrc.act.gov.au/humanrights/enforcing-human-rights/.

148. *Charter of Human Rights and Responsibilities Act 2006* (Vic), section 39(1); *Human Rights Act 2019* (Qld), section 59(1) and (2). However, the other cause of action need not be successful. *Goode v. Common Equity Housing Ltd* [2014] VSC 585, paras 28-42 (Bell J); *Kheir v. Robertson* [2019] VSC 422, para 101 (McDonald J); *Human Rights Act 2019* (Qld), section 59(2).
149. *Charter of Human Rights and Responsibilities Act 2006* (Vic), section 39(3); *Human Rights Act 2019* (Qld), section 59(3).
150. *Human Rights Act 2004* (ACT), section 40C(2)(a). See, for example, *Islam* [2018] ACTSC 322 where a Muslim prisoner commenced proceedings in the ACT Supreme Court alleging that his rights under section 14 of the *Human Rights Act 2004* (ACT) had been breached due to a failure to provide him with vegetarian food.
151. *Human Rights Act 2004* (ACT), section 40C(4). In *Islam*, the plaintiff sought an order that the defendant "take reasonable steps" to replace the current prison food ordering system with an approved, amended system. [2018] ACTSC 322 at para 4.
152. *Islam*, [2018] ACTSC 322 at para 71 (McWilliam AsJ).
153. *Islam*, [2018] ACTSC 322 at para 73 (McWilliam AsJ).
154. *Islam*, [2018] ACTSC 322 at para 72 (McWilliam AsJ).
155. [2012] VSC 582.
156. *Weaven v. The Secretary, Department of Justice* [2012] VSC 582, para 32 (Macaulay J) (original emphasis). In *Islam*, problems the plaintiff was "regularly experiencing" in obtaining vegetarian meals disappeared after the commencement of proceedings (and on 14 August 2017 he even received a vegetarian roll to replace one he had not received for lunch on 2 July 2017). [2018] ACTSC 322 at paras 98 and 129.

9. REFERENCES

A v. Dept. of School Education (2000) EOC 93-039.

ACT Human Rights Commission. "Enforcing Human Rights." Human Rights. Accessed August 22, 2020. https://hrc.act.gov.au/humanrights/enforcing-human-rights/.

Adelaide Company of Jehovah's Witnesses Inc. v. Commonwealth (1943) 67 CLR 116.

Age Discrimination Act 2004 (Cth).

Alger v. Australia, Communication 2237/2013, UN Human Rights Committee (July 13, 2017).

Animal Justice Party. "Human Diet and Animals." Humans. Accessed August 2, 2020. https://animaljusticeparty.org/policieslist/humans/human-diet-and-animals/.

Anti-Discrimination Board of NSW. *Annual Report 2018–19*. ttps://www.antidiscrimination.justice.nsw.gov.au/about-us/annual-reports.

———. "Discrimination and Religious Conviction: A Report of the Anti-Discrimination Board in Accordance with Section 119(a) of the Anti-Discrimination Act 1977." [1984] *IndigLRes* 4.

Anti-Discrimination Act 1977 (NSW).

Anti-Discrimination Act 1991 (Qld).

Anti-Discrimination Act 1992 (NT).

Anti-Discrimination Act 1998 (Tas).

Applicant A v. Minister for Immigration and Ethnic Affairs (1997) 190 CLR 225.

Australian Capital Television Pty Ltd v. Commonwealth (1992) 177 CLR 106.

Australian Constitution.

Australian Human Rights Commission. "Human Rights Explained: Case Studies: Complaints About Australia to the Human Rights Committee." Education. Published December 14, 2012. https://humanrights.gov.au/our-work/education/human-rights-explained-case-studies-complaints-about-australia-human-rights.

———. "Legislative and Other Measures for Implementation." Rights and Freedoms. Published May 1, 2013. https://humanrights.gov.au/our-work/rights-and-freedoms/legislative-and-other-measures-implementation.

Australian Human Rights Commission Act 1986 (Cth).

BBC. "Theravada Buddhism." Religions. Last modified October 2, 2002. http://www.bbc.co.uk/religion/religions/buddhism/subdivisions/theravada_1.shtml.

Bouma, Professor Gary, Professor Desmond Cahill, Dr Hass Dellal, and Athalia Zwartz. *2011: Freedom of Religion and Belief in 21st Century Australia*. Sydney: Australian Human Rights Commission, 2011. https://humanrights.gov.au/sites/default/files/content/frb/Report_2011.pdf.

Casamitjana v. The League Against Cruel Sports, ETCase No. 3331129/2018, Preliminary Hearing Judgment, January 21, 2020 (Employment Judge Postle).

Certain Children (by their Litigation Guardian, Sister Marie Brigid Arthur) v. Minister for Families and Children [2016] VSC 796.

Charter of Human Rights and Responsibilities Act 2006 (Vic).

Cheedy v. Western Australia (2011) 194 FCR 562.

Chiropedic Bedding Pty Ltd v. Radburg Pty Ltd (2008) 170 FCR 560.

Church of the New Faith v. Commissioner of Pay-Roll Tax (Vic) ("Scientology case") (1983) 154 CLR 120.

Church of Veganism. www.churchofveganism.org. Accessed November 28, 2020.

Constitution Act 1934 (Tas).

Corrections Act 1986 (Vic).

Council of Europe. Convention for the Protection of Human Rights and Fundamental Freedoms. 213 U.N.T.S. 221 (November 4, 1950). https://www.echr.coe.int/Documents/Convention_ENG.pdf.

CPS Management Pty Ltd v. Equal Opportunity Board [1991] 2 VR 107.

Department of Infrastructure, Transport, Regional Development and Communications. "Territories of Australia." Last modified May 12, 2020. https://www.regional.gov.au/territories/.

Dietrich v. The Queen (1992) 177 CLR 292.

Disability Discrimination Act 1992 (Cth).

Discrimination Act 1991 (ACT).

Duggan v. South Yarra Constructions Pty Ltd [1987] EOC 92–220.

Equal Opportunity Act 1984 (SA).

Equal Opportunity Act 1984 (WA).

Equal Opportunity Act 2010 (Vic).

Equality Act 2010 (UK).

Evershed v. City of Geraldton [1995] EOC 92–745.

Fair Work Act 2009 (Cth).

Georgiou, Elle. "Vegan Activist James Warden 'Forced to go Hungry' in Hakea Prison." The West Australian, April 19, 2019. https://thewest.com.au/news/wa/vegan-activist-james-warden-forced-to-go-hungry-in-hakea-prison-ng-b881174255z.

Goode v. Common Equity Housing Ltd [2014] VSC 585.

Hanes v. Human Rights and Equal Opportunity Commission [2007] FCA 751.

Hein v. Jacques (1989) EOC 91–188.

Hewitt, Anne. "Navigating the Maze of Australia's Complex Discrimination Legislation: A Case Study of Belief Discrimination." (2011) 24 Australian Journal of Labour Law: 24–44.

Human Rights Act 2004 (ACT).

Human Rights Act 2019 (Qld).

Human Rights and Equal Opportunity Commission. *Article 18: Freedom of Religion and Belief*. Sydney: Human Rights and Equal Opportunity Commission, 1998. https://humanrights.gov.au/sites/default/files/content/pdf/human_rights/religion/article_18_religious_freedom.pdf.

In the matter of Eric R Burns, Initial Order, Washington State Office of Administrative Hearings, Docket No. 094464, April 10, 2020.

In re South Place Ethical Society; Barralet v. Attorney-General [1980] 3 All ER 918.

Independent Broad-Based Anti-Corruption Commission Act 2011 (Vic).

International Labour Organization General Conference. Discrimination (Employment and Occupation) Convention (No. 111) (June 4, 1958), https://www.ilo.org/dyn/normlex/en/f?p=NORMLEXPUB:12100:0::NO::P12100_ILO_CODE:C111.

Islam v. Director-General Justice and Community Safety Directorate (No. 3) [2016] ACTSC 27.

Islam v. Director-General of the Department of Justice and Community Safety Directorate [2018] ACTSC 322.

Jones v. Jacobs & Clark [2004] QADT 34.

Karp, Paul. "Religious Discrimination Bill: What Will Australians Be Allowed to Say and Do if it Passes?" *The Guardian*, December 14, 2019. https://www.theguardian.com/world/2019/dec/14/religious-discrimination-bill-what-will-australians-be-allowed-to-say-and-do-if-it-passes.

Kheir v. Robertson [2019] VSC 422.

Kruger v. Commonwealth ("Stolen Generations case") (1997) 190 CLR 1.

LexisNexis. *Halsbury's Laws of Australia*. Last updated 7 March 2018. 80 Civil and Political Rights.

Mabo v. Queensland [No. 2] (1992) 175 CLR 1.

Mahommed v. State of Queensland [2006] QADT 21.

Malnak v. Yogi, 592 F.2d 197 (1979).

Minister of State for Immigration & Ethnic Affairs v. Ah Hin Teoh ("Teoh's case") (1995) 183 CLR 273.

Momcilovic v. R (2011) 245 CLR 1.

Nestle Australia Ltd v. Equal Opportunity Board [1990] VR 805.

Nevil Abolish Child Support v. Telstra Corporation Limited [1997] VADT 44.

Nationwide News Pty Ltd v. Wills (1992) 177 CLR 1.

Oldham v. Women's Information and Referral Exchange [1986] EOC 92–158.

Ombudsman Act 1973 (Vic).

PJB v. Melbourne Health (2011) 39 VR 373.

Racial and Religious Tolerance Act 2001 (Vic).

Racial Discrimination Act 1975 (Cth).

Ralph M Lee (WA) Pty Ltd v. Fort [1991] 4 WAR 176.

Re Minister for Immigration and Multicultural and Indigenous Affairs; Ex parte Lam (2003) 214 CLR 1.

Sex Discrimination Act 1984 (Cth).

State of Queensland v. Mahommed [2007] QSC 018.

Stratton, Jane. *Hot Topics: Human Rights: Chapter 4C: Implementing Treaties in Australian Law*. Sydney: Library Council of New South Wales, 2013. https://legalanswers.sl.nsw.gov.au/human-rights-australia/implementing-treaties-australian-law.

The Vegan Society. "Definition of Veganism." Accessed August 2, 2020. https://www.vegansociety.com/go-vegan/definition-veganism.

Thorne v. R [1986] EOC 92–182.

Toonen v. Australia, Communication 488/1992, United Nations Human Rights Committee (March 31, 1994).

UN General Assembly. Convention on the Rights of the Child A/RES/44/25 (November 20, 1989). https://undocs.org/en/A/RES/44/25.

———. Declaration on the Elimination of All Forms of Intolerance and of Discrimination Based on Religion or Belief. A/RES/36/55 (November 25, 1981). https://undocs.org/en/A/RES/36/55.

———. International Covenant on Civil and Political Rights. 999 U.N.T.S 171 (December 16, 1966). https://undocs.org/en/A/RES/2200(XXI).

———. [First] Optional Protocol to the International Covenant on Civil and Political Rights. A/RES/2200 A (XXI) (December 16, 1966). https://undocs.org/en/A/RES/2200(XXI).

UN Human Rights Committee. General Comment No. 22: The Right to Freedom of Thought, Conscience and Religion (Art. 18). CCPR/C/21/Rev.1/Add.4 (July 30, 1993).

United States v. Seeger, 380 U.S. 163 (1965).

Universal Military Training and Service Act of 1948, 50 U.S.C. (1958).

Weaven v. The Secretary, Department of Justice [2012] VSC 582.

Welsh v. United States, 398 U.S. 333 (1970).

Chapter Two

A Single Black Bean

Discrimination and the Protection of Ethical Vegans in Canada

Krystal-Anne Roussel and Camille Labchuk

1. INTRODUCTION

In the summer of 2017, firefighter Adam Knauff was dispatched to fight intense wildfires that were sweeping the province of British Columbia that season. Knauff is an Ethical Vegan, and despite working 14 to 16-hour days in physically-demanding conditions in a remote location, he was repeatedly denied vegan, nutritionally-adequate meals by his employer. At some meals, he was unable to eat any of the food on offer, and on one occasion, the only source of protein in his dinner was "a single black bean." It is still an open question as to whether Canada's human rights laws require many employers to respect and accommodate the beliefs of employees who happen to be Ethical Vegans. Yet, with more and more people identifying as Ethical Vegans, claims of discrimination related to a person's veganism are likely to arise with increasing frequency.[1]

As it stands today, vegetarians and vegans account for nearly 10 percent of Canada's population, and this is likely to increase in the next few decades.[2] People choose to be vegetarian or vegan for many reasons, including but not limited to: personal preference, ethical and moral beliefs, health, and environmentalism.[3] This chapter focuses exclusively on Ethical Veganism, generally understood to be more than simply a diet. Rather, Ethical Vegans believe that it is morally wrong to kill and harm non-human animals, and that human consumption or use of animal-derived products should be avoided. A commitment to Ethical Veganism is part of a comprehensive ethical and moral belief system that governs a person's daily conduct and practices. This chapter explores the extent to which Canadian human rights laws can and should protect people with a sincerely-held belief in Ethical Veganism.

Part two provides an overview of human rights law in Canada. Part three describes the beliefs and practices of Ethical Veganism. Part four addresses arguments in favour of expanding human rights protections to include secular ethical and moral belief systems like Ethical Veganism in Canada. Using the Knauff case as an example, this Part of the chapter examines whether and how Ethical Veganism fits into the definition of "creed" under the Ontario *Human Rights Code*.[4]

2. HUMAN RIGHTS LAW IN CANADA

2.1. The Canadian Charter of Rights and Freedoms

Canada is a federation, and the power to legislate respecting human rights is shared between the federal government and the provincial and territorial governments. At the federal level, the Canadian *Charter of Rights and Freedoms* enshrines constitutional protection for a variety of rights, guaranteeing "broad equality rights as well as fundamental freedoms, democratic rights, mobility rights, legal rights, and language rights."[5]

Under section 2(a) of the Charter, everyone has the right to freedom of conscience and religion.[6] The purpose of these protections is "to prevent interference with profoundly held personal beliefs that govern one's perception of oneself, humankind, nature, and, in some cases, a higher or different order of being."[7] In *R v Morgentaler*, the Supreme Court of Canada distinguished freedom of conscience from freedom of religion as follows:

> Certainly, it would be my view that conscientious beliefs which are not religiously motivated are equally protected by freedom of conscience in s. 2(a). [. . .] Indeed, as a matter of statutory interpretation, "conscience" and "religion" should not be treated as tautologous if capable of independent, although related, meaning.[8]

Freedom of conscience is therefore aimed at something beyond religious beliefs; its purpose is to protect secular beliefs based on strongly-held moral ideas of right and wrong.[9]

The protections for freedom of conscience afforded by section 2(a) of the Charter are not frequently considered by Canadian courts, but one of the leading freedom of conscience cases dealt squarely with what, if any, constitutional protections are to be afforded to those who eschew eating meat for moral reasons. In *Maurice v Canada*[10] a vegetarian inmate in the custody of the Correctional Service of Canada challenged the prison's refusal to provide him with vegetarian food.[11] Previously, Mr Maurice had identified as a member of the Hare Krishna faith, and had been provided with vegetarian meals by the prison in accordance with the tenets of his religion. He eventually renounced this faith, yet continued to request vegetarian meals based on his continuing belief that eating meat, fish, eggs, and poultry was "morally reprehensible and poisonous to society as a whole." The prison repeatedly denied his requests on the basis that special diets were only authorized for religious or medical reasons.[12] The Federal Court held that Mr. Maurice was entitled to vegetarian meals, stating that vegetarianism is a "dietary choice founded in a belief that consumption of animal products is morally wrong" and that the underlying belief system of vegetarians is an expression of conscience protected under section 2(a) of the Charter.[13] The Court went on to say that section 2(a) of the Charter protects both freedom of religion *and* conscience, and that conscientiously held beliefs not grounded in religion should not be ignored.[14]

Although *Maurice* dealt specifically with Ethical Vegetarianism (i.e., a philosophy that eating animal flesh should be avoided but that consuming other animal-derived products may be acceptable), there is no reason to believe the holding in the case would not extend to protect the belief systems of Ethical Vegans, too.

Charter rights, however, are limited in their application and cannot provide comprehensive protection to Ethical Vegans. Unlike provincial human rights legislation, which applies to both public and private bodies, the Charter applies only to government action.[15] While Charter protections are robust when they do apply, they offer no protection to Ethical Vegans who face discrimination in other circumstances that do not involve government action, such as private housing arrangements, service provision, and other commercial transactions. Non-governmental actions are the exclusive domain of provincial human rights laws.[16]

2.2. Provincial Human Rights Legislation

There is little consistency across provincial human rights legislation when it comes to protections for belief systems. Although every provincial human rights code in Canada prohibits discrimination on the basis of some variant of "religion,"[17] the details vary. New Brunswick, Quebec, and British Columbia use the term "religion."[18] Alberta uses the term "religious beliefs," and Nova Scotia, Prince Edward Island, and Saskatchewan each list "religion" and "creed" as separate grounds of discrimination.[19] Newfoundland refers to "religion" and "religious creed," and Manitoba provides the most extensive list of terms—"religion or creed, or religious belief, religious association, or religious activity."[20] Ontario is alone in prohibiting discrimination solely on the basis of "creed."[21]

No human rights statute in Canada defines any of the above-mentioned terms, and in practice, few Canadian decision-makers have had to wrestle with how to interpret them.[22]

3. DEFINING ETHICAL VEGANISM

Ethical Veganism is a comprehensive and overarching belief system grounded in an ethical and moral code about what is right and wrong, about the sanctity of life, and about the role of human beings in relation to other animals.[23] There is no single definition of veganism, but it has been described as "a way of living which seeks to exclude, as far as is possible and practicable, all forms of exploitation of, and cruelty to, animals for food, clothing or any other purpose."[24] A commitment to Ethical Veganism revolves around the fundamental principle that it is "immoral and unethical for humans to kill, harm, and exploit animals."[25] Generally, Ethical Vegans abstain completely (or to the extent possible) from eating, using, and purchasing products derived from animals, tested on animals, or otherwise acquired from practices that exploit animals.[26] For Ethical Vegans, the practice of abstention from animal products is not a mere dietary choice. It is a comprehensive and overarching system of belief that governs one's daily conduct and practices—from what they eat to what they wear, and much more.[27]

Though the "practice of abstention from the use of animal products may be the same or similar between Ethical Vegans and other vegans or vegetarians, the beliefs underlying those practices differ in significant ways."[28] Ethical Vegans must be distinguished from persons who merely subscribe to a vegan or vegetarian diet for other reasons, including personal preference, health, or environmentalism.[29]

4. DISCRIMINATION AND THE PROTECTION OF ETHICAL VEGANS IN CANADA

4.1. A Case Study: *Knauff v. Ministry of Natural Resources & Forestry*

In a novel case, a vegan firefighter based in the province of Ontario is suing his employer for failing to provide him with vegan food while he was deployed out-of-province in a remote location.

Adam Knauff was an 11-year veteran and team leader with Ontario's provincial forest firefighting force when he was sent to the Williams Lake region of British Columbia in 2017 to help extinguish the forest fires that ravaged the area that summer and forced the evacuation of thousands of residents. Mr. Knauff had been vegan for over 20 years to avoid causing suffering to animals. As a 13-year-old growing up in the northern-Ontario community of Thunder Bay—not a common time or place for vegetarians, let alone vegans—he gave up meat. At the age of eighteen, motivated by growing concern over the impact of his dietary choices on animals and the planet, he went fully vegan.[30]

Mr. Knauff's veganism was a fact well-known to his employer, the Ministry of Natural Resources and Forestry, and generally accommodated when he was on the job. Yet for ten days in a row while in Williams Lake, Mr. Knauff worked long hours in physically demanding conditions and faced a severe lack of vegan food in the basecamp where he was stationed.

Other non-vegan firefighter colleagues were provided with nutritionally adequate food that they could eat, but Mr. Knauff was frequently served either meals that contained meat or dairy products, which he cannot eat, or meals that were nutritionally inadequate and contained no source of protein. Sometimes he was provided with no food at all. He expressed his concerns to management and repeatedly attempted to work with management and caterers to improve the situation, but to no avail. At one point, he managed to source a block of tofu and asked that it be prepared for him, but the tofu disappeared, never to be seen again.[31] After ten days of frustration, Mr. Knauff verbally expressed his dismay at the conditions, and was met with retaliation by his supervisors—he was sent home, disciplined, and suspended without pay for a period of time, leaving him "humiliated."[32]

In Ontario, the *Human Rights Code*[33] ("the Code") prohibits actions that discriminate against people based on creed. Mr. Knauff's application to the Human Rights Tribunal of Ontario ("the Tribunal") raises a novel and often-theorized issue—whether his beliefs as an Ethical Vegan can be considered a form of "creed" and thus benefit from protection under the Code. The Tribunal has not yet ruled on this important issue, so Mr. Knauff's case could break new ground. Until relatively recently, creed was thought to be the same as religion, and the Ontario Human Rights Commission even stated explicitly in its previous creed policy that "creed does *not* include secular, moral or ethical beliefs or political convictions."[34] The Commission is a policy-making body that seeks to provide guidance to people about how to protect their rights, and guidance to employers, landlords, and service providers about how to respect the Code and protect the rights of others. Its policies are not binding law, but are generally considered influential, and are awarded a degree of deference by courts and the Tribunal.[35]

In 2011, the Commission began consultations aimed at developing a new creed policy seeking to clarify the nature and scope of rights and responsibilities based on creed, particularly in light of significant legal and social developments in Canada and internationally, including an increasing number of people identifying as non-religious, and courts and tribunals being asked to grapple with secular belief systems including Ethical Veganism.[36] The Commission consulted with a wide range of members of the public, scholars, civil society organizations, and other experts—including one of the authors of this chapter, who advanced the position that creed protections should be extended to encompass secular beliefs like ethical veganism.[37] The report produced as a result of the consultations repeatedly referenced the problems with leaving Ethical Vegans unprotected, and referred to legal advances in other countries, including the seminal *Hashman v Milton Park* case in the UK that saw the court afford legal protections to an individual with a philosophical belief in Ethical Veganism.[38]

In the end, the Commission listened to voices asking for inclusion of secular belief systems under the rubric of creed. It released its new creed policy late in 2015, stating that creed may include "non-religious belief systems that, like religion, substantially influence a person's identity, worldview and way of life."[39] The Policy also provided guidance for the Tribunal about which characteristics are relevant when considering if a belief system is a creed under the Code. According to the Policy, a creed should:

> 1. be sincerely, freely and deeply held;
> 2. be integrally linked to a person's identity, self-definition and fulfilment;
> 3. be a particular and comprehensive, overarching system of belief that governs one's conduct and practices;
> 4. address ultimate questions of human existence, including ideas about life, purpose, death, and the existence or non-existence of a Creator and/or a higher or different order of existence;
> 5. have some "nexus" or connection to an organization or community that professes a shared system of belief.[40]

The Policy goes on to state that, "given the breadth of belief systems that have been found to be a creed under the Code, [. . .] organizations should generally accept in good faith that a person practices a creed, unless there is significant reason to believe otherwise."[41]

For Mr. Knauff and others like him, Ethical Veganism is a comprehensive and overarching system of belief that governs their daily conduct and practices—from what they eat to what they wear, and much more.[42] The belief system addresses deep moral questions about human existence, and is linked to a broader vegan community, with Ethical Vegans increasingly making use of technology to find community and organize in-person events. These beliefs and practices can and should be protected by creed provisions under the Code.

Although the ultimate impact of the Policy on Mr. Knauff's case remains to be seen, the Policy has undoubtedly already had a "soft law" impact on the conduct of those governed by the Code in Ontario. Ethical Vegans and legal experts hailed the 2015 Policy upon its release, applauding it for bringing Ethical Veganism one step closer to being protected under Ontario's human rights laws.[43] The new Policy generated significant media coverage,[44] and employment and human rights law experts now regularly advise employers that they may be legally obligated to accommodate vegan employees.[45]

4.2. Arguments for Expanding Creed to Include Secular Ethical and Moral Beliefs

In recent years, an increasing number of human rights claims have been brought based on creed-based discrimination involving non-religious belief systems.[46] A number of cases have left open the possibility that secular ethical and moral beliefs may constitute a creed.[47]

4.2.1. Consistency with Principles of Statutory Construction and Interpretation

No adjudicator in Ontario has yet weighed in on the extent to which creed can encompass secular beliefs. Mr. Knauff's case is not the first to insist that Ethical Veganism is a form of creed,[48] but it may be the first case in which a decision-maker will evaluate the claim. This section will review several ways in which an interpretation of creed that includes ethical and moral secular belief systems like Ethical Veganism is consistent with well-established principles of statutory interpretation in Canada.[49]

First, the "presumption against tautology" assumes that the legislature has carefully chosen each word of a statute.[50] The related "presumption of consistent expression" assumes that, because words have been chosen carefully and consistently, identical words in a statute have the same meaning and different words have different meanings.[51] In *Canada v Canada*, the Federal Court held that the presumption of consistent expression applies not only within statutes but across statutes—especially ones that deal with the same subject matter.[52] Therefore, when interpreting the word "creed" in the Code, the Tribunal will have to compare the creed provision in the code to the wording used in the human rights legislation of other Canadian provinces. In Ontario, the Code uses only the word "creed" and makes no reference to "religion." In every other province, the terms "religion," "religious creed," or "religious belief" appear in addition to creed.[53] Based on the presumption of consistent expression, Ontario's decision to use only the term "creed" indicates a desire for it to mean something separate and apart from merely "religion," "religious creed," or "religious belief."[54]

Second, Canada is a bilingual country; statutes have both an English and a French version. The "shared meaning rule" of statutory interpretation for bilingual statutes requires that "where the words of one version may raise an ambiguity, one should look to the other official language version to determine whether its meaning is plain and unequivocal."[55] In the French version of the Code, "creed" is translated as "la croyance," which translates "belief" rather than merely "religion."[56] In *RC v District School Board of Niagara,* the Court held that this reflects a broader understanding of creed that includes secular beliefs as well as formal religious views.[57]

Third, the "principle of avoiding logical absurdities" provides that the best interpretation is one that does not result in inconsistent or absurd results.[58] One absurdity that may result from limiting creed protections to religion is that nearly identical beliefs in Ethical Veganism will be protected if they are founded in religion, but not if they are founded in secular reasoning.[59] Ethical Veganism is associated with many religions, such as Buddhism, Hinduism and Jainism.[60] Yet, it would be absurd to say that a vegan whose moral beliefs are rooted in organized religions deserves protection, while an Ethical Vegan who holds the same beliefs does not.[61] An interpretation of creed that excludes secular beliefs would result in precisely this kind of logical inconsistency.[62]

Religious beliefs have often played a central role in the structure and moral fabric of society, but religion may be declining as an organizational and motivational feature of belief. It is quickly becoming arbitrary and untenable to assume that beliefs based in religion should be protected, while beliefs based in reason or other secular motivations are not. Indeed, secular beliefs like Ethical Veganism will often play a role that is equally or even more profound than religious beliefs in the life of an adherent. In the face of statutory ambiguity, it is best to select an interpretation that avoids absurd results. This principle has been used to justify an expansive interpretation of a provision to avoid absurdity.[63]

Finally, it is a generally accepted principle of human rights legislation that rights are to be interpreted in a liberal and purposive way that reflects the spirit and intent of the legislation.[64] Any uncertainty about the scope of creed protections under the Code should "be resolved in a way that promotes the anti-discriminatory goals of the legislation."[65] Arguably, an interpretation of creed which includes secular ethical and moral belief systems would best reflect the objectives of the Code by ensuring that "similar beliefs are granted similar degrees of protection, regardless of whether they are rooted in religion or a secular basis."[66] This is consistent with a liberal, purposive interpretation of the Code[67] and the need to be maximally protective of human dignity.

4.2.2. Consistency with the Canadian Charter of Rights and Freedoms

Provincial human rights laws are also meant to be interpreted in a manner that is congruent with the Charter; this is particularly so in the context of freedom of religion.[68] The Canadian Supreme Court has ruled that protections available under human rights legislation for religious freedom may be informed by other constitutional values.[69]

Under this theory, Charter-protected rights to freedom of conscience obviously have significant bearing on the interpretation of creed. As the court ruled in *Maurice*, dietary choices to minimize animal suffering fall under an expression of conscience and give rise to Charter protection.[70]

Further, when two equally persuasive interpretations of legislation are available, a court should prefer an interpretation that promotes the principles and values underpinning the Charter over an interpretation that does not.[71] An expansive interpretation of creed that includes secular beliefs helps give full effect to the Charter right of freedom of conscience.

4.2.3. Consistency with Other Domestic Jurisprudence

The expanded definition of creed provided in the Commission's Policy is also consistent with domestic jurisprudence. A number of cases have affirmed or left open the possibility that non-religious beliefs may constitute a creed under the Code.[72] For example, in *Hendrickson Spring Stratford Operations v USWA, Local 8773*, the decision-maker held that:

> The term "creed" in the Code has a wide meaning and can "be taken to include almost any belief system that encompasses a set of particular religious beliefs but, as well, many other philosophical, secular and personal beliefs—the "isms" (such as are bound up in words like "environmentalism," "conservatism," "liberalism" or "socialism").[73]

Similarly, in *RC v District School Board of Niagara,* the Court held that creed protects secular beliefs as well as formal religious views.[74]

During public consultation regarding its updated Policy on creed, the Commission heard from a number of organizations that in order for secular beliefs to merit the same protection as religion under Ontario human rights legislation, they should meet the same or similar requirements.[75] For this reason, the Commission drew from some of the leading case law in Canada when developing the definition of creed in their updated Policy.[76]

First, the requirement that a creed "be sincere, freely and deeply held" and "integrally linked to a person's identity, self-definition and fulfilment" were drawn directly from the 2004 Supreme Court of Canada case, *Syndicat Northcrest v Amselem*.[77] The third characteristic, which requires that a creed be a "comprehensive, overarching system of belief that governs one's conduct and practices" comes from the 1986 Supreme Court case, *R v Edwards Books and Art Ltd.*[78] The fourth requirement set out in the Policy draws on indicators discussed in *Bennett v Canada.*[79] Specifically, the Federal Court held that section 2(a) protects "beliefs that coalesce to provide the believer with answers to many, if not most, of the problems and concerns that confront humans" including "ultimate ideas . . . about life, purpose and death."[80] This requirement also draws on statements in *Edwards Books*, where the court concluded that section 2(a) protects "profoundly personal beliefs that govern one's perception of oneself, humankind, nature, and, *in some cases*, a higher or different order of being."[81] The fifth and final characteristic set out in the Policy comes mainly from the 2015 Supreme Court case, *Loyola High School v Quebec*, where the court recognized the collective dimension of religious beliefs.[82] This means that the belief or practice must exist as part of a broader framework and not be simply a personal preference or opinion.[83]

While the Tribunal has not, as of writing, decided any cases involving non-religious beliefs since the release of the Commission's Policy in 2015, many of the Tribunal's decisions have made specific reference to the expanded definition of creed.[84] The Commission's policy statements are given great deference by the courts and the Tribunal, and this Policy should inform the Tribunal's interpretation of creed moving forward.[85]

4.3. The Knauff Case: Setting Precedent in Other Provinces

As noted in Part 2, Ontario is alone among provinces in prohibiting discrimination solely on the basis of creed. Human rights laws in British Columbia, Alberta, Quebec, New Brunswick, and Newfoundland appear to protect religious beliefs only, meaning that Ethical Vegans could avail themselves of protections only if their belief system was deemed to be a religion. Examining whether this could be the case is beyond the scope of this chapter, although we note that should Mr. Knauff's case be successful in Ontario, it could be persuasive in Manitoba, Saskatchewan, Nova Scotia, and Prince Edward Island, each of which lists "creed" as a separate ground of discrimination, distinct from religion.[86]

4.4. Other Issues

This chapter has emphasized how human rights laws may be used to protect the belief systems of Ethical Vegans, but this is far from the only legal issue facing vegans in Canada. This section will briefly survey another that arguably bears relation to protecting beliefs: the rise of so-called "ag gag" laws in Canada (i.e., agricultural gag laws) that seek to conceal the suffering of animals raised and killed for food, and chill vegan persuasion and advocacy efforts.

Late in 2019, the province of Alberta passed Canada's first ag gag law after the animal agriculture sector pressured the government to crack down on vegan activism. The legislation amended provincial trespass laws to effectively outlaw undercover investigations into farms and slaughterhouses.[87]

Ontario followed suit in June 2020 by passing similar legislation outlawing undercover investigations, and taking it one step further by outlawing peaceful protests outside slaughterhouses at which participants bear witness to farmed animals being trucked to their death, greeting them inside open-sided transport trucks, providing them with water on a hot day, and documenting the (often illegal) conditions under which they are being transported.[88]

Undercover investigations are a key tool for vegan advocates; they help shed light on the conditions that animals endure on farms and in slaughterhouses before they end up on the dinner plate, helping make the case that eliminating the use of animals is necessary to prevent animal suffering. Ag gag laws originated in the United States, where they were originally passed to shut down hidden-camera exposés that painted a truthful yet unflattering picture of modern industrial farming. Undercover investigations into Canadian farms have also revealed appalling suffering in the animal farming system, and have resulted in legal and policy changes, prosecutions, and significant publicity for the vegan cause. A statute outlawing citizens from gathering information and disseminating information in this manner is constitutionally problematic, and may run afoul of protections for freedom of expression under section 2(b) of the Charter.[89] Courts in Idaho,[90] Utah,[91] Iowa,[92] Kansas,[93] and North Carolina[94] have already struck down similar ag gag laws in those states as an unconstitutional restraint on freedom of speech under the First Amendment of the constitution of the United States.

The provisions in Ontario outlawing peaceful protest at slaughterhouses may also threaten the right to freedom of conscience as discussed above, and/or creed-based protections afforded by provincial human rights laws. Protests outside of slaughterhouses in Ontario often take the form of "vigils" organized by members of the Animal Save Movement, which holds that bearing witness to animal suffering is a core moral duty. Largely made up of Ethical Vegans who seek to convince other humans that animals deserve equal moral consideration, Animal Save Movement activists stand outside slaughterhouses on public property with signs urging people to consider animals by going vegan. They greet animals inside stopped trucks in their final moments before entering the slaughterhouse, often providing them with physical touch, water, or words of comfort. They regularly film the animals they witness confined inside transport trucks, often sharing the footage on social media platforms and revealing troubling fear and suffering, and conditions that are unethical and frequently unlawful.

Could the activities of bearing witness and exposing suffering also be considered manifestations of a conscientious belief in Ethical Veganism, thus potentially benefiting from protection as a creed and/or under section 2(a) of the Charter? This question has not yet been explored by a tribunal or court, but ag gag statutes in Canada will inevitably be subjected to a constitutional challenge, so the issue may soon be litigated.

5. CONCLUSION

Discrimination against vegans is an emerging legal issue that arises in a number of circumstances, including situations of fundamental significance such as in employment or housing. Ethical Vegans are still a numerical minority existing in a society where the human use of animals for food, clothing, entertainment, and scientific purposes is pervasive and so deeply entrenched that it goes largely unquestioned.

Ethical Vegans in Canada and beyond deserve clarity and certainty on the question of whether human rights laws can be used to protect their belief systems. Charter protections for freedom of conscience are capable of providing this protection, but in limited circumstances. The Knauff case may eventually confirm that Ethical Vegans in Ontario are protected, and those in the other four provinces that list creed as a protected ground may also benefit from protections. But what of those in the other half of the country who have no obvious legal recourse? With secular belief systems increasingly important to Canadians, and Ethical Veganism on the rise, legislatures should be mindful of this new reality and proactively legislate to ensure Ethical Vegans do not face discrimination and marginalization in Canada's dominant animal-using culture.

6. NOTES

1. Camille Labchuk, "Protecting Secular Beliefs: Should Creed Provisions Protect Ethical Vegans from Discrimination?" Paper delivered at the Ontario Human Rights Commission/York University Legal Workshop on Human Rights, Creed and Freedom of Religion, Toronto, Ontario (29–30 March 2012): 2, https://docs.google.com/file/d/0BwFvhg37TTCjMk84Q0l4QTdic3M/preview.
2. "More Than 3 Million Canadians Vegetarian or Vegan: Study," Ryan Flanagan, 2018, https://www.ctvnews.ca/canada/more-than-3-million-canadians-vegetarian-or-vegan-study-1.4027606.
3. Cara Hunt, "Vegan Values, Religious Rights: A Cultural Critique of Entrenched Ethics," (2010): 1, https://www.lclark.edu/live/files/6665-vegan-values-religious-rights.
4. *Human Rights Code*, RSO 1990, c H19.
5. Canadian Human Rights Commission, "Human Rights in Canada," 2020, https://www.chrc-ccdp.gc.ca/eng/content/human-rights-in-canada.
6. Canadian *Charter of Rights and Freedoms*, Part 1 of the *Constitution Act 1982* being Schedule B to the *Canada Act 1982* (UK), 1982, c 11 at s 2(a).
7. Department of Justice, "Section 2(a)—Freedom of Religion," 2020, https://www.justice.gc.ca/eng/csj-sjc/rfc-dlc/ccrf-ccdl/check/art2a.html; See also *R v Edwards Books and Art Ltd*, [1986] 2 SCR 713: 759; *R v Big M Drug Mart Ltd*, [1985] 1 SCR 295: 346; *Syndicat Northcrest v Amselem*, [2004] 2 SCR 551: 41; *Alberta v Hutterian Brethren of Wilson Colony*, [2009] 2 SCR 567: 32.
8. *R v Morgentaler*, [1988] 1 SCR 30: 178-179.
9. Department of Justice, "Section 2(a)—Freedom of Religion," https://www.justice.gc.ca/eng/csj-sjc/rfc-dlc/ccrf-ccdl/check/art2a.html.
10. *Maurice v Canada (Attorney General)*, 2002 FCT 69.
11. *Maurice v Canada (Attorney General)*.
12. *Maurice v Canada (Attorney General)*: 1.

13. *Maurice v Canada (Attorney General)*: 9.

14. *Maurice v Canada (Attorney General)*: 8.

15. Ontario Human Rights Commission, "Policy on Preventing Discrimination Based on Creed," 2015: 24, http://www.ohrc.on.ca/sites/default/files/Policy%20on%20preventing%20discrimination%20based%20on%20creed_accessible_0.pdf.

16. An exception is the federally-enacted *Canadian Human Rights Act*, RSC 1985, c H-6, which applies only to matters within the legislative purview of Parliament, including federally-regulated matters like First Nations governance, and industries including aviation, banking, and telecommunications. The Act is similar to provincial human rights codes yet seeks to prevent harassment and discrimination on the basis of a variety of grounds—none of which would obviously encompass Ethical Veganism.

17. Labchuk, "Protecting Secular Beliefs: Should Creed Provisions Protect Ethical Vegans from Discrimination?": 8.

18. Labchuk, "Protecting Secular Beliefs: Should Creed Provisions Protect Ethical Vegans from Discrimination?": 8.

19. Labchuk, "Protecting Secular Beliefs: Should Creed Provisions Protect Ethical Vegans from Discrimination?": 9.

20. Labchuk, "Protecting Secular Beliefs: Should Creed Provisions Protect Ethical Vegans from Discrimination?": 9.

21. Labchuk, "Protecting Secular Beliefs: Should Creed Provisions Protect Ethical Vegans from Discrimination?": 9.

22. Labchuk, "Protecting Secular Beliefs: Should Creed Provisions Protect Ethical Vegans from Discrimination?": 9.

23. Lisa Johnson, "The Religion of Ethical Veganism," *Journal of Animal Ethics* 5, no. 1 (2015): 59.

24. The Vegan Society, "Definition of Veganism," https://www.vegansociety.com/go-vegan/definition-veganism. Although note that there is no universally-accepted definition or practice of veganism. Much in the same way that those subscribing to a particular religion will vary in how they define the scope of its tenets and requirements, ethical vegans have varying beliefs. For example, some may find only harmful exploitation morally problematic, while considering exploitation *per se* to be acceptable so long as no harm or suffering is caused to animals (e.g., taking and sharing photos of animals housed in farm sanctuaries exploits their likeness, but does not cause physical or psychological harm to them).

25. *Friedman v S Cal Permanente Med Group*, 125 Cal Rptr 2d 663, 665-66 (Cal Ct App 2002) [*Friedman*] in Donna Page, "Veganism and Sincerely Held 'Religious' Beliefs in the Workplace: No Protection Without Definition," *University of Pennsylvania Journal of Labor and Employment Law* 7, no. 2 (2005): 388.

26. Labchuk, "Protecting Secular Beliefs: Should Creed Provisions Protect Ethical Vegans from Discrimination?": 4.

27. Page, "Veganism and Sincerely Held 'Religious' Beliefs in the Workplace: No Protection Without Definition": 390.

28. Johnson, "The Religion of Ethical Veganism": 31.

29. It is increasingly clear that raising and eating animals is a major contributor to climate change and other environmental degradation, and so-called "climate veganism" may be gaining in popularity. Choosing to adhere to veganism for moral reasons related to environmental protection, rather than animal protection, could be considered another form of Ethical Veganism, although this argument is beyond the scope of the present analysis.

30. Amy Dempsey, "Vegan firefighter suing the government says he didn't deserve hunger and humiliation: 'I'm tired of nice'," 2019, https://www.thestar.com/news/canada/2019/07/04/vegan-firefighter-suing-the-government-says-he-didnt-deserve-hunger-and-humiliation-im-tired-of-nice.html.

31. Adam Knauff Application under section 34 of the *Human Rights Code* (Form 1), (on file with author).

32. Adam Knauff Application: 30.

33. *Human Rights Code*: 4.

34. Ontario Human Rights Commission, "Policy on Preventing Discrimination Based on Creed": 15.

35. *Quesnel v London Educational Health Centre*, (1995) 28 CHRR D/474 (Ont Bd of Inquiry) [*Quesnel*]; See also Ontario Human Rights Commission, "Policy on Preventing Discrimination Based on Creed": 126.

36. Ontario Human Rights Commission, "Human Rights and Creed Research and Consultation Report," 2013, http://www.ohrc.on.ca/sites/default/files/consultation%20report_creed%20human%20rights%20research%20and%20consultation%20report.pdf.

37. Labchuk, "Protecting Secular Beliefs: Should Creed Provisions Protect Ethical Vegans from Discrimination?": 8.

38. Ontario Human Rights Commission, "Human Rights and Creed Research and Consultation Report," 2013: 49, 65. For *Hashman* case details, see Matthew Overton in this volume.

39. Ontario Human Rights Commission, "Policy on Preventing Discrimination Based on Creed": 1.

40. Ontario Human Rights Commission, "Policy on Preventing Discrimination Based on Creed": 1.

41. Ontario Human Rights Commission, "Policy on Preventing Discrimination Based on Creed": 2.

42. Page, "Veganism and Sincerely Held 'Religious' Beliefs in the Workplace: No Protection Without Definition": 390.

43. Animal Justice, "Veganism is One Step Closer to Becoming a Human Right in Ontario," 2016, https://www.animaljustice.ca/blog/veganism-is-one-step-closer-to-becoming-a-human-right-in-ontario.

44. See for example: Dan Taekema, "Vegans argue they're a 'creed' under Ontario human rights law," 2016, https://www.thestar.com/news/gta/2016/02/04/vegans-argue-theyre-a-creed-under-ontario-human-rights-law.html.

45. See for example: Benefits Canada, "Do employers have to accommodate vegans?" 2016, https://www.benefitscanada.com/news/do-employers-have-to-accommodate-vegans-79445; Vey Willets LLP, "Food for thought: Do employers need to accommodate ethical vegans in the workplace?" 2020, https://www.vwlawyers.ca/blog/food-for-thought-do-employers-need-to-accommodate-ethical-veganism-in-the-workplace; Petket Campbell Postnikoff LLP, "Employment Law: Firefighter Claims Veganism Is a Human Right," 2019, https://petkerlaw.com/employment-law-firefighter-claims-veganism-is-a-human-right/.

46. Ontario Human Rights Commission, "Human Rights and Creed Research and Consultation Report": 45, 64–65.

47. See for example: *RC v District School Board of Niagara*, 2013 HRTO 1382: 40–42; *Hendrickson Spring v United Steelworkers of America, Local 8773 (Kaiser Grievances)*, [2005] OLAA No 382, 142 LAC (4th) 159; *Rand v Sealy Eastern Ltd*, (1982) 3 CHRR D/938 (Ont Bd Inquiry); *Obdeyn v Walbar Machine Products of Canada Ltd* (1982) 3 CHRR D/712 (Ont Bd Inq); *Jazairi v Ontario Human Rights Commission* (1999), 175 DLR (4th) 302, 122 OAC 356 (ON CA).

48. See for example: *Hunter v Ontario (Ministry of Community Safety and Correctional Services)* 2010 HRTO 705, and *Ketenci v Yeates School of Graduate Studies at Ryerson University*, 2012 HRTO 994. In both cases, the question of whether Ethical Veganism constituted a form of creed was raised, but the cases were each decided on another basis.

49. Ontario Human Rights Commission, "Human Rights and Creed Research and Consultation Report": 47–52.

50. Ontario Human Rights Commission, "Human Rights and Creed Research and Consultation Report": 47.

51. Ontario Human Rights Commission, "Human Rights and Creed Research and Consultation Report": 47; See also *R v Zeolkowski, 1989 CanLII 72 (SCC) at 1387; Canada (Information Commissioner) v Canada (Minister of National Defence)*, [2009] 2 FCR 86: 47.

52. *Canada v Canada*: 47.

53. Ontario Human Rights Commission, "Human Rights and Creed Research and Consultation Report": 48.

54. Ontario Human Rights Commission, "Policy on Preventing Discrimination Based on Creed": 19.
55. *Reference re Supreme Court Act, ss 5 and 6*, [2014] 1 SCR 433: 32; *R v Daoust*, 2004 SCC 6: 28.
56. *Code des Droits de la Personne*, LRO 1990, chap H19.
57. *District School Board of Niagara*: 42.
58. *Unifor v Kuehne and Nagel Ltd*, 2019 CanLII 10485; See also *Campbell (GT) & Associates Ltd v Hugh Carson Co*, [1979] 99 DLR (3d) 529 (Ont CA).
59. Ontario Human Rights Commission, "Human Rights and Creed Research and Consultation Report": 49.
60. Page, "Veganism and Sincerely Held 'Religious' Beliefs in the Workplace: No Protection Without Definition": 407.
61. Page, "Veganism and Sincerely Held 'Religious' Beliefs in the Workplace: No Protection Without Definition": 407.
62. Ontario Human Rights Commission, "Human Rights and Creed Research and Consultation Report": 49.
63. See for example: *Campbell (GT) & Associates Ltd v Hugh Carson Co*: 57.
64. *Landau v Ontario (Finance),* 2011 HRTO 1521: 12; *Whiteley v Osprey Media Publishing*, 2010 HRTO 2152: 16.
65. Ontario Human Rights Commission, "Human Rights and Creed Research and Consultation Report": 52.
66. Ontario Human Rights Commission, "Human Rights and Creed Research and Consultation Report": 52.
67. See for example: *Dickason v University of Alberta* [1992] 2 SCR 1103; *Landau v Ontario (Finance)*: 12; *Whiteley v Osprey Media Publishing*: 16.
68. See *Ontario (Disability Support Program) v Tranchemontagne*, 2010 ONCA 593; *Ball v Ontario (Community and Social Services),* 2010 HRTO 360; *Mortillaro v Ontario (Transportation)*, 2011 HRTO 310.
69. *Syndicat Northcrest v Amselem*: 39.
70. *Maurice v Canada (Attorney General)*: 10.
71. *R v Zundel* [1992] 2 SCR 731: 772.
72. Ontario Human Rights Commission, "Human Rights and Creed Research and Consultation Report": 55; See also *RC v District School Board of Niagara*; *Hendrickson Spring v United Steelworkers of America, Local 8773 (Kaiser Grievances)*; *Rand v Sealy Eastern Ltd.*
73. *Hendrickson Spring v United Steelworkers of America, Local 8773 (Kaiser Grievances)* in Ontario Human Rights Commission, "Human Rights and Creed Research and Consultation Report": 56.
74. *RC v District School Board of Niagara*: 42.
75. Ontario Human Rights Commission, "Human Rights and Creed Research and Consultation Report": 45.
76. Ontario Human Rights Commission, "Policy on Preventing Discrimination Based on Creed": footnotes 69-72.
77. *Syndicat Northcrest v Amselem*: 39, 46; See also *Ktunaxa Nation v British Columbia (Forests, Lands and Natural Resource Operations)*, [2017] 2 SCR 386: 68.
78. *R v Edwards Books and Art Ltd*: 97.
79. *Bennett v Canada (Attorney General),* 2011 FC 1310: 55.
80. *Bennett v Canada (Attorney General)*: 55.
81. *R v Edwards Books and Art Ltd* [emphasis added].
82. *Loyola High School v Quebec (Attorney General),* [2015] 1 SCR 613: 59-62; See also *Alberta v Hutterian Brethren of Wilson Colony*: 182; *R v Edwards Books and Art Ltd*: 145.
83. *407 ETR Concession Co v CAW-Canada, Local 414*, 2007 CarswellOnt 422 (OAB) in Suzie Chiodo, "Conscience, Creed and the Code: Forthcoming Changes to the Ontario Human Rights Commission's Policy on Creed," 2012: 10, https://papers.ssrn.com/sol3/papers.cfm?abstract_id=2350268.
84. See *Lin v Toronto Court Services*, 2017 HRTO 1; *Everall v Donovan*, 2016 HRTO 957; *Vezina v Elections Ontario*, 2016 HRTO 994.

85. *Quesnel v London Educational Health Centre*: 35.

86. Labchuk, "Protecting Secular Beliefs: Should Creed Provisions Protect Ethical Vegans from Discrimination?": 9.

87. It does so by prohibiting citizens and organizations from using "false pretences" to obtain permission to be on property, which would effectively prevent a member of an animal protection organization from obtaining employment on a farm or at a slaughterhouse to investigate the conditions under which animals are kept. Employers in the animal agriculture sector are unlikely to hire animal advocates who are committed to exposing animal suffering in their operations. See s 2.4 of the *Petty Trespass Act*, RSA 2000 cP-11, and s. 2(4) of the *Trespass to Premises Act*, RSA 2000 cT-7.

88. See the *Security from Trespass and Protecting Food Safety Act*, 2020, SO 2020 c 9. Note that as of writing, regulations to accompany the legislation were still being drafted. The regulations will set out the scope of the prohibition on undercover investigations and peaceful protests.

89. Dozens of Canadian law professors and legal experts wrote to the provincial government to warn that Ontario's proposed ag gag law was unconstitutional. See: Animal Justice, "Letter from Richard Moon et al.," 2020, https://www.animaljustice.ca/wp-content/uploads/2020/02/2020-02-10-Bill-156-Sign-on-Letter-FINAL-UPDATED.pdf. Ag gag laws have already been struck down as unconstitutional in multiple US states, including Idaho, Utah, Iowa, Kansas, and North Carolina. See Animal Legal Defense Fund, "Ag Gag Laws," https://aldf.org/issue/ag-gag/.

90. *Animal Legal Def Fund v Wasden*, 878 F.3d 1184 (9th Cir 2018).

91. *Animal Legal Def Fund v Herbert*, 263 F Supp 3d 1193, 1198 (D Utah 2017).

92. *Animal Legal Def Fund v Reynolds*, No 417CV00362JEGHCA, 2019 WL 140069 (SD Iowa 9 Jan 2019); *Animal Legal Defense Fund et al. v Kimberly Reynolds et al.* No 4:19-cv-00124-JEG-HCA (SD Iowa 2 Jan 2020).

93. *Animal Legal Defense Fund et al. v Kelly*, 434 F Supp 3d 974 (D Kan 2020).

94. *People for the Ethical Treatment of Animals, Inc. et al. v Stein*, 1:16Cv25 (MDNC Jun 12 2020).

7. REFERENCES

407 ETR Concession Co v CAW-Canada, Local 414, 2007 CarswellOnt 422 (OAB).

Adam Knauff Application under section 34 of the *Human Rights Code* (Form 1), (on file with author).

Animal Justice. "Letter from Richard Moon et al." 2020. https://www.animaljustice.ca/wp-content/uploads/2020/02/2020-02-10-Bill-156-Sign-on-Letter-FINAL-UPDATED.pdf.

Animal Justice. "Veganism Is One Step Closer to Becoming a Human Right in Ontario." Accessed November 22, 2020. https://www.animaljustice.ca/blog/veganism-is-one-step-closer-to-becoming-a-human-right-in-ontario.

Animal Legal Defense Fund. "Ag Gag Laws." Accessed November 22, 2020. https://aldf.org/issue/ag-gag/.

Animal Legal Def Fund v Herbert, 263 F Supp 3d 1193, 1198 (D Utah 2017).

Animal Legal Defense Fund et al. v Kelly, 434 F Supp 3d 974 (D Kan 2020).

Animal Legal Def Fund v Reynolds, No 417CV00362JEGHCA, 2019 WL 140069 (SD Iowa 9 Jan 2019).

Animal Legal Defense Fund et al. v Reynolds et al., No 4:19-cv-00124-JEG-HCA (SD Iowa 2 Jan 2020).

Animal Legal Def Fund v Wasden, 878 F.3d 1184 (9th Cir 2018).

Alberta v Hutterian Brethren of Wilson Colony, [2009] 2 SCR 567.

Ball v Ontario (Community and Social Services), 2010 HRTO 360.

Benefits Canada. "Do employers have to accommodate vegans?" Accessed November 22, 2020. https://www.benefitscanada.com/news/do-employers-have-to-accommodate-vegans-79445.

Bennett v Canada (Attorney General), 2011 FC 1310.

Campbell (GT) & Associates Ltd v Hugh Carson Co, [1979] 99 DLR (3d) 529 (Ont CA).

Canada (Information Commissioner) v Canada (Minister of National Defence), [2009] 2 FCR 86.

Canadian *Charter of Rights and Freedoms*, Part 1 of the *Constitution Act 1982* being Schedule B to the *Canada Act 1982* (UK), 1982, c 11.

Canadian Human Rights Act, RSC 1985, c H-6.

Canadian Human Rights Commission. "Human Rights in Canada." Accessed November 22, 2020. https://www.chrc-ccdp.gc.ca/eng/content/human-rights-in-canada.

Chiodo, Suzie. "Conscience, Creed and the Code: Forthcoming Changes to the Ontario Human Rights Commission's Policy on Creed." 2012. https://papers.ssrn.com/sol3/papers.cfm?abstract_id=2350268.

Code des Droits de la Personne, LRO 1990, chap H19.

Dempsey, Amy. "Vegan firefighter suing the government says he didn't deserve hunger and humiliation: 'I'm tired of nice.'" 2019. https://www.thestar.com/news/canada/2019/07/04/vegan-firefighter-suing-the-government-says-he-didnt-deserve-hunger-and-humiliation-im-tired-of-nice.html.

Department of Justice. "Section 2(a)—Freedom of Religion." 2020. https://www.justice.gc.ca/eng/csj-sjc/rfc-dlc/ccrf-ccdl/check/art2a.html.

Dickason v University of Alberta [1992] 2 SCR 1103.

Everall v Donovan, 2016 HRTO 957.

Flanagan, Ryan. "More Than 3 Million Canadians Vegetarian or Vegan: Study." 2018. https://www.ctvnews.ca/canada/more-than-3-million-canadians-vegetarian-or-vegan-study-1.4027606.

Friedman v S Cal Permanente Med Group, 125 Cal Rptr 2d 663, 665-66 (Cal Ct App 2002).

Hendrickson Spring v United Steelworkers of America, Local 8773 (Kaiser Grievances), [2005] OLAA No 382, 142 LAC (4th) 159.

Human Rights Code, RSO 1990, c H19.

Hunt, Cara. "Vegan Values, Religious Rights: A Cultural Critique of Entrenched Ethics." 2010. https://www.lclark.edu/live/files/6665-vegan-values-religious-rights.

Hunter v Ontario (Ministry of Community Safety and Correctional Services) 2010 HRTO 705.

Jazairi v Ontario Human Rights Commission (1999), 175 DLR (4th) 302, 122 OAC 356 (ONCA).

Johnson, Lisa. "The Religion of Ethical Veganism" *Journal of Animal Ethics* 5, no. 1 (2015) 31.

Ketenci v Yeates School of Graduate Studies at Ryerson University, 2012 HRTO 994.

Ktunaxa Nation v British Columbia (Forests, Lands and Natural Resource Operations), [2017] 2 SCR 386.

Labchuk, Camille. "Protecting Secular Beliefs: Should Creed Provisions Protect Ethical Vegans from Discrimination?" Paper delivered at the Ontario Human Rights Commission/York University Legal Workshop on Human Rights, Creed and Freedom of Religion, Toronto, Ontario, 29–30 March 2012. https://docs.google.com/file/d/0BwFvhg37TTCjMk84Q0l4QTdic3M/preview.

Landau v Ontario (Finance), 2011 HRTO 1521.

Lin v Toronto Court Services, 2017 HRTO 1.

Loyola High School v Quebec (Attorney General), [2015] 1 SCR 613.

Maurice v Canada (Attorney General), 2002 FCT 69.

Mortillaro v Ontario (Transportation), 2011 HRTO 310.

Obdeyn v Walbar Machine Products of Canada Ltd (1982) 3 CHRR D/712 (Ont Bd Inq).

Ontario (Disability Support Program) v Tranchemontagne, 2010 ONCA 593.

Ontario Human Rights Commission. "Human Rights and Creed Research and Consultation Report." 2013. http://www.ohrc.on.ca/sites/default/files/consultation%20report_creed%20human%20rights%20research%20and%20consultation%20report.pdf.

Ontario Human Rights Commission. "Policy on Preventing Discrimination Based on Creed." 2015. http://www.ohrc.on.ca/sites/default/files/Policy%20on%20preventing%20discrimination%20based%20on%20creed_accessible_0.pdf.

Page, Donna. "Veganism and Sincerely Held 'Religious' Beliefs in the Workplace: No Protection Without Definition" *University of Pennsylvania Journal of Labor and Employment Law* 7, no. 2 (2005) 363.

People for the Ethical Treatment of Animals, Inc. et al. v Stein, 1:16Cv25 (MDNC Jun 12 2020).

Petket Campbell Postnikoff LLP. "Employment Law: Firefighter Claims Veganism Is a Human Right." 2019. https://petkerlaw.com/employment-law-firefighter-claims-veganism-is-a-human-right/.

Petty Trespass Act, RSA 2000 cP-11.

Quesnel v London Educational Health Centre, (1995) 28 CHRR D/474 (Ont Bd of Inquiry).

Rand v Sealy Eastern Ltd, (1982) 3 CHRR D/938 (Ont Bd Inquiry).

RC v District School Board of Niagara, 2013 HRTO 1382.

Reference re Supreme Court Act, ss 5 and 6, [2014] 1 SCR 433.

R v Big M Drug Mart Ltd, [1985] 1 SCR 295.

R v Daoust, 2004 SCC 6.

R v Edwards Books and Art Ltd, [1986] 2 SCR 713.

R v Morgentaler, [1988] 1 SCR 30.

R v Zeolkowski, 1989 CanLII 72 (SCC).

R v Zundel [1992] 2 SCR 73.

Security from Trespass and Protecting Food Safety Act, 2020, SO 2020 c 9.

Syndicat Northcrest v Amselem, [2004] 2 SCR 551.

Taekema, Dan. "Vegans argue they're a 'creed' under Ontario human rights law." 2016. https://www.thestar.com/news/gta/2016/02/04/vegans-argue-theyre-a-creed-under-ontario-human-rights-law.html.

The Vegan Society. "Definition of Veganism." https://www.vegansociety.com/go-vegan/definition-veganism.

Trespass to Premises Act, RSA 2000 cT-7.

Unifor v Kuehne and Nagel Ltd, 2019 CanLII 10485.

Vey Willets LLP. "Food for thought: Do employers need to accommodate ethical vegans in the workplace?" 2020. https://www.vwlawyers.ca/blog/food-for-thought-do-employers-need-to-accommodate-ethical-veganism-in-the-workplace.

Vezina v Elections Ontario, 2016 HRTO 994.

Whiteley v Osprey Media Publishing, 2010 HRTO 2152.

Chapter Three

Vegetarian and Vegan Litigation in the United States

Adam P. Karp

1. INTRODUCTION

The 2008 *Vegetarian Times* poll, collected by the Harris Interactive Service Bureau, surveying 5,050 respondents, found that 3.2 percent of the American population (7.3 million) is vegetarian-inclined [meaning vegetarian or vegan], of which 15.6 percent, or 0.5 percent of the entire population (about 1 million), are vegans. In 2011, the Vegetarian Resource Group commissioned Harris to perform another survey of 1,010 adults. In three short years, the percentages jumped to approximately 5.0 percent vegetarian-inclined (with about half, or 2.5 percent, vegan [or about 7.8 million]). A 2018 Gallup poll suggests little movement (5.0 percent vegetarian-inclined, 3.0 percent vegan [about 9.8 million]).[1]

Dietary vegans abstain from the consumption of animal products. Ethical vegans extend their commitment beyond dietary choices to avoidance of cosmetics, clothing, and vaccines. Animal lawyer and named plaintiff in *Friedman v. S. Cal. Permanente Med. Gp.,* 102 Cal.App.4th 39 (2002) described Ethical Veganism this way:

> Ethical Veganism extends beyond trivial dietary preferences. Diet is merely a small part of observing a non-exploitive relationship with the people and animals of this world. Ethical Veganism is a relational lens through which to view the world. Ethical Vegans are not "speciesist" and value the sanctity of all life, seeking to exclude from their life, as far as possible and practical, all forms of exploitation of, and cruelty to, animals for food, clothing or any other purpose. Consequently, Ethical Vegans do not eat meat, fish or poultry, and do not use other animal products and by-products including eggs, dairy products, honey,

> leather, fur, wool, soaps and toothpastes which contain lard, etc., and Ethical Vegans do not participate in the biomedical experimentation on animals and avoid activities or products which encourage it. As can be seen from this "list" of prohibited activities, being vegetarian is only one small part of being an Ethical Vegan. While being a Vegan or Ethical Vegan necessarily implies that one is a vegetarian, the opposite is not true; being a vegetarian does not imply one is an Ethical Vegan, let alone a Vegan. . . . There is a common ethical principle shared by all Vegans which is a reverence for life and desire to live with, as opposed to depending upon, the other species of the planet.[2]

Legal issues pertaining to vegans and vegetarians relate predominantly to accommodation in employment, education, medical care, and institutionalized meals. Though adherents to particular faith systems may find support and even prescription for vegetarianism in religious canons, others embrace such multifaceted conscientious views from a secular, humanist, or nonreligious perspective. Certainly, one may choose veganism without possessing proper religious credentials or pious calibration of soul. Yet it also finds refuge in Buddhism, Christianity, Hinduism, Judaism, Wicca, and Spiritual Veganism.[3]

In *Belonging, Vol. I of Faith in the Neighborhood*,[4] Lucinda Mosher, Th.D., surveys and illustrates the personal impacts and struggles that adherents to diverse faiths have within desegregated American neighborhoods. The following excerpt from this text raises an interesting hypothetical:

> A homeowner in an American suburban [*sic*] is expected to maintain a well-manicured lawn. But manicuring one's lawn presents a challenge to the devout American Jain, says Arvind Vora, president of the Long Island Multi-Faith Forum. Arvind owns a home in the small city of Kings Park. To "belong" in an American neighborhood as a Jain is a moral compromise, he stresses. "When you mow the lawn, you know, so many insects will be killed," his wife Ila explains, "and so that is a very difficult situation for us." Killing insects willfully is a violation of *ahimsa* (non-harming)—Jainism's highest principle.
>
> Well then, do the Voras mow their lawn? Yes, Arvind assures us, but if they could figure out a way to have an acceptable yard without having to mow the lawn, they both agree, that would be more Jain. "It is one of those unfortunate things that we humans have to live someplace, and that there are no houses available without lawns here. But I think there are, of course, many nice groundcovers available where you don't have to cut the lawn and all those things. So perhaps that could be the compromise." Arving continues, "Some of our Jain friends here believe in not mowing the lawn. They do not care whether the house prices go down on their block. They just let the grass grow. They give it freedom; they do not cut it."[5]

What if Kings Park passed a law requiring the Voras and their Jain friends to mow their lawns to a length of no longer than two inches between the months of May and September? Would the First Amendment, or federal or state antidiscrimination laws, protect their right to not cut the grass?

2. EMPLOYMENT

2.1. Title VII of the Civil Rights Act of 1964

Title VII of the Civil Rights Act of 1964 ("CRA") renders unlawful the employment practice of discriminating against an employee or prospective employee on the basis of "such individual's race, color, religion, sex, or national origin . . ."[6] Employers may not fail or refuse to hire or to discharge any individual, or otherwise discriminate against any individual with respect to such protected classifications.[7] Further, they must reasonably accommodate the employee's "religious observance or practice" unless doing so would be an "undue hardship on the conduct of the employer's business."[8] The Equal Employment Opportunity Commission ("EEOC") has established a more informative administrative definition that elucidates the situation where the issue of whether or not a practice or belief is "religious" exists. It provides:

> In most cases whether or not a practice or belief is religious is not at issue. However, in those cases in which the issue does exist, the Commission will define religious practices to include moral or ethical beliefs as to what is right and wrong which are sincerely held with the strength of traditional religious views. This standard was developed in United States v. Seeger, 380 U.S. 163 (1965) and Welsh v. United States, 398 U.S. 333 (1970). The Commission has consistently applied this standard in its decisions. [FN 1 See CD 76-104 (1976), CCH ¶ 6500; CD 71-2620 (1971), CCH ¶ 6283; CD 71-779 (1970), CCH ¶ 6180.] The fact that no religious group espouses such beliefs or the fact that the religious group to which the individual professes to belong may not accept such belief will not determine whether the belief is a religious belief of the employee or prospective employee. The phrase "religious practice" as used in these Guidelines includes both religious observances and practices, as stated in section 701(j), 42 U.S.C. 2000e(j).[9]

Title VII and Rule 1605.1 only apply to employers with fifteen or more employees.[10]

Title VII religious accommodation claims follow a two-part, burden-shifting analysis. The employee must establish a *prima facie* case by proving (1) an employment obligation interferes with her religious practice; (2) she has informed the employer of same; (3) the employer subjected her to an adverse employment action due to her inability to perform as required. Then the burden shifts to the employer to rebut one or more elements of the *prima facie* case, show it offered a reasonable accommodation, or show that accommodation would constitute an undue hardship.[11] Claims under Title VII must be brought within 300 days of the unlawful employment practice in jurisdictions that enforce a law prohibiting discrimination on the same basis. Otherwise, the deadline is 180 days. Before initiating litigation, one must obtain a "Notice of Right to Sue" letter from the EEOC. If the EEOC fails to complete its investigation within 180 days of the filing of the employee's complaint, then one can immediately request a right to sue letter at that time. Suits must be filed within 90 days of receiving the right to sue letter.

Perhaps the earliest known Title VII case claiming vegan workplace discrimination concerned Bruce Anderson of San Diego. Anderson drove buses for public transit. When his strict vegan views compelled him to refuse to hand out Carl's Jr. coupons to passengers so they could claim free hamburgers, the Orange County Transit Authority fired Anderson for insubordination—even though he offered to place the coupons in a basket so passengers could take them as they wished.[12] On August 20, 1996, the Equal Employment Opportunity Commission ("EEOC") held that Anderson's vegan beliefs rose to the level of a protected religion under Title VII.[13]

Michael E. Reilly filed a grievance with the West Virginia Public Employees Grievance Board against former employer West Virginia University in 2018 after being fired when he refused to work as an industrial hygienist at WVU's farms and vivisection laboratories due to his veganism, stating, "I would not participate in activities where animals are being subjected to exploitation and murder."[14] The Board denied his request for position reinstatement and payment of lost wages, finding that he was terminated short of his annual appointment for insubordination related to failure to perform his duties in WVU's farms and labs. Though the Board lacked jurisdiction to hear his claim under the CRA, it was considered as a defense to the charge of insubordination and, in that respect, Reilly did not succeed. Without explanation, the Board held that his refusal could not be viewed as protected under the CRA, and that as up to half of his duties included work around animals, it would be an undue hardship for WVU to assign all such tasks to other specialists, particularly in the case of emergency.[15]

2.2. State Antidiscrimination Laws

State antidiscrimination laws may also protect religiously-based dietary preferences in the employment context. In 2014, the Washington Supreme Court decided *Kumar v. Gate Gourmet, Inc.,* 180 Wn.2d 481 (2014). It held that there existed a *prima facie* case for a religious accommodation claim under the Washington Law Against Discrimination ("WLAD") where airport employees' sincerely held religious beliefs mandating a vegetarian diet conflicted with the employer's requirement that they all eat nonvegetarian, company-provided food (citing security concerns). The plaintiffs informed the employer of the conflict, to which it responded by first deceiving the employees into dining on fare prohibited by their religions and then refusing to entertain any of the employees' proposed accommodations, thereby compelling them to eat forbidden meals or work hungry. Specifically, and putting aside that turkeys are not vegetables, Gate Gourmet switched from beef-pork meatballs to turkey meatballs to ostensibly accommodate their vegetarian requirements but then switched back to beef-pork mixtures without telling them. *Kumar* reversed *Short v. Battleground Sch. Dist.,* 169 Wash. App. 188 (2012), which held no duty existed for an employer to accommodate an employee's religion under the WLAD.

When Jerry Friedman, an ethical vegan of nearly ten years, refused to receive a mumps vaccination, a mandatory condition of permanent employment with Kaiser Permanente Medical Group, on the basis that it used a chicken embryo for culturing, Kaiser withdrew its offer of employment. Friedman then sued for religious creed discrimination under the California Fair Employment and Housing Act ("FEHA"), Govt. Code § 12940 and Regulation 7293.1, defining "religious creed" as "any traditionally recognized religion as well as beliefs, observations, or practices which an individual sincerely holds and which occupy in his or her life a place of importance parallel to that of traditionally recognized religions."[16]

Although California decisional law had not then formally construed "religious creed" under the FEHA or administrative regulations established by the Employment and Housing Commission for purposes of implementing the FEHA, its holdings in other contexts did "point away from a strictly theistic definition of religion. A belief in a Supreme Being is not required."[17] United States Supreme Court decisions also broadened protections from those with belief in a Judaeo-Christian Creator and a system of after-death punishments and rewards to religions "which do not teach what would generally be considered a belief in the existence of God," such as "Buddhism, Taoism, Ethical Culture, Secular Humanism and others."[18]

After surveying California decisional authority, the hallmark United States Supreme Court cases of *U.S. v. Seeger,* 380 U.S. 163 (1965) (conscientious objection to military service); *Welsh v. U.S.,* 398 U.S. 333 (1970) (conscientious objector status applies to "all those whose consciences, spurred by deeply held moral, ethical, or religious beliefs, would give them no rest or peace if they allowed themselves to become a part of an instrument of war"); and *Wisconsin v. Yoder,* 406 U.S. 205 (1972) (Amish families convicted for refusing to allow their children to attend public high school), federal Title VII employment discrimination law, and federal non-employment discrimination law, the court embraced Third Circuit Court of Appeals Judge Arlin M. Adams's objective test for determining whether a belief "plays the role of a religion and functions as such in an individual's life."

Originally articulated in *Malnak v. Yogi,* 592 F.2d 197 (3rd Cir.1979), and later adopted in five other circuits, the test follows:

> First, a religion addresses fundamental and ultimate questions having to do with deep and imponderable matters. Second, a religion is comprehensive in nature; it consists of a belief-system as opposed to an isolated teaching. Third, a religion often can be recognized by the presence of certain formal and external signs.[19]

Before applying the three-prong test, the court admitted that the EEOC definition of religion was more expansive than Regulation 7293.1 and, perhaps, than the statutory interpretation in *Seeger*, which protects strictly moral or ethical beliefs held with the "strength of traditional religious views." Reg. 7293.1 requires that said beliefs carry not only the import and weight of traditional religious views but must *occupy in his or her life a place of importance parallel to that of traditionally recognized religions.*

As applied, Friedman lost, the court determining that (1) Friedman's veganism did not address "meaning of human existence; purpose of life; theories of humankind's nature or its place in the universe." Arguably, classical Darwinism would begin to address these issues. The court then found a lack of comprehensivity (2) in that there was no "apparent spiritual or otherworldly component" and that the veganism is "limited to the single subject of highly valuing animal life and ordering one's life based on that perspective." But what of parallels to the Jewish doctrine of *tikkun olam* (without the overt messianic component which is, of course, critical to this prong) or similar "reverence of life" belief systems? Why is the tethering to a supreme being or power so critical? Because the *Malnak* test requires not just an "isolated teaching" but a full "belief system." On the last point, Friedman's veganism did not possess sufficient indicia of religious formality and externality, having not found teachers, services, holidays, or other organizational structures. Does this suggest that no *religions of one* qualify under this statute? The court concluded that veganism inspired or required by a traditionally recognized religion or quasi-religion qualifying under *Malnak* may be protected as "religious belief" under 7293.1.

Since *Friedman,* another court examined veganism in an employment discrimination dispute. Sakile Chenzira, a hospital customer service representative working for Cincinnati Children's Hospital for over a decade, was discharged due to a refusal to receive a non-vegan flu vaccine.[20] She sued under Title VII of the Civil Rights Act of 1964, Ch. 4112 of the Ohio Revised Code, and tortious wrongful discharge in violation of public policy. At the motion to dismiss stage, the court rejected the hospital's contention that veganism was "no more than a dietary preference or social philosophy" or that Chenzira's essay response, "The Biblical Basis of Veganism," was nothing more than "strategically cherry-picked Bible verses":

> The Court finds that in the context of a motion to dismiss, it merely needs to determine whether Plaintiff has alleged a plausible claim. The Court finds it plausible that Plaintiff could subscribe to veganism with a sincerity equating that of traditional religious views. The Sixth Circuit's decision in Spies in no way bars such conclusion. In Spies, the Court found that a Buddhist inmate's dietary request was adequately met by the provision of a vegetarian diet, as the inmate himself conceded that a more restrictive vegan diet was not a religious requirement of his faith. 173 F.3d 398, 407.[3] The Court's conclusion is further bolstered by Plaintiff's citation to essays and Biblical excerpts. Although the Code makes it clear that it is not necessary that a religious group espouse a belief before it can qualify as religious, 29 C.F.R. 1605.1, the fact here that Plaintiff is not alone in articulating her view lends credence to her position. Accordingly, at this early stage of the litigation, the Court finds it inappropriate to dismiss Plaintiff's claims for religious discrimination based on her adherence to veganism.[21]

Occasionally, the sexual politics of meat[22] manifest as discrimination based not on vegetarianism or veganism, but on gender. *Catalanello v. Kramer,* 18 F.Supp.3d 504 (S.D.N.Y. May 7, 2014) concerned managing director of Credit Agricole CIB Robert Catalanello, who sued Arizona State University Associate Dean and Professor of Law Zachary Kramer for defamation and related dignitary torts for statements made in the article *Of Meat and Manhood,* 89 Wash. U. L. Rev. 298 (2011) and the lecture "Of Meat and Manhood/The New Sex Discrimination," in which Kramer examined the lawsuit by Ryan Pacifico, a former junior foreign exchange trader at Credit Agricole, who sued Catalanello, his former supervisor, for creating a hostile work environment by harassing him for not eating meat and referring to him as "gay" or "homo" in front of coworkers. When Catalanello told the traders they were dining at a Brazilian steakhouse, someone asked what Pacifico could eat there, to which Catalanello responded, "Who the fuck cares? It's his fault for being a vegetarian homo." Three years after filing suit, Pacifico nonsuited his case with prejudice. While the case pended, Kramer submitted an article on the law's refusal to treat gender stereotyping as a form of sexual orientation protection under title VII. He regarded Pacifico's case as a "case study" to "highlight [] the messiness of modern sex discrimination." He concludes stating that Pacifico's case demonstrates how sex discrimination occasionally manifests in other forms, such as a "hybrid of vegetarian and sexual orientation discrimination." In 2012, Kramer presented a lecture at Western New England University School of Law, arguing that Catalanello viewed Pacifico's vegetarianism as a proxy for effeminacy and that male vegetarianism is, wrongly, an unprotected trait in federal employment discrimination law. The trial court dismissed the lawsuit, finding Kramer's statements to be nonactionable opinions and fair accounts of an official proceeding.

2.3 Discrimination by Vegans

For an interesting twist, consider claims made *against* vegan *employers* who proselytize nonvegetarian *employees*. Commissioner Mary Wendy Roberts decided *In the Matter of Sapp's Realty, Inc.*,[23] a case alleging that Gloria and Bob Sapp, Seventh Day Adventists, had created an intimidating and offensive work environment by subjecting 19-year-old Caroline Armon to an "intolerable atmosphere of religious harassment and intimidation, causing her to refuse to continue working, and thus constructively discharged her." Specifically, the Sapps allegedly made "unwelcome religious advances, proselytizing, and other verbal conduct of a religious nature or term or condition of Complainant's employment." The commissioner ordered the Sapps to pay $10,477.45 to Caroline Armon, representing $4477.45 in wage loss and $6000 in mental distress, to deliver a favorable reference for her, and to cease and desist from discriminating against any employee based on religion. The thrust of the charge had nothing to do with the vegetarian tenets of Seventh Day Adventism, but the commissioner did address one encounter in the kitchen:

> Based upon all relevant evidence on the record, this forum concludes that Seventh Day Adventists believe in not consuming alcohol or coffee, and that many, but not all, Seventh Day Adventists are vegetarians. Respondents Sapp explained to Complainant during her employment at Respondent Sapp's what food one should eat and tried to influence her dietary habits. For example, once, when Complainant was preparing to eat a meat sandwich for lunch in the office's kitchen. Respondent B. Sapp told her that meat eaters had bad breath because they used their stomachs as graveyards for dead animals. (Even though Complainant understood Respondent B. Sapp's comments to be in jest on occasion, they seemed to her more in the nature of ridicule, as exemplified by the preceding comment)
>
> Respondent G. Sapp maintained at hearing and, since there is no evidence to the contrary, this forum finds, that her vegetarianism was based primarily upon health, as opposed to religious, concerns and that her comments concerning vegetarianism were made strictly from a health standpoint. As there was no specific first or even second-hand evidence that the comments of Respondent B. Sapp to Complainant about diet were based upon his religious beliefs or practices (rather than upon health considerations), this forum declines to find that they were.[24]

The concept of religious intimidation has been examined by the EEOC[25] and it has been held that allowing a supervisor to occasionally discuss religious beliefs on the job with his co-workers (one of whom felt his job could be threatened by his reaction to those discussions, one of whom believed he was trying to be converted, and both of whom felt it interfered with their job performance) created a working environment that was not free of religious intimidation.

In *Grimsley v. Charles River Laboratories, Inc.*, 564 Fed.Appx. 333 (9th Cir. 2014), Guy Grimsley was terminated as Director of Laboratory Sciences for making comments that several scientists found derogatory and based on gender stereotypes. He asserted employment discrimination based on "national origin," pursuant to 42 U.S.C. § 2000e-2(a)(1), and the implementing regulations prohibiting discrimination on the basis of "cultural . . . characteristics of a national origin," 29 C.F.R. § 1606.1. Specifically, he contended that his critical "views on the treatment of animals" at Charles River, a perspective purportedly steeped in his British heritage, furnished the true, discriminatory basis for ending his employment. The Ninth Circuit disagreed, finding no evidence to support such a claim of pretextual discrimination. It did not determine whether, as a matter of law, a cultural objection to animal mistreatment would state a claim under Title VII of the Civil Rights Act.

2.4. FIRST AMENDMENT

First Amendment retaliation jurisprudence also speaks to vegan workplace discrimination claims. Consider the case of Keith Allison of Ohio, a vegan second grade teacher fired in 2014 for posting a picture on his personal Facebook page depicting a local dairy farm with crates used to house babies separated from their mothers at birth. PETA attorney Gabriel Walters (along with other counsel at PETA and ACLU) sued the Board of Education of Green Local School District, and various officials on behalf of Allison in *Allison v. Besancon,* N.D.Ohio 5:15-cv-00416-DAP. On Apr. 14, 2015, a voluntary dismissal with settlement agreement was filed.[26] In addition to monetary settlement, Mr. Allison achieved reinstatement (at a middle school in the same district, rather than the elementary school at which he previously taught) and a written policy clarifying that district teachers have a right to engage in protected speech on matters of public concern in their role as private citizens. It should be noted that Allison was not engaging in vegan advocacy on class time and was using his personal computer. This case was styled not as a Title VII accommodation claim, but First Amendment claim based on *Pickering v. Board of Education,* 391 U.S. 563 (1968).[27]

Also consider the matter of Karen Coyne, a vegan high school English teacher for more than a decade at Newport-Mesa Unified School District. Coyne sued the District after being forced to take the 2013-14 year off. In early 2012, she had informed teachers and the principal that requiring students to perform animal dissections broke state educational law. She collaborated with a campus group, Compassion in Action, to educate the staff and administrators about alternatives. The principal allegedly changed her schedule so she could not meet with the club, then changed it back. Students began acting out, some posing with dead animals on Facebook, another holding up a cat's head and pretending to lick it, and yet another putting a dissected cat's head in a student's locker.[28] Coyne's attorney Cheryl Konell Ruggiero sued for a lost year of salary and benefits and unspecified general damages.

3. CONSUMERS

While not presenting as a free exercise or religious discrimination claim, vegans duped by health care providers and manufacturers into ingesting or implanting animal products may state a claim under unfair business practice acts. Mystie Michael, likely a vegan and suffering from a severe Lidocaine allergy, specifically asked that no animal products or xenografting "parts" be used as part of a bone grafting procedure performed by periodontist Dr. Mosquera-Lacy of Bright Now! Dental. Months prior to the procedure, Michael specifically requested non-animal bone (allograft or synthetic graft). And moments before the procedure, Michael said, "Dr. Lacy, I said I didn't want cow bone . . . I just can't fathom the thought of animal parts being in my body. . . . Do you have human bone?" Dr. Lacy had given her seven Lidocaine caplets as an anesthetic and confirmed that she would use human bone. After the procedure, Michael vomited, lost consciousness, and was rushed to the ER for treatment of conditions arising from the Lidocaine allergy. When Dr. Lacy called to check on Michael, she admitted that she used cow bone because she did not have enough human bone material to finish Michael's procedure. Michael sued for negligence, medical battery, and CPA violations. The trial court dismissed the Consumer Protection Act ("CPA") claim on summary judgment. Michael nonsuited her remaining claims and appealed the trial court's order. At issue was whether Michael suffered "injury to business or property," a key element of a CPA claim. She asserted that the cow bone inserted into her jaw was defective and an unlawful "substitution of products." The Washington Court of Appeals agreed that the injury was the type that, if proven, would be subject to the CPA, and added that, "If her only injury was gum swelling or complications from the bone grafting surgery, then the CPA would not apply. Here, as in *Tallmadge*, Michael thought she was purchasing one product but was given another."[29] Merely proving a nonquantifiable deprivation of use and enjoyment of property (e.g., the graft and her jaw) sufficed.

The court next dismissed the assertion that the lack of evidence of advertising or promotional activities negated Michael's claim, finding that "advertising is [not] necessary to satisfy [the unfair or deceptive act element] of a CPA claim."[30] While the "learned professions" are typically not subject to the CPA except for their "entrepreneurial activities," the court found that a material issue of fact existed as to whether Dr. Lacy's representations and use of cow bone related to how Bright Now! obtained, retained, and dismissed its clients. The final element of the CPA—public interest impact—also resolved in favor of Michael, the court noting that the factors informing the traditional distinction between a "consumer transaction" or "private dispute" are not dispositive in order to demonstrate public interest, and since Bright Now could not demonstrate that "the only reasonable conclusion from the evidence was that the transaction involved did not affect the public interest," the matter should go to the jury. *Michael v. Mosquera-Lacy,* 140 Wash.App. 139, 153 (2008). Judge Bridgewater dissented, noting that Michael's case turned on personal injury, not property damage, and did not demonstrate how cow bone was less valuable or enduring, or more prone to repair, than human bone. The Washington Supreme Court reversed, finding that the defendant's misconduct did not involve the entrepreneurial aspects of practice germane to the CPA.[31]

Other unfair business practice litigation revolving around nondisclosure or misrepresentation of the inclusion of animal products in items marketed to end-consumers include the use of cochineal extract (pulverized beetle carcasses) in 'frappuccinos', smoothies, cakes, and doughnuts;[32] the sale of cosmetics as "vegetarian";[33] a pharmaceutical company's failure to label its B-12 tablets "recommended . . . for vegetarians and vegans" as coated in gelatin;[34]; a tuberculosis test distributor's representation that it did not contain animal products and was "Vegan 'safe'" and "Vegan 'friendly'"[35] and a historic class action lawsuit on behalf of 16 million vegetarian and Hindu consumers seeking accountability from McDonald's for false advertisement and using beef tallow in French fries.[36]

4. STUDENT VEGANISM

4.1. School Lunch Programs

When Congress passed the National School Lunch Act of 1946, 42 U.S.C. §§ 1751-1769j, it established the National School Lunch Program, administered by the USDA. Accepting federal funding required that schools serve USDA-approved lunches, which mandate offering students dairy milk.[37] Come 2004, Congress amended the Act to require the offering of dairy substitutes to meet dietary needs of students.[38] On July 19, 2012, Susan Levin, M.S., R.D., of the Physicians Committee for Responsible Medicine ("PCRM"), filed a petition with the USDA seeking to exclude dairy milk as a required component of the federal school lunch program, contending that it does not improve bone health or reduce osteoporosis risk but actually creates new risks.[39]

4.2. Dissection and Vivisection

In 2013, Active Learning Elementary School in the Queens borough of New York City became the first public school in the country to serve only vegetarian meals for breakfast and lunch.[40] Compare this shift to a plant-based diet with the State of Washington's closure of a vegan-only preschool, kindergarten, and elementary school. For twenty years, Ellouise Carroll, PhD, directed a trilingual State-approved K-6 Early Education Center Academy in Puyallup, Wash. Dr. Carroll stated:

> I couldn't, in good conscience, feed the children in my care in a way that I now knew was not healthy for them. . . . We were not allowed to be vegan (in order to be licensed in the State of Washington, you *must* serve dairy products and, if you don't serve meat, you actually have to serve twice as many dairy products: one as a liquid dairy and one as a substitute for the meat).

The school closed in 2003 after she could not afford to fight the State.[41] In the last decade, focus on the health benefits of plant-based diets and deleterious effects of animal products, coupled with recognition of lactose intolerance among non-European American students, led to codified requirements to promote dairy and meat alternatives.[42] For instance, the District of Columbia Healthy Schools Act of 2010, Sec. 205(b)(2), requires that schools "inform families that vegetarian food options and milk alternatives are available upon request."

Tenth-grader Jenifer Graham, a vegetarian sophomore opposed to killing animals for scientific purposes, enrolled at Victor Valley Union High School, objected to dissecting a frog in her biology class. She received a zero for the assignment, lowering her grade from A to B. The school rejected her request to use a frog model, claiming it would give her an advantage over other students and jeopardize its academic rigor and credibility among universities and colleges. She later filed a federal lawsuit, *Graham v. Bd. of Trustees of the Victor Valley Union H.S. Dist.,* C.D.Cal. CV-87 03764 (1987), which U.S. District Court Central District of California Judge Manuel L. Real dismissed, stating, "I don't think she has any choice in this," adding, "She can't take this to absurdity. The Constitution is not meant to be absurd."[43] However, he did tell the school to provide her with a frog who died from natural causes and allow her to identify internal organs from photographs.[44] The school failed to provide her with such a frog, and she appealed.

Subsequently, the district settled, removing all negative marks from her record, and paying her legal fees.[45] But changes did not end with litigation. *CBS School Break* aired a special titled "Frog Girl: The Jenifer Graham

Story" and the California Legislature passed a law that mandated alternatives to dissection for elementary and secondary students who object on moral grounds.[46] The District of Columbia and seventeen other states have given students the choice—Connecticut, Florida, Illinois, Louisiana, Maine, Maryland, Massachusetts, Michigan, New Hampshire, New Jersey, New Mexico, New York, Oregon, Pennsylvania, Rhode Island, Vermont, and Virginia.[47] Even Apple featured her in a television ad showcasing a computer-generated frog model.[48]

Approaching the subject from the perspective of school districts uniformly prohibiting vivisection or dissection in the classroom, instead of from that of an individual conscientious objector, one finds that eleven States[49] presently mandate humane education.[50]

4.3. Postsecondary Education

After admission to Ohio State University's College of Veterinary Medicine, student Jennifer Kissinger received an Admission Acceptance Form stating that the faculty believed "the use of live animals in the teaching program is essential" and that, "Objection to the use of live animals will not be grounds for excuse from class." In her second year, the College required that she take Operative Practice and Techniques, a surgical course involving the anesthetization, operation, and swift euthanization of healthy animals. Citing her religious beliefs, Kissinger requested an alternative curriculum to fulfill the surgical requirement. The College refused. When she enrolled in her third-year classes but did not participate in such sacrificial surgeries, the College said she could withdraw from the Operative Practice class, but then no longer continue with subsequent courses, at which point she would have to petition for readmission. After filing suit on various grounds, including 42 U.S.C. § 1983 (relative to First and Fourteenth Amendment violations), state common-law and constitutional theories, the College offered an alternative curriculum. After fine-tuning, she accepted the revised offer, completed matriculation, obtained her degree, and practiced veterinary medicine. Her request for prevailing party attorney's fees[51] under 42 U.S.C. § 1988, however, failed.[52] Without examining whether Kissinger's veganism amounted to a religion, the Sixth Circuit appeared to assume as much, yet concluded, "Ohio State's curriculum did not violate Kissinger's right to exercise freely her religion" and she "was not legally entitled to force Ohio State to exempt her from taking Operative Practice and Techniques."[53]

Modern free exercise jurisprudence[54] requires the complaining party to demonstrate that her religious convictions are sincerely held and central to religious practice. Courts will not delve into the truth or rationality of those beliefs, so long as "arguably religious."[55] To merit First Amendment protection, such beliefs need not cling to a traditional religious dogma or tenet, but "[p]urely secular views do not suffice."[56]

Next, the party must demonstrate that the challenged act or legislation burdens the free exercise of religion through its coercive effect. Thus, a facially neutral, nonselectively enforced statute may still violate the constitutional right to free exercise if it indirectly burdens religion. The Supreme Court has rejected the indirect-direct burden dichotomy. If the government does burden religious belief, it must identify a compelling government interest that justifies such imposition and that the burden imposed represents the least restrictive means of satisfying it.[57]

5. PRISONERS

By far, the greatest number of vegetarian or vegan rights cases arise from our nation's jails and prisons. Inmates cannot simply travel to the restaurant or supermarket of their choosing but must rely on what the commissary and cafeteria provide. But because putatively "religious" demands might jeopardize legitimate penal objectives (e.g., a Sikh demands a ceremonial sword or dagger, named a kirpan), reasonable debate ensues—though it is hard to see how perishable foodstuffs could ever present a security risk. Vegan prisoner challenges typically invoke the First and Eighth Amendments to the federal constitution and the Religious Land Use and Institutionalized Persons Act of 2000, 42 USC 2000cc et seq. ("RLUIPA"), which superseded the since-overturned 1993 Religious Freedom Restoration Act, 42 USC 2000bb et seq. ("RFRA").[58]

In October 2016, the Federal Bureau of Prisons unfurled a new menu offering a vegan entrée for each meal in its 102 facilities. In 2018, the State of California enacted SB 1138, requiring that state prisons, hospitals, and health care facilities provide at least one vegan option at every meal. While these accommodations benefit animal rights activists convicted under the federal Animal Enterprise Terrorism Act and other federal laws, inmates serving time in any of the over 1700 state prisons may find themselves in a vegan food desert, and because incarceration prevents them from nomading to vegan oases, they rely exclusively on what the government furnishes.[59]

The Eighth Amendment provides, in relevant part, that "No [] cruel and unusual punishments [shall be] inflicted." *Rhodes v. Chapman,* 452 U.S. 337 (1981), held that though inmates are not entitled to luxurious prison accommodations, correctional facilities are nonetheless governed by the Eighth Amendment's efforts to safeguard the evolving standards of decency that mark the progress of a maturing society. But to bring a viable Eighth Amendment claim requires proof of deliberate indifference by prison officials and employees, a high hurdle to surmount.[60] It is extremely unlikely that a vegan inmate could prevail under the Eighth Amendment even in the shadow of *Holt v. Hobbs,* 574 U.S. 352 (2015), a favorable RLUIPA decision by Gregory Holt, a Muslim prisoner who wished to grow a half-inch beard as required by his faith and finding protection by the Supreme Court of the United States, which held that while the government has a compelling interest in security and avoiding inmates hiding contraband in their beards, it was not the least restrictive means to that end.

The Fourteenth Amendment's Equal Protection Clause may be applicable if dietary accommodations are made to one religion but not another.[61] However, the Equal Protection approach is less favorable (unless a protected class status can be invoked), as the basis of judicial review in such instances is the more deferential rational relationship to legitimate penological interests standard, versus strict scrutiny analysis governed under the RLUIPA.

The First Amendment commands that "Congress shall make no law respecting an establishment of religion, or prohibiting the free exercise thereof." RLUIPA defines "religious exercise" to include "any exercise of religion, whether or not compelled by, or central to, a system of religious belief." This standard relaxed a previous requirement of compulsoriness or centrality. Oft-cited, *Spies v. Voinovich,* 173 F.3d 398 (6th Cir.1999) articulates the First Amendment free exercise position typically taken as to incarcerees demanding meals without animal products. Douglas Spies, an ordained Zen Buddhist serving time at Marion, Ohio's North Central Correctional Institution, began guiding fellow Buddhists in meditation. The prison permitted him to use the chapel and religious icons, but would not honor his request for a vegan diet. A prison chaplain contacted the International Buddhist Meditation Center in Los Angeles and learned that while Buddhism counseled abstention from animal flesh, veganism was not a required tenet. Accordingly, NCCI rejected his request and he sued. In light of Spies's admission that "a vegan diet is not a requirement for Zen Buddhist practice," and that the prison did furnish him with a vegetarian meal, the Sixth Circuit held that he had no First Amendment right to a vegan meal.[62] In so ruling, however, the majority made clear that "We are not stating that Spies's veganism is not a sincerely-held religious belief. Rather, we are stating that because the prison has already provided him with a vegetarian meal, we believe, in this instance, that the prison's decision to deny him a vegan meal is reasonably related to legitimate penological interests."[63]

Dissenting Circuit Judge Moore differed, stating that the prison's defense that veganism was not mandated by Spies's religion was "inadequate as a matter of law," for Spies was entitled to prove that accommodation of his own sincerely held beliefs would not unreasonably burden the prison resources.[64]

Had Spies filed his lawsuit after Sept. 22, 2000, when the Religious Land Use and Institutionalized Persons Act ("RLUIPA"), 42 U.S.C. § 2000cc et seq., became effective, the outcome may have been more aligned with that in *Borkholder v. Lemmon*, 983 F.Supp.2d 1013 (N.D.Ind.2013): "It is not every day that someone makes a federal case out of ramen noodles. But unfortunately, that's what Joshus Borkholder had to do" after the prison officials revoked his vegan diet upon learning that he ordered chicken-flavored ramen noodles from the prison commissary. Borkholder became vegan while imprisoned after "continual study" of religious beliefs and concluded that it was immoral "to slaughter harmless animals for food when there [are] other natural foods being grown for human consumption." The commissary did not sell vegetarian noodles, so he resorted to buying chicken-flavored ramen noodles, discarding the flavoring packet, and adding peanut butter to the boiled noodles—or eating them plain. Judge Philip P. Simon granted him declaratory and injunctive relief to restore his vegan diet and provide him with vegetarian ramen. Aside from the standard First Amendment analysis, the court invoked the Religious Land Use and Institutionalized Persons Act, 42 U.S.C. § 2000cc.[65] Pursuant to the Prison Litigation Reform Act, Judge Simon narrowed the injunction to precluding the prison from revoking Borkholder's vegan diet simply because he buys chicken-flavored ramen noodles from the commissary or a similar product with a separately packaged meat flavoring that can be readily discarded, when no vegetarian alternative exists.[66]

6. CHILD ABUSE

African-American couple Jade Sanders, 27, and Lamont Thomas, 31, only gave their newborn son Crown Shakur soy milk and apple juice. He died at six weeks of age due to bronchopneumonia secondary to extreme malnourishment and starvation. He presented dead to the emergency room. Sanders and Thomas reportedly showed no emotion. At trial, Thomas volunteered that food was very expensive and the prosecution presented evidence of nearly empty cupboards. Sanders conceded that she did not tell her coworkers about her pregnancy.[67] Thomas asked, "Why would I do something with his body? We are against animals being murdered, why would we be cruel to him and try to do something to his body?" Crown Shakur's mother said, "they did what they thought was right," speaking of their motivation to raise Crown as a vegan. The prosecution insinuated that Sanders and Thomas invoked veganism as an afterthought to avoid prosecution for the intentional starvation of their child. Both were convicted of malice murder and sentenced to life in prison. After three convictions of vegan parents in four years, the *New York Times* published an op/ed by Nina Planck, entitled "Death by Veganism," claiming that vegan diets imperil infants, though not even the prosecution made such a connection in the Crown case. The American Dietetic Association and Dieticians of Canada stated in 2003 that well-planned vegan diets are "appropriate for all stages of the life cycle, including during pregnancy, lactation, infancy, childhood and adolescence."[68]

7. MEDIA

In 1949, the Federal Communications Commission required broadcast licenseholders to present controversial issues of public importance honestly and equitably—in short, fairly. The "Fairness Doctrine" required providing airtime to contrasting viewpoints on matters of public interest.[69] As of August 2011, the FCC eliminated language implementing the Doctrine.[70] Before its repeal, however, complaints were lodged with the FCC concerning vegetarianism.[71]

Yet when criticism of meat-eating, or more accurately meat-producing, comes under scrutiny, libel litigation against television show personalities has commenced. In *Texas Beef Group v. Winfrey*, 11 F. Supp. 2d 858 (N.D. Tex. 1998), a number of cattle companies sued Oprah Winfrey, Harpo Productions, Inc., and Howard "Mad Cow" Lyman for false disparagement of perishable food products under the Texas False Disparagement of Perishable Food Products Act (T.C.P.R.C. 96.002), common law business disparagement; common law defamation; statutory libel; negligence and negligence *per se* arising from Apr. 11, 1996 and Apr. 16, 1996 shows discussing Bovine Spongiform Encephalopathy ("BSE") and its link to a variant of Creutzfeld-Jakob Disease ("V-CJD"). Running through the program was the key assumption that the American cattlemen's feeding practices (ruminant-to-ruminant) contributed to the danger of BSE and V-CJD in the United States. Plaintiffs claimed that "malicious editing" of factual and scientific information presented through counterpoint by Drs. Hueston and Weber would have calmed the hysteria of the "mad cow" scare. Additional defamatory/disparaging comments alleged included:

1. Winfrey's allegedly damaging "never eating a hamburger again" comment;
2. Lyman's "Mad Cow Disease could make AIDS look like the common cold" statement; and
3. Lyman's "The United States is treating BSE as a public relations issue, as Great Britain did, and failing to take any 'substantial' measures to prevent a BSE outbreak."

On motion for summary judgment, the trial court dismissed the defendants' statutory food disparagement claim, and their defamation, statutory libel, and negligence claims, but retained the common law business disparagement claim. As to allegedly false statements, the court held that the defendants' speech occupied the "highest rung" of First Amendment values given its coverage of "matters of public concern" and factual basis. Lyman's comments had a factual basis—ruminant-to-ruminant feeding was an existing practice in the United States. Exaggeration does not equal defamation. It deemed the Perishable Food Products Act ("PFPA") inapplicable as: (1) the statute does not apply to live "fed cattle"; (2) the plaintiffs' cattle had not "perished" or "decayed beyond marketability"; and, alternatively, (3) the plaintiffs proffered insufficient proof tending to show that the defendants knowingly disseminated false information. Moreover, the statute required actual knowledge of falsity, the highest standard available under defamation law.

The submitted jury instruction for this remaining claim stated: "Did a below-named defendant publish a false, disparaging statement that was of and concerning the cattle of a below-named plaintiff as those terms have been defined for you?" The jury found for the defendants. The group appealed and lost in *Texas Beef Gp. v. Winfrey,* 201 F.3d 680 (5 Cir., 2000). As to the PFPA, the Fifth Circuit examined whether the defendants knowingly disseminated false information tending to show American beef was not fit for public consumption. It concluded that while Lyman and Winfrey melodramatized the scare, it was Winfrey's "stopped cold from eating another burger" nonactionable comment that had the greatest fallout. "Lyman's opinions, though strongly stated, were based on truthful, established fact, and are not actionable under the First Amendment." As to the assertion of malicious editing:

> Stripped to its essentials, the cattlemen's complaint is that the 'Dangerous Food' show did not present the Mad Cow issue in the light most favorable to United States beef. This argument cannot prevail. . . . So long as the factual underpinnings remained accurate, as they did here, the editing did not give rise to an inference that knowingly false information was being disseminated.[72]

Concurring Judge Edith Jones nonetheless held that live, fed cattle are "perishable food products":

> While recognizing this diminution in value, the district court found that live cattle do not decay "beyond marketability" because they may still be sold for uses other than USDA prime beef—e.g., hamburger or dog food. This interpretation, however, would seem to vitiate the applicability of the statute to food products that were undoubtedly intended to fall within the protective reach of the Act. For example, bananas are undoubtedly a food product that will decay over time. Yet, bananas with brown spots have uses beyond consumption as fresh bananas—e.g., when processed in banana bread and certain non-food uses. The Act, properly construed, does reach fed cattle.[73]

She relied upon the definition of "perishable food product":

> A perishable food product is "a food product of agriculture or aquaculture that is sold or distributed in a form that will perish or decay beyond marketability within a limited period of time." Tex. Civ. Prac. & Rem. § 96.001.*Id.* . . . The evidence adduced at trial demonstrates that live cattle appear to decay steadily in value from their optimum date of sale (perish beyond marketability) just as an apple hanging from a tree might rot. That the decay occurs pre-slaughter does not detract from the protections of the statute. An apple will rot on the tree as easily as it will rot in the grocer's produce section.[74]

As to the single claim going to the jury, the plaintiffs appealed the "of and concerning" language, asserting that the instruction improperly required it to find (1) that defendants made false, disparaging statements regarding *specific cattle*, and (2) that defendants made false, disparaging statements "of and concerning cattle," as opposed to *beef*. The appellate court affirmed as the plaintiffs failed to object with sufficient specificity or state the grounds of their objection or offer a proposed alternate instruction.

8. LANDLORD AND TENANT

Where a landlord refuses to rent, lease, or sell realty to a vegetarian or vegan, a viable discrimination claim may arise by equating such belief with "religion," as discussed above. But would a reciprocal prohibition against carnists state a claim? Not unless a prospective tenant could source her carnism in creed. In 2015, Seattleite Jinesh Varia offered to let his three-bedroom townhome for $2200, or $2000 for tenants who did not eat meat. "Ethically and morally, it's extremely important to be vegetarian," Varia told KING 5 news. "This appears to be a facially neutral policy, giving vegetarian and vegan tenants a discount on rent," Lee Jones, United States Department of Housing and Urban Development Public Affairs director for the Northwest Region, told FoxNews.com. However, if it were a pretext to disparately impact a protected class, a possible violation of the federal Fair Housing Act might exist.[75] Such practice is not uncommon in parts of India, where the Gujarati never rent to meat-eaters, forcing some to lie or eat meat outside their homes.

9. ORGAN DONATION

The Uniform Anatomical Gift Act (UAGA) applies to all or part of a human body used for transplantation, therapy, research, or education and governs the gifting, revocation, and refusal to make an anatomical gift. If the gift's purpose is not specified, it must first be used only for transplantation or therapy, and then to research or education. Buying or selling parts for transplantation or therapy is a crime, as is, in order to obtain financial gain, intentionally falsifying, forging, concealing, defacing, or obliterating a document of gift, an amendment or revocation of a document of gift, or a refusal. As of 2017, the UAGA has been adopted in one of its forms (1968, 1987, 2006) in every American State and the District of Columbia. Presently, nine states have organ transplant antidiscrimination laws (California, Delaware, Kansas, Maryland, Massachusetts, New Jersey, Ohio, Oregon, and Pennsylvania), which seek to prohibit discrimination based on patient disability.[76] California's 1996 law prohibits hospitals, physicians, surgeons, procurement organizations, and others from denying a gift based on physical or mental disability unless, after case-by-case evaluation, it is one medically significant to its provision to the potential recipient. Government agencies and transplant centers cannot discriminate based on race, sex, religion, and other suspect classifications as qualifying entities in receipt of federal funding assistance (see Title VI of Civil Rights Act of 1964).

But what of a vegan who directs that her organs only go to fellow vegans? Can such conditional gift stand? Would it not endorse an insufferable form of social or religious discrimination with life-and-death consequences similar to that of a Ku Klux Klan member only donating to a white person?[77] In 1999, British Health Secretary Frank Dobson ordered an inquiry into organs gifted to Northern General Hospital in Sheffield, South Yorkshire when a family of a kidney donor from northern England restricted the use of his organs against going to "coloured people."[78] Does it matter if the donor altruistically donates while alive, as in the case of a 50-year-old American ordained Buddhist nun who required that "the recipient be a person who is not associated with a killing vocation of any type (e.g., hunter, fisherman, military person)" and who "preferred that the recipient be of an ethnic or racial minority"?[79]

Although it did not answer the above questions, the case of Robert Colavito, who was in end-stage renal disease and on a kidney transplant waiting list, suggests that mishandling of a directed gift would not state a viable claim. When Colavito's longtime friend Peter Lucia died, his wife asked that his kidneys be given to Colavito as a directed donation. However, the hospital sent one kidney to a patient in Florida and the other was unsuitable for transplant due to an aneurysm in the renal artery and, further, did not match in any event. Colavito sued the New York Organ Donor Network, Inc. for giving away the compatible kidney. Claims for fraud (no reliance), conversion (matter of first impression, body not property and against public policy to assign economic value thereto as personality), and an implied cause of action under New York's AGA were dismissed.[80]

While this area of law will require further development, generally one may direct that an *inter vivos* anatomical gift be given to whomever the donor pleases for any reason (whether identifiable individually or as a conditional gift to a class). However, where a conditional gift made after the donor's passing violates antidiscrimination laws, the donor's desire may be thwarted. Veganism, if not a "religion" or "creed," would not trigger such proscriptions and would appear to be as legitimate a way to reject potential donees as one to condition receipt on political affiliation or membership in a club or organization like National Rifle Association or American Civil Liberties Union. If veganism is deemed a religion, however, then choosing only to donate to fellow vegans might be challenged on similar grounds as one might dispute a restricted donation between Catholics or Muslims.

10. NOTES

1. "Gallup News Service, Gallup Poll Social Series: Consumption Habits," accessed December 5, 2020, https://news.gallup.com/file/poll/238346/180801Vegetarians.pdf.

2. Pet. for Rev. at 17 (Oct. 23, 2002) (No. S110916); *see* generally Erik Marcus, *Meat Market: Animals, Ethics, & Money* (Boston: Brio Press, 2005); Sarah Soifer, "Vegan Discrimination: An Emerging and Difficult Dilemma," 36 Loy. L.A. L. Rev. 1709 (2003); Karen Iacobbo & Michael Iacobbo, *Vegetarians and Vegans in America Today* (Westport, CT: Praeger Publishers, 2006).

3. Stanley M. Sapon, "Is Veganism a Religion?," VegNews (Dec. 2002) and *Vegan Ethics,* at www.veganforlife.org/ethics.htm and International Vegetarian Union, *Religion and Vegetarianism,* www.ivu.org/religion.

4. Lucinda Mosher, *Belonging*, Vol. I of Faith in the Neighborhood (Church Pub. 2005).

5. Mosher, *Belonging,* 137–38.

6. 42 U.S.C. § 2000e-2(a).

7. 42 U.S.C. § 2000e-2(a).

8. 42 U.S.C. § 2000e(j) (circularly defining "religion" as "all aspects of religious observance and practice, as well as belief").

9. 29 CFR § 1605.1.

10. 42 U.S.C. § 2000e(b).

11. *See EEOC v. Union Independiente de la Autoridad de Acueductos y Alcantarillados de Puerto Rico,* 279 F.3d 49, 55 (1 Cir.2002).

12. David Haldane, "Vegetarian Bus Driver Settles Suit Against Agency for $50,000," Los Angeles Times (Nov. 20, 1996), at A3.

13. *Anderson v. Orange Cy. Transit Auth.,* EEOC Charge No. 345960598 (1996). For further discussion, see Donna D. Page, "Veganism and Sincerely Held 'Religious' Beliefs in the Workplace: No Protection without Definition," 7:2 U. Pa. J. of Labor & Emp. L. 363 (2005).

14. *Reilly v. WVU,* 2018 WL 6037410, *1 (W.Va.Educ.St.Empl.Griev.Bd.)

15. *Id.*, *6.

16. *Friedman v. So. Cal. Kaiser Permanente Gp.,* 125 Cal.Rptr.2d 663 (2002).

17. *Id.,* at 49.

18. *Torcaso v. Watkins,* 367 U.S. 488, 495 fn. 11 (1961).

19. *Africa v. Com. of Pa.,* 662 F.2d 1025, 1032 (3rd Cir.1981).

20. *Chenzira v. Cincinnati Children's Hospital Medical Ctr.*, 2012 WL 6721098 (S.D. Ohio Dec. 27, 2012).

21. *Id.*, at *4.

22. Carol J. Adams authorized the both widely acclaimed and reviled critical feminist/ animal studies text Carol J. Adams, *The Sexual Politics of Meat: A Feminist-Vegetarian Critical Theory* (Continuum: 2000).

23. 4 Boli 232 (Or Boli), 1985 WL 1134246 (1985).

24. 4 Boli, at 15.

25. EEOC Dec. 72-1114 (1972).

26. https://assets.documentcloud.org/documents/1873593/aclu-settlement.pdf.

27. The employee must prove (1) he spoke as a private citizen on a matter of public concern; (2) his First Amendment interests, combined with interest of the public, outweigh the government's legitimate interest in the efficient performance of the workplace; and (3) even if the balance of interests favors the employee, he must still prove that protected speech was a substantial or motivating factor in the employer's adverse employment action. The 9th Circuit has refined the three-step *Pickering* inquiry into five steps: (1) whether the plaintiff spoke on a matter of public concern; (2) whether the plaintiff spoke as a private citizen or public employee; (3) whether the plaintiff's protected speech was a substantial or motivating factor in the adverse employment action; (4) whether the state had an adequate justification for treating the employee differently from other members of the general public; and (5) whether the state would have taken the adverse employment action even absent the protected speech. *Dahlia v. Rodriguez,* 735 F.3d 1060, 1067 (9th Cir.2010) (quoting *Eng v. Cooley,* 552 F.3d 1062 [9th Cir.2009]).

28. To learn more, see: http://www.psmag.com/nature-and-technology/battle-high-school-animal-dissection-92391.

29. *Id.*, at 148.

30. *Id.*, at 149.

31. *Michael v. Mosquera-Lacy,* 165 Wn.2d 595 (2009).

32. *Anderson v. Starbucks Corp.,* Los Angeles Cy. Sup. Ct. BC485438 (filed May 25, 2012).

33. *Balser v. Hain Celestial Gp., Inc.,* C.D.Cal. No. 2:13-cv-05604, 2013 WL 6673617.

34. *Lateef v. Pharmavite LLC,* 2013 WL 1499029 (N.D.Ill.2013) (dismissing claim because label did not assert a fact concerning presence or absence of gelatin in its supplements).

35. *Friedman v. Merck & Co.*, 107 Cal.App.4th 454 (2003) (dismissed as no duty to warn existed, foreseeability of harm was too remote, and California law did not recognize negligent misrepresentation for risk of emotional harm alone).

36. *Sharma v. McDonald's Corp.,* King Cy. Sup. Ct. (Wash.) No. 01-2-12267-3SEA. The matter ultimately settled as part of the contemporaneous class action filed in Cook Cy., Ill. *Block v. McDonald's Corp.,* 01-CH-9137, Cook Cy. Circ. Ct. (2001).

37. 42 U.S.C. § 1758(a)(2).

38. Child Nutrition and WIC Reauthorization Act of 2004, P.L. No. 108–265.

39. On file with author.

40. Cheryl K. Chumley, "Where's the beef? Bloomberg launches vegetarian-only school lunch," The Washington Times (May 1, 2013).

41. Karen Iacobbo and Michael Iacobbo, *Vegetarians and Vegans in America Today* (Praeger 2006), 142–43.

42. Monica Eng, "Lactose intolerance: When drinking school milk makes students feel sick," Chicago Tribune (Nov. 26, 2012).

43. United Press International, "Suit on Frog Dissection Rejected," Los Angeles Times (Aug. 1, 1988). Judge Real was later investigated for judicial misconduct by the Ninth Circuit Court of Appeals. Terry Carter, "Real Trouble, " ABA Journal (Sept. 1, 2008).

44. Joe Menosky, "Down in the Swamps, a 'Natural' Death for a Frog Is, Well, Just Not Natural, " Los Angeles Times (Aug. 22, 1988).

45. Associated Press, "Student Who Sued School Isn't Required to Cut Frog," New York Times (Aug. 3, 1988).

46. Cal. Educ. Code § 32255.1.

47. http://www.aavs.org/site/c.bkLTKfOSLhK6E/b.6457903/k.BF6/Student_Choice_Laws.htm#.VA04xvmwL4g.

48. Apple II ad featuring Jenifer Graham—Frog (1987) https://www.youtube.com/watch?v=MhwWuLlzBpI; see also www.animalearn.org. See also Marcia Goodman Kramer, "Humane Education, Dissection, and the Law," 13 Animal L. 281 (2007) (discussing *Graham* and other antidissection cases).

49. N.D. Political Code 884 (1905, ch. 108) required teaching of humane education of "not less than two lessons of ten minutes each per week." That provision appears to have been repealed.

50. California Edu. Code 51540 and 233-233.5, Florida Educ. Code 233.061(2)(j), 233.09 and Flor. Stat. 1003.42(2)(k) and 1001.01(2), 105 Ill. Comp. Stat. 5/27-13.1, 5/27-14, 5/27-15, 5/27-18; Louisiana Stat. Ann. 17:266, N.Y. Educ. Law 809, RCW 28A.230.020, Maine Code ch. 20 § 1221, Mass. Gen. Stat. Ch. 272 § 80G; N.J. Educ. 18A:35-4.1, N.H. Crim. Code 644:8-c; ORS 336.067, Penn. Public Sch. Code of 1949 § 1514.

51. Rutgers University Law Professor Gary L. Francione represented Kissinger and wrote this accessible text with Anna E. Charlton, Gary L. Francione and Anna E. Charlton, *Vivisection and Dissection in the Classroom: A Guide to Conscientious Objection* (American Anti-Vivisection Society: 1992).

52. *Kissinger v. OSU,* 5 F.3d 177 (6th Cir. 1993).

53. *Kissinger,* at 179, 181.

54. Note that Title VII only applies in the employment context. Hence, Kissinger could not invoke the CRA's protection but sought a remedy under the federal constitution.

55. *International Soc. for Krishna Consciousness, Inc. v. Barber,* 650 F.2d 430, 439 (2nd cir. 1981).

56. See *Frazee v. Illinois Department of Employment Security*, 489 U.S. 829, 833-35 (1989); *Dettmer v. Landon,* 617 F. Supp. 592 (E.D.Va.1985) (issue is not substance of belief system but function or role of it as part of a person's "ultimate concern"; ordering that prison official's refusal to give inmate access to candles, salt or sulfur, incense, kitchen timer, and white robes impermissibly infringed upon his First Amendment right).

57. *See Thomas v. Review Board,* 450 U.S. 707, 717–718 (1981).

58. RFRA was deemed unconstitutional in *City of Boerne v. Flores,* 521 U.S. 507 (1997). Congress passed the RLUIPA as a narrowed legislative repeal of *Flores. Holt v. Hobbs,* 135 S.Ct. 853 (2015) set forth the test for whether a prison policy implicates the prisoner's religious exercise: if the relevant exercise is grounded in a sincerely held religious belief, and the policy substantially burdens it, the burden shifts to the state to prove that its policy furthered a compelling governmental interest and was the least restrictive means to further it, specific to the burdened plaintiff. *Id.*, at 863 (quoting Burwell v. *Hobby Lobby Stores, Inc.*, 134 S.Ct. 2751, 2779 [2014]).

59. For a cogent analysis of inventive approaches to ensure vegan prisoners have access to savory and nutritious fare, see David B. Rosengard, "'Three Hots and a Cot and a Lot of Talk': Discussing Federal Rights-Based Avenues for Prisoner Access to Vegan Meals," 23 Animal L. 355 (2017).

60. *Wilson v. Seiter,* 501 U.S. 294 (1991).

61. See, for instance, *Turner v. Safley*, 482 U.S. 78 (1987), and the refinement of *O'Lone v. Estate of Shabazz*, 482 U.S. 342 (1987), concerning giving Jewish inmates kosher meals but not halal meals to Muslim inmates.

62. *Spies,* at 406.

63. *Spies,* at 407.

64. *Spies,* at 410.

65. *See Koger v. Bryan,* 523 F.3d 789, 796 (7 Cir. 2008) (contrasting RLUIPA with First Amendment, which requires only that the prison provides an "adequate justification" premised on "legitimate penological interests" as opposed to the higher burden of showing that the action presents the least restrictive means to further a compelling government interest); see also *Reed v. Faulkner,* 842 F.2d 960, 963 (7 Cir. 1988). ("It would be bizarre for prisons to undertake in effect to promote strict orthodoxy, by forfeiting the religious rights of any inmate observed backsliding, thus placing guards and fellow inmates in the role of religious police.")

66. See also *Goodman v. Carter,* 2001 WL 755137 (N.D. Ill. 2001) (Wiccan inmate sought and initially obtained vegan diet from prison but then tried to supplement by purchasing items containing eggs and dairy from the commissary, at which point the defendants removed him from the vegan diet and would not offer him a vegetarian diet; court "does not understand why Goodman is being denied eggs and milk products—which he is willing to pay for himself—for no articulated reason. . . . As far as appears on this record, denying Goodman the privilege of purchasing these foods from the commissary has no rational relationship to any legitimate purpose whatever.").

67. Associated Press, "Vegan couple will serve life sentences for starving baby to death, court rules," NY Daily News (Sept. 12, 2011); *Sanders v. State,* 289 Ga. 655 (2011) (affirming convictions).

68. *Position of the American Dietetic Association and Dieticians of Canada: vegetarian diets,* 64(2) Can. J. Dietetic Prac. & Res. 62 (2003).

69. *Red Lion Broadcasting Co. v. FCC,* 395 U.S. 367 (1969) (upholding doctrine's constitutionality).

70. *FCC Chairman Genachowski Continues Regulatory Reform to Ease Burden on Businesses; Announces Elimination of 83 Outdated Rules,* 2011 WL 3679221 (F.C.C. Aug. 22, 2011).

71. *In re Shriver Concerning the Fairness Doctrine,* 46 F.C.C.2d 1121 (May 10, 1974) (claiming that Merv Griffin Show episode featuring animal protein advocates and that refused to allow her to appear because "vegetarians have been represented" did not violate the Doctrine as she failed to provide reasonable grounds proving that "the issue of an animal protein diet versus a vegetarian diet is a controversial issue of public importance"); *In re American Vegetarian Union Concerning Fairness Doctrine,* 38 F.C.C.2d 1024 (Dec. 13, 1972) (accord in context of The Phil Donahue Show disparaging vegetarian diet without offering vegetarian viewpoint).

72. *Texas Beef,* at 689.

73. *Texas Beef,* at 691.

74. *Texas Beef,* at 691.

75. Sky McCarthy, "Washington state landlord offers $200 discount to vegetarians," Fox News (Nov. 25, 2016).

76. National Council on Disability, "Organ Transplant Discrimination Against People with Disabilities" (Sept. 25, 2019, p. 57).

77. Discussed in Hanto DW, "Ethical challenges posed by solicitation of deceased and living organ donors," N. Engl. J. Med. 2007; 356: 1062–66.

78. *Dobson: 'No health apartheid',* BBC News (7.7.99); *See also* T M Wilkinson, "What's not wrong with conditional organ donation?," J. Med. Ethics 2003; 29: 163–64.

79. Gohh RY, Morrissey PE, Madras PN, Monaco AP, "Controversies in organ donation: the altruistic living donor," Nephrol Dial Transplant. 2001 Mar; 16(3): 619–21.

80. *Colavito v. New York Organ Donor Network, Inc.,* 356 F.Supp.2d 237 (EDNY 2005), appealed, 438 F.3d 214 (2 Cir.2006), question certified to 6 N.Y.3d 820 (N.Y.C.A.2006) and 8 N.Y.3d 43 (2006), and final federal court decision, 486 F.3d 78 (2 Cir.2007).

11. REFERENCES

Adams, Carol, *The Sexual Politics of Meat: A Feminist-Vegetarian Critical Theory* (Continuum: 2000).

Associated Press, "Student Who Sued School Isn't Required to Cut Frog," New York Times (Aug. 3, 1988).

Associated Press, "Vegan couple will serve life sentences for starving baby to death, court rules," NY Daily News (Sept. 12, 2011).

Carter, Terry, "Real Trouble," *ABA Journal* (Sept. 1, 2008).

Chumley, Cheryl, "Where's the beef? Bloomberg launches vegetarian-only school lunch," The Washington Times (May 1, 2013).

Dobson: 'No health apartheid,' BBC News (7.7.99); *See also* T M Wilkinson, "What's not wrong with conditional organ donation?," J. Med. Ethics 2003; 29: 163–64.

Eng, Monica, "Lactose intolerance: When drinking school milk makes students feel sick," Chicago Tribune (Nov. 26, 2012).

Francione, Gary and Charlton, Anna, *Vivisection and Dissection in the Classroom: A Guide to Conscientious Objection* (American Anti-Vivisection Society: 1992).

Frog (1987) https://www.youtube.com/watch?v=MhwWuLlzBpI.

Gohh RY, Morrissey PE, Madras PN, Monaco AP, "Controversies in organ donation: the altruistic living donor," Nephrol Dial Transplant. 2001 Mar; 16(3): 619–21.

Goodman Kramer, Marcia, "Humane Education, Dissection, and the Law," 13 Animal L. 281 (2007).

Haldane, David, "Vegetarian Bus Driver Settles Suit Against Agency for $50,000," Los Angeles Times (Nov. 20, 1996), at A3.

Hanto DW, "Ethical challenges posed by solicitation of deceased and living organ donors," N. Engl. J. Med. 2007; 356: 1062–66.

Marcus, Erik, *Meat Market: Animals, Ethics, & Money* (Boston: Brio Press, 2005)

McCarthy, Sky, "Washington state landlord offers $200 discount to vegetarians," Fox News (Nov. 25, 2016).

Menosky, Joe, "Down in the Swamps, a 'Natural' Death for a Frog Is, Well, Just Not Natural," Los Angeles Times (Aug. 22, 1988).

Mosher, Lucinda, *Belonging*, Vol. I of *Faith in the Neighborhood* (Church Pub. 2005).

National Council on Disability, "Organ Transplant Discrimination Against People with Disabilities" (Sept. 25, 2019).

Page, Donna, "Veganism and Sincerely Held 'Religious' Beliefs in the Workplace: No Protection Without Definition," 7:2 U. Pa. J. of Labor & Emp. L. 363 (2005).

Position of the American Dietetic Association and Dieticians of Canada: vegetarian diets, 64(2) Can. J. Dietetic Prac. & Res. 62 (2003).

Rosengard, David, "'Three Hots and a Cot and a Lot of Talk': Discussing Federal Rights-Based Avenues for Prisoner Access to Vegan Meals," 23 Animal L. 355 (2017).

Sapon, Stanley, "Is Veganism a Religion?," VegNews (Dec. 2002).

Soifer, Sarah, "Vegan Discrimination: An Emerging and Difficult Dilemma," 36 Loy. L.A. L. Rev. 1709 (2003); Iacobbo, Karen and Michael, *Vegetarians and Vegans in America Today* (Westport, CT: Praeger Publishers, 2006).

United Press International, "Suit on Frog Dissection Rejected," Los Angeles Times (Aug. 1, 1988).

Chapter Four

Vegan Legal Issues in Germany

Ralf Müller-Amenitsch

1. INTRODUCTION

This chapter examines the scope of protection for vegans under German law and explains the legal challenges undertaken by the author for specific vegan clients. It also briefly discusses laws restricting the labeling of vegan food products in Germany.

Unlike Great Britain, Germany does not protect vegans under antidiscrimination law. Section 2 of this chapter describes how, nonetheless, vegans in specific public sectors have a right to vegan food or, at least, monetary compensation for a lack thereof. Section 3 explains the rights of parents to feed their children a vegan diet, and how veganism can affect custody rights. Section 4 discusses consumer rights regarding the quality of vegan food. Section 5 discusses discrimination protections for vegan jobseekers, students, and employees within German labor law. Section 6 explains two aspects of social welfare benefits relating to veganism. Section 7 describes German antidiscrimination law and how veganism is not currently considered a protected characteristic in the same way as religion or sexual identity. This section also examines existing legal claims for 'moral damage.' The final section, 8, is not about vegan rights, but instead restrictions on vegan businesses: it discusses German laws restricting the labeling of vegan products with words traditionally associated with the 'livestock' industry.

For readers more familiar with Anglo-American legal texts in particular, in order to understand the law in the Federal Republic of Germany, it is necessary to understand that the German law is based primarily on the principle of the separation of powers. The law in the Federal Republic of Germany is also fully codified.

The German legal system works with the 'indefinite legal terms' concept. Indefinite legal terms are vague notions like 'important reasons' which give the judiciary some scope for interpretation whilst minimizing the accumulation of case law as a source of law. These indefinite legal terms enable the independent individual judges to bring justice in individual cases.

When considering vegan rights, a law must always be analyzed first to see whether favorable outcomes for vegans can result from the interpretation of the indefinite legal term. For example, vegans can be exempted from the obligation to finance general non-vegan school meals if there is an important reason for this. The exception to the general obligation is enabled in the relevant law via the indefinite legal term 'important reason.'

2. ACCESS TO VEGAN FOOD IN PUBLIC INSTITUTIONS

2.1. General Explanation of the Legal Background

Veganism is protected under Article 9 of the European Convention on Human Rights (the right to freedom of thought, conscience, and religion).[1] In the German constitution, a limited concept of veganism is protected by Article 4 Grundgesetz (freedom of conscience, religion, or belief). Religious plant-based dietary needs are protected by the notion of religion or belief, secular vegans by the notion of conscience. The definition of 'belief' in the German constitution is narrower than the definition used by the European Court of Human Rights to decide cases brought under Article 9 of the European Convention and does not cover secular vegans.[2] Nevertheless, constitutional protection means that the state needs important reasons to interfere with the exercise of veganism. However, the constitutional right alone does not provide a claim against the state to provide vegan food in the same way as provided in Portugal, where the provision of 'strict vegetarian' food, i.e., vegan food, is mandatory.[3] The German state also has no duty to avoid discriminating against vegans in the provision of food as is provided under the Equality Act 2010 of Great Britain.

2.2. Apportionment of Costs for Non-Vegan Meals or Sharing of Costs for School Meals

In the state of Berlin, a judge ruled that a father did not have to pay a lunch fee for non-vegan school lunches at the primary school his vegan daughter was attending.[4] Following this ruling, most other parents of vegan children are exempt from paying lunch fees for food their children cannot eat.[5] The arguments in this case were based on:

1. Manifest error of assessment.

2. Article 4 GG: Violation of freedom of conscience, religion, or belief (empathy and antispeciesism).
3. The plaintiff follows the gastrosophic rules of the Frankfurt school of philosophy and sociology.
4. The right to equal treatment with children who are provided with a Kosher or Halal diet, and whose parents did not have to pay the lunch fee.

The State of Berlin cancelled the apportionment and recognized, thereby, ethical veganism as being an important reason for the exemption of costs. Since this court case, most parents of vegan children are now exempt from sharing the total cost of school lunches. Rather than contribute to the school lunch fund, parents can now use their own money to self-supply lunches for their children.

2.3. Access to Vegan Food in Kindergartens

No legal protections exist for vegan children in kindergartens and nurseries. Very often parents experience difficulties with their claims, which are based on anti-discrimination rules and equal treatment and are sometimes hindered by contractual clauses. If they ask for legal help, they can at least self-supply food to their children based on their fundamental rights, as guaranteed by the aforementioned judicial ruling, but they are obliged to follow hygiene regulations regarding the food brought into school.[6] Due to the difficulties they have faced, some vegan parents have felt forced to move their children to alternative kindergartens, citing 'other' reasons than structural discrimination. Luckily, in many cases kindergarten administrations can be convinced to provide vegan food, and more and more caterers are starting to add vegan dishes to their menus.

2.4. Access to Vegan Food in Schools

Vegan children have to self-supply food when it is not available at school in Germany. They have to either bring their own food to school or obtain it from an external caterer. This creates a situation of outsidership and isolation, making them appear and feel different from other children.

For this reason, a model case was launched by the present author's law firm Müller-Amenitsch. The case was against the State of Berlin with a special court situation. This legal approach enables the plaintiff to get a legal opinion from the court with minimal cost risk; the court gives a legal opinion on the questions of the case, free of charge, before the case is opened as a full case.

In the case itself, the court had to decide whether to grant legal aid so that the plaintiff could make a claim to get vegan food at a school in Berlin. The claim in the model case was based on:

1. Equal treatment under Article 3 of the German Constitution (other children get financial support for their meals, vegans do not).
2. Violation of Article 9 of the European Convention on Human Rights (the right to freedom of thought, conscience and religion).
3. Violation of the right to conscience, religion, and belief under Article 4 of the German Constitution.
4. The right to education under Article 12 of the German Constitution.

The Administrative Court of Berlin decided that there is no likelihood of success for the claim and therefore no legal aid should be granted. The decision was based on the argument that the Berlin School regulations[7] confer discretionary power to the local authority. The court could only examine, therefore, whether there was a manifest error of assessment.

The court concluded that there was no error of assessment, since the local authority had applied the recommendations of the German food authority (DGE), which did not recommend vegan food for children without taking special care of potential nutritional deficiencies. The court had to check only if a reasonable amount of effort to provide vegan food by the authority had been made. The court concluded that reasonable effort had been made. Denial of vegan food would be in accordance with the law, since vegan food has to be specially prepared by the caterer which, in the opinion of the court, is not reasonable.[8]

The case was, thus, brought to the Oberverwaltungsgericht Berlin, which is the Higher Administrative Court. This higher court decided that there is no right to claim vegan food, since the constitutional rights do not provide a 'status activus,' i.e., a positive claim against the state.[9] The case was then presented to the German Constitutional Court, which gave a legal opinion.[10] The short decision can be summarized as follows:

- Freedom rights are not concerned, since the plaintiff has been given the right to self-supply.
- Right of 'freedom of conscience' does not, per se, give a claim against the state to supply vegan food.
- Equality rights were not violated in this case, since other minorities were not granted (burden of proof problem) special food.
- The plaintiff has the right to self-supply (as a minimum).
- The plaintiff has the right to be exempted from apportionment for non-vegan food.

- There is a general right of access to vegan food when other minority foods are provided.
- There is a right to receive financial support for food if vegan food is not available and other food is funded and provided, such as in the army, police force, etc.

This decision reflects the author's assessment in the first German publication on vegan law[11] and confirms the general right to self-supply in all public institutions. As a minority, people who eat vegan food for secular ethical reasons can claim equal rights for dietary needs alongside religious groups. Further, under Article 3 of the German Grundgesetz (Constitution), which confirms the principle of equality, vegans in school have the right to be provided for in the same way as other minorities. Therefore, in the author's professional opinion, if a child requiring halal or kosher food is provided for under the terms of relevant legislation, then the same legislative rights would also apply to vegan children eating a diet according to secular ethics.

2.5. Access to Vegan Food at Universities

No right to vegan food exists for vegan students in German universities, even though the food at university canteens is subsidized by the sixteen German states. Vegan students, therefore, by paying taxes, pay for nonvegan food to be provided to their nonvegan colleagues. In canteens of universities, vegan options are not always available. In Berlin, however, one university canteen exclusively and successfully provides vegan food. Vegans who don't have access to vegan food in university canteens have the right to self-supply as described above, but if halal and or kosher food is served in public canteens vegans could go to an administrative court to present a claim for equal treatment. In private canteens, they could claim discrimination under the conditions explained in section 7 below.

2.6. Access to Vegan Food in Prisons

Since the prison administration is organized under federal authority in Germany, the provision of vegan food to prisoners differs in the different states.

In Berlin, the prison authority granted a component-choosing right based on the interpretation of federal law. For example, a prisoner can take two portions of potatoes instead of one portion of meat. In addition, prisoners have the right to self-supply, although this is not always practicable due to lack of money or to bureaucratic burdens. So far, it has not been possible to launch a model case to support vegan prisoners, since the possible plaintiffs ended their service before a case could be brought to court.

In some federal states, the supply of vegan food is insufficient and problematic under the claim of human rights.[12] Some vegan prisoners have no access to vegan food, since neither are they provided with it nor do they have a right to self-supply.

2.7. Access to Vegan food in the Military and Police Force

In the German federal army (Bundeswehr), volunteer draftees have the right to self-supply and receive daily financial support for vegan food. Professional soldiers have the right to self-supply and can be exempted from apportionment of costs for the provision of common food.

Individual cases for exemption of apportionment for non-vegan food have been successful for police officers on special assignments—for example, those tasked with ensuring security at a demonstration, or those in training. In these cases, the police officers were provided with a daily budget for the provision of meals when omnivore meals were funded for colleagues.

2.8. Access to Vegan Food in Hospitals

Vegan patients in hospital also have the right to self-supply if no vegan food is available.

Another issue of interest regarding vegan patients is the fact that German residents are required to purchase health insurance. Since the health insurance pays a daily sum for food to the hospital, in a case where vegan food was not provided, a claim for reimbursement could be a possible model case for the courts to consider.

Tube feeding for vegan patients is a challenge, since there are very few products for enteral and parenteral nutrition. If possible, patients should make sure in advance that they will have access to available options. Subject to discussion with health care providers about the suitability of those available, vegan patients have the right—based on their fundamental rights, as described in 2.1 above—to choose suitable vegan remedies when there is a vegan option and, if they wish, can refuse a non-vegan treatment.

Vegans can also appoint a power of attorney to ensure that they will continue to be provided with vegan food when they suffer from dementia or other disorders that prevent autonomous food choice.

To support vegans in Germany, a white list of hospitals that serve vegan food, and a list of vegan remedies, and remedies that fall under the 'grandfather' rule' of animal testing is available.[13] The 'grandfather rule' considers that those remedies that do not need any further animal testing are to be preferred to those that are still in the process of regular testing.

2.9. Summary

In general, German law grants the right to self-supply with vegan food in every German public institution, based on the European Convention of Human Rights and on the German Constitution. However, there is need for improvement in the practical application of this fundamental right in prisons, schools and kindergartens. In some prisons, vegan prisoners have no access to vegan food because they are denied the right to self-supply. In kindergartens, the problem is that when parents attempt to achieve their aim with legal help, very often their children suffer from tensions with the kindergarten nannies.

There is nonetheless a trend of improved provision of vegan food by caterers, although vegans continue to struggle to obtain vegan food and to secure a fundamental right to vegan food.

Vegans can claim under legal provisions for equal treatment for vegan food to be supplied in public institutions by the state. However, these claims will likely only succeed if it can be shown that other minorities are provided with food that meets their dietary needs—for example, Jews receiving kosher food and Muslims receiving halal food. This would be based on the sixteen special federal laws of the sixteen federal countries in Germany, in combination with Article 4 of the German constitution (equal treatment).

In addition, many changes are needed for vegan public sector employees in areas other than food provision—for example, vegan employees who are required to wear uniforms and standard issue personal protective equipment are not consistently provided for.

3. VEGANS IN FAMILY LAW

3.1. General Explanation of Legal Background

In Germany, family law is regulated in the civil code [Bürgerliches Gesetzbuch] (BGB),[14] which is based on the idea of consensual agreements in order to promote children's welfare.

3.2. A Right to Determine the Choice of Food

It is not uncommon for couples, especially if separated, to argue over whether their child should be vegan or not. This problem is referred to in the specialist literature as the 'right to determine food choice.'[15]

According to the relevant regulations,[16] divorced and separated parents have to exercise joint custody. They have to agree on financial, medical, religious and educational matters such as the choice of doctors, schools, etc. If one parent is not available, the other parent needs a power of attorney for contracts relating to the child—for example, contracts with a doctor or school. In matters of considerable importance, both parents have a veto right. In disputes about the food given to the child which they cannot solve, they can apply to the family court for a formal decision. In the case of separated and divorced parents, the parent with whom the child is habitually and regularly resident decides what diet the child will follow. So, should that parent wish to raise the child vegan, the parent who has only the right of contact has to respect the choice of vegan food during the contact.[17]

3.3. Deprivation of Custody

Some parents appeal to German family courts to withdraw custody from the other parent because the other parent feeds the child a vegan diet. Veganism as such is no reason for the withdrawal of custody, but symptoms of malnutrition are. In general, custody of a child is only withdrawn from German parents if there is a risk to the child's welfare. According to the case law of the Federal Court of Justice, this is only the case if 'there is a current risk to such an extent that considerable damage is almost certainly to be expected in the further development' of the child.[18] In the case of vegan children, a child's welfare risk can only be determined by a doctor. German doctors tend to follow the nutrition advice of the Deutsche Gesellschaft für Ernährung, the German Society for Nutrition (DGE), a mostly government-funded body. The DGE enjoys similar credibility to that of national bodies in other countries, such as the British Dietetic Association.

3.3.1. Deficiency Symptom as a Custody Indicator

The DGE has declared that deficiency symptoms can occur with vegan nutrition. They state that there is certainly a vitamin B12 deficiency without supplementation, and a risk of vitamin D deficiency, which should be prevented by supplementation in winter. Regarding vitamin A, the DGE is uncertain whether the vegan diet provides adequate carotene and advises that in cases of doubt it should be supplemented. The DGE also believes that those following a vegan diet are at risk of iodine and calcium deficiency and, thus, advises that both iodine and calcium levels are checked and supplemented if necessary. They also advise that protein levels are monitored regularly because protein deficiency can lead to growth retardation in children.

The German Nutrition Society's summary of its statement on vegan diets translates as follows:

> With a purely plant-based diet, an adequate supply of some nutrients is not possible without supplements or is difficult. The critical nutrient is vitamin B12. The potentially critical nutrients in a vegan diet also include protein or indispensable amino acids and long-chain N-3 fatty acids as well as other

> vitamins (riboflavin, vitamin D) and minerals (calcium, iron, iodine, zinc, selenium). For pregnant women, nursing mothers, infants, the DGD does not recommend a vegan diet to children and adolescents, but if you still want to eat vegan, you should take a vitamin B12 supplement permanently, make sure you have an adequate supply of critical nutrients and use fortified foods and nutrient preparations. If necessary, advice should be given by a qualified nutritionist and the supply of critical nutrients should be checked regularly by a doctor.[19]

In matters of family law, it is recommended that vegan parents adhere to these guidelines so they can demonstrate in court that they do not endanger the well-being of their child. Following this advice, they should, if necessary, be able to provide medical evidence that there are no symptoms of nutritional deficiency in the child.

3.3.2. Special Case When Vegan Mothers Cannot Breastfeed

Some vegan mothers are unable to breastfeed. This could be due to health reasons, or they might be taking medication where breastfeeding is contraindicated, or they might simply be unable to breastfeed for physiological reasons.

In these situations, according to the current assessment of the DGE, there is no suitable commercially available infant formula to adequately feed the babies. Vegan parents are strongly advised not to argue with the authorities in this regard, but to find a way of obtaining breast milk via a breast milk exchange (human milk bank).

3.4 Summary

The vegan diet of children is viewed critically by the official German nutritionist and the jurisprudence,[20] but there is no risk of custody deprivation for parents who consistently make sure that their children do not show symptoms of deficiencies.[21] All other questions of family law, such as the question of the right to determine the food, are to be resolved pragmatically, so that in summary it can be said that the situation for vegan parents in the Federal Republic of Germany is limited to the marginal areas of structural discrimination, which other minorities also have to suffer.[22]

4. CONSUMER AND TRAVEL LAW

4.1. General Explanation of Legal Background

Although hotels and tour operators offer special travel programs for vegans, they often serve vegan food below the quality of nonvegan alternatives. In such cases, the German legal system grants a price reduction under the following conditions:[23]

- Vegan food is a warranted characteristic (there is only a serious deficiency to the holiday if warranted characteristics are lacking).[24]
- The traveler complains immediately. (The burden of proof is on the traveler.)[25]
- The traveler lodges a legal claim within one month.[26]

4.2. Court Decisions

So far, one decision has been made by the Civil Court of Bremen. The court did not award a price reduction.[27] In this case, a mother and daughter went on an eleven-day cruise and the tour operator guaranteed vegan food. The price per person was 5600 Euro. At almost every meal, they received assorted vegetables, while nonvegan guests were given a choice from two different menus. For a gala dinner, they were provided with an onion filled with chopped vegetables and a melted block of couverture chocolate as dessert. For her birthday, the daughter was provided with a birthday cake containing butter and egg.

Since they were not satisfied with the quality of the food provided for the price they had paid for the cruise, they sued the travel operator, claiming a price reduction.

The court based its decision on the German BGB civil code. It decided the tour operator had to supply vegan food of average kind and quality, and that a dish of assorted vegetables on a daily basis with little variation would fulfil this standard. The judge stated that an onion stuffed with vegetables contained 'important biovital ingredients' for vegans. A birthday cake was not part of the contract, so no price reduction could be claimed for it.[28] The court formulated the following guiding principle:

> If a special agreement is made on a cruise that offers vegan food specifically for the traveler, only a food offer of average type and quality will be owed and not a comparable food range with that offered to the other cruise guests in the context of mass catering.

This decision was criticized on the following points:[29]

- Monotonous food generally gives the right to price reduction of about 15%. This is also applicable for vegan food. The court ignored this typical category for price reduction.
- Stuffed onion is not average quality on a three-star gala dinner level.
- The serving of allergens like egg and butter in the birthday cake without declaration is an administrative offense.[30]

- Administrative offences are illegal; therefore, the service cannot be considered as being of average kind and quality even though the cake was an additional service.
- If the customers had eaten the cake, they could claim moral damage.[31]

4.3. New Quality Standards for Vegan Food

Because of this court decision, a proposition for vegan quality standards and table for claims for defects pursuant to Section 437 BGB has been developed by the present author, Ralf Müller-Amenitsch, in cooperation with the Austrian vegan cook Siegfried Kröpfl. The recommendations are based on the recommendations of the international hotel organization 'Stars Alliance' and provide guidance for 'basic' to 'five-star' hotel level restaurants.[32] For example:[33]

> Food availability and quality:
>
> - If no vegan food is available, then the vegan customer can expect a 50 percent price reduction per day.
> - If only monotonous vegan food is provided a customer can expect a 15 percent price reduction per day.
>
> In each inn it should be possible to purchase:
>
> - A soup,
> - a simple salad, and
> - a main course—this could be a pasta dish, baked vegetables or a risotto. (The dishes should also reflect what would customarily be available in the given region.)
> - various spreads, and
> - a cake or cream.
>
> In the category of '1 star' it should be possible to purchase:
>
> - Simple appetizers, spreads and salads,
> - cream soup—seasonally matched,
> - at least two different main courses—these can be pasta dishes, risottos, curries etc.
> - Two different desserts—as a cream or cake.
>
> For breakfast, the following products should be offered:
>
> - different vegan yoghurts, muesli, fresh fruits, cut fruit, various pastries, jams,
> - milk alternatives—at least two varieties,
> - two spreads, vegetable margarine.

5. LABOR LAW

5.1. General Explanation of Legal Background

Vegans can be affected by various employment-related situations. If vegans are excluded in the job advertisement as potential applicants, a fact of discrimination would have to be examined according to German antidiscrimination law (Allgemeines Gleichbehandlungsgesetz).

Another problem area is when vegans have to carry out employment tasks that, as vegans, they find objectionable. One example is a supermarket employee who is transferred from the drinks department to the meat department. Even employees in non-food-related employment contexts can experience conflicts with their ethical orientation, such as a translator who is instructed to translate contract texts for clients in the meat industry. In some cases, instructing employees to undertake tasks that conflict with their ethical beliefs could amount to 'illegal instruction,' discussed below.

5.2. Illegal Instruction

In these employment cases, the question arises as to whether the employer is entitled to assign employees to work that violates their ethical or religious beliefs, or conscience. To deal with these cases, the German legislator has developed the principle of 'illegal instruction.'[34]

For those affected, this means that, for example, if the employer instructs them to be transferred from the beverage department of a supermarket to the meat department, they can have the labor court check whether the request is an arbitrary instruction that the employee does not have to follow. In these cases, the burden of proof is on the employer, who must show that there is an operational necessity to assign the employee to the work they do not wish to do.

5.3. Veganism as an Obstacle to Training and Professional Practice

In some cases, vegans have problems entering professional fields of employment due to compulsory elements of training programs contradicting their ethical beliefs. The job descriptions of chef, baker and confectioner, housekeeper and nutritionist are particularly well known. In all these professions vegans do not like to process or recommend non-vegan products during training.

For those affected, this often means that they cannot achieve their professional goal, or they suffer serious ethical conflicts during training and their professional practice. In the long term, it is desirable that the training regulations change. Those affected have, in individual progressed cases, already claimed to be exempted from the non-vegan part of the curriculum. For example, it was confirmed in the case of a trainee confectioner that she did not have to prepare non-vegan products to be licensed as a confectioner under an exemption permitted by Article 8 of the German Handicrafts Ordinance, on the grounds of unreasonable burden.[35]

Alternative approaches are certainly possible. For example, housekeeping teachers could use substitute vegan products in order to demonstrate the preparation of conventional non-vegan dishes; when providing a practical lesson on how, for example, to fry a steak, the vegan teacher could use a vegan steak replacement.

For German vegans wishing to pursue certain professions that in Germany have training programs containing 'non-vegan' elements, there is also the possibility to register and train abroad and then come back to work in Germany, for example as a vegan cook.

6. SOCIAL LAW

6.1. Limiting Social Welfare

In 2015, a social court ruled that the German state is not allowed to cut benefits for low-income employees because they get free food at work.[36] This is particularly important for low-income vegans who cannot eat workplace food or can do so only partially. This was confirmed in the case of a German employee who had been given financial support (social welfare) by the state of Berlin, on the grounds of low income. When the employee was offered a free lunch at work, the state of Berlin cancelled the lunch part of the social welfare benefits. However, the food provided consisted mainly of meat products which were unsuitable and, therefore, the employee did not want to partake of the free daily lunch.

The social court considered this case and ruled that "The reduction of welfare benefit was a violation of her right to a personal sphere ('Allgemeines Persönlichkeitsrecht') and was, therefore, prohibited. ('Allgemeines Persönlichkeitsrecht' is a construction of the highest courts to provide protection for intimate personal decisions.)"

6.2. Entitlement to Vitamin B12 Test and Vitamin B12

To check if they have a B12 deficiency, many vegans undergo a Vitamin B12 test. In Germany, health insurance companies have to cover the medical costs of patients. Since German citizens are required to obtain health insurance, the covering of the costs of vitamin B12 tests and vitamin B12 supplementation by health insurance companies is a legal issue for vegans.

According to the case law in the Federal Republic of Germany, there is no entitlement to reimbursement of the cost of a vitamin B12 preparation as a dietary supplement. However, if symptoms of deficiency occur, vitamin B12 can be prescribed as a medication and is then paid for by the insurance company for the vegan patient.

7. DISCRIMINATION AGAINST VEGANS

7.1. Scope of Protection

The German Antidiscriminatory Act [Allgemeines Geichbehandlungsgesetz] (AGG) protects individuals against discrimination on the grounds of sex, age, sexual orientation, race and ethnic origin, physical handicap, belief (Weltanschauung) and religious belief. In contrast to religious requirements for plant-based food, secular ethical veganism does not fall under the scope of the General Equal Treatment Act, according to the guidelines of the Federal Anti-Discrimination Agency.

According to the notion of belief the European Union, based on the Directive 2000/78 / EC of 27 November 2000,[37] a broad conception of belief is to be used.[38] However, the European notion of belief is translated in German as 'Weltanschauungsbegriff,' and, as such, is most likely to be interpreted as the German concept of 'conviction.'

According to general interpretation of 'Weltanschauung,' not every conviction is protected, and ethical veganism, in the opinion of many academic commentators, does not fall under the protective scope of the General Equal Treatment Act.[39] This limited scope of protection is not fully developed in relation to the convictions that underlie veganism. For example, pacifism is considered sufficient for the application of the concept of Weltanschauung.[40]

Ethical veganism can be classified as pacifist-antispeciesist because vegans have the same basic outlook as pacifists, which are a protected group. The difference is that vegans have included nonhuman animals in their pacifism because they are vulnerable and in need of protection. Vegan pacifists have so far remained out of the jurisprudential view and should, in the author's opinion, also fall under the narrow concept of Weltanschauung of the AGG. The restrictive view of the German General Equal Treatment Act compared to the wider scope of the European term leads to inconsistent jurisprudence in the European Union, which conflicts with legal harmonization. Accordingly, the limited application of Weltanschauung is criticized by Petra Kudelka, Felix Hnat and the present author.[41] Ultimately, the progressive standardization of European law will probably lead to a clarification, either through further regulations or case law of the European Court of Justice.

7.2. Moral Damage in Civil Law for Application of Non-Vegan Food and Substances

In German civil law to date, two cases have been clarified by the German courts. In one case, a vegetarian patient asked her dermatologist to treat her with only vegetarian products, but her doctor performed an allergy test by injecting her with a product that contained animal ingredients. The client sued the doctor for moral damage, and the court ruled that the injection constituted a bodily injury that was not covered by the patient's consent and, therefore, led to moral damage.[42]

Regarding a claim for moral damage for serving nonvegan food to a vegan, or nonvegetarian food to a vegetarian, there has not been any court decision yet. Generally, though, serving the wrong kind of food is not considered an offence as such, but the undeclared serving of allergens is an administrative offence that can lead to claims for moral damage. Moral damage is also granted when the court agrees that there has been a violation of important personal rights protected under Article 823 II BGB (German Civil Code). The personal sphere (Allgemeines Persönlichkeitsrecht) of a vegan is considered within the scope of the meaning of this right. Therefore, involuntary consumption of non-vegan products by a vegan can lead to claims for moral damage.[43]

8. VEGAN PRODUCT LABELING: FORBIDDEN DENOMINATIONS OF PLANT-BASED MEAT. EGG AND DAIRY-LIKE PRODUCTS

In Germany, misleading food product denominations or other denominations that are forbidden by the law can lead to actions for a prohibitory injunction combined with fines of up to 250,000 euros. The courts have already decided many cases and the rulings impact negatively on plant-based food producers:

- 'Veierlikör' ('Vegg liqueur') was judged misleading for giving the impression it could be egg liqueur.[44]
- 'Natur ('yoghurt')' was judged misleading since there was no declaration of the ingredients being purely plant-based.[45]
- 'Pflanzenkäse' ('plant cheese') was judged as illegal.[46]
- 'Wie Frischkäse' (similar to 'cream cheese') was judged as illegal.[47]
- 'Cashew cheese' was judged as illegal.[48]
- 'Zu verwenden wie Crème Fraiche,' (replacement for 'crème fraiche') was judged as illegal.[49]

The most famous case was heard at the European Court of Justice.[50] The Court had to decide whether a product can be given the name of 'Tofubutter.'

The court decided that '[t]erms such as "milk," "cream," "butter," "cheese" or "yoghurt" may only be used for animal products.' The court stated that:

> Article 78(2) and Annex VII, Part III, to Regulation (EU) No 1308/2013 of the European Parliament and of the Council of 17 December 2013 establishing a common organization of the markets in agricultural products and repealing Council Regulations (EEC) No 922/72, (EEC) No 234/79, (EC) No 1037/2001 and (EC) No 1234/2007 must be interpreted as precluding the term 'milk' and the designations reserved by that regulation exclusively for milk products from being used to designate a purely plant based product in marketing or advertising, even if those terms are expanded upon by clarifying or descriptive terms indicating the plant origin of the product at issue, unless that product is listed in Annex I to Commission Decision 2010/791/EU of 20 December 2010 listing the products referred to in the second subparagraph of point III(1) of Annex XII to Council Regulation (EC) No 1234/2007.[51]

Thus, consumer protection of omnivore consumers from potentially misleading denominations is considered to be of greater importance than the interests of vegan consumers in making a quick and safe purchase decision. In contrast, however, German courts have decided recently that the denomination 'alternative to cheese' is permitted:[52] 'The designation of a vegan cashew product as a "cheese alternative" does not constitute an inadmissible use of the designation "cheese," which is reserved exclusively for milk products according to . . . EU (VO) No. 1308/2013.'[53]

Currently, despite an EU-based initiative,[54] labeling vegan products with meat-like or fish-like terms is not prohibited by law. On October 23, 2020, the European Parliament voted against the so-called 'burger ban,' thus allowing meaty denominations of plant-based food.[55] On the same day, the European Parliament voted to ban descriptive terms for vegan alternatives to dairy products like "alternative to cheese." These restrictions will have to be followed when the new EU Regulation is published.

9. NOTES

1. C.W. v the United Kingdom, ECtHR App. No. 18187/91, decision 10th February 1993, available at https://hudoc.echr.coe.int/eng#{%22itemid%22:[%22001-1503%22]}.
2. See Elisabeth Gottwald und Ralf Müller-Amenitsch, *Urteilssammlung Veggie Food* [*Veggie Food Judgment Collection*] (Hamburg: Behrs Verlag, 2020), 59.
3. Portuguese Law Nr. 10/2017 Art. 3 grants the provision of at least one strict vegetarian i.e., a vegan meal in every public canteen.
4. The ruling followed legal action by the author's Law Firm Müller-Amenitsch (Vater Vs. State of Berlin—VG 37 K 621.14).
5. The judicial ruling has little implication in the 15 other states since each of them has its own education system and law.
6. The German Nahrungsmittelhygieneverordnung [Food Hygiene Regulation] (LMHV) sets minimal standards for food safety.
7. Article 19.3.1 of the School Act for the state of Berlin.

8. Verwaltungsgericht [Administrative court] of Berlin AZ VG 3 K 503.15, decision of 09. May 2016.

9. Oberverwaltungsgericht [higher administrative court] of Berlin AZ OVG 3M 65.15 decision 27 July 2016.

10. Bundesverfassungsgericht [German constitutional court] 1 BvR 1981/16 / decision of 09 August 2018.

11. See Ralf Müller-Amenitsch, "*Vegan im Recht" ["Vegan Rights"*], 2nd ed. (Mainz: Ventil Verlag), 22.

12. For a discussion of how the European Court of Human Rights has ruled on cases concerning a prisoner's right to be provided with food that aligns with their vegan beliefs see Jeanette Rowley, "The Right to Vegan Food in Prison in Europe" (Conference presentation, Vienna, November, 2017), accessed November 1, 2019, https://www.academia.edu/35161387/The_Right_to_Vegan_Food_in_Prison_in_Europe_November_2017_Vienna_.

13. This list is supplied by PETA Germany.

14. https://www.gesetze-im-internet.de/bgb/.

15. Müller-Amenitsch, "*Vegan im Recht,"* (*"Vegan Rights"*), 2nd ed., 48.

16. Article1627 BGB (German Civil Code).

17. See Müller-Amenitsch, "*Vegan im Recht"* (*"Vegan Rights"*), 2nd ed., 48–49.

18. See, for example BGH 14.07.1956 AZ IV ZB 32/56 (German Federal Court of Justice).

19. See German Nutrition Society: accessed December 22, 2019, https://www.dge.de/wissenschaft/weitere-publikationen/dge-position/vegane-ernaehrung/.

20. Regarding veganism as a custody indicator, and if veganism alone could be a cause of custody deprivation, see also Clausius, Monika, "Vegane Ernährung als Sorgerechtsindikator" ["Vegan Diet as a Custody Indicator"], *Familienrechtsberater,* ['*Family Law Advisor'*] no. 1 (2017) 19-20.

21. See Müller-Amenitsch, "*Vegan im Recht,"* (*"Vegan Rights"*), 2nd ed. 47.

22. Further court decisions and comments can be found in Ralf Müller-Amenitsch, and Gottwald, *Urteilssammlung Veggy-Food,* 89–96.

23. Article 651cI,651dI,638III and IV BGB Civil Code.

24. Article 651C BGB Civil Code.

25. 651 d II BGB.

26. Article 651g BGB.

27. Civil Court Bremen, judgment of 26.01.2016—5 C 188/16.

28. Civil Court Bremen, judgment of 26.01.2016—5 C 188/16.

29. Ralf Müller-Amenitsch, and Elisabeth Gottwald, *Urteilssammlung Veggy-Food,* 74–80.

30. Article 10 Abs. 3 LKMV ivm. Art. 9 Abs. 1c LMIV (German Food Act).

31. Further court decisions and comments can be found in Ralf Müller-Amenitsch, and Elisabeth Gottwald, *Urteilssammlung Veggie Food,* 69–85.

32. For further details see Ralf Müller-Amenitsch and Elisabeth Gottwald *Urteilsammlungsammlung Veggie Food,* 82.

33. The full categories can be found on the PETA Blog "*Veganes Recht*" (Vegan Rights") https://veganes-recht.de/qualitaetskriterien-fuer-veganes-essen-und-reisen.

34. BGB Article 315 and Article 106 (sentence1) Gewerbeordnung (German Trade Regulations).

35. Article 8 Handwerksordnung (German Handicrafts Ordinance). Example cases were dealt with by the author.

36. Social court of Berlin Az. AS 15482/14, Judgement from 23.03.2015.

37. Establishing a general framework for equal treatment in employment and occupation Official Journal L 303 , 02/12/2000 P. 0016—0022.

38. Thomas Heinrichs and Heike Weinbach, "*Weltanschauung als Diskriminierungsgrund-Begriffsdimensionen und Diskriminierungsrisiken,*" ["*World View as Grounds of Discrimination—Conceptual Dimensions and Risks of Discrimination"*] (Berlin: Antidiskriminierungsstelle des Bundes, 2016), 21.

39. Ralf Müller-Amenitsch, "*Vegan im Recht"* (*"Vegan Rights"*), 2nd ed. (Mainz: Ventil Verlag), 85–86.

40. Heinrichs and Weinbach, *Weltanschauung als Diskriminierungsgrund-Begriffsdimensionen und Diskriminierungsrisiken*." ["*World View as Grounds of Discrimination—Conceptual Dimensions and Risks of Discrimination*"], 22.

41. Ralf Müller-Amenitsch, Felix Hnat and Petra Kudelka, "*Vegan im Recht Austrian Edition*, 103, or Müller-Amenitsch, *Vegan im Recht* (*"Vegan Rights"*), 2nd ed., 82 ff. For a wider discussion about the status of veganism to law see the work of Jeanette Rowley, and specifically *Towards a Vegan Jurisprudence: The Need for a Reorientation of Human Rights* (Lexington, 2020).

42. Civil Court of Düren Decision from 13.09.1999 Nr. 47C 301/98.

43. See Müller-Amenitsch, "*Vegan im Recht,"* (*"Vegan Rights"*), 2nd ed., 67.

44. Landgericht Trier [Trier district court] 20. December 2018, 7 HK 0 13/18.

45. Oberlandesgericht Nürnberg [Higher Regional Court of Nuremberg], 17 April 2018, AZ 3 U 2083/17.

46. Offending Art 78 Abs, II EU directive 1380/2013 (Landgericht (district court) Trier, 24 March 2016, AZ 7HKO 58/15.

47. Offending Art 78 Abs, II EU directive 1380/2013 (Landgericht Koblenz 22 July 2017, AZ 0 25/16.

48. Offending Art 78 Abs, IIEU directive 1380/2013 (Landgericht Trier, 24 August 2017, 7HK O 20/16).

49. Offending Art 78 Abs, II EU directive 1380/2013 (Landgericht Hamburg, 13 July 2018.

50. ECJ v. 14.06.2017.

51. Judgment of 14.06.2017—C-422/16. https://eur-lex.europa.eu/legal-content/EN/SUM/?uri=CELEX:62016CJ0422.

52. Landgericht Stade, 28 March 2019, AZ 8 O 64/18.

53. Not Offending Art 78 Abs, II EU directive 1380/2013 (Landgericht Stade 28.March 2019, AZ 8O 64/18.

54. See for example, Damien Carrington, "Battle Over EU Ban on 'Veggie Burger' Label Reaches Key Vote," *The Guardian*, accessed December 23, 2020, https://www.theguardian.com/environment/2020/oct/16/eu-ban-veggie-burger-label-parliament-vote-meat.

55. See Maria Chiorando, "EU Parliament Rejects 'Veggie Burger Ban' But Supports 'Dairy Ban' Against Vegan Producers" October 23, 2020 accessed January 14, 2020, https://plantbasednews.org/culture/dairy-ban-voted-in-veggie-burger-ban-rejected/.

10. REFERENCES

Carrington, Damien. "Battle Over EU Ban on 'Veggie Burger' Label Reaches Key Vote." *The Guardian*. Accessed December 23, 2020. https://www.theguardian.com/environment/2020/oct/16/eu-ban-veggie-burger-label-parliament-vote-meat.

Chiorando, Maria. "EU Parliament Rejects 'Veggie Burger Ban' But Supports 'Dairy Ban' Against Vegan Producers," October 23, 2020. Accessed January 14, 2020. https://plantbasednews.org/culture/dairy-ban-voted-in-veggie-burger-ban-rejected/.

Clausius, Monika. "Veganes Recht als Sorgerechtsindikator." *Familienrechtsberater*, no.1 (January 2017): 19–20.

Gottwald, Elisabeth and Ralf Müller-Amenitsch. "*Urteilssammlung Veggie Food."* Hamburg: Behrs Verlag, 2020.

Heinrichs, Thomas and Heike Weinbach. *Weltanschauung als Diskriminierungsgrund-Begriffsdimensionen und Diskriminierungsrisiken*." Berlin: Antidiskriminierungsstelle des Bundes, 2016.

Kudelka, Peter and Felix Hnat and Ralf Müller-Amenitsch. "*Vegan im Recht Austrian Edition."* Wien: Vegane Gesellschaft Wien, 2017.

Müller-Amenitsch Ralf. *Vegan im Recht* ("Vegan Rights"), 2nd ed. Mainz: Ventil Verlag, 2018.

Rowley, Jeanette. "The Right to Vegan Food in Prison in Europe" (Conference presentation, Vienna, November 2017). Accessed November 1, 2019. https://www.academia.edu/35161387/The_Right_to_Vegan_Food_in_Prison_in_Europe_November_2017_Vienna_

Rowley, Jeanette. *Towards a Vegan Jurisprudence: The Need for a Reorientation of Human Rights*. Lexington, 2020.

Chapter Five

Veganism and Law in Italy

Carlo Prisco

1. INTRODUCTION

Discrimination against vegans in Italy is widespread despite constitutional equality and published ministerial food guidelines that promote the need to provide for religious, ethical, and cultural dietary requirements. This chapter explains the relationship between veganism and law in Italy, how Italian authorities have dealt with vegans and how grounding a defense in scientific facts about veganism and health has had a positive impact for vegans in Italy.

2. THE RIGHTS OF VEGAN PEOPLE

2.1. Veganism and the Italian Constitution

The Italian approach to veganism is based on the fact that the Italian Constitution guarantees to provide protection for ethical, as well as religious, convictions. More specifically, Article 3 states that: 'Everyone has the right to freely express their thoughts with the word, the written word and any other means of diffusion.'[1] Theoretically, and considering that eating a vegan diet is a way an individual expresses their values and convictions, this constitutional provision should be enough to recognize and protect what I call 'the right to vegetarianism.'[2] In reality, however, in Italy, this is not the case.

Where veganism is concerned, there is no equality of provision for religious and ethical expression. The convictions expressed through eating a vegan diet are considered insignificant and not as important as a religious habit or belief. Although some relevant principles for the protection of non-religious convictions have been set out in the Constitution, the common law practice in Italy shows how hard it is to translate such principles into actual rights, even at a basic level.

In my experience, the judges in Italy are worried when they are required to make practical use of the Constitution. This may be a consequence of centralized Constitutional control that, in Italy, entitles only the Constitutional Court to determine whether a law infringes the Constitution, while other Courts cannot. Where there are potential opportunities for pioneering interpretations, common Courts just prefer to avoid making any statement: this leads to the aforementioned result, rendering the Constitution a dead letter.

2.2. Dietary Guidelines

Many obstacles to the eradication of discrimination against vegans derive from nutritional concerns that regard a vegetarian or (particularly) a vegan diet unbalanced and unhealthy. In 2010, the Italian government approved dietary guidelines to set common principles for public institutions (e.g., hospitals, schools, etc.) regarding food and food administration. The guidelines emphasized the need for young children to develop healthy eating habits and set this statement in the context of the fundamental right of the child to a healthy and proper diet.[3]

Although the guidelines are not binding, if followed properly, they represent a good point of reference in the most controversial cases of discrimination against vegans. Further, the common principles reference the right to health.

One of the main reasons for the publication of dietary guidelines is concern about the growing phenomenon of childhood obesity, typical of the Western societies and largely caused by the spread of erroneous eating patterns and high-calorie foods combined with widespread low levels of physical activity. The Italian guidelines positively embrace these concerns:

> The Guidelines for the national school food move from the need to facilitate, since childhood, adoption of healthy eating habits for health promotion and prevention of chronic degenerative diseases (diabetes, cardiovascular disease, obesity, osteoporosis, etc.) caused by bad nutrition. On the other hand, the profound changes in lifestyle of families and individuals have led to an increasing number of individuals with the need to consume at least one meal away from home, using collective and commercial food services.[4]

Scientists from all around the world, especially in the West, are trying to understand the relationship between meat consumption and the obesity rate of the population. A study published in June 2009 analyzed historical data and identified that the consumption of meat could increase the risk of developing obesity by as much as 30%.[5]

Childhood is particularly sensitive with regard to food issues in the context of the natural exposure of children to specific disorders or diseases and the development of eating habits which, if incorrect, may accompany the individual for most or the whole of their life.

From a nutritional perspective, the ministerial Guidelines did not consider the issue of whether vegetarianism or veganism supported good health, but focused instead on the properties of individual foods and, in particular, on the contribution of nutrients to good health.

Even though vegetarianism or veganism are not specifically mentioned, the ministerial guidelines contain a generic reference to providing for '*ethical-religious*' needs. In this regard, the dietary element of vegetarian and vegan practice is undoubtedly as relevant as the dietary practice of those with religious convictions and, therefore, should be recognized and protected in the same way:

> The standard of the service, the right of access for users with special health care and ethical-religious needs, must be maintained and defined in each business model, and declared to all users, to official control, to canteen committees, through a service charter.[6]

Further, the guidelines state that '[t]he operating model required to be identified in relation to the needs of the population should provide for the numerical size of the users, ages, physiological, pathological and ethical-religious needs, and for those with disabilities.'[7]

The protected interest is, of course, respect for opinions, which may also be expressed as the 'values' or 'convictions' of those with dietary and health needs; in this respect, the scope of the reference appears to be deliberately broad and undefined and, thus, has potentially unlimited application.

What appears to be of undoubted importance is the obligation to provide information to an entire population; often the exercise of a right, especially if it is not well-known or easily knowable, depends on the awareness of the right-owner, as it is evident that no one can exercise a right of which they know nothing about.

On purely legal grounds, it may be asked if such provisions in ministerial guidelines can establish a genuine right, or simply convey the need to promote the importance of providing an alternative option for those who do not wish to consume products derived from other animals. It seems that they accurately represent fundamental constitutional principles but, as such, cannot be considered real sources in establishing those rights. They do, however, transpose those relevant constitutional rights in an appropriate technical and systematic manner.

On the grounds of relevant constitutional statements regarding equality, and the importance given to accommodating individuals with ethical-religious dietary needs, it can be argued that a strict vegetarian or vegan meal option should be included in the school feeding program in the same way that options for those who wish to abstain from certain foods on religious grounds already are. Furthermore—at least theoretically—the school menu should also provide for lesser-known ethical positions, such as, for example, fruitarianism.

The ministerial food guidelines also assure the provision of adequate food replacements required for ethical, religious or cultural reasons. Requests for suitable food replacements for children do not require medical certification, just a simple request by the parents.[8] This explicit support for cultural dietary needs would seem correct and appropriate, given that many eating habits depend not only on ethical or religious beliefs, but also on cultural traditions.

The scope of provision for an individual's dietary needs, is, therefore, broad and unambiguous. The ministerial food guide provides a point of reference for the importance of ensuring that all those with dietary needs are accommodated, whether those needs be grounded in religion, ethics, or culture. Public canteens are required to ensure the presence of an 'adequate replacement,' which must be nutritionally adequate and therefore qualitatively and quantitatively similar to 'normal' dishes.

Since the criteria to be observed in nutritional composition of meals are provided and described in the guidelines, it seems clear that the assessment of adequacy is to be made on the basis of these parameters, allowing each user to enjoy the same number of courses and a similar nutritional intake.

Considering vegetarian and vegan alternatives, it should be emphasized that the proper replacements should also include a wide variety of foods groups, and this is not only to ensure proper nutrition, but also to address social and psychological issues. The significance of these issues cannot be neglected, especially in the school context, where young pupils with dietary needs could potentially be exposed to continuous confrontation with their classmates.

Moreover, the provision of vegetarian and vegan options should not be considered just as a matter of respect for the opinions and choices of the individuals concerned, but also as a matter of health benefits and ecological implications, which are also referred to repeatedly in the ministerial document: It seems contradictory that even the management of waste is inspired by ecological need, while nothing is said about the environmental impact of food derived from nonhuman animals.

The omission of any reference to the health aspects of vegetarianism and veganism seems unreasonable, both in terms of nutritional education and the many benefits of a meat-free and dairy-free diet for growing children and adults. In this regard, it should be noted that the erroneous conviction that it is dangerous for children to eat a vegetarian diet often prevails in school environments, which results in prejudice and 'tolerance,' sometimes combined with an ill-concealed concern for the (alleged) health problems of the children.

2.3. A Mandatory Vegetarian/Vegan Option?

In 2006, the Italian association LAV (Anti-Vivisection League) promoted a bill for mandatory vegetarian and vegan options.[9] This was the first example, in Western society, of a proposal for a law to protect vegetarian and vegan people with regard to their dietary practice. The bill was presented for the first time in the Italian Senate, in the XV Legislature, identified as DDL 1879, November 13, 2007, and was signed by Senator Valpiana. The title chosen, 'Rules for the Protection of Vegetarian and Vegan Food Choices,' clearly shows the purpose and aims of the project, which takes into account the dietary practices of both vegetarians and vegans.

The bill's preamble contains many insights drawn from ethical, environmental, cultural, and health perspectives, stating in part: 'Only in Italy, food consumption implies the death of more than 600 million animals from land and incalculable numbers of aquatic animals (fish, mollusks, crustaceans).[10] Factory farms are also a major source of pollution of groundwater and of the atmosphere.'[11] In addition to recognizing animal sentience, the bill references well-known environmental and social issues:

> The vegetarian or vegan lifestyle also helps to promote a more equitable distribution of resources that could help fight world hunger. Much cereal production in the Southern Hemisphere, in fact, is intended to feed animals for meat production in Western countries, when they could cover local needs.[12]

The bill also discusses health issues related to diet:

> Science, both official and independent, recognizes in a healthy, well-balanced vegetarian and vegan diet the capacity to ensure a better state of health than a diet that includes meat (eighty pounds a year per capita) or fish (more than twenty pounds per year). It is shown that a vegetarian diet, rich in fruits and vegetables, protects against cardiovascular disease by 24 percent and decreases the chances of heart attack, one of the leading causes of death in Western countries and linked to a diet too rich in fats and animal proteins. The incidence of the most prevalent cancers (colorectal, breast, prostate, pancreas) is much higher among people who eat animal foods (70 percent of people affected by these diseases) rather than among vegetarians (only 30 percent). Western vegetarians also have a lower incidence of obesity and diabetes in comparison to omnivores.[13]

The need to provide legislative protection for vegetarianism, however, is not based solely on ethical consideration or health benefits, but also on the values of a relevant proportion of the population. The bill states that:

In Italy, the number of vegetarians and vegans is rapidly increasing, rising from three million to six million since 2002.[14]

Failing to find complete and balanced meals without meat, fish, or ingredients of animal origin, vegetarians and vegans are forced to eat frugal and nutritionally unbalanced meals in contradiction with the principles of equality enshrined in the Constitution, according to which the state and the government must ensure the same treatment of all citizens, regardless of gender, religion, and every other kind of guidance. This principle should ensure access to healthy vegetarian food.[15]

On the aforementioned premises, the bill's core is as follows:

Article 1 (Purposes)

This law protects vegetarian and vegan diets and Citizens who follow them and affirms and promotes ethical and scientific aspects of such choices.

Article 2 (Definitions)

For the purposes of this Act the following definitions apply:

1. a vegetarian diet excludes meat, fish, and other foods derived from the killing of animals;
2. a vegan diet excludes meat, fish, and other foods derived from the killing of animals, milk and dairy products, eggs, honey, and other foods of animal origin.

Article 3 (Refectories)

1. In all public refectories, affiliated and private, or exercising any kind of public service, refectories performing service for schools of all levels, including nurseries, universities, and places where workers who are unable to return home to eat lunch, such as bars and restaurants attached to workplaces, there will always be offered and advertised at least one vegetarian option and a vegan alternative to foods or products containing animal ingredients provided in the conventional menu.
2. The vegetarian and vegan menu offered must be structured in such a way as to ensure a balanced intake of all nutrients as indicated by official science of nutrition and considering scientific advances in this field.
3. The vegetarian and vegan food should not even contain ingredients of animal origin used in the preparation and unidentifiable organoleptically, listed in the Annex.

4. In order to ensure an adequate service to users, the staff responsible for the administration must be adequately informed of the purposes of this law.
5. The eggs present in vegetarian food must come from hens raised organically or outdoors.

Article 4 (Education and Schooling)

1.
    a. Within the school year following the year in progress at the date of issue of this Act, the Ministry of Education, University, and Research places the teaching of fundamentals of nutrition, food, and vegetarian and vegan food in the teaching programs for vocational institutes and vocational institutes for hotel services and catering.
    b. Students who, in obedience to conscience, in the exercise of the right to freedom of thought, conscience and religion, recognized by the Universal Declaration of Human rights, the Convention for the Protection of Human Rights and Fundamental Freedoms and the International Covenant on Civil and Political Rights, are opposed to violence against all living beings, can declare their conscientious objection to lessons teaching practices regarding food animals.
    c. The institutions indicated in paragraph 1 shall be obliged to make known to all students their right to exercise conscientious objection referred to in paragraph 2.
    d. No student objector may suffer adverse consequences due to the exercise of the right indicated in paragraph 2.
    e. Students objectors are offered a proposal to integrate alternative study for the number of hours required by the school curriculum.

After 14 years, the bill is still pending in Parliament, and the real prospects of approval are unknown. The bill is not given special attention by Parliament and is the subject of debates between those with conflicting interests, predominantly from within the food industry.

3. CASE LAW

When it comes to case law on veganism, Italy has a sad outlook. Prejudice and ignorance about vegan diets are often spread within courts, as well as between professionals such as doctors and attorneys.

In many cases, vegans are scared by professionals and public officials, who openly instruct them to avoid feeding their children a vegan diet. In cases of divorce or separation, vegan parents frequently submit to authority because they are afraid of losing custody.

Other cases are connected with vegan options at school. Once again, these cases involve children, and this leads many people, including pediatricians, to fiercely oppose the provision of vegan food on principle. The most frequent accusation, also shared by the media, is that 100% vegan plant-based food is not suitable for children and is dangerous to their growth. Courts, doctors and social services support what they consider to be the best interests of children. For that reason, it is also common to find that schools independently refuse to provide vegan options.

3.1. The Suspension of Parental Authority for Vegetarian Parents

A well-discussed case occurred in Milan in 1999, when Chiara, a one-year-old baby, was brought by her vegetarian parents to the emergency room with respiratory problems. The doctors diagnosed malnutrition, decided to keep her for investigation and treatments, and also brought the case to the attention of the Juvenile Court of Milan.[16]

The judge decided that the parents were not fulfilling their care obligations and consequently had caused serious damage to the child's health. On the basis of this finding, the child was put under the custody of the Municipality of Milan, with the suspension of all parental rights.

Of course, the Court's decision was highly publicized, and it sharpened the contrast between proponents and opponents of vegetarianism, and, in legal terms, compounded the assumptions of the court in its pronunciation of the circumstances.

Dr. Livia Pomodoro, then president of the Juvenile Court of Milan, defended the decision and made the point that although the courts respect the choices of parents, it is not appropriate for the court to intervene when the authorities make decisions to protect the child's right to health: parents have responsibilities, not a right to the life or death of the child.

The debate from the courtroom soon moved to the media and was furthered by doctors and nutritionists for both parties—the first to support the correctness of the judges and the latter, on the contrary, to contest it. Doctors opposed to the parental choices stated that:

> The so-called vegans derive their name from the Englishman who was the initiator of this philosophy of food; his followers exclude from their diet any animal food, including milk and eggs. Despite being aware that eggs and milk cannot be considered strictly 'animals,' they exclude them anyway because their production causes suffering to animals themselves. . . . You can live well eating vegetarian, without risk to health. Plant proteins are more than suffi-

> cient for the needs of a human organism. For someone who eats too many eggs or cheese too, there may be a risk of an excessive consumption of saturated fats. . . . When a population is accustomed to eating little and following a vegetarian diet, it's bad when it suddenly begins to eat protein foods, which Westerners have become accustomed to. . . . Personally, I think that the ideal diet is fish-vegetarian diet, based on plants and fish, with the addition of yogurt.[17]

The same nutritionist, after explaining the above, and warning against the consumption of foods of animal origin, said, 'before two years of age, the vegetarian diet, especially if in the strict sense, is absolutely not recommended. After weaning, children become omnivores, but have to supplement their diet with milk.'[18] Giorgio Calabrese, a famous nutritionist also speaking against the choice of vegetarian parents, said:

> The vegetarian diet that these two parents follow is totally unbalanced for their child . . . because it lacks proteins resulting primarily from foods of animal origin and at the same time lacks Vitamin B12 and Folic Acid, Calcium, Vitamin D, Vitamin B2, and iodine. The first two elements are essential for the balance of the production of red blood cells and to make them work well, avoiding severe anemia and preventing damage to the nervous tissue. Calcium is essential for the integrity and the formation of bones and teeth, both in the nursing mother and in children and is also used for the proper functioning of muscles, including the heart and nervous system. Vitamin D helps to prevent rickets in children; Vitamin B2 deficiency can cause damage to the skin, especially around the nose and mouth and can give eye disorders. Iodine balances the thyroid which, if altered, causes so many troubles that it is better to avoid.[19]

Dr. Riccardo Trespidi, supporting the vegetarian diet for infants and children, argued:

> It is scientifically proven that a vegetarian diet is recommended, as it helps to reduce certain diseases such as cancer, high blood pressure, obesity. . . . Eating vegetarian, in a proper way, means health. This is also true for infants: if breast milk is not available, there is soy milk. At weaning, add vegetable purees supplemented with barley, rice, or millet. And a lot of fruit. Following this regime, the kids are fine. I hope that the judges will intervene to terminate the parental rights also to the parents who give their children snacks and burgers until they become obese.[20]

From a legal perspective, the matter focuses on the protection of the right to health, and, therefore, on the way to ensure it. The medical, scientific, and historical documentation, now part of the Western cultural heritage, does not consider vegetarianism and veganism harmful to health; rather, in fact, the opposite. However, the Milan case resulted in the mistaken attribution of the child's illness to the vegetarian diet, while, if anything, the problem originated in malnutrition, which can occur both in omnivorous and vegetarian or vegan diets.

The outcome of this case manifested the erroneous classification of the problem, which led to the wrong conclusion that a change in the diet was required, rather than a correction of the diet already adopted. As many have suggested, the decision of the court should have taken into consideration the parents' ethical values, while also requiring compliance with the measures that the court deemed the most appropriate for the child's health, whether that be hospitalization or other forms of medical and therapeutic interventions.

Following the Milan case, there was a similar case in Lecce (Southern Italy), where the court withdrew the parental rights of a vegetarian couple and placed their two-year-old daughter in a religious institution. The mother was permitted to stay with the child to be 're-educated.' The couple were only able to regain custody of the child after approximately a year, after which they emigrated to Switzerland.[21]

3.2. Vegan Meals at Kindergarten

In 2015, in my capacity as an attorney, I was contacted by a woman, a single parent, whose two-year-old son had been expelled from a public nursery because she was a vegan and had asked for a vegan option for her son. In order to obtain vegan food, the school had required a medical certificate attesting the child's good health and confirming a periodical analysis. None of those stipulations had been placed on the other parents, and that, of course, represented a clear discrimination. After the woman refused to provide the requested certification, the school had expelled her child.

Subsequently, I filed a claim at the Administrative Court (T.A.R.), stating that such a decision was clearly disproportionate and constituted unjustified discrimination. Our counterpart, the town of Merano, stated that the decision was intended to protect the child's health and that this primary interest prevailed over the mother's dietary choice.

My argument was grounded in scientific evidence and relevant publications by the American Dietetic Association. I was able to prove that a vegan diet is not only complete and proper for people of any age, but it is also better than the omnivorous diet, as it promotes good health and prevents many diseases, not to mention obesity. Within a few days, I obtained an interim order by the court that obliged the school to re-enroll the child during the trial, while waiting for the final decision.

On 24 July 2015, the Administrative Court of Bolzano upheld the claim in ruling no. 245/15, which declared the school's request unjust and undue. It also confirmed the child's re-enrollment at school.

Even though the court did not enter into discussion of the health question, it is very important to observe that the town's argument was clearly discarded, given that, if the child's health had been in danger, the court should have observed the *ubi maior, minor cessat* rule, recognizing as predominant the interest to life and health in place of ethics. That did not happen, and the town defense was not able to give any evidence in support of its statement that a vegan diet would have harmed the child.

The child remained vegan and went on to attend the same nursery. This happy ending shows how a well-organized defense, grounded in facts and scientific evidence, can overcome the prejudice against vegans in a courtroom.

The key to this success was, of course, correct knowledge of the matter. Attorneys are usually scared to defend a vegan diet and are often the first to condemn it, considering it inappropriate for children. The American Dietetic Association publications were especially useful in this case, as they presented unequivocal scientific arguments.

3.3. Vegan Parent v Omnivorous Parent

In 2016, I was contacted by a vegan woman who was very worried about her child (age 8). Her child had been raised vegan until she and her partner had separated (in 2011). At that point, the child's father had changed his mind and had asked the Milan Juvenile Court to forbid the mother from feeding their child a vegan diet.

The expert appointed by the court, a doctor, was openly against vegan diets, especially for children. The woman's own attorney was also very worried and suggested that she give omnivorous food to her son, warning her about consequences of maintaining the child's vegan diet, such as losing custody.

After a two-year trial, the woman was condemned to feed her son an omnivorous diet, and this caused some health issues: the boy was sick from ingesting dairy products. As many vegans know, after weaning, humans (better to say: mammals) are no longer meant to consume milk, so their normal physiology is simply not agreeable to it. On the other hand, people who continue to drink milk after weaning can maintain their enzyme lactase activity: in this case, the consequences for consuming dairy are minor or negligible.

Luckily, in this case, sickness was clear and provable. As such, I was able to file a new lawsuit to revert the first pronunciation. Once again, the court appointed a doctor. Once again, the doctor was against vegan diets. The difference, in this case, was that another doctor, appointed as an expert by my vegan client, was able to challenge all the misleading information about veganism put forward by the court expert. Eventually, the doctor appointed by the court had to admit that a vegan diet is suitable for children, and, in particular, for that child. Considering the well-documented diseases caused by milk, the court concluded that the only way to protect the child's interests and health was to accept his mother's request.

This was the first time ever, at least in Italy, that a vegan parent has obtained an order from the court to overrule the omnivorous parent's choice.

Obviously, in this case the health issue was fundamental, although—theoretically—it would be easy to prove on a scientific basis that vegan diets are better for health than omnivorous ones. Clearly, when it comes to non-vegan junk food, it is now well-known and recognized by professionals that it is very harmful for children. On the other hand, we still see—in Italy, at least—an overwhelming number of proceedings against vegan parents compared with omnivorous parents who widely use junk food.

4. A CLOUDY FUTURE?

In 2016, a member of Parliament issued a bill of law to punish vegan parents by taking away their parental authority.[22]

The bill's preamble was very clear: based on news, many vegan children were sick and their lives were endangered because of their parents' choices.[23] This statement was wrong: although many cases were actually reported by national media, none of the reports were accurate or true. In some cases, children were simply not vegan; in other cases, they were vegan, but the illness they presented with was not connected with their diet. The most discussed case pertained a child with a congenital heart malformation. I was contacted by the hospital doctor who was treating him, who informed me that the disease had absolutely no relation to diet or food. The story told by the media, however, was different, and the public had no doubt that it was vegan food that was causing harm to that child.

The bill was never approved, and it never became law. As a result of inaccurate media reporting, however, it was considered as a law by many, and, of course, it conveyed the message that vegan food is not suitable for children.

It is interesting to note how that bill addressed the issue of diet and health. The word 'vegan' was never mentioned but it described a diet, missing 'essential elements for healthy and balanced growth.' It is ironic that such a statement could easily refer to a typical omnivorous diet more than to a well-balanced vegan diet. Should that bill ever become law, omnivorous parents should be more scared than vegans.

Unfortunately, another heavy menace to veganism in Italy came about in 2020 in the form of 'the dietary guidelines reform proposal.'[24] While the 2010 dietary guidelines were the most effective tool in any vegan attorney's hands, the new ones literally overturn them, by stating that any kind of 'restrictive' diet at school can be allowed only and if it is prescribed by a doctor. This chapter was hoping to conclude with more information about the new guidelines and their possible implications, but due to the Covid-19 pandemic, Italy, for now, has more immediate concerns. What will undoubtedly be significant, however, is that the vegan diet is far from restrictive and replaces products derived from nonhuman animals with a rich variety of nutritious and healthy plant alternatives.

NOTES

1. Senato della Repubblica, "Costituzione della Repubblica Italiana," 2012, https://www.senato.it/documenti/repository/istituzione/costituzione.pdf.
2. 'Vegetarianism' originally indicated what today is called 'veganism,' as any and all animal products were excluded. The use of the word 'vegetarianism' shifted toward the so called 'lacto-ovo-vegetarianism,' and ultimately became identified with 'lacto-ovo vegetarianism.' Keeping in mind the origin of the principle is useful to understand that nobody ever suggested that it was possible to eat animal derivatives while claiming to respect other animals.
3. National Nutritional Guidelines, 2010, http://www.salute.gov.it/imgs/C_17_pubblicazioni_1248_allegato.pdf 4.
4. National Nutritional Guidelines, 2010, 5.
5. Y. Wang and M. Beydoun, "Meat Consumption is Associated with Obesity and Central Obesity Among US Adults," *Int J Obes*ity, 33, 621–628 (2009). https://doi.org/10.1038/ijo. 45.
6. National Nutritional Guidelines, 2010, 18.
7. Ibid., 20.
8. Ibid., 22.
9. Senato della Repubblica, XV Legislatura 2006-2008, "Norme per la tutela delle scelte alimentari vegetariana e vegana," http://www.senato.it/service/PDF/PDFServer/BGT/00297146.pdf.
10. Ibid., 2.
11. On the unsustainability of eating meat/animal products, see: Henk, W., *Soy Protein and Formulated Meat Products* (Cambridge, MA: Cabi Publishing, 2005); Y. H. Hui, W.K. Nip, R.W. Rodgers and Owen A. Young, *Meat Science and Applications* (New York: Marcel Dekker, 2005). See also Food and Agricultural Organization of the United Nations, "Livestock's Long Shadow," 2006, http://www.fao.org/3/a0701e/a0701e00.htm; Worldwatch Institute, *State of the World: Confronting Climate Change 2009* (London: Earthscan, 2009). See also: Norman Myers, "The Hamburger Connection: How Central America's Forests Became North America's Hamburgers," *Ambio*, 10, n. 1, (1981) 3–8, and David Kaimowitz, Benoit Mertens, Sven Wunder and Pablo Pacheco, "Hamburger Connection Fuels Amazon Destruction," Center for International Forestry Research, April 2003, http://www.cifor.org/publications/pdf_files/media/Amazon.pdf.
12. Frances Moore Lappé, *Diet For a Small Planet* (New York: Ballantine Books, 1982), 69–71. See also, Helen Burley, "What Feeds Our Food? The Environmental and Social Impacts of the Livestock Sector," *Friends of the Earth* (London, UK, 2008), 17.
13. Senato della Repubblica, XV Legislatura 2006-2008, "Norme per la tutela delle scelte alimentari vegetariana e vegana," http://www.senato.it/service/PDF/PDFServer/BGT/00297146.pdf.. 2. See alsoAmerican Dietetic Association, "Position of the American Dietetic Association: Vegetarian Diets," 2009, https://www.vrg.org/nutrition/2009_ADA_position_paper.pdf
14. Senato della Repubblica, XV Legislatura 2006-2008, "Norme per la tutela delle scelte alimentari vegetariana e vegana," http://www.senato.it/service/PDF/PDFServer/BGT/00297146.pdf. 2.

15. Ibid., 2.
16. Marco Piazzi, "Tolta la Figlia ai Genitori Vegetariani," *Corriere della Sera*, October 8, 1999, 17.
17. Ibid., 9/10/99, 14.
18. Ibid., 9/10/99, 14.
19. Brunella Giovara, "Siamo Pentiti, Quella Dieta Poteva Ucciderla," *La Stampa*, October 9, 1999, 12.
20. Marco Piazzi, "Dietologo Imposto ai Genitori Vegetariani," *Corriere della Sera*, October 9, 1999, 14.
21. Paolo Berizzi, "Bambini in Casa-famiglia Business da un Miliardo All'anno," *la Repubblica*, April 29, 2011, http://www.repubblica.it/cronaca/2011/04/29/news/inchiesta_italiana-15507476/.
22. La Repubblica, "Proposta di legge Fi: 'Reato imporre dieta vegana ai figli sotto i 16 anni,'" *La Repubblica* August 7, 2016, https://www.repubblica.it/salute/alimentazione/2016/08/07/news/proposta_di_legge_fi_per_punire_genitori_che_impongono_dieta_vegana_a_figli-145539707/.
23. House of Representatives, "Law Proposal on the Initiative of the Deputy Elvira Savino," July 7, 2016, https://www.camera.it/_dati/leg17/lavori/stampati/pdf/17PDL0043930.pdf.
24. Maria Luisa Amerio, et al, "Ministerio Della Salute: Linee Di Indrizzo Per La Risarazione Ospedaliera Assistenziale Scolastica, Rome, 2016, http://www.quotidianosanita.it/allegati/allegato5559931.pdf?fbclid=IwAR3JAMBcNh502_Y0_gs7uvB-WACztofp1ieXjjCs1ubo6g8SF7QaAFNWekQ.

REFERENCES

American Dietetic Association, "Position of the American Dietetic Association: Vegetarian Diets," 2009, https://www.vrg.org/nutrition/2009_ADA_position_paper.pdf

Amerio, Maria Luisa, et al. "Ministerio Della Salute: Linee Di Indrizzo Per La Ristorazione Ospedaliera Assistenziale Scolastica." Rome, 2016. http://www.quotidianosanita.it/allegati/allegato5559931.pdf?fbclid=IwAR3JAMBcNh502_Y0_gs7uvB-WACztofp1ieXjjCs1ubo6g8SF7QaAFNWekQ.

Berizzi, Paolo. "Bambini in Casa-famiglia Business da un Miliardo All'anno." *la Repubblica*, April 29, 2011. http://www.repubblica.it/cronaca/2011/04/29/news/inchiesta_italiana-15507476/.

Burley, Helen. "What Feeds Our Food? The Environmental and Social Impacts of the Livestock Sector," *Friends of the Earth* (London, UK, 2008), 17.

Food and Agricultural Organization of the United Nations. "Livestock's Long Shadow." 2006. http://www.fao.org/3/a0701e/a0701e00.htm

Giovara, Brunella. "Siamo Pentiti, Quella Dieta Poteva Ucciderla." *La Stampa*. October 9, 1999, 12.

Hoogenkamp, Henk W. "Soy Protein and Formulated Meat Products." Cambridge, MA: Cabi Publishing, 2005.

House of Representatives. "Law Proposal on the Initiative of the Deputy Elvira Savino." July 7, 2016. https://www.camera.it/_dati/leg17/lavori/stampati/pdf/17PDL0043930.pdf.

Hui, Y. H., W.K. Nip, R.W. Rogers, and Owen A. Young. *Meat Science and Applications*. New York: Marcel Dekker, 2005.

Kaimowitz, David Benoit, Mertens, Sven Wunder and Pablo Pacheco. "Hamburger Connection Fuels Amazon Destruction." Center for International Forestry Research. April 2003. http://www.cifor.org/publications/pdf_files/media/Amazon.pdf.

La Repubblica. "Proposta di legge Fi: 'Reato imporre dieta vegana ai figli sotto i 16 anni.'" *La Repubblica*. August 7, 2016. https://www.repubblica.it/salute/alimentazione/2016/08/07/news/proposta_di_legge_fi_per_punire_genitori_che_impongono_dieta_vegana_a_figli-145539707/.

Moore Lappé, Frances. *Diet for a Small Planet*. (New York: Ballantine Books, 1982) 69–71.

Myers, Norman. "The Hamburger Connection: How Central America's Forests Became North America's Hamburgers." *Ambio*, 10, no. 1 (1981) 3–8.

National Nutritional Guidelines. 2010. http://www.salute.gov.it/imgs/C_17_pubblicazioni_1248_allegato.pdf

Piazzi, Marco. "Dietologo Imposto ai Genitori Vegetariani." *Corriere della Sera*. October 9, 1999, 14.

Piazzi, Marco. "Tolta la Figlia ai Genitori Vegetariani." *Corriere della Sera*. October 8, 1999. 17.

Senato della Repubblica, XV Legislatura 2006-2008, "Norme per la tutela delle scelte alimentari vegetariana e vegana," http://www.senato.it/leg/15/BGT/Schede/Ddliter/29259.htm

Wang, Y., Beydoun, M. "Meat Consumption Is Associated with Obesity and Central Obesity Among US Adults." *Int J Obesity* 33, 621–628 (2009). https://doi.org/10.1038/ijo.2009.45.

Worldwatch Institute. *State of the World: Confronting Climate change*. London: Earthscan, 2009.

Chapter Six

The Protection of Vegans in Portugal

Law and Progress

Nuno Alvim

1. INTRODUCTION

Portugal is a small southwestern European country with a population of just over ten million people. In recent years, veganism has become an increasingly popular lifestyle, following a similar pattern to many other countries across Europe. According to the latest statistical study from 2017, there are at least 120,000 vegetarian individuals living in Portugal, of which at least 60,000 follow a vegan lifestyle.[1] By comparing this data with the previous study results from 2007,[2] which reported the existence of 30,000 vegetarians, it is estimated that the number of vegetarians has grown 400% in just a decade (2007-2017). There are no estimates for the growth of the vegan population over the period. However, we also know from the previous 2007 study that at least 5% of the population exclude meat, fish, eggs, or dairy from their daily diet and 2% never consume any kind of meat.

Other available data also points towards a fast growth in veganism in Portugal—especially the fact that the number of vegetarian or vegan shops and restaurants has increased about 513% in the last decade.[3]

Whilst the number of vegans living in Portugal has been increasing, there is little protection against discrimination afforded to them by the Portuguese government or equality bodies. Vegans in Portugal are subjected to multiple forms of discrimination. This goes largely unreported and takes place in a rather systematic way. Examples include explicit refusal to serve animal-derived food alternatives (i.e., vegan meals) and forceful imposition of a single dietary regime in public institutions, bullying and psychological abuse related to vegan beliefs, and exclusion and stigmatization at work and in schools, etc.[4]

Veganism, which can be defined as an ideological belief involving the practice of abstaining from the use of all commodities produced through the exploitation of other animals, is within the scope of the meaning of the right to freedom of belief under the European Convention of Human Rights[5] and is protected under British equality law.[6] However, it has been afforded little attention or effective protection by Portugal's government policies or its equality laws stemming from international treaties, despite the country having a very advanced legal framework and pioneering several socially progressive movements.

In 2017, the Portuguese government approved a bill[7] legislating for the provision of strict vegetarian (i.e., vegan) meals in all public facilities. This new law has been the object of international attention and acclaim and is the main topic of discussion in this chapter.

This chapter firstly introduces the Portuguese legal framework and explains how it relates to veganism. It also explains the role that equality bodies have played in protecting vegetarians or vegans from discrimination. Secondly, the aforementioned legislation on the provision of strict vegetarian food is assessed, and its strengths and shortcomings explained. Finally, there is a discussion about the possible solutions for overcoming the observed shortcomings of the law's implementation.

2. FRAMING VEGANISM IN PORTUGAL'S LEGAL FRAMEWORK

Portugal is renowned worldwide for its progressive stance on human rights and on several social issues (e.g., drug policy). It has ratified the International Covenant on Civil and Political Rights (ICCPR), the International Covenant on Economic, Social and Cultural Rights (ICESCR), the European Convention of Human Rights (ECHR) and the Charter of Fundamental Rights of the European Union (CFREU). These treaties contain important legal principles concerning the human right to freedom of thought, conscience and religion and require all signatories to prohibit unlawful interference with this primary human right and ensure that it is made available to all people equally. The right to freedom of conscience is stated under Article 18 of the ICCPR:

> 1. Everyone shall have the right to freedom of thought, conscience and religion. This right shall include freedom to have or to adopt a religion or belief of his choice, and freedom, either individually or in community with others and in public or private, to manifest his religion or belief in worship, observance, practice and teaching.

2. No one shall be subject to coercion which would impair his freedom to have or to adopt a religion or belief of his choice.
3. Freedom to manifest one's religion or beliefs may be subject only to such limitations as are prescribed by law and are necessary to protect public safety, order, health, or morals or the fundamental rights and freedoms of others.
4. The States Parties to the present Covenant undertake to have respect for the liberty of parents and, when applicable, legal guardians to ensure the religious and moral education of their children in conformity with their own convictions.

The Constitution of the Portuguese Republic[8] explains how these legal principles are incorporated into Portuguese law. The right to freedom of conscience is explained in Article 41. Given that veganism is the expression of an ideological belief grounded on ethical convictions against the exploitation of other animals, 41.1–3 (freedom of conscience, of religion and of form of worship) are relevant to the protection for vegans.

1. The freedom of conscience, of religion and of form of worship is inviolable.
2. No one may be persecuted, deprived of rights or exempted from civic obligations or duties because of his convictions or religious observance.
3. No authority may question anyone in relation to his convictions or religious observance, save in order to gather statistical data that cannot be individually identified, nor may anyone be prejudiced in any way for refusing to answer.
4. The right to be a conscientious objector, as laid down by law, is guaranteed.

The right of resistance, under Article 21, is also arguably relevant to the practice of veganism:

> Everyone has the right to resist any order that infringes their rights, freedoms or guarantees and, when it is not possible to resort to the public authorities, to use force to repel any aggression.

Additionally, Article 13 (principle of equality) is relevant when considering equal treatment for vegans:

1. All citizens possess the same social dignity and are equal before the law.

2. No one may be privileged, favored, prejudiced, deprived of any right or exempted from any duty for reasons of ancestry, sex, race, language, territory of origin, religion, political or ideological beliefs, education, economic situation, social circumstances or sexual orientation.

Portugal has reported to the United Nations that Portugal is 'a country strongly committed to ensuring the highest levels of the promotion and protection of all human rights, civil, cultural economic, political and social.'[9] Regarding the implementation of anti-discriminatory rules, Portugal also confirmed that its Constitution clearly confirms that there can be no form of discrimination on any ground, stating that:

> A structuring principle of the Portuguese legal system is the principle of equality enshrined in article 13 according to which "every citizen shall possess the same social dignity and shall be equal before the law" and "no one shall be privileged, favored, prejudiced, deprived of any right or exempted from any duty on the basis of ancestry, sex, race, language, place of origin, religion, political or ideological beliefs, education, economic situation, social circumstances or sexual orientation."[10]

However, while Portugal's report refers to rights and equality considerations for 'foreigners,' 'children,' the 'elderly,' 'women,' 'immigrants' and 'ethnic minorities,' and on issues of 'gender,' 'disability,' 'maternity' and 'paternity,' it does not specifically discuss measures taken to secure equality of practice for those with 'religious,' 'political' or secular 'ideological beliefs' and, therefore, does not reference specific issues such as the accommodation of the needs of vegans.

Portugal also claims to have fully transposed European Union Equality Directive of 2000/78/EC[11] to its national legislation, in the Work Code and Law 99/2003.[12] In this document, it is stated that no worker should suffer discrimination on the basis of political or ideological convictions.[13] Article 23 of this code sets out the meaning of discrimination applicable to matters of occupation and training:

a. direct discrimination shall be considered where, by reason of a factor of discrimination, a person is treated less favorably than that which is, has been or will be given to another person in a comparable situation;
b. indirect discrimination where an apparently neutral provision, criterion or practice is capable of placing a person, on grounds of a discrimination factor, in a position of disadvantage compared to others, unless that provision, criterion or practice is objectively justified for a legitimate purpose and the means to achieve it are appropriate and necessary . . .

However, there is no available information on the application of this Directive to the accommodation of the specific needs of those with secular, ideological beliefs, such as veganism.

Discrimination against vegan individuals, by either denying them the right to live according to their ethical convictions or neglecting to give due regard to accommodating their needs, clearly violates the primary human right to be free to live according to one's conscience. Moreover, such a violation is clear when the discrimination is routinely perpetuated, as observed in Portugal. Nevertheless, the needs of vegans in Portugal often go unnoticed, and Portugal's report to the UN makes no reference to their needs as a matter of the right to freedom of conscience. Hence, we may question whether these constitutional assurances, reflective of international directives, are effective in their aim to ensure the protection of fundamental rights and freedoms for individuals belonging to secular and cultural minorities, such as vegans.

Regarding the provision of food in public establishments, if a state does not consider its equality duty and provides only a conventional dietary option, which vegans reject on the grounds of conscience, it is arguably falling short of its international and domestic legal obligations. This situation raises questions about the 'structuring principle of the Portuguese legal system,' and, thus, about its expressed constitutional duty.

Despite widespread discrimination against vegans, their needs are not recognized and addressed by equality bodies, which seem to either ignore or underestimate the issue as one relevant to the development of equality measures. Furthermore, the Portuguese government has not allocated time to discuss discrimination against vegans, despite having recently approved a bill for the provision of vegan food, which raises and partially addresses the issue.

3. THE POSITION OF EQUALITY BODIES REGARDING VEGANISM

According to the European Network of Equality Bodies (EQUINET), the Portuguese national equality bodies that assure the enforcement of equality policies are The Commission for Equality at the Workplace, The Commission for Gender Equality and the High Commission for Migration.

Equality bodies across Europe exist to promote equality and tackle discrimination on grounds of gender, race, age, sexual orientation, religion and belief, disability, or other grounds. Their role is defined in accordance with EU equal treatment legislation, and they play a fundamental role in the nondiscrimination architecture of the European Union (EU).

Equality bodies oversee and monitor the implementation of national equality measures and are authoritative voices in matters of discrimination.[14]

From an overview of the work and investigations performed by these equality bodies, it appears that there is no information concerning the discrimination that vegans experience in their daily lives, in the workplace, at school, at university and within other public institutions. The only exception, as far as the Portuguese bodies are concerned, appears to relate to the High Commission for Migration, which has developed some documents to support social workers in their efforts to integrate immigrant families. This context predicts the existence of dietary needs on religious grounds, specifically mentioning vegetarianism as one of the considerations in the provision of food.

Despite the Portuguese legal system not explicitly recognizing veganism, the needs of vegans being largely ignored, and widespread discrimination against vegans, Portugal has, nevertheless, legislated that 'strict vegetarian' (i.e., 'vegan') food must be made available in public institutions. This achievement was not an outcome of government equality considerations but was largely the result of a powerful and popular public campaign that highlighted the power of the collective action of Portuguese citizens.

4. A PARADIGM SHIFT: LAW MANDATING THE PROVISION OF VEGAN FOOD

In February 2015, the Portuguese Vegetarian Association started a petition asking for an alternative meal to be provided in all public catering facilities. The petition was popular and collected over 15,000 signatures from Portuguese citizens. With the support of a limited number of Parliamentarians, in April 2017, Law No. 11/2017 was approved, establishing the mandatory provision of a 'strict vegetarian' (i.e., a vegan) option on the menus of all public canteens and refectories.[15] The law came into effect within six months of its approval to allow time for public authority catering establishments to prepare and adapt.[16]

Regarding the provision of vegan food, Article 3 law states that all public canteens must have at least one vegetarian option in their daily menus. It goes on to define a 'vegetarian option' as a meal that does not contain any animal products whatsoever, which in practice means that the meal should be strictly vegetarian, i.e., vegan:

1. The service of the canteens and public cafeterias referred to in the previous article includes, in all daily menus, at least one vegetarian option.

2. For the purposes of the preceding paragraph, 'vegetarian option' means that it is based on meals which do not contain any products of animal origin.

This law applies to the canteens of all public administration entities and services, namely:

- Health care units;
- Nursing homes;
- Primary and secondary schools;
- Universities;
- Prison facilities and guardianship facilities;
- Social services.

4.1. Analyzing the Law's Strengths

Law 11/2017 has been the subject of much international attention and acclaim, and in part, rightfully so; as a piece of legislation, it is unprecedented at a worldwide level, and it is an important breakthrough in terms of the protection of human rights, as it provides for a very specific population group—vegetarians or vegans—who have been (and still are) much neglected, as previously noted.

One of the critical strengths of this law is that it asserts that the alternative meal to be provided should be strictly vegetarian (Article 3.2), rather than merely ovo-lacto-vegetarian or any other variant. This is clearly a positive element of the law, as it aims to guarantee a more inclusive approach that takes into consideration the vegan demographic, as well as any other people who do not consume eggs or milk due to allergies or other health reasons. A strict vegetarian menu is the only effective way of providing an alternative that is inclusive and more accessible to a wide range of individuals.

But perhaps the most fundamental reason that this bill is important is that it provides vegan citizens with a legal instrument which they can use to protect themselves from discrimination: in this case, the refusal by a public institution to provide a vegan meal in their respective canteen.

Of significance is that Article 5 states that the fulfillment of the law should be guaranteed by the National Authority on Food and Economical Safety (ASAE), which has the responsibility to inspect public canteen facilities and enforce the application of the law. Therefore, any citizen may present a formal complaint to this authority and denounce a violation of the law, which the ASAE is obliged to investigate. This is a highly significant measure because, prior to this law, there were no legal arguments that could be used in favor of a citizen claiming the right to an alternative to the conventionally imposed meal containing meat, eggs and dairy.

4.2. Analyzing the Law's Shortcomings

Whilst this legislation has been groundbreaking in its support of vegans and a transition to widespread plant-based eating, several limitations and shortcomings have come to light following its implementation.

Article 3.3 states that public institutions may be exempted from offering a strict vegetarian option on their menus if there is no demand for it. This applies to health care units as well as primary and secondary school institutions. This provision is justified under a food waste prevention policy, and at first glance, appears reasonable and sensible. However, this provision could be used by institutions that will never provide vegan meals because they have not properly surveyed the needs of their users, be they students or patients. Further, if an alternative meal is not promoted, the consumer may not know that alternative food is available.

In Portugal, many people who choose to have a vegetarian or vegan meal are not necessary vegetarians or vegan themselves and are likely to have made their choice out of curiosity or because they regard the alternative food offered as a healthier choice. Exempting a school or hospital from providing vegan food in the absence of any apparent demand may contribute to depriving vegan and vegetarian users of that choice and could also lead to situations of enduring discrimination.

Article 3.4 of Law 11/2017 may also be perceived as a significant limitation and has in fact been proved to produce several constraints in the implementation of the law. Article 3.4 states that '[i]n case of reduced demand for the vegetarian option, canteen management entities may establish a system for the prior registration of vegetarian option consumers.' Since the law does not clarify what 'reduced demand' means, that is, it does not provide a numerical and objective measure of 'reduced,' both public institutions and the enforcement authorities are left to speculate on what it actually means and can apply discretionary criteria in assessing demand and act accordingly. In practice, it has been reported that some public institutions, particularly schools, have interpreted the law as allowing them to adopt a long-term prior subscription scheme. These schemes force students to opt between a conventional dietary regime and a vegan regime at the beginning of the school year which they then have to maintain throughout the whole academic year. This also means that children who transition to veganism part way through a school year do not have the option to eat an alternative vegan meal at school until the following year.

4.3. Analyzing the Law's Implementation

As previously mentioned, the law came into effect in June 2017, with a period of six months for adaptation, during which all public facilities' canteens were required to prepare to provide strict vegetarian meals. Since then, the Portuguese Vegetarian Association has been committed to supporting and assisting public institutions by providing training and consultancy services to canteen staff to help ensure timely compliance.

While not providing an exact measure of the implementation of this law, there is some available data from 2018 which may suggest the extent to which vegan meals are being served.[17] According to an article by the newspaper *Público*:[18]

- A total of 10% of the meals served in universities are vegetarian. All public universities adhered to the law. Some don't yet serve strictly vegan meals.
- A total of 1% of the 270,000 meals served in schools are vegetarian. That is three vegetarian meals per school;
- Around 14% of the meals served in public hospitals and health care units are vegetarian;
- Around 10% of the 600,000 meals served in social services facilities are vegetarian.

As can be seen, the percentage of vegan meals served in public facilities in Portugal varies considerably across different types of institution. While the option is more popular in public hospitals or health care units, it is much less commonly served in schools, which could suggest resistance to implementation of the law in this type of public facility.

The Portuguese Vegetarian Association produced a report in June 2018, one year after the law came into effect, to publicise some of the main challenges and difficulties that have come to light since its implementation. The report was based on evidence collected through a survey, which collected 97 answers from students, parents, patients, and other citizens.[19] Among others, the main challenges identified were:

- By choosing the vegan option at the beginning of a school year, where there is a subscription system in place, many students report that they become bound to follow it throughout the year, and do not have the option to change their initial choice until the next academic year.
- It is common for parents to report that schools' officials indicate that they must present a medical report that justifies the adoption of a vegetarian regime, although the law does not require this.
- Frequently, the meal that is provided is not strictly vegetarian, but rather ovo-lacto-vegetarian, which is an infringement of the law.
- Very often the vegetarian meal is not properly balanced, demonstrating a lack of proper training for preparing these meals.

- Some institutions deny the provision and justify it by stating that the demand is very low, which is clearly an infringement of the law.
- Several institutions deny the provision due to the alleged existence of a sub-contract with a meal provision company that is not qualified to prepare vegan meals. This may not be fully in contradiction with the law.

4.4. Discussion of Possible Solutions

Overall, the implementation of Law 11/2017 has suffered from some deficiencies and has met with some resistance. Partially, the difficulties in fully implementing the law are caused by its own limitations: namely, the fact that it is somewhat ambiguous in defining what reduced demand means, and when 'reduced demand' justifies an exemption from providing a vegan meal or the implementation of a long-term subscription system. Several institutions, schools in particular, have shown signs of high resistance to this new legislation.

Possible modifications to the law concerning the ambiguity of Articles 3.3 and 3.4, and the lack of an objective definition of reduced demand, have been recommended by the Portuguese Vegetarian Association to several political parties. However, it is generally felt that more time is required to properly assess a full-scale implementation of the new law. Some have even voiced concerns that an open call for early modifications may lead to a detrimental setback, as the law would have to be discussed and voted on once again by all parliamentary parties across the political spectrum.

One of the main issues identified has been subjective interpretation by some schools leading to the potential unlawful implementation of a subscription system. Very often, students feel that they have no choice but to follow a conventional dietary regime during the whole school year because the alternative would be being served vegan meals throughout the year, every day, which may not be easily adopted by everyone interested in adopting a vegan way of life. This practice discourages students from having a strict vegetarian meal, which they could otherwise choose occasionally. This could be possibly resolved by more frequent subscription enquiries, such as daily or weekly subscription options that give the students the option of choosing a vegetarian meal just for days or weeks, rather than a year in advance.

Furthermore, preparing a slightly larger quantity of the vegan meal, in relation to the logistics calculation, and having the meal openly available to any interested student would also encourage them to choose an alternative meal which otherwise they might not be actively looking for.

As previously noted, there are other serious issues reported by surveyed participants, such as clear infringements of the law, for which there are no penalties. The only remedy available is communicating the breach of regulations to the enforcement authority and demanding that the situation is investigated and corrected. This limitation does little to ensure effective equality for vegans.

It has also been noted that there is widespread ignorance of the law. Many users of public institutions, along with their staff, are not aware that such a law exists, or of the full extent of its application and scope, making it increasingly important for the government and non-government organizations to cooperate in bringing that information to the attention of Portuguese citizens.

5. CONCLUSION

The moral commitment of vegans to live without exploiting other animals is protected in the European system of human rights, under the Human Rights Act in the United Kingdom, and under equality legislation in Great Britain. This protection clearly relates to international legal principles regarding the right to be free to live according to sincerely held moral values, but such protection does not explicitly feature in Portuguese rights and equality legislation, nor is it considered in the published literature of the relevant Portuguese equality body. Nevertheless, largely through the power of petitioning, Portugal has legislated that strict vegetarian food must be made available in all public institutions. However, this legislation is not well-known in Portugal, is partially open to subjective interpretation and has not fully eliminated situations of discrimination towards consumers. Furthermore, there are no penalties for non-compliance—at least none that have been made known.[20]

In the absence of state promotion and proper enforcement of the law, and given the lack of penalties for non-compliance, it is the Portuguese Vegetarian Association (along with other non-governmental organizations and advocates) that works to raise awareness of the legislation, provides training services in order to qualify caterers to adequately prepare strict vegetarian meals, and provides Portuguese citizens with the information and necessary tools to make use of this law, thus improving its application and ensuring the effective protection of vegan rights.

Of course, the implementation of rights and equality measures should be the business of state authorities, but despite clear infringements of relevant legal principles and provisions, the needs of vegans go largely unnoticed and are not cited in current rights and equality policies. Although the eyes of the world have been on the successful development of legislation for strict vegetarian food in public canteens, it is a measure that addresses the issue of food inequality only and that receives little government attention. It is, for the most part, left to invested non-government organizations and other individuals to ensure it is implemented in practice. Clearly, much more must be achieved for the growing Portuguese vegan community to benefit from the international right to freedom of conscience and the prohibition of discrimination.

6. NOTES

1. Centro Vegetariano, "Nielsen Study for the Vegetarian Center," accessed March 13, 2021, https://www.centrovegetariano.org/Article-620-Numero-vegetarianos-quadruplica-10-anos-Portugal.html.

2. Centro Vegetariano, "Study by AC Nielsen, for the Vegetarian Center," accessed March 13, 2021, https://www.centrovegetariano.org/Article451Portugal:%2030%20000%20Vegetarianos-Portugal%253A%2B30%2B000%2BVegetarianos.html.

3. Associação Vegetariana Portuguesa, "Vegetarian Food Market in Portugal Increased By 514% in the Last Ten Years," 2018, accessed March 13, 2021, https://www.avp.org.pt/mercado-de-alimentacao-vegetariana-em-portugal-aumentou-514-nos-ultimos-dez-anos/.

4. For more information about discrimination of vegans in Portugal, see Elisa Nair, "State Discrimination Against Vegans in Portugal," International (Vegan) Rights Network conference presentation, posted by The Vegan Society 2021, accessed March 13, 2021, https://www.vegansociety.com/elisa-nair-ferreira.

5. Article 9 the right to freedom of thought, conscience, and religion. See H v United Kingdom (1993) 16 EHRR.

6. Mr J Casamitjana Costa v The League Against Cruel Sports: 3331129/2018—Preliminary ((UK Employment Tribunal: For further details see Jeanette Rowley and Edie Bowles, and Matthew Overton in this volume).

7. Diário da República, Law no. 11/2017, https://dre.pt/web/guest/pesquisa/-/search/106886578/details/normal?l=1.

8. Parlamento, "Constitution of The Portuguese Republic Seventh Revision [2005]," https://www.parlamento.pt/sites/EN/Parliament/Documents/Constitution7th.pdf.

9. United Nations, "Committee on Economic, Social and Cultural Rights Concludes Consideration of Report of Portugal," 12 November, 2014, accessed March 13, 2021, https://www.ohchr.org/EN/NewsEvents/Pages/DisplayNews.aspx?NewsID=15283&LangID=E.

10. United Nations, "Fourth Periodic Reports Submitted by States Parties Under Articles 16 and 17 of the Covenant: Portugal," 28 January 2011, accessed March 13, 2021, https://docstore.ohchr.org/SelfServices/FilesHandler.ashx?enc=4slQ6QSmlBEDzFEovLCuW0NfjzXH%2bfptLhwAM98g4AmcIRHSoAuozIABX4oveSYiJ2U5qgTvMfnzJLzXgtn1cwIq1DFeM7PcifaYcBGonz7WgwpdKxvvudIboyRXiclT.

11. Information and link to the Directive: European Commission, "Employment, Social Affairs & Inclusion," accessed March 13, 2021, https://ec.europa.eu/social/main.jsp?catId=166&langId=en.

12. Assembleia Da República, Law 99/2003, accessed March 13, 2021, https://dre.pt/application/dir/pdf1sdip/2003/08/197A00/55585656.pdf (Revised: Law 7/2009).

13. Assembleia Da República, Law No. 7/2009, http://www.pgdlisboa.pt/leis/lei_mostra_articulado.php?nid=1047&tabela=leis&ficha=1&pagina=1&so_miolo=S.

14. EQUINTET, "Equality Bodies," accessed March 13, 2021, https://equineteurope.org/what-are-equality-bodies/.

15. Diário da República, Law no. 11/2017: https://dre.pt/web/guest/pesquisa/-/search/106886578/details/normal?l=1.

16. See Nuno Alvim, "Law and Mandatory Access to Vegan Food in Portugal," International (Vegan) Rights Network conference presentation, posted by The Vegan Society 2021, accessed March 13, 2021, https://www.vegansociety.com/nuno-alvim.

17. At the time of preparing this draft for publication in 2020/2021, this data appears to remain unchanged.

18. Margarida David Cardoso, "Almost 10% of Meals Served at Universities Are Vegetarian," *Público* February 13, 2018, accessed March 13, 2021, https://www.publico.pt/2018/02/13/sociedade/noticia/quase-10-das-refeicoes-servidas-nas-universidades-sao-vegetarianas-1802926.

19. Associação Vegetariana Portuguesa, "Vegetarian Option in Portuguese Canteens: Reality or Intention? An Evaluation Study of Law No. 11/2017," 2018, accessed March 13, 2021, https://www.avp.org.pt/opcao-vegetariana-estudo-avaliacao/.

20. No data on this matter was available at the time of preparing this final draft chapter for publication in March 2021.

7. REFERENCES

Alvim Nuno. "Law and Mandatory Access to Vegan Food in Portugal." International (Vegan) Rights Network conference presentation. Posted by "The Vegan Society" 2021 Accessed March 13, 2021. https://www.vegansociety.com/nuno-alvim.

Assembleia Da República. Law No. 7/2009. http://www.pgdlisboa.pt/leis/lei_mostra_articulado.php?nid=1047&tabela=leis&ficha=1&pagina=1&so_miolo=S.

Assembleia Da República. Law 99/2003. https://dre.pt/application/dir/pdf1sdip/2003/08/197A00/55585656.pdf (Revised: Law 7/2009).

Associação Vegetariana Portuguesa. "Vegetarian Food Market in Portugal Increased by 514% in the Last Ten Years." 2018. Accessed March 13, 2021. https://www.avp.org.pt/mercado-de-alimentacao-vegetariana-em-portugal-aumentou-514-nos-ultimos-dez-anos/.

Associação Vegetariana Portuguesa. "Vegetarian Option in Portuguese Canteens: Reality or Intention? An Evaluation Study of Law No. 11/2017." 2018. Accessed March 13, 2021. https://www.avp.org.pt/opcao-vegetariana-estudo-avaliacao/.

Cardoso, Margarida David. "Almost 10% of Meals Served at Universities Are Vegetarian." *Público.* February 13, 2018. Accessed March 13, 2021. https://www.publico.pt/2018/02/13/sociedade/noticia/quase-10-das-refeicoes-servidas-nas-universidades-sao-vegetarianas-1802926.

Centro Vegetariano. "Nielsen Study for the Vegetarian Center." Accessed March 13, 2021. https://www.centrovegetariano.org/Article-620-Numero-vegetarianos-quadruplica-10-anos-Portugal.html.

Centro Vegetariano. "Study by AC Nielsen, for the Vegetarian Center." Accessed March 13, 2021. https://www.centrovegetariano.org/Article451Portugal:%2030%20000%20Vegetarianos-Portugal%253A%2B30%2B000%2BVegetarianos.html.

Constitution of The Portuguese Republic Seventh Revision [2005]. https://www.parlamento.pt/sites/EN/Parliament/Documents/Constitution7th.pdf.

Diário da República. Law no. 11/2017: https://dre.pt/web/guest/pesquisa/-/search/106886578/details/normal?l=1.

EQUINTET. "Equality Bodies." Accessed March 13, 2021. https://equineteurope.org/what-are-equality-bodies/.

European Commission. "Employment, Social Affairs & Inclusion." Accessed March 13, 2021. https://ec.europa.eu/social/main.jsp?catId=166&langId=en.

H v United Kingdom (1993) 16 EHRR.

Mr J Casamitjana Costa v The League Against Cruel Sports: 3331129/2018—Preliminary (UK Employment Tribunal).

Nair, Elisa. "State Discrimination Against Vegans in Portugal." International (Vegan) Rights Network conference presentation. Posted by The Vegan Society 2021. Accessed March 13, 2021. https://www.vegansociety.com/elisa-nair-ferreira.

Parlamento. "Constitution of The Portuguese Republic Seventh Revision [2005]," https://www.parlamento.pt/sites/EN/Parliament/Documents/Constitution7th.pdf.

United Nations. "Committee on Economic, Social and Cultural Rights Concludes Consideration of Report of Portugal." November 12, 2014. Accessed March 13, 2021. https://www.ohchr.org/EN/NewsEvents/Pages/DisplayNews.aspx?NewsID=15283&LangID=E.

United Nations. "Fourth Periodic Reports Submitted by States Parties Under Articles 16 and 17 of the Covenant: Portugal." 28 January, 2011. Accessed March 13, 2021. https://docstore.ohchr.org/SelfServices/FilesHandler.ashx?enc=4slQ6QSmlBEDzFEovLCuW0NfjzXH%2bfptLhwAM98g4AmcIRHSoAuozI-ABX4oveSYiJ2U5qgTvMfnzJLzXgtn1cwIq1DFeM7PcifaYcBGonz7WgwpdKxvvudIboyRXiclT.

Chapter Seven

Animal Agriculture, the Right to Food and Vegan Dietary Solutions

Joe Wills

1. INTRODUCTION

There is wide acceptance amongst environmental and food security experts that present patterns of animal product consumption in Western countries are unsustainable and are undermining global food security. The system of industrialized animal agriculture, which enables the mass consumption of animal products, is both grossly inefficient in its use of natural resources and hugely detrimental to the environment we rely on to harvest sufficient qualities and quantities of food.[1] Yet far from taking steps to address this mounting food security crisis, most Western states are adding fuel to the fire by adopting laws and policies designed to prop up industrialized animal agriculture at the expense of alternative plant-based food systems.[2]

This chapter will argue that the policies and laws of Western states[3] are undermining the enjoyment of the internationally-protected human right to food for both present and future generations. The right to food is by no means the only internationally recognised human right that industrial animal agriculture undermines,[4] but for reasons of space, this right will be the focus of the chapter. Part 2 details the myriad ways in which Western states provide material, legal and ideological support to industrial animal agribusiness industries. Part 3 discusses how the animal agribusiness industries undermine people's enjoyment of the right to food. Part 4 discusses how present state policies are at odds with such duties in relation to the right to food. The chapter concludes with proposals for alternative policies of re-directing subsidies to plant-based foods to ensure progressive realization of the right to food.

2. WESTERN STATES: THE SHIELD AND SWORD OF THE ANIMAL AGRIBUSINESS INDUSTRIES

It might be thought that animal product consumption does not raise any human rights concerns. After all, human rights impose legal duties on the state. As the animal agribusiness industry is made up of private companies and the consumers of their products are non-state subjects, so the thought goes, human rights are simply not engaged. Such a view is mistaken for two reasons. For a start, it is well-established in human rights law that states are not merely under a negative obligation to abstain from directly violating the rights of individuals under their jurisdictions; they also have positive duties to, amongst other things, protect individuals from the actions of private actors who undermine the enjoyment of their rights.[5]

Moreover, to view the animal agribusiness industries as constituting a private sphere entirely independent from the state is to fall for 'the myth of the free market.' According to this mythology, market economies in modern capitalist societies are defined by an absence of government intervention. In reality, most developed capitalist economies are characterized by their use of industry bailouts, subsidization programs and industry-specific protective legislation.[6] Nowhere is this observation truer than in relation to Western animal agribusiness industries (AAI), who are not merely the recipients of huge sums of public money, but also the beneficiaries of a raft of other policies and laws that maintain their privileged position in society. This section will provide a few examples of the royal treatment AAI receive.

2.1. State Subsidies

Perhaps the most blatant form of state support for AAI is in the form of vast public subsidies. It is estimated that Organization for Economic Cooperation and Development members pay up to $52 billion to subsidize animal products, including support for animal feed, animal housing and transport infrastructure.[7] In the United States, the biggest food industry recipients of state largesse are the meat and dairy sectors, receiving $38.4 billion annually, nearly two thirds of all agricultural subsidies. Fruits and vegetables, by contrast, are categorized as 'specialty crops' ineligible for direct subsidies.[8] In Europe, Greenpeace estimate that the European Union (EU) spends between $28.5 billion and $32.6 billion on payments to the livestock industry, comprising between 18% and 20% of its total annual budget.[9]

2.2. Marketing Campaigns

Over the past four decades, AAI 'have had to respond to an avalanche of public concerns about health, environmental and ethical problems with their products.'[10] In response, they have launched a counter-offensive via marketing campaigns, often with the support of public authorities. In the United States, this is done through 'commodity checkoff programs.' These are programs subsidized through the United States Department of Agriculture (USDA) that collect funds from producers of an agricultural commodity for promoting that commodity. The USDA oversees checkoff programs that spend $557 million per year on promoting animal product consumption. As Simon notes, checkoff programs are 'remarkably effective,' boosting sales by $38 for every checkoff dollar spent.[11] A similar policy exists in Australia.[12] In the EU, state involvement in marketing campaigns is even more direct. A report by the Dutch Animal Welfare Organization Wakker Dier found that the EU has directly subsidized meat advertising in Europe to the tune of at least €60 million since 2017.[13]

2.3. 'Ag-gag Laws'

Just as governments have assisted animal agribusiness in presenting their industry and products in a positive light, so too have they attempted to suppress alternative narratives. The most infamous mechanism through which they have done this is so-called 'ag-gag laws.' The term 'ag-gag' refers to laws designed to limit public access to information about practices in animal agriculture. These laws impose criminal and civil penalties for groups and individuals who gather evidence without an owner-operator's consent, gain employment under false pretenses or fail to disclose the evidence within a narrow timeframe.[14] Such laws inevitably create a 'chilling effect' for reporting and investigation,[15] making it more 'difficult to expose any kind of wrongdoing, including animal cruelty, environmental violations, labor violations, safety violations, or other illegal activity.'[16]

Although the United States is most well-known for its state-level anti-whistleblower legislation, similar laws have recently been proposed in Australia[17] and introduced in Canada.[18] Whilst 'ag-gag' laws have not made their way to Europe, prosecution authorities in some instances use similar 'anti-trespass' logics to shield animal agribusiness from investigation. For example, in England and Wales, the Department for the Environment, Food and Rural Affairs (DEFRA) has declined to pursue prosecutions for breaches in animal welfare law where evidence of this is obtained through trespass,[19] despite there being no general evidentiary rule prohibiting the admissibility of such evidence in court.[20]

2.4. Exemptions from Environmental and Animal Welfare Law

Another means by which Western states uphold the interests of AAI is through exempting them from standard forms of criminal and civil liability.

The most infamous example of this is encapsulated in 'right to farm' legislation developed in the USA,[21] Canada,[22] and Australia.[23] Though they differ in terms of scope and applicability, the goals of these laws, broadly stated, involve shielding farmers from private nuisance suits, effectively granting them 'de facto immunity' from liability.[24]

AAI are also largely exempt from animal cruelty liability. In the United States, the farmed-animal industry 'has persuaded the majority of state legislatures to actually amend their criminal anticruelty statutes to simply exempt all "accepted," "common," "customary," or "normal" farming practices.'[25] Furthermore, the recently passed Federal Preventing Animal Cruelty and Torture Act forbids acts that cause serious bodily injury to animals but exempts 'customary and normal' practices of agricultural husbandry as well as 'the slaughter of animals for food.'[26] Similar exemptions exist in most states and territories in Australia[27] and provinces in Canada.[28]

In European states, the *de facto* exemption of animal agribusiness from most forms of animal welfare liability takes less explicit forms. In England and Wales for example, courts have historically been loath to find conventional farm practices to breach animal welfare standards, regardless of how much suffering they cause animals. For example, in *Roberts v. Ruggiero*, Stocker J insisted that criminal prosecution is not the appropriate method by which 'the legality of the system of husbandry should be established.'[29] In determining whether suffering inflicted on farm animals is 'unnecessary' and hence unlawful, the courts consider whether the conduct which caused the suffering was in compliance with relevant codes of conduct and regulations governing their treatment. Such codes and regulations invariably sanction the various horrors of industrial agriculture, leaving them outside the scope of liability.[30]

2.5. Repressive State Responses to Opponents of Animal Farming

Whilst AAI are largely immune from criminal and civil liability, their opponents are often the victims of draconian laws and state harassment. In the United States, the Federal Bureau of Investigation has classified the animal rights movement as '[o]ne of today's most serious domestic terrorism threats,' despite its admission that animal rights activists had not taken a single life.[31] Such 'green scare' sentiments, combined with industry lobbying, culminated in the federal Animal Enterprise Terrorism Act, which reclassified non-violent property offences targeting animal exploitation industries as forms of 'terrorism' incurring higher penalties than other property offences.[32] In response to animal rights activism in Australia and Canada, new laws creating harsher penalties for non-violent protest and civil disobedience against animal farming have been introduced.[33]

In Britain, animal rights groups have been subject to 'sustained and intense undercover infiltration' by state agents.[34] In 1986, Special Branch set up the Animal Rights National Index and by 1998 it was running over 100 informers on an annual budget of £140,000.[35] Undercover police officers who infiltrated animal rights and environmental groups went as far as engaging in deceptive romantic relationships with women involved in the groups, before abruptly disappearing into thin air. Such techniques have been described by one victim of this deception as 'abusive, cold-hearted, psychological torture.'[36]

This section has highlighted a few of the ways Western states prop up AAI. The next will demonstrate some of the ways in which animal agriculture is undermining enjoyment of the right to food.

3. ANIMAL AGRIBUSINESS AND THE RIGHT TO FOOD

3.1. The Right to Food under International Law

The right to adequate food is set out in Article 25 of the Universal Declaration of Human Rights in the context of the right to an adequate standard of living.[37] This formulation is repeated in the International Covenant on Economic, Social and Cultural Rights (ICESCR),[38] which also recognises the 'fundamental right of everyone to be free from hunger.'[39] The right to food is also contained in international human rights treaties aimed at protecting specific groups, including the Convention on the Elimination of All Forms of Discrimination against Women,[40] the Convention on the Rights of the Child[41] and the Convention on the Rights of Persons with Disabilities.[42]

These treaties have been ratified by all the Western states discussed in the previous section except the United States. Indeed, the United States has repeatedly emphasized that it regards the right to food as 'a goal or aspiration to be realized progressively that does not give rise to any international obligation.'[43]

However, a number of international law scholars have argued that the right to food is now part of customary international law and maybe even a *jus cogens* (i.e. non-derogable by agreement), based upon the multiple international documents that explicitly and implicitly grant the right to food and accepting this right as a norm of international law.[44] This means that all states have duties in relation to the right to food regardless of whether they have ratified any particular treaty or even whether they recognise the right. Consequently, the United States' near-unilateral rejection of the right to food does not mean that it does not have any international obligations in relation to it.

3.2. The Normative Content of the Right to Food

Though there are numerous sources for the right to food under international law, the United Nations Committee for Economic, Social and Cultural Rights (UNCESCR) General Comment 12 (hereafter GC12) on the right to adequate food under article 11 of the ICESCR is regarded as 'the most authoritative interpretation of the right to food within the UN human rights system and reflects the present state of international law.'[45] Accordingly, this section will rely on GC12's analysis of the normative content of the right to food and will illustrate how people's enjoyment of the right is being undermined by industrial animal product consumption.

GC12 states that the normative content of the right to adequate food has four components: adequacy, sustainability, availability, accessibility. Each of these will now be considered in turn.

3.2.1. *Adequacy*

For food to be adequate, it must be 'sufficient to satisfy the dietary needs of individuals, free from adverse substances and acceptable within a given culture.'[46] According to GC12, the notion of dietary needs 'implies that the diet as a whole contains a mix of nutrients for physical and mental growth, development and maintenance, and physical activity that are in compliance with human physiological needs at all stages throughout the life cycle.'[47]

Whilst animal products can form part of a balanced diet, the current quantities consumed in Western countries are contributing to negative net health impacts and chronic diseases 'including obesity, type 2 diabetes, cardiovascular diseases and cancer.'[48] As Simon notes, artificially low prices of animal foods and government-led marketing programs encourage citizens in high-income countries to consume animal products 'at levels much higher than normal market forces would dictate.'[49] Consequently, state support for the animal agribusiness industries is contributing to excesses of animal proteins, fats and cholesterol in the standard Western diet, promoting chronic degenerative diseases detrimental to human health and well-being.[50] By contrast, well-planned plant-based diets have not only been shown to be healthful and nutritionally adequate for all stages of the life cycle, but also likely to reduce the risk of such diseases.[51]

To be adequate, food must also be free from adverse substances, including those that originate through contamination or adulteration in the food chain, but also naturally occurring toxins.[52] Present intensive animal agribusiness operations contribute to contamination of both food and water.[53] In relation to food, animal products are the sources and carriers of a wide variety of deadly viruses, including campylobacter, nipah virus and hepatitis E.[54] The dramatic rise in meat consumption increases the likelihood of exposure to dangerous foodborne pathogens, and risks of E.coli and salmonella infection are often greater in intensive production systems.[55] These viruses do not only affect animal products. For example, leafy green vegetables can be infected by airborne transmission of E.coli from cattle feedlots.[56] In addition, the production of animal food products is the greatest agricultural cause of water pollution.[57] In addition, the pollution is caused by animal wastes, wastes from livestock processing and feed and fodder production.[58] A review by Heredia and Garcia concludes that food-producing animals are the major reservoirs for many foodborne pathogens and that this 'will continue causing outbreaks and deaths throughout the world, because no effective interventions have eliminated them from animals and food.'[59]

Finally, cultural acceptability involves taking account of perceived values and informed consumer concerns attached to food.[60] It must be noted that whilst most people in most cultures accept some forms of animal product consumption, there are some groups who don't. Most obviously here are vegetarians and vegans. Indeed, the former European Commission of Human Rights recognised that veganism is capable of concerning 'conscience' or 'belief' within the meaning of Article 9 of the European Convention on Human Rights and is accordingly protected.[61] Moreover, there are also many followers of religious faiths for whom the consumption of all or certain animals is prohibited, or certain methods of rearing and slaughtering animals are prohibited. The right to have access to a vegetarian diet for Buddhists has been recognized by the European Court of Human Rights.[62] State support for animal products does therefore potentially, although not inevitably, raise issues concerning cultural acceptability and indirect discrimination in a way that subsidization of plant-based products would not.

GC12 states that 'The precise meaning of "adequacy" is to a large extent determined by prevailing social, economic, cultural, climatic, ecological and other conditions.'[63] The ecological and climatic effects of animal agriculture will now be considered in relation to sustainability.

3.2.2. Sustainability

GC 12 states that 'the notion of sustainability is intrinsically linked to the notion of adequate food or food security, implying food being accessible for both present and future generations.'[64] There is now abundant evidence that AAI are the most resource-intensive and environmentally-destructive food sector. A recently published meta-analysis of 38,000 farms producing forty different agricultural goods around the world by Oxford researchers Poore and Nemecek showed that meat, farmed fish, eggs and dairy use 83% of the world's farmland and contribute 56 to 58% of food's different emissions.[65] The livestock sector is responsible for 18% of total greenhouse gas emissions in C02 equivalent—more than the entire transport sector and second only to the burning of fossil fuels. It also emits 35-40% of anthropogenic methane and 65% of anthropogenic nitrous oxide, which have 23 and 296 times the global warming potential of CO_2 respectively.[66]

Animal agribusiness is 'by far the single largest anthropogenic user of land,'[67] and is also responsible for 20% of the world's pastures and rangelands being degraded due to overgrazing, compaction and erosion.[68] Animal agriculture is not only inefficient in its use of land, but also in its production of calories. When cereals are fed to farm animals rather than directly to humans, a significant amount of energy and resources are lost in converting grain calories to 'meat' calories. Farm animals need to consume on average 7 kcal of cereal grain feed for every kcal generated in meat, ranging from 16 kcal for beef to 3 kcal for broiler chickens. This loss in calories is known as the 'diet gap.' The United States, China, Western Europe, and Brazil account for 26, 17, 11, and 6% of the global diet gap, respectively.[69] With meat consumption predicted to rise by 15kg per person a year by 2050, cereals will increasingly get diverted away from the mouths of humans.[70]

A similar story is true of water consumption. Per ton of product, animal products—especially beef cattle—generally have a larger water footprint than plant products. The average water footprint per calorie for beef is twenty times larger than for cereals and starchy roots. The water footprint per gram of protein for milk, eggs and chicken meat is about 1.5 times larger than for pulses and for beef, it is 6 times larger.[71]

Lastly, a further word needs to be said about zoonotic diseases as well as the concomitant problem of antibiotic resistance—two significant and growing risks associated with AAI that threaten its sustainability as a means of supplying food. According to the Centers for Disease Control and Prevention, '3 out of every 4 new or emerging infectious diseases in people come from animals.'[72] Many of the deadliest zoonotic diseases, including BSE, HIV, tuberculous, SARS, Ebola and all strains of swine and avian flu are believed to have their origins in animal consumption practices and industries.

As this chapter goes to press (December 2020) the world is in the grip of the SARS-CoV-2 pandemic, which has already killed almost 1 and half million people globally and has wreaked havoc on national economies. A live animal 'wet market' in China is cited as relevant to the investigation into the outbreak.[73] However, as many commentators have pointed out, the same type of conditions that make this type of market an ideal breeding ground for the spread of novel viruses—animals confined in extremely cramped conditions in close proximity to humans, large amounts of blood, excrement and other bodily fluids etc.—are also present in Western 'factory farms' and industrial slaughterhouses. Indeed, it is beyond doubt that intensification of animal farming is associated with increased risk of zoonotic disease emergence.[74]

A related—and potentially even more catastrophic—threat posed by AAI is antibiotic resistance. Because animals confined in intensive systems are reared in cramped conditions, farmers attempt to avoid them getting sick by routinely administering antibiotics.[75] As a result, the majority of the world's antibiotics are now consumed by farm animals, with 80% of antibiotic consumption in the US attributable to animal agriculture.[76] There is growing evidence that this widespread nontherapeutic use of antibiotics in livestock is promoting antibiotic resistance in humans. This threat, if left unchecked, could mean public health becoming 'catastrophically affected,'[77] leading to a return to 'the pre-antibiotics era, in which people died in droves from infections that have been effectively treated since the discovery of penicillin.'[78]

Given the extreme threats to ecosystem survival, access to food and water, and public health outlined in this section, it is beyond doubt that present trends in animal product consumption are entirely unsustainable from a food security perspective.

3.2.3. *Availability*

Availability refers to the possibilities either for feeding oneself directly from productive land or other natural resources, or for well-functioning distribution, processing and market systems that can move food from the site of production to where it is needed in accordance with demand.[79] Industrial animal agribusiness undermines access to available food in both the short and long-term through its contribution to global warming. As just noted above, AAI is one of the main contributors to greenhouse gases. Global warming in turn increases the occurrence and intensity of extreme weather events such as heatwaves, droughts, hurricanes, tsunamis and flooding.[80] Due to the geographical distribution of climate change impacts, these extreme weather events hit the poorest and most food-insecure populations the hardest, further undermining the availability of food for them.[81]

3.2.4. *Accessibility*

For food to be accessible, it must be affordable,[82] yet increased demand for animal products is driving up the cost of food worldwide. The principal reason for this relates to the need to produce more crops every year to feed farm animals. This in turn leads to an increase in demand for crops and consequently increases prices. As Professor Stefan Dercon, the former chief economist at the United Kingdom (UK) Department of International Development points out, 'We know in the context of rising food prices in recent years, that the livestock demand clearly is a factor in getting prices very high.'[83] This can place basic food stuffs beyond the affordability of the poorest. As De Schutter notes, 'Demand for meat diverts food away from poor people who are unable to afford anything but cereals.'[84]

4. STATE DUTIES CONCERNING THE RIGHT TO FOOD

Thus far, this chapter has demonstrated that industrial animal agriculture is being assisted by Western states and that animal agriculture is undermining enjoyment of the right to adequate food for both present and future generations. This final section will show that present state policies are contrary to their obligations to progressively realize the right to food under the ICESCR.

4.1. General Obligations under the ICESCR

Under article 2(1) of the ICESCR, a state party is required to

> take steps, individually and through international assistance and co-operation, especially economic and technical, to the maximum of its available resources, with a view to achieving progressively the full realization of the rights recognized in the present Covenant by all appropriate means, including particularly the adoption of legislative measures.

For the purpose of this section I will focus on three dimensions of this complex obligation: progressive realization, maximum available resources and the international (or 'extraterritorial') dimensions of the obligation.

4.2. Progressive Realization

The requirement of 'progressive realization' imposes an obligation on States Parties 'to move as expeditiously and effectively' towards ensuring the fulfilment of the right to food. An implicit corollary entailed by this requirement is a *prima facie* duty to avoid enacting deliberately 'retrogressive measures' that reduce the level of protection already achieved.[85]

As Part 3 argued, mass consumption of animal products in Western societies is undermining food security for present and future generations, especially in poorer countries in the Global South. The state subsidies directed towards AAI therefore militate against progressive realization of the right and, if present consumption trends continue, will over time reduce existing levels of enjoyment of the right as the availability and accessibility of food become less for the global poor. In the short term, some of these negative impacts of supporting AAI could theoretically be offset by countervailing measures designed to ensure continued enjoyment of the right to food. But over the longer term, the types of environmental destruction wrought by AAI, and their manifold negative impacts of food security, will become irreversible and non-compensable. As such, continued state support for AAI over time should be regarded as a retrogressive measure.

4.3. Maximum Available Resources

The obligation of governments to realize socioeconomic rights requires that they mobilize resources within their country to their utmost availability.[86] These include natural, financial, human and organizational resources.[87] Taxation is an important source of revenue, and the design and structure of a taxation framework are critically important in utilizing maximum available resources.[88]

Given that state subsidies to agriculture are paid for through taxes, one must question whether handing the lion's share of them to the food sector that is doing most to undermine food security is compatible with state duties to mobilize resources to the maximum of their ability.

State subsidies also impact upon how natural resources are used. As documented above, animal agriculture is very inefficient and intensive in its use of natural resources to produce food. As the Special Rapporteur on poverty has pointed out, states allowing natural resource exploitation without ensuring a fair share of its proceeds are taxed and allocated towards advancing human rights could be failing to mobilize adequate resources.[89] Likewise, former Special Rapporteur on the right to food Oliver De Schutter recommended that Cameroon reconsider the tax policy on concessions of agricultural land and for exploitation of natural resources to optimize the revenue earned from these resources to improve food security for vulnerable groups.[90] State subsidies and other forms of support to AAI are in effect doing the opposite of this, pouring public money into industries that require intensive resource exploitation that undermines the right to food.

4.4. Duties to Respect, Protect and Fulfil & Extraterritorial Obligations

The CESCR have used General Comments to advance a tripartite typology of state obligations. This imposes three levels of obligations on state parties: to *respect*, *protect* and *fulfil*.[91] Importantly, these obligations apply at both the domestic level and extraterritorially, meaning that states have obligations to individuals based outside of their territories[92] including in the context of business activities.[93] This is significant, given that most of the negative effects of Western agricultural policy occur in the poorer countries in the Global South, where food security is most precarious.

States' obligations to respect entail avoidance of measures that prevent existing access to the right to food.[94] States should also take steps to respect the enjoyment of the right to food in other countries and this 'requires States parties to refrain from interfering directly or indirectly with the enjoyment of the Covenant rights by persons outside their territories.'[95] As Skogly points out, this means that measures taken by foreign states in terms of subsidies and market access should not lead to a violation of the right to food for individuals in third states, whose right to food was previously enjoyed by them.[96] As discussed above, AAI is undermining the accessibility and availability of food. By continuing to adopt policies that favour these industries, Western states are making existing access to the right to food harder for many people, especially in poorer countries.

The duty to protect requires states to ensure that private actors do not deprive individuals of their access to adequate food.[97] Internationally, states parties are required 'to take steps to prevent and redress infringements of Covenant rights that occur outside their territories due to the activities of business entities over which they can exercise control.'[98] The responsibility of the state can be engaged even if other causes also contributed to the violation and even if states had not foreseen that a violation would occur, provided such a violation was reasonably foreseeable.

The CESCR has noted that states violate their duty to protect the right to food 'by granting exploration and exploitation permits for natural resources without giving due consideration to the potential adverse impacts of such activities on the individual and communities' enjoyment of Covenant rights.'[99]

A comparable claim is applicable to the context of financial and other support for AAI, given the harmful natural resource exploitation associated with the practice. Giving subsidies and other forms of support to industries that require exploitation of natural resources is more causally remote than granting permits for such exploitation, but in terms of downstream effect, both produce similar outcomes.

Finally, the duty to fulfil requires proactively adopting policies to either strengthen people's access to the means of procuring food or, where they are unable, to directly provide them with food.[100] The extraterritorial duty to fulfil requires states parties to 'contribute to creating an international environment that enables the fulfilment of' the right to food. To that end, states parties must 'take the necessary steps in their legislation and policies, including diplomatic and foreign relations measures, to promote and help create such an environment.'[101] As already documented, present Western consumption of animal products, abetted by the policies of Western governments, is undermining global food security in the short and long term. As such, present policies are incompatible with state obligations to fulfil the right to food.

In summary, it is arguable that Western states' ongoing support for animal agriculture is most clearly at odds with the obligation to fulfil the right to food, but also at least in tension with the obligations to respect and protect.

5. CONCLUSION: TOWARD A PLANT-BASED FOOD SYSTEM

As Hilal Elver—the former UN Special Rapporteur on the Right to Food—has noted,

> Realizing the right to food . . . requires us to realize that our consumption of meat, at its current rate, stands as a major barrier to both our own human rights and the rights of future generations.[102]

This chapter concurs and has suggested that current Western government policies in relation to AAI are in violation of their obligations relating to the right to food. What alternative policies could be pursued instead to better progressively realize this right?

There is growing consensus amongst food security and environmental experts that to address long-term threats of hunger and ecosystem collapse, a radical restructuring of our food system and transition towards predominantly plant-based food consumption are necessary.[103] As Baroni et al. note, 'vegetarian and vegan diets could play an important role in preserving environmental resources and in reducing hunger and malnutrition in poorer nations.'[104]

Governments have a role to play in helping to shift this paradigm. A range of options are open for consideration. The first obvious step that could be taken would be to remove the subsidies currently directed to AAI. Additionally, the money currently spent on subsidizing AAI could instead be given to plant-based protein alternatives or transitioning animal farmers to crop agriculture. Public grants or low-interest loans could also be granted to companies developing plant-based meat alternatives. Indeed, support for developing plant-based meats could be critical to encouraging transition to a predominantly plant-based diet as they replicate the taste and texture of animal-derived meats and approximate their macro- and micro-nutrient profiles. A recent survey of existing plant-based meats found that they use 47-99% less land, produce 30-90% lower GHG emissions, use 72-99% less water, produce 51-91% less nutrient pollution and use 100% less antibiotics than their animal-based counterparts.[105]

Other strategies might involve a prohibition on advertising animal products or the creation of public campaigns encouraging and promoting more consumption of plant foods. A more radical solution would be to increase taxes on animal products to incorporate the cost of their environmental and public health externalities, or even to ban the most intensive and environmentally destructive farming sectors. There are clearly a range of options available to states, and the viability of each will vary from country to country. There is not space in this chapter to offer any detailed proposals. However, it is obvious that business as usual cannot continue. In the future, food security and progressive realization of the right to food will require a significant transformation in Western food consumption habits, and governments have an important role to play in making this a reality.

Unfortunately, given the realities of lobbying and political and regulatory capture, government action against animal farming is unlikely at present. Moreover, most states—including Britain, Canada and Australia—have not ratified the Optional Protocol to the International Covenant on Economic, Social and Cultural Rights (OP-ICESCR), which establishes complaint and inquiry mechanisms for the ICESCR.[106] In the light of this, it is hoped that the recently appointed UN Special Rapporteur on the right to food—Michael Fakhri—will build upon and accentuate the brief and scattered observations of former Special Rapporteurs concerning the threat posed to the right to food by the AAI. Human rights, environmentalist and food justice academics and campaigners also have a vital role to play highlighting the threats posed by AAI to sustainable food systems. It is largely down to civil society actors to engage creative legal and non-legal strategies to promote a shift toward plant-based eating. The community coalitions resisting right to farm laws in the US, the animal rights/environmentalist coalition behind the upcoming ballot initiative on factory farming in Switzerland, and vegan advertising campaigns such as the UK- and Ireland-based Go Vegan World all provide examples of possible ways forward.

6. NOTES

1. See Part 3.
2. See Part 2.
3. This chapter primarily focuses on North America, Europe and Australasia for reasons of space, but many of the same criticisms would apply to countries like China, Japan, India and Brazil.
4. Charlotte E Blattner, and Ammann Odile. "Agricultural Exceptionalism and Industrial Animal Food Production: Exploring the Human Rights Nexus," *Journal of Food Law & Policy* 15, no. 2 (2019): 92–151.
5. Sandra Fredman, *Human Rights Transformed: Positive Rights and Positive Duties* (Oxford: Oxford University Press, 2008).
6. Mark Martinez, *The Myth of the Free Market: The Role of the State in a Capitalist Economy* (Sterling: Kumarian Press, 2009), 4.
7. Susanne Stoll-Kleemann & Tim O'Riordan, "The Sustainable Challenges of Our Meat and Dairy," *Environment: Science and Policy for Sustainable Development* 57, no 3 (2015): 43.
8. Doris Lin, "Ag-gag Laws and Farming Crimes Against Animals," In *The Routledge International Handbook of the Crimes of the Powerful,* ed. Gregg Barak (London: Routledge, 2015), 471.
9. Greenpeace, *Feeding the Problem: The Dangerous Intensification of Animal Farming in Europe* (Brussels: Greenpeace Publishing Unit 2019), 5
10. Lin, "Ag-gag Laws and Farming Crimes Against Animals," 472 (quoting David Robinson Simon).
11. David Robinson Simon, *Meatonomics: How the Rigged Economics of Meat and Dairy Make You Consume Too Much—and How to Eat Better, Live Longer, and Spend Smarter* (Newburyport: Conari Press, 2013), 5.

12. Elle Hunt, 'Meatonomics Author Says Government Working With Meat and Dairy Industry to Boost Consumption,' *Guardian*, May 5, 2017, accessed April 23, 2020https://www.theguardian.com/science/2017/may/06/meatonomics-author-says-government-working-with-meat-and-dairy-industry-to-boost-consumption.

13. Wakker Dier, "EU-Subsidies voor 'eet meer vlees-campagnes': onderzoek naar een onhoudbaar subsidiesysteem," accessed April 21, 2020, https://www.wakkerdier.nl/persberichten/eu-subsidies-voor-vleesreclame-haaks-op-nederlands-beleid/

14. Caitlin A. Ceryes and Christopher D. Heaney, "'Ag-Gag' Laws: Evolution, Resurgence and Public Health Implications," *New Solutions: A Journal of Environmental and Occupational Health* 28, no. 4 (2019): 666.

15. Ceryes and Heaney, ""Ag-Gag" Laws: Evolution, Resurgence and Public Health Implications," 664.

16. Lin, "Ag-gag laws and farming crimes against animals," 473.

17. Elizabeth Englezos, "Ag-gag in Australia: Activists under Fire May Not Be out of the Woods Yet," *Griffith Journal of Law & Human Dignity* 6, no. 2 (2018): 272–93.

18. Camille Labchuk, "U.S.-Style Ag-gag Laws Come to Canada," *Policy Alternatives*, March 2 2020, accessed April 21, 2020, https://www.policyalternatives.ca/publications/monitor/us-style-ag-gag-laws-come-canada. See also, Labchuk in this volume.

19. DEFRA, "Animal Aid Abattoir Cruelty Footage: Myth Busted," *DEFRA*, July 29, 2011, accessed April 21, https://www.gov.uk/government/news/animal-aid-abattoir-cruelty-footage-myth-busted (2020).

20. See, e.g., *Singh v Singh* [2016] EWHC 1432.

21. Loka Ashwood, Danielle Diamond and Fiona Walker, "Property Rights and Rural Justice: A Study of U.S. Right-to-Farm Laws," *Journal of Rural Studies* 67 (2019): 120–29.

22. Laura Alford and Sarah Berger Richardson, "Right-to-Farm Legislation in Canada: Exceptional Protection for Standard Farm Practices," *Ottawa Law Review* 50, no. 1 (2018): 131–62.

23. Gareth Griffith, "Right to farm laws," *NSW Parliamentary Research Service*, June 2015 e-brief 5/2015.

24. Blattner and Odile, "Agricultural Exceptionalism and Industrial Animal Food Production: Exploring the Human Rights Nexus," 107.

25. David J. Wolfson and Mariann Sullivan, "Foxes in the Hen House: Animals, Agribusiness and the Law: A Modern American Fable," in *Animal Rights: Current Debates and New Directions*, eds. Cass Sunstein and Martha Nussbaum (Oxford: Oxford University Press, 2005), 205–33.

26. Pub.L. 116-72, § 48(a)(1) & 48(d)(1)(A)&(B).

27. Aimee Mundt, "Australia's Need for An Independent Office of Animal Welfare," *Global Journal of Animal Law*. 1 (2015): 3.

28. David Fraser, Katherine E. Koralesky and Geoff Urton, "Toward a Harmonized Approach To Animal Welfare Law in Canada," *The Canadian Veterinary Journal* 59, no.3 (2018): 297.

29. *Roberts v. Ruggiero* (3 April 1985) per Stocker J, unreported (Q.B.) Lexis Citation 892.

30. Joe Wills, 'Our Fellow Animals and the Law,' *Sarx,* April 13 2020, accessed April 23, 2020, https://sarx.org.uk/articles/animal-issues/our-fellow-creatures-and-the-law/.

31. Kimerly McCoy, "Subverting Justice: An Indictment of the Animal Enterprise Terrorism Act," *Animal Law* 14, no. 1 (2007): 54.

32. Kimberly McCoy, "Subverting justice: An Indictment of the Animal Enterprise Terrorism Act," 58.

33. Piero Moraro, 'It Isn't Clear How the New Bill Against Animal Rights Activists Will Protect Farmers,' *The Conversation*, July 22 2019, accessed April 21, 2020, https://theconversation.com/it-isnt-clear-how-the-new-bill-against-animal-rights-activists-will-protect-farmers-120588; Laura O'Neil, 'New Ontario law seeks to protect farmers from animal rights activists' *BlogTO*, December 3 2019, accessed April 21, 2020, https://www.blogto.com/city/2019/12/new-ontario-law-protects-farmers-animal-rights-activists/.

34. Conor Woodman, *Spycops in Context: A Brief History of Political Policing in Britain* (London: Centre for Crime and Justice Studies, 2018), 21.

35. Woodman, *Spycops in Context*, 22.

36. Rob Evans, 'Woman Who Was Engaged to Police Spy Sues Met Over 'Psychological Torture',' *Guardian*, May 5, 2017, accessed April 21, 2020, https://www.theguardian.com/uk-news/2016/jan/18/police-spy-carlo-neri-woman-sues-psychological-torture.

37. Universal Declaration of Human Rights (adopted 10 December 1948), UNGA Res 217 A(III) (UDHR) article 25.

38. International Covenant on Economic, Social and Cultural Rights (adopted 16 December 1966, entered into force 23 March 1976) 993 UNTS 3 (ICESCR) article 11(1).

39. Ibid article 11(2).

40. 1979, UN Doc A/34/46, article 12(2).

41. 1989, UN Doc A/44/49, articles 24(2)(c) and (e) and 27(3).

42. 2007, UN Doc A/RES/61/106, articles 25(f) and 28(1). The right is also enshrined in a number of regional human rights instruments including the Additional Protocol on Economic, Social and Cultural Rights (San Salvador Protocol), OAS Treaty Series No 69 (1988), articles 12 and 17(a); African Charter on the Rights and Welfare of the Child, OAU Doc CAB/LEG/24.9/49 (1990), articles 14 (2) (c), (d) and (h); Protocol to the African Charter on Human and People's Rights on the Rights of Women in Africa, Maputo, 11 July 2003, articles 15 and 14(2) (b), available at https://www.un.org/en/africa/osaa/pdf/au/protocol_rights_women_africa_2003.pdf.

43. United States of America 'Reservation' FAO, Annex II: Explanatory Notes and Reservations, accessed April 22, 2020, http://www.fao.org/docrep/MEETING/005/Y7106E/Y7106E03.htm#TopOfPage.

44. Anthony Paul III Kearns, "The Right to Food Exists via Customary International Law," *Suffolk Transnational Law Review.* 22 no. 1 (1998): 223–258; Laura Niada, "Hunger and International Law: The Far-Reaching Scope of the Human Right to Food," *Connecticut Journal of International Law.* 22, no. 1 (2006): 131–202; Hilal Elver, "Interim report of the Special Rapporteur on the right to food," (2017) UN Doc.A/72/188.

45. Sven Sollner, "The "Breakthrough" of the Right to Food: The Meaning of General Comment No.12 and the Voluntary Guidelines for the Interpretation of the Human Right to Food," *Max Planck Yearbook of United Nations Law* 11 (2007): 396.

46. UN Committee on Economic Social and Cultural Rights (UNCESCR), "General Comment 12: The Right to Adequate Food (Art.11)," (1999) UN Doc E/C.12/1999/5, para. 8.

47. UNCESCR, "General Comment 12," para. 9.

48. Olivier De Schutter, "Report of the Special Rapporteur on the right to food, Olivier De Schutter. Final Report: The transformative potential of the right to food," (2014) UN Doc.A/HRC/25.57, para. 9.

49. David Robinson Simon, *Meatonomics,* 91.

50. Polly Walker, Pamela Rhubart-Berg, Shawn McKenzie, Kristin Kelling and Robert S Lawrence, "Public health implications of meat productions and consumption," *Public Health Nutrition* 8, no. 4 (2005): 348–56.

51. Vesanto Melina and others, "Position of the Academy of Nutrition and Dietetics: Vegetarian Diets." *Journal of the Academy of Nutrition and Dietetics* 116, no. 12 (2016): 1970–80.

52. UNCESCR, "General Comment 12," para. 10.

53. Former Special Rapporteur on the right to food, Jean Ziegler, has argued that the right not merely covers solid foods but also the nutritional aspects of drinking water. See Jean Zeigler, Christophe Golay, Claire Mahon and Sally-Anne Way, *The Fight for the Right to Food: Lessons Learned* (London: Palgrave Macmillan, 2011), 357.

54. Rob Wallace, *Big Farms Make Big Flu: Dispatches on Infectious Disease, Agribusiness and the Nature of Science* (New York: NYU Press, 2016).

55. Compassion in World Farming, *Zoonotic Diseases, Human Health and Farm Animal Welfare* (London: Compassion in World Farming, 2013).

56. Elaine D Berry and others, "Effect of Proximity to a Cattle Feedlot on Escherichia coli 0157:H7 Contamination of Leafy Greens and Evaluation of the Potential for Airborne Transmission," *Applied and Environmental Microbiology* 81, No. 3 (2015): 1101–10.

57. Ramona Cristina Ilea, "Intensive Livestock Farming: Global Trends, Increased Environmental Concerns, and Ethical Solutions," *Journal of Agricultural and Environmental Ethics* 22 (2009): 153–167, 161 (quoting the Livestock, Environment, and Development Virtual Center).

58. Food and Agriculture Organization (FAO), *Livestock's long shadow: environmental issues and options* (Rome: Food and Agriculture Organization, 2006), 133–61.

59. Norma Heredia and Santos Garcia, "Animals as Sources of Food-Borne Pathogens," *Animal Nutrition* 4, No. 3 (2018): 253.

60. UNCESCR, "General Comment 12," para.11.

61. *CW v United Kingdom*, Application No. 18187/91.

62. *Jakóbski v Poland*, Application no. 18429/06; *Vartic v Romania (no. 2)*, Application 14150/08.

63. UNCESCR, "General Comment 12," para.7.

64. UNCESCR, "General Comment 12," para.7.

65. Joseph Poore and Thomas Nemecek, "Reducing Food's Environmental Impacts Through Producers and Consumers," *Science* 360 (2018): 987–92.

66. FAO, *Livestock's Long Shadow*, 112–14.

67. FAO, *Livestock's Long Shadow*, xxi; Stoll-Kleemann & Tim O'Riordan, "The Sustainable Challenges of Our Meat and Dairy," 36.

68. FAO, *Livestock's Long Shadow*, xxi.

69. Paul C. West and others, "Leverage Points for Improving Global Food Security and the Environment," *Science* 345, no. 6194 (2014): 326.

70. Teja Tscharntke and others, "Global Food Security, Biodiversity Conservation and the Future of Agricultural Intensification," *Biological Conservation* 151 (2012): 55.

71. Mesfin Mekonnen and Arjen. Y Hoekstra, *The Green, Blue and Grey Water Footprint of Farm Animals and Animal Products* (Delft: UNESCO-IHE Institute for Water Education, 2010), 5.

72. Centers for Disease Control and Prevention. "Zoonotic Diseases," accessed April 21, 2020, https://www.cdc.gov/onehealth/basics/zoonotic-diseases.html.

73. Report of the WHO-China Joint Mission on Coronavirus Disease 2019 (COVID-19), https://www.who.int/docs/default-source/coronaviruse/who-china-joint-mission-on-covid-19-final-report.pdf.

74. See, for example, Jay P. Graham and others, "The Animal-Human Interface and Infectious Disease in Industrial Food Animal Production: Rethinking Biosecurity and Biocontainment," *Public Health Reports* 123, no. 3 (2008): 282–99; Stephen Cutler, Anthony Fooks and Willem van der Poel, "Public Health Threat of New, Reemerging, and Neglected Zoonoses in The Industrialized World," *Emerging Infectious Diseases* 16, no. 1 (2010): 1–7; T. W Drew, "The Emergence and Evolution of Swine Viral Diseases: To What Extent Have Husbandry Systems and Global Trade Contributed to their Distribution and Diversity?" *Revue Scientifique et Technique* 30, no. 1 (2011): 95–106; Bryony Jones and others, "Zoonosis Emergence Linked to Agricultural Intensification and Environmental Change," *Proceedings of the National Academy of Sciences of the United States of America* 110, no. 21 (2013): 8399–404.

75. Julia A. Barrett, "Airborne Bacteria in CAFOs: Transfer of Resistance from Animals to Humans," *Environmental Health Perspectives* 113, no. 2 (2005): 116–17.

76. Michael J Martin, Sapna E Thottahil and Thomas B. Newman, "Antibiotics Overuse in Animal Agriculture: A Call to Action for Health Care Providers," *American Journal of Public Health* 105, no. 12 (2015): 2409–10.

77. Martin, Thottahil and Newman, "Antibiotics Overuse in Animal Agriculture: A Call to Action for Health Care Providers," 2409.

78. David Banatar, "Our Cruel Treatment of Animals Led to the Coronavirus," *New York Times*, April 13, 2020, accessed April 23, 2020, https://www.nytimes.com/2020/04/13/opinion/animal-cruelty-coronavirus.html.

79. UNCESCR, "General Comment 12," para. 12.

80. Michael Tippett, "Extreme Weather and Climate," *Climate and Atmospheric Science* 1, no. 45 (2018): 1–2.

81. Food and Agriculture Organization, *Climate Change and Food Security: A Framework Document* (Rome: Food and Agriculture Organization, 2008).

82. UNCESCR, "General Comment 12," para. 13.

83. House of Commons International Development Committee, *Global Food Security: First Report of Session 2013–14* (London: House of Commons, 2013), para. 12.

84. Olivier De Schutter, "Report of the Special Rapporteur on the right to food, Olivier De Schutter. Final Report: The transformative potential of the right to food," para. 8.

85. UN Committee on Economic Social and Cultural Rights (UNCESCR), "General Comment 3: The Nature of State Parties Obligations." UN Doc E/1991/23, para. 9.

86. Magdalena Carmona Sepúlveda, *The Nature of the Obligations under the International Covenant on Economic, Social and Cultural Rights* (Antwerp: Intersentia, 2003), 313–19.

87. Diane Elson, Radhika Balakrishnan and James Heintz, "Public Finance, Maximum Available Resources and Human Rights" in *Human Rights and Public Finance: Budgets and the Promotion of Economic and Social Rights*, eds Aoife Nolan, Rory O'Connell and Colin Harvey (Oxford: Hart 2013), 15.

88. Ben Saul, David Kinley and Jaqueline Mowbray, *The International Covenant on Economic, Social and Cultural Rights: Commentary, Cases, and Materials* (Oxford: Oxford University Press, 2014), 144.

89. Magdalena Carmona Sepúlveda, "Report of the Special Rapporteur on extreme poverty and human rights, Magalena Carmona Sepúlveda," (2014) UN doc.A/HRC/26/28, para.72.

90. Olivier De Schutter, "Report of the Special Rapporteur on food, Olivier De Schutter' (Mission to Cameroon) (2013)," (2013) UN Doc A/ HRC/22/50/Add.2., para.73.

91. Henry Shue, "Rights in Light of Duties" in *Human Rights and U.S. Foreign Policy*, eds. Peter G. Brown and Doughlas MacLean (Lanham MD: Lexington, 1979), 51–64; Asbjørn Eide, "The International Human Rights System" in *Economic, Social and Cultural Rights: A Textbook*, eds. Asbjørn Eide, Catarina Krause, & Allan Rosas (Dordrecht: M. Nijhoff, 1995): UNCESCR, "General Comment 12," para. 15.

92. UNCESCR, "General Comment 12," para. 15.

93. UN Committee on Economic Social and Cultural Rights (UNCESCR), "General Comment 24: State Obligations under the International Covenant on Economic, Social and Cultural Rights in the Context of Business Activities," (2017) UN Doc.E/C/GC/24, paras. 29–37.

94. UNCESCR, "General Comment 12," para. 15.

95. UNCESCR, "General Comment 24," para. 29.

96. Sigrun I Skogly, "Right to Adequate Food: National Implementation and Extraterritorial Obligations," *Max Planck Yearbook of United Nations Law* 11 (2007): 13–14.

97. UNCESCR 1999, "General Comment 12," para. 15.

98. UNCESCR, "General Comment 24," para. 30.

99. UNCESCR, "General Comment 24," para. 18.

100. UNCESCR, "General Comment 12," para. 15.

101. UNCESCR, "General Comment 24," para. 37.

102. Hilal Elver and Melisa Shapiro, "No, You Don't Have a Right to Eat Meat," *Hilalelver.org*, September 11, 2019, accessed April 22, 2020, https://hilalelver.org/no-you-dont-have-a-right-to-eat-meat/.

103. Stoll-Kleemann & O'Riordan, "The Sustainable Challenges of Our Meat and Dairy," 45–46.

104. Luciana Baroni and others, "Evaluating the Environmental Impact of Various Dietary Patterns Combined with Different Food Production Systems," *European Journal of Clinical Nutrition* 61 (2007): 285.

105. Good Food Institute, "Plant Based Meat for a Growing World" (2020), accessed April 23, 2020, https://www.gfi.org/files/pb-meat-sustainability.pdf.

106. Adopted 10 December 2008, entered into force 5 May 2013, UN Res. A/RES/63/117.

7. REFERENCES

Alford, Laura, and Sarah Berger Richardson. "Right-to-Farm Legislation in Canada: Exceptional Protection for Standard Farm Practices." *Ottawa Law Review* 50, no. 1 (2019): 131–62.

Ashwood, Loka, Danielle Diamond, and Fiona Walker. "Property Rights and Rural Justice: A Study of U.S. Right-to-Farm Laws." *Journal of Rural Studies*. 67 (2019): 120–29.

Banatar, David. "Our Cruel Treatment of Animals Led to the Coronavirus." *The New York Times*. April 13, 2020. Accessed April 22, 2020. https://www.nytimes.com/2020/04/13/opinion/animal-cruelty-coronavirus.html.

Baroni, Luciana and others. "Evaluating the Environmental Impact of Various Dietary Patterns Combined with Different Food Production Systems." *European Journal of Clinical Nutrition*. 61 2007: 279–86.

Barrett, Julia A. "Airborne Bacteria in CAFOs: Transfer of Resistance from Animals to Humans." *Environmental Health Perspectives*. 113, no. 2 (2005): 116–17.

Berry, Elaine D and others. "Effect of Proximity to a Cattle Feedlot on Escherichia coli 0157:H7 Contamination of Leafy Greens and Evaluation of the Potential for Airborne Transmission." *Applied and Environmental Microbiology*. 81 No. 3 (2015): 1101–10.

Blattner, Charlotte E and Odile Ammann. "Agricultural Exceptionalism and Industrial Animal Food Production: Exploring the Human Rights Nexus." *Journal of Food Law & Policy* 15, no. 2 (2019): 92–151.

Centers for Disease Control and Prevention. N/A. "Zoonotic Diseases." Accessed April 22, 2020.https://www.cdc.gov/onehealth/basics/zoonotic-diseases.html.

Ceryes, Caitlin A. and Christopher D. Heaney. "'Ag-Gag' Laws: Evolution, Resurgence and Public Health Implications." *New Solutions: A Journal of Environmental and Occupational Health* 28, no. 4 (2019): 664–82.

Compassion in World Farming. 2013. *Zoonotic Diseases, Human Health and Farm Animal Welfare*. London: Compassion in World Farming, 2013.

Cutler, Stephen, Anthony Fooks and Willem van der Poel. "Public Health Threat of New, Reemerging, and Neglected Zoonoses in the Industrialized World." *Emerging Infectious Diseases*. 16, no. 1 (2010): 1–7.

DEFRA. 2011. "Animal Aid Abattoir Cruelty Footage: Myth Busted." *DEFRA*, July 29 2011. Accessed April 21, 2020.https://www.gov.uk/government/news/animal-aid-abattoir-cruelty-footage-myth-busted

De Schutter, Olivier. "Report of the Special Rapporteur on Food, Olivier De Schutter' (Mission to Cameroon) (2013)" UN Doc A/ HRC/22/50/Add.2.

De Schutter, Olivier. "Report of the Special Rapporteur on the Right to Food, Olivier De Schutter. Final Report: The transformative potential of the right to food." 2014. UN Doc.A/HRC/25.57.

Drew, T. W. "The Emergence and Evolution of Swine Viral Diseases: To What Extent Have Husbandry Systems and Global Trade Contributed to Their Distribution and Diversity?" *Revue Scientifique et Technique* 30, no. 1 (2011): 95–106.

Eide, Asbjørn. "The International Human Rights System" in *Economic, Social and Cultural Rights: A Textbook*, edited by Asbjørn Eide, Catarina Krause, & Allan Rosas. Dordrecht: M. Nijhoff, 1995.

Elson, Diane, Radhika Balakrishnan, and James Heintz. "Public Finance, Maximum Available Resources and Human Rights" in *Human Rights and Public Finance: Budgets and the Promotion of Economic and Social Rights*, edited by Aoife Nolan, Rory O'Connell and Colin Harvey. 13–40. Oxford: Hart, 2013.

Elver, Hilal. 2017. "Interim Report of the Special Rapporteur on the Right to Food." UN Doc.A/72/188.

Elver, Hilal and Melissa Shapiro. "No, You Don't Have a Right to Eat Meat." *Hilalelver.org*, September 11, 2019. Accessed April 22, 2020. https://hilalelver.org/no-you-dont-have-a-right-to-eat-meat/.

Englezos, Elizabeth. "Ag-gag in Australia: Activists under Fire May Not Be out of the Woods Yet." *Griffith Journal of Law & Human Dignity* 6, no. 2 (2018): 272–93.

Evans, Rob. "Woman Who Was Engaged to Police Spy Sues Met over 'Psychological Torture.'" *Guardian*, May 5, 2017. Accessed April 23, 2020. https://www.theguardian.com/uk-news/2016/jan/18/police-spy-carlo-neri-woman-sues-psychological-torture.

Food and Agriculture Organization. *Livestock's Long Shadow: Environmental Issues and Options*. Rome: Food and Agriculture Organization, 2006.

Food and Agriculture Organization. *Climate Change and Food Security: A Framework Document.* Rome: Food and Agriculture Organization, 2008.

Fraser, David, Katherine E. Koralesky and Geoff Urton, 'Toward a Harmonized Approach to Animal Welfare Law in Canada.' 2018. *The Canadian Veterinary Journal* 59, no. 3: 293–302.

Fredman, Sandra. *Human Rights Transformed: Positive Rights and Positive Duties*. Oxford: Oxford University Press, 2008.

Good Food Institute. "Plant Based Meat for a Growing World." 2019. Accessed April 23, 2020.https://www.gfi.org/images/uploads/2019/08/GFI-Plant-Based-Meat-Fact Sheet_Environmental-Comparison.pdf?utm_source=blog&utm_medium=website&utm_campaign=pb-meat-sustainability.pdf.

Graham, Jay P., and others. "The Animal-Human Interface and Infectious Disease in Industrial Food Animal Production: Rethinking Biosecurity and Biocontainment." *Public Health Reports* 123, no. 3 (2008): 282–99.

Greenpeace. *Feeding the Problem: The Dangerous Intensification of Animal Farming in Europe*. Brussels: Greenpeace Publishing Unit, 2019.

Griffith, Gareth. "Right to Farm Laws." NSW Parliamentary Research Service June 2015 e-brief 5/2015.

House of Commons International Development Committee. *Global Food Security: First Report of Session 2013–14*. London: House of Commons, 2013.

Hunt, Elle. 'Meatonomics Author Says Government Working With Meat and Dairy Industry to Boost Consumption.' *Guardian*, May 5, 2017. Accessed April 23, 2020. https://www.theguardian.com/science/2017/may/06/meatonomics-author-says-government-working-with-meat-and-dairy-industry-to-boost-consumption.

Ilea, Ramona Cristina. "Intensive Livestock Farming: Global Trends, Increased Environmental Concerns, and Ethical Solutions." *Journal of Agricultural and Environmental Ethics* 22 (2009): 153–167.

Jones, Bryony and others. "Zoonosis Emergence Linked to Agricultural Intensification and Environmental Change." *Proceedings of the National Academy of Sciences of the United States of America* 110, no. 21 (2013): 8399–404.

Kearns, Anthony Paul III. "The Right to Food Exists via Customary International Law," *Suffolk Transnational Law Review* 22, no. 1 (1998): 223–258.

Labchuk, Camille. "U.S.-style ag-gag laws come to Canada," *Policy Alternatives*, March 2 2020. Accessed April 21, 2020. https://www.policyalternatives.ca/publications/monitor/us-style-ag-gag-laws-come-canada.

Lennon, Jonathan and Aziz Rahman. "The Exclusion of Unlawfully Obtained Evidence." *Rahmanraveppi.co.uk* N/D. Accessed April 21, 2020. https://www.rahmanravelli.co.uk/pr/pr-07-08.pdf.

Lin, Doris. "Ag-gag Laws and Farming Crimes Against Animals." In *The Routledge International Handbook of the Crimes of the Powerful,* edited by Gregg Barak, 466–78. London: Routledge, 2015.

Martin, Michael J, Sapna E Thottahil and Thomas B. Newman. "Antibiotics Overuse in Animal Agriculture: A Call to Action for Health Care Providers." *American Journal of Public Health* 105, no. 12 (2015): 2409–10.

Martinez, Mark, A. *The Myth of the Free Market: The Role of the State in a Capitalist Economy.* Sterling: Kumarian Press, 2009.

McCoy, Kimerly. "Subverting justice: An indictment of the Animal Enterprise Terrorism Act." *Animal Law* 14, no. 1 (2007): 53–70.

Mekonnen, Mesfin and Arjen. Y Hoekstra. *The Green, Blue and Grey Water Footprint of Farm Animals and Animal Products*. Delft: UNESCO-IHE Institute for Water Education, 2010.

Melina, Vesanto and others. "Position of the Academy of Nutrition and Dietetics: Vegetarian Diets." *Journal of the Academy of Nutrition and Dietetics* 116, no. 12 (2016): 1970–80.

Moraro, Piero. 'It Isn't Clear How the New Bill Against Animal Rights Activists Will Protect Farmers,' *The Conversation*, July 22 2019. Accessed April 21, 2020.https://theconversation.com/it-isnt-clear-how-the-new-bill-against-animal-rights-activists-will-protect-farmers-120588.

Mundt, Aimee. "Australia's Need for An Independent Office of Animal Welfare." *Global Journal of Animal Law*. 2015, 1–26.

Niada, Laura. "Hunger and International Law: The Far-Reaching Scope of the Human Right to Food," *Connecticut Journal of International Law* 22, no. 1 (2006): 131–202.

O'Neil, Laura. 'New Ontario Law Seeks to Protect Farmers From Animal Rights Activists' *BlogTO*, December 3 2019. Accessed April 21, 2020. https://www.blogto.com/city/2019/12/new-ontario-law-protects-farmers-animal-rights-activists/.

Poore, Joseph, and Thomas Nemecek. "Reducing Food's Environmental Impacts Through Producers and Consumers." *Science* 360 (2018): 987–92.

Report of the WHO-China Joint Mission on Coronavirus Disease 2019 (COVID-19). https://www.who.int/docs/default-source/coronaviruse/who-china-joint-mission-on-covid-19-final-report.pdf.

Saul, Ben, David Kinley and Jaqueline Mowbray. *The International Covenant on Economic, Social and Cultural Rights: Commentary, Cases, and Materials*. Oxford: Oxford University Press, 2014.

Sepúlveda Carmona, Magdalena. *The Nature of the Obligations under the International Covenant on Economic, Social and Cultural Rights.* Antwerp: Intersentia, 2003.

Sepúlveda Carmona, Magdalena. "Report of the Special Rapporteur on Extreme Poverty and Human Rights, Magalena Sepúlveda Carmona." (2014) UN doc.A/HRC/26/28.

Shue, Henry. "Rights in Light of Duties" in *Human Rights and U.S. Foreign Policy* edited by Peter G. Brown and Doughlas MacLean, 51–64. Lanham MD: Lexington, 1979.

Simon, David Robinson. *Meatonomics: How the Rigged Economics of Meat and Dairy Make You Consume Too Much—and How to Eat Better, Live Longer, and Spend Smarter*. Newburyport: Conari Press, 2013.

Skogly, Sigrun I. "Right to Adequate Food: National Implementation and Extraterritorial Obligations." *Max Planck Yearbook of United Nations Law* 11 (2007): 339–58.

Sollner, Sven. "The 'Breakthrough' of the Right to Food: The Meaning of General Comment No. 12 and the Voluntary Guidelines for the Interpretation of the Human Right to Food." *Max Planck Yearbook of United Nations Law* 11 (2007): 392–415.

Stoll-Kleemann, Susanne and Tim O'Riordan. "The Sustainability Challenges of Our Meat and Dairy Diets." *Environment: Science and Policy for Sustainable Development* 57, no. 3 (2015): 34–48.

Tippett, Michael. "Extreme weather and climate." *Climate and Atmospheric Science* 1, no. 45 (2018): 1–2.

Tscharntke, Teja and others. "Global Food Security, Biodiversity Conservation and the Future of Agricultural Intensification." *Biological Conservation* 151 (2012): 53–59.

UN Committee on Economic Social and Cultural Rights. "General Comment 3: The Nature of State Parties Obligations." (1990) UN Doc E/1991/23.

UN Committee on Economic Social and Cultural Rights. "General Comment 12: The Right to Adequate Food (Art. 11)." (1999) UN Doc E/C.12/1999/5.

UN Committee on Economic Social and Cultural Rights. "General Comment 24: State obligations under the International Covenant on Economic, Social and Cultural Rights in the context of business activities." (2017) UN Doc.E/C/GC/24.

Wakker Dier. 2020. "EU-Subsidies voor 'eet meer vlees-campagnes': onderzoek naar een onhoudbaar subsidiesysteem." Accessed April 21, 2020. https://www.wakkerdier.nl/persberichten/eu-subsidies-voor-vleesreclame-haaks-op-nederlands-beleid/.

Walker, Polly, Pamela Rhubart-Berg, Shawn McKenzie, Kristin Kelling and Robert S Lawrence. "Public Health Implications of Meat Productions and Consumption." *Public Health Nutrition* 8, no. 4 (2005): 348–56.

Wallace, Rob. *Big Farms Make Big Flu: Dispatches on Infectious Disease, Agribuisness and the Nature of Science*. New York: NYU Press, 2016.

West, Paul C. and others. "Leverage Points for Improving Global Food Security and the Environment." *Science*. 345 no. 6194 (2014): 325–28.

Wills, Joe. 2020. 'Our Fellow Animals and the Law,' *Sarx,* April 13, 2020. Accessed April 23, 2020. https://sarx.org.uk/articles/animal-issues/our-fellow-creatures-and-the-law/.

Wolfson, David J., and Mariann Sullivan. "Foxes in the Hen House: Animals, Agribuisness and the Law: A Modern American Fable." In *Animal Rights: Current Debates and New Directions* edited by Cass Sunstein and Martha Nussbaum, 205–33. Oxford: Oxford University Press, 2005.

Woodman, Conor. *Spycops in context: A Brief History of Political Policing in Britain.* London: Centre for Crime and Justice Studies, 2018.

Zeigler, Jean, Christophe Golay, Claire Mahon and Sally-Anne Way. *The Fight for the Right to Food: Lessons Learned.* London: Palgrave Macmillan, 2011.

Chapter Eight

The Growth of Veganism in France

Law and Current Challenges

Marie Laffineur-Pauchet

1. INTRODUCTION

This chapter explores how human rights laws and consumer law in France affect the exercise of vegan freedom of conscience and the potential for the growth of veganism. In doing so, it contextualises veganism within the dominant, oppositional traditional food culture and within a legal framework that is confused in relation to the protection of both nonhuman animals and of vegans themselves.

The chapter begins with an examination of veganism in France and the challenge that veganism represents to France's traditional food culture. It then considers the issue of an emerging framework regulating plant-based products and how it is problematic for vegan freedom of conscience.

Prior to the main discussion below, it should be noted that English and French vocabulary relating to the exclusion of animal products from diets differ slightly. The term 'plant-based' can be translated into French in two different ways: (1) *à base de plantes,* meaning a diet or product based on plants; and (2) *végétalien or végétalienne,* meaning a diet or product based on plants or referring to a person adopting such a diet. In the same way that 'plant-based' does not include ethical considerations and does not necessarily mean vegan, the concept of *végétalisme* refers solely to the exclusion of animal products from the diet.

In this chapter, 'plant-based' will, therefore, refer to both *végétalien* and *à base de plantes.* The word 'vegan' is to be understood as meaning 'plant-based' when it is used specifically in relation to food products (e.g., use of the term 'vegan burger' does not imply any ethical dimension).

For the sake of simplicity, in 'animal products,' the word 'animal' is to be understood as referring to non-human animals.

In addition, the words 'meat,' 'fish,' 'milk,' 'cheese,' 'butter' and other expressions traditionally used to identify animal products do not refer to plant-based products, except where preceded by the words 'plant-based,' 'vegetarian' or 'vegan.'

2. CONTEXT: VEGANISM IN FRANCE

Internationally, in relation to food, France is particularly known for its *cuisine*, *gastronomy* and *arts de la table* ('arts of the table'). The latter has such importance in France that the 'gastronomic meal of the French,' referring to a social practice of enjoying together a meal normally containing animal products, was included on UNESCO's List of the Intangible Cultural Heritage of Humanity in 2010.[1] With this context in mind, it appears that consideration of non-human animals and plant-based food in France is interlinked with the recognition of its traditional food culture and social norms linked to it. The controversial practice of force-feeding ducks for the production of foie gras, traditionally consumed for Christmas in France, undeniably illustrates this statement.

Nevertheless, according to recent studies, 89% of French people consider the protection of animals as an important cause.[2] The 2020 citizen initiative *Référendum pour les Animaux*,[3] which proposes new measures for non-human animal protection, is supported by 73% of French people.[4] This evidences a general determination to improve the condition of non-human animals. In addition, legislation aimed at protecting non-human animals has evolved and been strengthened in the recent past. Even though French Animal Law is subject to a number of incoherencies, the withdrawal of animals from the Civil Code category of 'things' in 2015 constitutes a major step towards animal protection.[5] Moreover, the law proposal of 29 January 2021 titled *Lutte contre la maltraitance animale* ('Fight against animal mistreatment'),[6] which was adopted by an accelerated procedure,[7] also seems to support the view that concern for non-human animals is a high priority in the public and political debates.

In addition, even though there are currently no official legal definitions of vegetarianism or veganism in France, nor the European Union (EU), the legal framework related to the consumption and labeling of vegetarian and vegan products is also rapidly evolving.[8] This is, for instance, the case with the 2018 new food and agricultural law, also known as EGalim Law,[9] which introduced, as an experimental measure, at least one weekly vegetarian option in public schools.

From a social standpoint, a survey from 2015 shows that 62% of French people declare themselves ready to reduce their meat consumption for environmental reasons,[10] and another conducted in 2017 shows that 41% have declared that they consume more plant-based food, mainly for health reasons.[11]

From a market share standpoint, the vegetarian and vegan markets in France grew by 24% in 2018,[12] which constitutes, at first sight, a favourable context for plant-based food. However, the recent prohibitions of the use of traditional milk and meat product names for the purpose of describing plant-based alternatives in France, as well as the opening of an inquiry into vegetarian and vegan businesses by the *Direction générale de la concurrence, de la consommation et de la répression des fraudes* (DGRCC, Directorate-General for Competition, Consumer Affairs and Prevention of Fraud) in 2020,[13] need to be considered when evaluating the French context for veganism.

In reality, the development and recognition of rights for those who wish to live with respect for non-human animals and consume plant-based food in France encounter considerable difficulties that are possibly not entirely unrelated to the deeply-anchored practice of the consumption of animal products. The violent activism of a minority of non-human animal advocates, vegans and anti-speciesists may also have created negative impressions and feelings in both society and government for the successful development of rights for vegans: as discussed below, the French government recently created the *Cellule Demeter* ('Demeter Cell'),[14] which aims to identify and combat potential threats caused by the vegan movement. An unfortunate consequence is that even though France is often referred to as the 'home of human rights' on account of its historic past, civic and economic fundamental liberties related to the rights to live, eat, and market products with compassion for other animals may appear to be at risk.

3. VEGANISM AS A CHALLENGE TO THE FRENCH TRADITIONAL FOOD IDENTITY

An examination of the specific place of animal products in French traditional culinary culture illustrates that practices linked to their consumption are subject to identity, policy and juridical difficulties.

3.1. Animal Products as a Fundamental Component of French National Identity

As stated in the introduction, food has such an important place in France that the 'gastronomic meal of the French,' which contains animal products, such as meat and/or fish as well as cheese, was included in UNESCO's List of the Intangible Cultural Heritage of Humanity in 2010.[15]

This recognises that French *traditional food culture* and gastronomy—which is constituted, amongst others, of the *art de vivre* ('art of living'), *arts de la table* and *culinary hedonism*[16] traditions—are an inherent part of its culture.[17] The latter food tradition could even have a specific foundational value for the French identity.[18] In fact, having in mind Ernest Renan's definition of a nation in his 1882 famous lecture at the Sorbonne, French traditional food practices could be identified as one of the fundamental components of the French nation:[19]

> A nation is a soul, a spiritual principle. Two things which, properly speaking, are really one and the same constitute this soul, this spiritual principle. One is the past, the other is the present. One is the possession in common of a rich legacy of memories; the other is present consent, the desire to live together, the desire to continue to invest in the heritage that we have jointly received.[20]

Applying the above criteria of Renan's definition of a nation, French food culture and in particular the traditions of *art de vivre, arts de la table* and *culinary hedonism* appear to be (1) parts of French legacy of memories[21] and (2) a heritage in which the state and society are investing in order to pass it on and safeguard it.[22] It could, therefore, be argued that they are constitutive elements of the French nation.

Furthermore, as French food is generally rich in animal products, and the 'French gastronomic meal' contains such products,[23] it could also be argued that a variety of French traditionally consumed animal products are constitutive elements of the French heritage.

The latter would explain, amongst other things, the financial investments in and valorization of animal products by policymakers, especially since the inclusion of the French gastronomic meal on the aforementioned UNESCO list may have legal consequences related to the conservation and promotion of such heritage.[24]

This specific importance of animal products in French cuisines may explain the difficulty in abolishing certain controversial practices related to non-human animals that are considered to be part of the French culinary patrimony and culinary traditions, such as the production of foie gras,[25] which involves the force-feeding of ducks and geese. This practice is already prohibited by a number of EU countries.[26]

This anchoring of traditional food, with its high density of animal products, in French national identity may also have resulted in the association of such food with feelings of national pride, whereby negative perceptions could emerge towards people manifesting moral convictions for animals. Since foods dense in animal products are an important part of the French national culture and way of living, eliminating consumption of them from its own diet can be seen as rejecting cultural and social norms and pride in national identity.

The important place of animal food products in the definition of the French nation seems to dissonate with the public opinion in favour of more protection of non-human animals.[27] On the one hand, the French wish to be more compassionate towards animals. On the other hand, changing or abandoning traditions linked to food consumption—and, therefore, animal products—appears difficult. Such traditions could be so anchored in France that incoherencies emerge when the question of protection of animals exploited and killed for food consumption arises.[28] Legislatively, this also leads to a dissonant and partly-blinded reconsideration of practices related to the consumption of animal products.

3.2. A Difficult Legal Reconsideration of Practices Linked to Animal Consumption

The difficult reconsideration of practices linked to animal consumption in France is mirrored in its legal framework. First, despite recent legislative developments for animal welfare, the animal law framework is dissonant. Second, with only a few texts mentioning vegans or vegan food, the status of vegans in French law is at an embryonic stage, and the legal protection of vegans is uncertain, as discussed next.

4. A DISSONANT FRENCH ANIMAL LAW FRAMEWORK

French animal law is fragmented into different pieces of legislation and is constantly evolving. The framework was, firstly and unofficially, codified in the *Code de l'Animal* (Animal Code),[29] first published in 2018. The Code shows the diversity of provisions applying to non-human animals with regard to our relationship with them.[30] Since our relationship with non-human animals is dissonant,[31] the provisions sometimes require care and respect—for example, for companion and protected wild animals—but are also contradictory and sometimes permit treatment involving suffering and/or killing in the name of food, science, clothing, entertainment and/or tradition. For example, 'farm' animals, 'laboratory' animals, animals used for entertainment (cockfighting or bullfighting), and those exploited for the production of foie gras are subject to a varied and inconsistent degree of welfare protection.

Nevertheless, in relation to the protection of nature, France was the first to legally acknowledge animal sensitivity through a law passed on 10 July 1976.[32] A major step in the evolution of French animal law was the removal of non-human animals from the category of 'things' in 2015 by means of Article 515-14 of the Civil Code, which recognized them as *êtres vivants doués de sensibilité* ('sensitive living beings'). The question of 'sentience,' being a concept inspired by Anglo-Saxon literature, does not seem to appear yet in French legal texts. In fact, before the introduction of the word 'sentience' in a French dictionary in 2020,[33] there was no exact equivalent in the French language[34] and the term 'sensitive beings' has been used in legal provisions at French or European level, when using the French language.[35] In additional to the legal recognition of animals as 'sensitive living beings,' the Economic Commission of the French National Assembly also recently acknowledged their status as *êtres vivants doués de conscience* ('conscious living beings').[36]

However, Article 515-14 of the Civil Code confers a 'hybrid' legal status on non-human animals, who no longer fall under the category of things but can be submitted to the regime of things. This double-edged sword status is explained by scholar J-P. Marguénaud as animals being in a situation of 'juridical levitation.'[37] Since '[t]his provision means that the animal is an object (not subject) of protection, with the effect that legal persons can bear and exercise property rights over it,'[38] non-human animals can still be legally considered as things according to the specific laws and provisions applying to them (e.g., for animals used for food, entertainment, and domesticated animals, etc.).

While French animal law remains fragmented and dissonant, some positive developments can be observed for the protection and welfare of non-human animals. In this regard, the EGalim Law[39] tightens animal welfare provisions and sanctions for certain offences committed against animals and opens the way to vegetarian and plant-based alternatives in collective catering. This legislation extends the offence of animal abuse to slaughter establishments and to the transport of live animals, doubles penal sanctions for animal abuse and extends the role of animal protection associations, allowing them to join criminal proceedings as civil parties for the latter offences (article 67). It also prohibits the establishment of new batteries for keeping laying hens in cages (article 68). Furthermore, the EGalim Law introduces a mandatory vegetarian option in schools at least once a week for a period of two years and obliges certain catering establishments (i.e. schools, universities, pre-schools, and health and socio-medical establishments) with more than 200 seats to establish protein-diversification plans with plant-based alternative food items (article 24). Nevertheless, since most amendments of the law that intended to introduce truly effective measures in relation to the suffering of farm animals were rejected by the French deputies,[40] the EGalim Law was not seen as a victory by animal protection associations.

As scholar S. Canselier stated when researching the development of animal protection in French and European law, 'the impression of constant improvement . . . may be tempered by the persistence of exceptions and by the ambiguity of case-law.'[41] One of these exceptions or ambiguities surely made in the name of tradition or economy in France, as noted earlier, is the persistence of the practice of force-feeding for foie gras despite the legal obligation for policy-makers to take into account the suffering of ducks and geese.[42] Furthermore, this impression of tempered improvement is clearly illustrated by the recent proposal for a law against animal mistreatment that excludes from its scope of application sensitive topics such as foie-gras, corrida, hunting and intensive farming.[43] The versatility of the development of French animal law may give the impression that traditions and/or the economic value of animal products are superior to the legal status of sensitive living beings attributed to them in the Civil Code.[44]

The 'hybrid' legal status of non-human animals is exacerbated by the situation for veganism, which challenges the current accepted French food culture and identity in France, and initiatives relating to the legal consideration of vegans.

5. THE AMBIVALENT STATUS OF VEGANS ACCORDING TO PUBLIC POWERS: BETWEEN DISCRIMINATION AND PROTECTION

The French legal framework recognises human rights as some of the highest-ranked legal principles. In this regard, the *bloc de constitutionnalité* ('block of constitutionality') has the highest legal value in the French legal system order and includes a number of texts which could constitute an implicit recognition of rights for vegans at different levels. The block of constitutionality includes the Declaration of Human and Civil Rights ('DDHC'), the Constitution of 4 October 1958, the Preamble of the Constitution of 1946 enouncing the fundamental principles recognised by French law, and the Charter for the Environment of 2005. Such texts with constitutional value contain relevant provisions for vegans and people aiming to protect animals. For example, the right to freedom of belief and the correlative obligation of the French Republic to respect all beliefs (Article 1 of the Constitution of 1958 and the Preamble of the Constitution of 1946), which are intrinsically linked to the right to not be disquieted on account of opinions (Article 10 DDHC) and the right to freedom of expression of thoughts and opinions (Article 11 DDHC). The right to freedom of association, which can be important for people aiming at protecting animals, was also recognised by the *Conseil Constitutionnel* (French Constitutional Council) as a principle with constitutional value.[45]

At the international level, France is also party to a number of conventions which could be interpreted as conferring explicit rights on vegans. In terms of human rights, this *bloc de conventionnalité* ('bloc of conventionality') includes the 1948 Universal Declaration of Human Rights ('UDHR'), the International Covenant on Civil and Political Rights ('ICCPR') and the International Covenant on Economic, Social and Cultural Rights ('ICESCR'). At the European level, France is also subject to the European Convention on Human Rights ('ECHR') and to the Charter of Fundamental Rights of the European Union ('CFR').[46] Having in mind that veganism is a moral conviction,[47] certain provisions of the latter texts clearly apply to vegans. For example, the right to freedom of belief (Article 18 UDHR, Article 18 ICCPR, Article 9 ECHR and Article 10 CFR), which provides the right to believe in this conviction, practice it and revendicate it, and the right to not be subject to coercion which could impair this freedom or prevent one from adopting such a conviction.

Nevertheless, in view of some statements, documents and decisions from public authorities, it may be perceived that the rights of vegans, vegetarians and anti-speciesists under existing legal provisions are currently at risk in France.

For example, vegetarianism was compared to an eating disorder on the website of the Ministry of Education and Youth.[48] This clearly constituted an offence against the freedom of conviction due to its interference with the rights to not be disquieted on account of opinions and to practice moral convictions. Following a letter of the *Association Végétarienne de France* to the Ministry in June 2020,[49] the comparison was removed from the Ministry's website.

Furthermore, people who wish to protect animals, vegans and anti-speciesists in general have reported to be subject to intimidation from the French state authorities. Such intimidation would put at risk their right to practice their beliefs and convictions, their right to not be disquieted on account of their opinions and their freedom to associate. Further, in relation to the freedom of expression, it could also endanger their right to communicate information, for instance about cases of animal abuse.[50]

A particularly worrying development is that French vegans have been targeted as extremists. A 2019 National Assembly report, conducted on behalf of the Commission of Inquiry on the Fight Against Extreme Right-wing Groups in France, recommended that the state organization in charge of dealing with radical groups should include the vegan movement in its scope of application.[51] Even though some deputies and the president of the Commission expressed their disagreement with this recommendation on the basis that it was not linked to the initial scope of the Commission,[52] it might constitute a discomfort and a threat to vegans wishing to freely and lawfully express their beliefs within the confines of the rule of law.[53]

Another example of an act that could be perceived as a threat to the rights of vegans is the creation of the *Cellule Demeter* ('Demeter Cell')[54] in 2019, following a Convention signed by the French Interior Ministry, the National Federation Farmer Unions (NFSEA) and Young Agricultors (JA). The Demeter Cell aims to cooperate with agricultural professionals in order to create awareness of and prevent threats from those referred to as 'animal rights militants.'[55] Subsequent to the creation of the Demeter Cell, several employees and volunteers from animal protection and ecologist associations reported to have been investigated by the police and, apparently, subject to intimidation.[56] For this reason, a French animal defence association, *L214 Ethique & Animaux*,[57] with the support of the League of Human Rights, recently filed a complaint against the Demeter Cell.[58]

On a more positive note, the Tribunal of Lille *Vegan Calais Festival* case,[59] which related to the organization of a vegan event in a French city, shows some positive developments for the protection of the rights of vegans. The details of this case are as follows. In 2018, the animal protection association 'Farplace' obtained the city's agreement to organize a vegan festival in Calais. In response, groups of hunters and marketers of animal products informed the press that they wanted to organize a big meat-based barbecue in front of the festival. This, and developments subsequent to the initiatives of a minority of animal rights activists, created tension and disputes around the planned vegan festival. As a result, the mayor of Calais decided to prohibit the vegan festival from taking place on the basis that it could disrupt public order. Several animal protection associations made requests for the judge to annul the order of the mayor who had prohibited the festival, stating that it violated their freedom of expression and association, as well as the freedom of commerce and industry.[60] The judge found that the aforementioned freedoms were critically at risk. Moreover, the allegation of disruption to public order (1) was not accepted, as it was only based on press articles, (2) was countered by the fact that the festival was to be held indoors and the organizers had hired security services and (3) in any case, did not justify such restriction of fundamental rights.[61] By ordinance of September 4, 2018, the Tribunal of Lille, therefore, annulled the decision of the mayor of Calais to prohibit the vegan festival, which finally took place.[62]

The example above shows how the rights of vegans were put at risk by a public servant and how this was rectified by the legal recognition that the fundamental freedoms, including those of vegans, must be protected. While the recognition of protection for the fundamental rights of vegans has been formally acknowledged, rules relating to vegetarian and vegan products and provisions for vegans in France can be regarded as a sign that France is still to find its way to address the growth of the vegan movement and related demand for plant-based products.

6. THE DIFFICULTIES OF AN EMERGING VEGETARIAN AND VEGAN FOOD LAW

As mentioned earlier, the obligation to provide a weekly vegetarian option in the public sector under EGalim law (France's 2018 food and agricultural food law)[63] and the rules around the marketing and labelling of such options establish the emergence of a vegetarian and perhaps vegan food law in France, but also reveal some legal difficulties and incoherencies which have implications for the growth of veganism in France.

6.1. The Obligation to Provide a Weekly Vegetarian Option in Schools as a First Step in Establishing a Right to be Offered Plant-Based Food?

France's traditional food culture, which is based on animal products, is entrenched in French legislation. For example, legislation obliges schools to serve animal products with each meal according to the legal framework on the nutritional quality of meals in school and university catering.[64]

This legislation was, however, recently reconsidered by some French deputies, who denounced its discriminating character and the need to educate young people and the general population about the ecological and nutritional impacts of their diets and about the availability of a diverse range of proteins.[65] As a result of this reconsideration, the EGalim law achieved some positive steps in favour of vegetarian and vegan options.

Since 1 October 2020, the law requires school catering facilities (from kindergarten to high school) to provide a vegetarian option once a week for a period of two years. This is an experimental measure that will be evaluated at the end of this period. In addition, all public entities, as well as public and private schools, universities, hosting facilities for children under 6 years of age, health establishments, and socio or socio-medical establishments with more than 200 seats will have to 'present to their governing bodies a multi-year plan for protein diversification including vegetable protein alternatives in the meals they offer' with the state's support from 2022 (Article 24 of the EGalim law). In other words, these institutions, with the support of public powers, must start thinking about including vegan alternatives in their menus.

Nevertheless, these provisions are clearly inadequate in view of the composition of vegan meals, which must be free of animal products. On the one hand, a vegetarian option will be provided only once a week and may include animal *or* plant-based proteins; the law does not currently provide any option for vegans. It should also be noted that schools are allowed to adopt vegetarian options every day, but must also provide meat and fish-based options in line with legislation on the nutritional quality of meals in school and university catering.[66] Recently, in Lyon, in a context where 50% of students were not eating meat at school, the mayor decided to provide a single pesco-vegetarian menu to comply with the food choices of students. In response to this case, which was seen as polemical by certain French farmers and citizens, the Minister of Agriculture declared to have referred the matter to the competent authority. [67] This case clearly illustrates that the legislation and the decisions of some public authorities (i.e., the Minister of Agriculture) do not align with the food choices of what is arguably a significant proportion of young people in France.[68] Such a political scene could also create difficulties for the introduction of vegan options in schools and universities.

Additionally, the obligation to include a weekly vegetarian option in schools is not permanent; it is merely a two-year experiment which will then be evaluated by the *Conseil National de la Restauration Collective* (National Council for Collective Catering) and which may be adapted if necessary.[69] With regard to the protein diversification plans in collective catering services, there are no follow-up measures to secure the right to a vegan or vegetarian option. In this regard, the 2019 report of the *Défenseur des Droits*, titled *Un droit à la cantine scolaire pour tous les enfants* ('A right to a school canteen for all children') points out the increase in demands related to the elimination of meat and animal proteins in schools and notes the need to align food menus with the human right to freedom of conscience by including meals free from meat and other animal proteins.[70]

In terms of marketing practices, since no definitions of 'vegetarian' or 'vegan' are currently provided in the French legal framework, and since vegan labels, certifications and logos can be useful guarantees but are only provided on a voluntary basis, the offer of vegetarian and vegan products is subject to a diversification of practices which could potentially lead to confusion and fraudulent practices, even at public level. As such, the absence of legal definitions for vegetarian and vegan products means that there is no precise legal basis for the relevant authority[71] to promote, control and enforce compliance with consumer law—to effectively verify that products labelled as veg(etari)an do not include animal ingredients in their composition or manufacturing process—even though such products are subject to consumer law and it is a requirement that their labelling should not mislead consumers or prevent them from making an informed choice.[72]

6.2. The 'Saga' of Plant-Based Food Denominations

The denominations of available vegetarian and vegan products have become a true phenomenon in French society and have led to a restructuring of food labelling rules, allegedly aiming at the protection of consumers. This issue is directly relevant to the adoption and growth of veganism in France.

The 'saga'[73] started in 2017 at European Union level. Following a complaint made by a German competition association against an online vegan shop which was marketing its plant-based products using names traditionally used by the dairy industry, the European Court of Justice ruled in *Verband Sozialer Wettbewerb eV v TofuTown.com GmbH*[74] that EU rules 'must be interpreted as precluding the term 'milk' and the designations reserved by that regulation exclusively for milk products from being used to designate a purely plant-based product in marketing or advertising.'[75] Practically, the decision prohibited the use of marketing names that are traditionally used for dairy products (milk, cream, butter, cheese, etc.) by producers of plant-based food. The decision, however, also highlighted that exceptions to the general rule could be added by member states on a discretionary basis or by the European Commission 'to satisfy demonstrated needs resulting from evolving consumer demand, technical progress or the need for product innovation.'[76] Lawyers defending the rights of vegans made the point that by failing to rule in the light of this measure, this case enforced a political decision to give dairy a monopoly on the words in question.[77]

European rules are not as precise when it comes to labelling meat-like plant-based products. Unlike the definition of 'milk,'[78] the definition of 'meat' provided in Regulation (EC) No 853/2004 of the European Parliament and of the Council[79] is not exclusive and could therefore be interpreted as not excluding meat-like products made of plants from its scope of application. This inconsistency, however, has led to formal uncertainty around the use of the meat-like denominations for plant-based products in some EU member states. Perhaps inspired by the European Court of Justice *TofuTown* ruling, French deputy Jean-Baptiste Moreau, cow-breeder by profession, seized the opportunity to seek to prohibit the use of meat-like denominations for plant-based products in France in an adopted amendment to the new food and alimentation law (EGalim Law) in 2018.[80] Nevertheless, the *Conseil Constitutionnel* declared this amendment unconstitutional on the basis that it had no direct link to the original purpose of the law.[81]

The saga was revived a year later during debates concerning proposed legislation on the transparency of information of food products. During the debates, several deputies proposed an amendment to prohibit the use of meat-like denominations for vegetarian and vegan products.[82] The amendment was adopted, and the Consumer Code now states in Article L. 412-10 that 'the names used to designate foodstuffs of animal origin may not be used to describe, market or promote foodstuffs containing vegetable proteins.' A decree implementing the law could be imminent,[83] and meanwhile uncertainty on the issue of lawful denominations and labelling for plant-based products prevails. For example, it is unclear whether similar phonetic denominations, similar graphic designs or even cellular meat would be exempt from the prohibition.

Regarding meat-like denominations, there is no legal text in the European Union that prevents plant-based products from being labeled with meat-like denominations such as 'vegan sausage' or 'vegan burger.' On the contrary an amendment aiming at such prohibition at EU level was rejected during the latest debates of the Common Agricultural Policy.[84] The adoption of diverging legislations by member states on the labelling of vegetarian and vegan products—illustrated by France's prohibition on the use of meat-like names for plant-based products—could create legal and competition divergences,[85] and has to be considered in relation to the principle of free competition on the EU market.[86] A particularly worrying point regarding the safeguard of free competition is that France's prohibition on the use of meat-like names for plant-based products was adopted before the end of the standstill period required by EU legislation to anticipate or prevent any commercial barriers under the TRIS notification system.[87] Such procedural defect could have prevented contributors to submit their observations and might even mean that the prohibition to use meat-like names is inapplicable and unenforceable.[88]

As reflected by the European Vegetarian Union in the context of the prohibition of the use of meat-like names for plant-based products,[89] it may be argued that vegetarian and vegan labelling rules can impact negatively on businesses selling such products. For instance, the rules may create additional administrative burdens for producers wishing to sell their plant-based products in different EU member states; producers have to research the applicable rules, which are unclear in the non-harmonised framework, and may possibly be required to label their products differently to comply with the requirements of the member state in which they are reselling.

At French level, it has been confirmed by official controls that denominations are an important issue for veg(etari)an products producers, manufacturers and resellers. In January 2020, the Directorate-General for Competition, Consumer Affairs and Prevention of Fraud of the French Ministry of Economy of Finance launched an inquiry specifically targeting vegetarian and vegan food products.[90] This inquiry follows up on the 2018 controls and sanctions of the same Directorate related to new alimentary consuming practices, which penalized several businesses selling vegetarian and vegan products on account of 'deceptive' and 'fraudulent marketing practices'[91] and reported that the majority of anomalies relating to vegetarian and vegan products concerned the use of denominations traditionally reserved to animal products.

Furthermore, it could be perceived that consumers of veg(etari)an products are not protected by labelling rules prohibiting names with which they are more familiar. For instance, although this statement necessitates more research, they may be confused by the lack of accurate descriptive names and feel frustrated to be unable to find on the market the names that they are using in their daily language to designate the products (for example, when looking for soya 'cream' or vegan 'cheese' in the EU or meat substitutes in France).[92] Consumers who wish to purchase plant-based products according to their ethical or religious beliefs may also argue that rules restricting the use of familiar food names (such as 'milk') in marketing and labelling constitute interference with their freedom of belief and a restriction on their related freedom of speech. This is an interesting perspective given the international principle intrinsic to the human right to freedom of conscience that there should be no interference, and everyone should be free to adopt a belief of choice.

Due to the difficult context related to veganism in France, it is essential to question whether these confused rules, which cause inconvenience for vegans and inquiries into vegan food producers and sellers, may reflect biased policy choices and target the growth of vegan plant-based consumerism. An important long-standing issue raised for many years with the European Commission is the composition and reliability of products marketed as 'vegetarian' and 'vegan,' and the inadequacy of a policy of voluntary rather than mandatory labelling, which results in uncertainty for vegetarian and vegan consumers who cannot be sure whether the products they wish to purchase are in fact truly vegetarian or vegan.[93]

7. CONCLUSION

Although the opinion of French citizens is favourable to the protection of non-human animals and to an increase in the consumption of plant-based products, the complicated French legal frameworks hinder proper protection for non-human animals and the growth of veganism.

Of significance is that French identity is based on the consumption of animal products. This negatively impacts the reconsideration of practices linked to the consumption of non-human animals, consideration for them, and the inclusion of vegetarian and vegan diets in the French legal frameworks. These circumstances create many difficulties for animal liberation and incoherencies in the development of favourable law, policy and practice.

Clearly incoherent is the ambivalence of laws protecting non-human animals that are, on the one hand, considered as sentient and living beings deserving moral consideration and, on the other hand, subject to rules that treat them as things or products.

Since veganism has not yet been explicitly recognised as fundamentally protected in the French legal framework, the scope of legal protection of vegans is unclear. A positive step for vegans was the outcome of the 2018 Calais Vegan Festival tribunal, which recognised and protected the rights of vegans. However, despite this protection afforded to vegans, the controversial actions of a minority of activists have inspired political measures to prohibit the growth of veganism and fostered antagonistic social conditions that are likely to manifest in further discriminatory social circumstances for vegans.

As observed by the *Défenseur des Droits,*[94] in the context of school catering, and regardless of the increase of demands for vegetarian and vegan meals, legislation regarding the provision of suitable vegan, plant-based food options in schools is, at the moment, inadequate and hinders the adoption of compassionate, plant-based living.

Additionally, recent French and EU developments in food law arguably impede the smooth development of the vegetarian and vegan markets. Businesses and consumers are also negatively impacted by the confusion surrounding plant-based food labelling, and vegetarian and vegan businesses are particularly at risk of penal sanctions for using the descriptive words that are helpful for consumers wishing to make compassionate food choices. Consumers are further impacted by the current absence of a definition of vegetarian and vegan products and clear labeling rules.

Nevertheless, despite the complexities, difficulties and unfair treatment, there is some hope for the growth of veganism and the protection of vegan freedom of conscience in France. French people have registered their interest in the well-being of other animals, there is widespread interest in plant-based living, and vegetarian and vegan associations and consumers groups do not remain silent in response to adverse social, political, and legal circumstances. The recent complaint against the *Cellule Demeter* ('Demeter Cell'), which aims to identify and combat potential threats caused by the vegan movement, and the new legislation on plant-based products labelling show that inconveniences faced by vegans and consumers who care about the environment and their health can be reconsidered favorably and balanced with fundamental liberties.

8. NOTES

1. UNESCO, "Convention for the Safeguarding of the Intangible Cultural Heritage," Decision of the Intergovernmental Committee: 5.COM 6.14, Fifth session Nairobi, Kenya, November 15 to 19, 2010, https://ich.unesco.org/en/decisions/5.COM/6.14.

2. Ifop, "La sensibilité des Français à la cause animale à la veille de la séquence électorale," JF/PC no. 116072, accessed March 14, 2021, https://www.ifop.com/wp-content/uploads/2019/02/116072-R%C3%A9sultats-Collectif-AnimalPolitique.pdf.

3. Référendum pour les animaux, accessed March, 2021, https://referendumpourlesanimaux.fr/. The *Référendum pour les animaux* is an initiative from French citizens supported by associations and personalities aiming at organizing a referendum in application of article 11 of the Constitution for a new law relative to the environmental responsibility of humankind towards animals and their welfare. More details on this law proposal and the measures it contains for animals are available on the website.

4. Ifop/Caniprof, "Référendum sur la cause animale Les Français soutiennent les animaux," accessed March 14, 2021, https://www.ifop.com/publication/les-francais-soutiennent-ils-le-projet-de-referendum-pour-les-animaux/.

5. However, even though animals have been removed from the category of things in 2015, they can still be subject to laws considering them as things. For more information see section 4 of this chapter detailing the legal status and regime of non-human animals in France.

6. Assemblée nationale, "Proposition de loi, adoptée, par l'Assemblée nationale après engagement de la procédure accélérée, visant à renforcer la lutte contre la maltraitance animale," January 29, 2021, T.A. no. 558, https://www.assemblee-nationale.fr/dyn/15/dossiers/maltraitance_animale.

7. The accelerated procedure ('procedure accélérée') for the adoption of laws is laid out in Article 45 of the French Constitution. It aims at reducing the times of parliamentary debates for a law proposal by submitting the text only once at the National Assembly (and then Senate) in order to debate its adoption. Such procedure was engaged for the law proposal "Lutte contre la maltraitance animale" (Fight against animal mistreatment) as explained in the National Assembly dossier of this law proposal: https://www.assemblee-nationale.fr/dyn/15/dossiers/maltraitance_animale.

8. See section 6 of this chapter.

9. Loi no. 2018-938 du 30 Octobre 2018 pour l'équilibre des relations commerciales dans le secteur agricole et alimentaire et une alimentation saine, durable et accessible à tous, *JORF* no. 0253 of November 1, 2018, text no. 1, NOR: AGRX1736303L.

10. Yougov/L214, "Etude élevage et climat," accessed March 14, 2021, https://visuels.l214.com/sites/www.l214.com/2015/12-communique-presse/Sondage-Youogov-viande-climat-nov2015.jpg.

11. Ifop/Lesieur, "Le végétal dans l'alimentation des français," *Observatoire des cuisines populaires*, accessed March 14, 2021, https://www.restauration21.fr/files/Etude%20IFOP-LESIEUR%20pour%20l%27OCPop%20-%20Le%20v%C3%A9g%C3%A9tal%20dans%20l%27alimentation%20des%20Fran%C3%A7ais.pdf. According to the same survey, 82% of those having declared to increase their plant consumption did it for health-related reasons.

12. Van Overstraeten, Benoit, "Le marché végétarien et végan a augmenté de 24% en 2018, selon une étude," éd. Jean-Michel Bélot, *Capital*, January 8, 2019, https://www.capital.fr/economie-politique/le-marche-vegetarien-et-vegan-a-augmente-de-24-en-2018-selon-un-etude-1322408.

13. Ministère de l'économie, des finances et de la relance, Direction générale de la concurrence, de la consommation et de la répression des fraudes (DGCCRF), "Programme national d'enquêtes 2020," accessed March 14, 2021, 6, https://www.economie.gouv.fr/files/files/directions_services/dgccrf/dgccrf/pne/2020/pne-2020.pdf.

14. See section 5 of this chapter.

15. UNESCO, *op. cit.*, note 1.

16. In my view, the importance of the *art de vivre, arts de la table* and *culinary hedonism* traditions for France is reflected in the UNESCO List of Mundial Patrimony. In this sense, the 'gastronomic meal of the French' is described with the following sentences: "It is a festive meal bringing people together for an occasion to enjoy the art of good eating and drinking. The gastronomic meal emphasizes togetherness, the pleasure of taste, and the balance between human beings and the products of nature.." The latter description clearly highlights that food is viewed as an art and a philosophy of life by the French. For the full reference, see: UNESCO, *loc. cit.*, note 1, point 4.

17. See Priscilla Ferguson, "Identité et culture: La gastronomie en France," *Revue De La BNF* 49, no. 1 (2015): 12–17, https://doi-org.ezpum.biu-montpellier.fr/10.3917/rbnf.049.0012; Francis Chevrier, *Notre gastronomie est une culture: le repas gastronomique des Français au patrimoine de l'humanité* (Paris: F. Bourin, 2011).

18. Food, cuisine and gastronomy are important for the identity of many nations or cultures in the world. I here argue that they have a specific foundational value for the French nation and without excluding the same for other nations, although this statement might need more research on national food identity. The importance of the food component in the French identity has developed through a series of political, artistic and perhaps religious conditions. For example, France is historically linked to Catholicism in which the consumption of animal products is promoted for certain rites. On this view, history teaches us that the French monarchy used

cuisine as a way to develop and enshrine a common national culture and to promote the supremacy of French cuisine on the international scene with French *art de vivre*, *art de la table* and *culinary hedonism*. The example of "*Dîners d'Epicure*" which consists in dinners organized in different countries at the same time and first launched by French cook Auguste Escoffier (1846–1935) to promote French *cuisine* in the world supports this idea. We may compare this foundational value of food, cuisine and gastronomy with, for instance, one of its neighbors, Italy which has a similar religious background linked to Catholicism, and for which it could also be argued that traditional food is an essential component of the nation. France benefited from favorable political conditions thanks to a relative population unity and artistic initiatives aiming at promoting French national food culture. In Italy the foundational element of food in the definition of nation could in any way not be brought to its full geographical potential before its unification, and internationally with the mundialization of Italian products allowed amongst others by the exodus of part of the Italian population to the United States.

19. See Roland Barthes, "Pour une psycho-sociologie de l'alimentation contemporaine," *Annales: Histoire, Sciences Sociales* 5, no. 16 (1961): 983–84, https://doi.org/10.3406/ahess.1961.420772.

20. Ernest Renan, "What Is a Nation?" trans. Ehan Rundell from Renan Ernest's "Qu'est-ce qu'une nation?" conference delivered at the Sorbonne, March 11, 1882, Paris: Presses-Pocket, 1992, http://ucparis.fr/files/9313/6549/9943/What_is_a_Nation.pdf.

21. UNESCO, "Convention for the safeguarding of the intangible cultural heritage," Decision of the Intergovernmental Committee: 5.COM 6.14, Fifth session Nairobi, Kenya, 15 to 19 November 2010, https://ich.unesco.org/en/decisions/5.COM/6.14, point 2, R.1: 'The gastronomic meal of the French plays an active social role within its community and is transmitted from generation to generation as part of its identity.'

22. UNESCO, *Ibid.*, point R3: "Safeguarding measures reflect the commitments of the community, the French authorities and NGOs to reinforce its transmission, particularly through the education system, while encouraging research and promotion."

23. UNESCO, *Ibid.*, point 1, "The gastronomic meal should respect a fixed structure, commencing with an apéritif (drinks before the meal) and ending with liqueurs, containing in between at least four successive courses, namely a starter, fish and/or meat with vegetables, cheese and dessert. Individuals called gastronomes who possess deep knowledge of the tradition and preserve its memory watch over the living practice of the rites, thus contributing to their oral and/or written transmission, in particular to younger generations."

24. For more information on French measures on the safeguard of cultural patrimony, see UNESCO, "Periodic reporting on the Convention for the Safeguarding of the Intangible Cultural Heritage," No. 00824/France, 2014; Ministère de la culture, "La législation sur le patrimoine culturel immatériel en France," accessed March 14, 2021, https://ich.unesco.org/en/state/france-FR?info=periodic-reporting&cp=FR&topic=fr-etat.

25. Matthieu Ferry, "Le foie gras sous la mitraille," review of "Contested Tastes: Foie Gras and the Politics of Food" by DeSoucey Michaela, *La Vie des idées*, October 16, 2017, https://laviedesidees.fr/Le-foie-gras-sous-la-mitraille.html.

26. At the EU level, the practice of force-feeding of ducks and geese necessary to obtain *foie-gras* is already prohibited in Germany, Denmark, Finland, Ireland, Italy, Luxembourg, The Netherlands, Poland, Czech Republic, Sweden, United Kingdom and in certain provinces of Austria and Belgium. For more information on the prohibition of force-feeding of non-human animals in the world, see L214 Ethique & Animaux, "Foie gras. Le gavage interdit (presque) partout," accessed March 14, 2021, https://www.l214.com/stop-foie-gras/le-gavage-interdit-a-travers-le-monde/.

27. See Ifop/Caniprof, "Référendum sur la cause animale Les Français soutiennent les animaux," accessed March 14, 2021, https://www.ifop.com/publication/les-francais-soutiennent-ils-le-projet-de-referendum-pour-les-animaux/.

28. As further discussed in section 4 of this chapter: incoherence regarding protecting animals is supported by the fact that most amendments aimed at improving the conditions of farm animals were rejected by deputies during the debates of the EGalim Law in 2018. During the debates of the 2021 law proposal aimed at reinforcing penalties for animal mistreatment there

were no discussions concerning farming, fishing nor hunting of animals for food consumption nor towards the practice of gavage.

29. Jean-Pierre Marguénaud and Leroy Jacques (dir.), *Code de l'animal* (Paris: LexisNexis, 1st ed., 2018).

30. For more information on the French Animal Code, see Laffineur-Pauchet Marie, "First Animal Code in France: A Response to a Dissonant Animal Law," *Derecho Animal (Forum of Animal Law Studies)* 10, no. 2 (2019): 83–106, https://doi.org/10.5565/rev/da.359.

31. This dissonant relation towards non-humans is the result of what Gary Francione refers to as 'moral schizophrenia' in his book *Introduction to Animal Rights: Your Child or the Dog?*

32. Loi no. 76-629 du 10 juillet 1976 relative à la protection de la nature. The latter law was repealed in 2010. The sensitivity of animals is now codified at Article L214-1 of the *Code Rural et de la pêche maritime*.

33. Fondation Droit Animal, 'Le mot sentience entre dans le Larousse 2020," accessed March 14, 2021, https://www.fondation-droit-animal.org/102-le-mot-sentience-entre-dans-le-larousse-2020/.

34. On vocabulary explanations in relation to sentience, see Estiva Reus, "Sentience!," *Cahiers antispécistes*, no. 26, November, 2005, https://www.cahiers-antispecistes.org/sentience/.

35. For instance, the English version of Article 13 of the Treaty on the Functioning of the European Union ('TFEU') refers to 'sentient beings' while the French version refers to 'sensitive beings': Treaty on the Functioning of the European Union, Article 13, French and English version, Consolidated version, https://eur-lex.europa.eu/legal-content/EN/TXT/?uri=celex%3A12012E%2FTXT.

36. The acknowledgment of animals as 'conscious living beings' by French National Assembly is based on political and philosophical history, scientific discoveries and aligns with the Declaration of Cambridge on Consciousness of 2012 quoted in the report Assemblée Nationale, "Rapport fait au nom de la Commission des affaires économiques sur la proposition de loi *visant à* renforcer *la* lutte *contre la* maltraitance animale (no. 3661 rectified)," January 20, 2021, Part I, https://www.assemblee-nationale.fr/dyn/15/rapports/cion-eco/l15b3791_rapport-fond#_Toc256000003.

37. Jean-Pierre Marguénaud, "Une révolution théorique : l'extraction masquée des animaux de la catégorie des biens," *Recueil Dalloz, JCP G*, no. 305 (2015): 501, https://hal.archives-ouvertes.fr/hal-01872337.

38. Cédric Riot, "Legal Personhood of Animals (I): The Case for the Legal Personhood of Companion Animals," *dA. Derecho Animal (Forum of Animal Law Studies)* 9, no. 2 (2018): 57, https://doi.org/10.5565/rev/da.341.

39. *Op. cit.,* note 9.

40. For more information on the EGalim Law, see Marie Laffineur-Pauchet, "New Food & Agricultural Law in France: Progress for Animals and Plant-Based Food?" *The Vegan's Society Research News*, accessed March 14, 2021, https://www.vegansociety.com/about-us/research/research-news/new-food-agricultural-law-france-progress-animals-and-plant-based-food; "Most deputies have been insensitive to farm animals' suffering by voting against amendments aiming at improving their lot. An amendment prohibiting factory-farming was introduced but rejected during debates. As a result, on almost 100 articles, only seven concern 'animal welfare' and delay the adoption of truly effective measures."

41. Sonia Canselier, "Les grands progrès de la protection animale en droit français et européen," *Histoire de la recherche contemporaine* IV, no. 1 (2015): 54–57, 8, https://doi.org/10.4000/hrc.977. S. Canselier makes this remark about the ambivalence of French Animal Law's development regarding legislation and case-law of 2015 or before. Nevertheless, the same could still be affirmed today.

42. At the European Union level, foie gras production is covered by Council Directive 98/58/EC of 20 July 1998 aligning with Recommendation of 22 June 1999 of the Standing Committee of the European Convention for the Protection of Animals Kept for Farming Purposes. In relation to foie gras, the latter Directive states that "Animals must be fed a wholesome diet which is appropriate to their age and species and which is fed to them in sufficient quantity to maintain them in good health and satisfy their nutritional needs. No animal shall be provided

with food or liquid in a manner, nor shall such food or liquid contain any substance, which may cause unnecessary suffering or injury." (Annex, point 14) and that "All animals must have access to feed at intervals appropriate to their physiological needs" (Annex, point 15), which appears contradictory to the practice of force-feeding deliberately damaging animals' livers and is therefore an incompatible feeding in view of their physiological needs. Furthermore, paragraph (8) of the Preamble of the aforesaid Recommendation explicitly state that force-feeding does not respect applicable welfare requirements.

43. Assemblée nationale, "Proposition de loi, adoptée, par l'Assemblée nationale après engagement de la procédure accélérée, visant à renforcer la lutte contre la maltraitance animale," January 29, 2021, T.A. no. 558, https://www.assemblee-nationale.fr/dyn/15/dossiers/maltraitance_animale?etape=15-AN1.

44. At Article 515-14 of the Civil Code as explained at the beginning of this section.

45. Conseil constitutionnel, Décision no. 71-44 DC du 16 juillet 1971, Loi complétant les dispositions des articles 5 et 7 de la loi du 1er juillet 1901 relative au contrat d'association. *JORF* of July 18, 1971. Rec. 29, ECLI:FR:CC:1971:71.44.DC.

46. For more information on the rights of vegans in International and European Law, see The Vegan Society, "What rights do vegans have?," accessed March 14, 2021, https://www.vegansociety.com/get-involved/international-rights-network/what-rights-do-vegans-have#european-law.

47. Jeanette Rowley, *Towards a Vegan Jurisprudence: The Need for a Reorientation of Human Rights* (London: Lexington, 2020), 53.

48. See Association Végétarienne de France, "Lettre ouverte de l'AVF à Jean-Michel Blanquer, ministre de l'Éducation nationale et de la Jeunesse," June 2020, accessed March 14, 2021, https://www.vegetarisme.fr/communiques/lettre-ouverte-ministre-education-nationale/?highlight=jeunes.

49. *Ibid.*

50. For an overview and commentary of case-law related to the right of animal protection's activists or whistle-blowers to communicate information and their freedom of expression, see Jean-Pierre Marguénaud, "Les militants de l'association L 214 devant le tribunal correctionnel," *Revue Semestrielle de Droit Animalier—RSDA*, no. 1 (2017): 15–24, https://idedh.edu.umontpellier.fr/files/2017/12/RSDA_1_2017-1.pdf and cited case-law.

51. Assemblée Nationale, "Rapport fait au nom de la Commission d'enquête sur la lutte contre les groupuscules d'extrême droite en France," June 6, 2019, Recommendation no. 31, http://www.assemblee-nationale.fr/15/rap-enq/r2006.asp.

52. Assemblée Nationale, *Ibid.*, section "Examen en Commission."

53. On this point, Article 10 of the 1789 Declaration of Human and Civil Rights states that "No one may be disturbed on account of his opinions, even religious ones, as long as the manifestation of such opinions does not interfere with the established Law and Order." The latter therefore recognises the right of freedom of opinion and of non-discrimination for them as well as the freedom of speech, in the limit of the respect of the law and public order.

54. For more information on "Cellule Demeter," see Ministère de l'intérieur, "Présentation de « DEMETER », la cellule nationale de suivi des atteintes au monde agricole," accessed March 14, 2021, https://www.interieur.gouv.fr/Archives/Archives-ministres-de-l-Interieur/Archives-Christophe-Castaner/Dossiers-de-presse/Presentation-de-DEMETER-la-cellule-nationale-de-suivi-des-atteintes-au-monde-agricole.

55. *Ibid.*

56. L214, "Cellule Demeter: stop à la répression des lanceurs d'alerte!" accessed March 14, 2020, https://www.l214.com/lettres-infos/2020/07/31-recours-justice-cellule-demeter-ligue-droits-homme/.

57. L214 Ethique & Animaux is a French animal defence association created in 2008 to expose animal suffering in farming, fishing, transport, slaughter. It is particularly known for its graphic undercover footage and investigations inside farms and slaughterhouses. Its name is inspired by Article L214-1 of the Rural Code recognising for the first time animals' sensitivity. For more information on L214, see L214 Ethique & Animaux, "L214 ÉTHIQUE & ANIMAUX: PRESENTATION," accessed March 14, 2021, https://www.l214.com/L214-french-vegan-animal-protection-NGO.

58. Ligue des Droits de l'Homme, "L214, avec le soutien de la ligue des droits de l'homme, attaque la Cellule Demeter en justice," accessed March 14, 2021, https://www.ldh-france.org/l214-avec-le-soutien-de-la-ligue-des-droits-de-lhomme-attaque-la-cellule-demeter-en-justice/.

59. Tribunal Administratif de Lille, Ordonnance du 4 septembre 2018, *Association L214 et autres*. No.1807923, http://lille.tribunal-administratif.fr/content/download/151875/1538369/version/2/file/1807923.pdf.

60. In application of article L-521-2 of the Code of administrative justice stating that when a fundamental freedom is urgently at risk, the judge [*juge des référés*] can order measures aiming at the safeguard of this fundamental freedom.

61. *Op. cit.*, note 59, paragraphs 3 to 6.

62. Tribunal Administratif de Lille, "Le Calais Vegan Festival aura bien lieu." Communiqué, September 4, 2018, http://lille.tribunal-administratif.fr/Actualites/Communiques/Le-Calais-Vegan-Festival-aura-bien-lieu.

63. Loi no. 2018-938 du 30 Octobre 2018 pour l'équilibre des relations commerciales dans le secteur agricole et alimentaire et une alimentation saine, durable et accessible à tous, *JORF* no. 0253 of 1 November 2018, text no.1, NOR: AGRX1736303L.

64. See Article D230-25 of the Rural and Maritime Fishery Code. For schools in particular see Décret no. 2011–1227 du 30 septembre 2011 relatif à la qualité nutritionnelle des repas servis dans le cadre de la restauration scolaire, *JORF* no. 0229 of October 2, 2011, text no. 29, NOR: AGRG1032342D; Arrêté du 30 septembre 2011 relatif à la qualité nutritionnelle des repas servis dans le cadre de la restauration scolaire, *JORF* no. 0229 of October 2, 2011, text no. 34, NOR: AGRG1032380A. For universities, see Décret no. 2012-141 du 30 janvier 2012 relatif à la qualité nutritionnelle des repas servis dans le cadre de la restauration universitaire, *JORF* no. 0026 of January 31, 2012, text no. 49, NOR: AGRG1134513D. Please note that it is probable that the legal framework related to the nutritional quality of meals in schools and universities will be updated soon.

65. Assemblée Nationale, "Equilibre dans le secteur agricole et alimentaire (No. 627)—Amendement no. CE1248 présenté par Mme Valetta Ardisson et M. Trompille," April 18, 2018, http://www.assemblee-nationale.fr/dyn/15/amendements/0627/CION-ECO/CE1248.pdf; Assemblée Nationale, "Equilibre dans le secteur agricole et alimentaire (No. 1175)—Amendement no. 792 présenté par Mme Cazebonne et al.," September 7, 2018, http://www.assemblee-nationale.fr/dyn/15/amendements/1175/AN/792.

66. *Op. cit.*, note 64.

67. Julien De Normandie (@J_Denormandie), "Arrêtons de mettre de l'idéologie dans l'assiette de nos enfants ! Donnons-leur simplement ce dont ils ont besoin pour bien grandir. La viande en fait partie. J'ai saisi le Préfet du Rhône," Quote Tweet, February 21, 2021, https://twitter.com/J_Denormandie/status/1363432191888416769.

68. See Association Végétarienne de France, "À Lyon, polémique hors sol sur le menu sans viande," accessed March 14, 2021, https://www.vegetarisme.fr/communiques/lyon-menu-sans-viande-polemique/.

69. Ministère de l'agriculture et de l'alimentation, "Les mesures de la loi EGalim concernant la restauration collective," accessed March 14, 2021, https://agriculture.gouv.fr/les-mesures-de-la-loi-egalim-concernant-la-restauration-collective.

70. Défenseur des droits, "Un droit à la cantine pour tous," June 19, 2019, 38–39, https://www.defenseurdesdroits.fr/sites/default/files/atoms/files/rapport-cantine-num-19.06.19.pdf.

71. *Direction générale de la concurrence, de la consommation et de la répression des fraudes* (Directorate-General for Competition, Consumer Affairs and Prevention of Fraud: DGCCRF).

72. In accordance with the provisions in Article L120-1 of the Code de la consommation.

73. According to the expression used by Clémence Landeau of the *Association Végétarienne de France expression* in: V-label. "Les steaks végétaux: une véritable saga," accessed March 14, 2021, https://v-label.fr/2018/11/06/les-steaks-vegetaux-une-veritable-saga/.

74. European Court of Justice, Judgment of 14 June 2017, *Verband Sozialer Wettbewerb eV v TofuTown.com GmbH*, Case C-422/16, ECLI:EU:C:2017:458.

75. *Ibid.*, last paragraph. The interpretation of the judge was in particular based on Regulation (EU) No. 1308/2013 of the European Parliament and of the Council of 17 December 2013

establishing a common organization of the markets in agricultural products which provides in point 1 of part III of Annex VII that ""Milk" means exclusively the normal mammary secretion obtained from one or more milkings without either addition thereto or extraction therefrom." The Court also stated that the latter Regulation reproduced, without making substantive changes, the provisions of Council Regulation (EEC) No. 1898/87 of 2 July 1987 on the protection of designations used in marketing of milk and milk products.

76. *Op. cit.*, paragraph 39.

77. See Barbara Bolton, "The TofuTown Decision: What does dairy's monopoly on words mean for plant-based businesses in the UK?" November 3, 2017, https://www.lexology.com/library/detail.aspx?g=5229937c-2a93-4308-8ee6-b71c5ebbb0a9.

78. Regulation (EU) No. 1308/2013 of the European Parliament and of the Council of 17 December 2013 establishing a common organization of the markets in agricultural products. *OJ L 347*, 20.12.2013, 671–854, Annex VII, part III, point 1.

79. Article 1.1 of Annex I of Regulation (EC) No 853/2004 provides that "1.1. 'Meat' means edible parts of the animals referred to in points 1.2 to 1.8, including blood."

80. Assemblée Nationale, "Equilibre dans le secteur agricole et alimentaire (No. 627), Amendement adopté no. CE2044 présenté par M. Moreau," April 13, 2018, http://www.assemblee-nationale.fr/dyn/15/amendements/0627/CION-ECO/CE2044.

81. Conseil constitutionnel, Décision no. 2018-771 DC du 25 octobre 2018, *Loi pour l'équilibre des relations commerciales dans le secteur agricole et alimentaire et une alimentation saine, durable et accessible à tous. JORF* no. 0253, November 1, 2018, text no. 2, NOR: CSCL1829418S.

82. Assemblée nationale, "Proposition de loi no. 2441 modifiée par le Sénat relative à la transparence de l'information sur les produits agricoles et alimentaires. Amendement no. CE-22 [adopted] visant à interdire les dénominations carnées pour les produits végétaux." March 5, 2020. http://www.assemblee-nationale.fr/dyn/15/amendements/1786/CION-ECO/CE22.

83. Loi no. 2020-699 du 10 juin 2020 relative à la transparence de l'information sur les produits agricoles et alimentaires, *JORF* no. 0142 of June 11, 2020, text no. 1, NOR: AGRX1935395L, Article 5.

84. European Parliament, Common agricultural policy—amendment of the CMO and other Regulations. Texts adopted, October 23, 2020, P9_TA(2020)0289, last modified February 3, 2021, https://www.europarl.europa.eu/doceo/document/TA-9-2020-0289_EN.html.

85. In this sense Article 45 of Regulation (EU) No 1169/2011 on the provision of food information to consumers obliges member states of the European Union to publicly notify any new food information national legislation to anticipate and prevent commercial barriers.

86. See Treaty on the Functioning of the European Union, consolidated version. *OJ C 326*, 26.10.2012, 47–390, articles 34 to 37.

87. Directive (EU) 2015/1535 of the European Parliament and of the Council of 9 September 2015 laying down a procedure for the provision of information in the field of technical regulations and of rules on Information Society services. *OJ L 241*, 17.9.2015, p. 1–15. The notification for the provisions related to the French meat-like names prohibition was received on 5 June 2020 while the related transparency law was adopted on 10 June 2020 therefore not complying with the three months standstill period required in Article 6.1 of Directive (EU) 2015/1535. See European Commission. Act on the transparency of information on agricultural and food products, 2020/338/F (France), date received June 5, 2020, https://ec.europa.eu/growth/tools-databases/tris/en/search/?trisaction=search.detail&year=2020&num=338.

88. See European Court of Justice, judgment of 16 July 2015, *UNIC and Uni.co.pel*, C-95/14, EU:C:2015:492, paragraphs 29 and 30.

89. European Commission, act on the transparency of information on agricultural and food products, 2020/338/F (France), Stakeholders Contributions, European Vegetarian Union, June 16, 2020, https://ec.europa.eu/growth/tools-databases/tris/en/index.cfm/search/?trisaction=search.detail&year=2020&num=338&mLang=FR or https://ec.europa.eu/growth/tools-databases/tris/en/index.cfm/search/?trisaction=search.detail&year=2020&num=338&mLang=FR#.

90. Ministère de l'économie, des finances et de la relance, Direction générale de la concurrence, de la consommation et de la répression des fraudes (DGCCRF), *op. cit.*, note 13. However, this inquiry was suspended due to the Covid-19 crisis.

91. Ministère de l'économie, des finances et de la relance, Direction générale de la concurrence, de la consommation et de la répression des fraudes (DGCCRF), "Rapport annuel 2018 du plan national de contrôles officiels pluriannuels (PNCOPA) 2016-2020," accessed March 14, 2021, 39, TN27KC, https://www.economie.gouv.fr/files/files/directions_services/dgccrf/securite/produits_alimentaires/rapport-annuel_2018.pdf; Ministère de l'économie, des finances et de la relance, Direction générale de la concurrence, de la consommation et de la répression des fraudes (DGCCRF), "Résultats 2018 de la DGCCRF," accessed March 14, 2021, 33, https://www.economie.gouv.fr/files/files/directions_services/dgccrf/dgccrf/rapports_activite/2018/resultats-dgccrf-2018.pdf.

92. See, for example, *Ibid.* or Association Végétarienne de France and European Vegetarian Union, "France to privilege meat over reason. EVU and AVF oppose forthcoming French ban on 'meaty names' for vegetarian food," press release, accessed March 14, 2021, https://www.euroveg.eu/wp-content/uploads/2020/06/Press-Release-French-TRIS-notification_EN.pdf; "the new legislation on labelling vegetarian and vegan products leads to more confusion of consumers by breaking with already well-established plant-based denominations."

93. See for example, European Citizen Initiative, "Mandatory food labelling Non-Vegetarian / Vegetarian / Vegan," last modified November 12, 2019, ECI(2018)000007, https://europa.eu/citizens-initiative/initiatives/details/2018/000007_en [Unsuccessful collection].

94. Défenseur des droits, *op. cit.*, note 70.

9. REFERENCES

Arrêté du 30 septembre 2011 relatif à la qualité nutritionnelle des repas servis dans le cadre de la restauration scolaire. *JORF* no. 0229 of October 2, 2011, text no. 34, NOR: AGRG1032380A.

Assemblée nationale. "Proposition de loi, adoptée, par l'Assemblée nationale après engagement de la procédure accélérée, visant à renforcer la lutte contre la maltraitance animale." January 29, 2021. T.A. no. 558. https://www.assemblee-nationale.fr/dyn/15/dossiers/maltraitance_animale?etape=15-AN1.

Assemblée Nationale. "Rapport fait au nom de la Commission des affaires économiques sur la proposition de loi *visant à* renforcer *la* lutte *contre la* maltraitance animale (no. 3661 rectified)." January 20, 2021. https://www.assemblee-nationale.fr/dyn/15/rapports/cion-eco/l15b3791_rapport-fond#_Toc256000003.

Assemblée nationale. "Proposition de loi no. 2441 modifiée par le Sénat relative à la transparence de l'information sur les produits agricoles et alimentaires. Amendement no. CE-22 [adopted] visant à interdire les dénominations carnées pour les produits végétaux." March 5, 2020. http://www.assemblee-nationale.fr/dyn/15/amendements/1786/CION-ECO/CE22.

Assemblée nationale. "Rapport fait au nom de la Commission d'enquête sur la lutte contre les groupuscules d'extrême droite en France." June 6, 2019. http://www.assemblee-nationale.fr/15/rap-enq/r2006.asp.

Assemblée nationale. "Equilibre dans le secteur agricole et alimentaire (No. 1175)—Amendement no. 792 présenté par Mme Cazebonne et al." September 7, 2018. http://www.assemblee-nationale.fr/dyn/15/amendements/1175/AN/792.

Assemblée nationale. "Equilibre dans le secteur agricole et alimentaire (No. 627)—Amendement adopté no.CE2044 présenté par M. Moreau." April 13, 2018. http://www.assemblee-nationale.fr/dyn/15/amendements/0627/CION-ECO/CE2044.

Assemblée nationale. "Equilibre dans le secteur agricole et alimentaire (No. 627)—Amendement no. CE1248 présenté par Mme Valetta Ardisson et M. Trompille." April 18, 2018. http://www.assemblee-nationale.fr/dyn/15/amendements/0627/CION-ECO/CE1248.pdf.

Association Végétarienne de France. "À Lyon, polémique hors sol sur le menu sans viande." Accessed March 14, 2021. https://www.vegetarisme.fr/communiques/lyon-menu-sans-viande-polemique/.

Association Végétarienne de France. "Lettre ouverte de l'AVF à Jean-Michel Blanquer, ministre de l'Éducation nationale et de la Jeunesse." Accessed March 14, 2021. https://

www.vegetarisme.fr/communiques/lettre-ouverte-ministre-education-nationale/?highlight=jeunes.

Association Végétarienne de France and European Vegetarian Union. "France to privilege meat over reason. EVU and AVF oppose forthcoming French ban on 'meaty names' for vegetarian food." Accessed March 14, 2021. https://www.euroveg.eu/wp-content/uploads/2020/06/Press-Release-French-TRIS-notification_EN.pdf.

Barthes, Roland. "Pour une psycho-sociologie de l'alimentation contemporaine." *Annales. Economies, sociétés, civilisations* 5, no. 16 (1961): 977–86. https://doi.org/10.3406/ahess.1961.420772.

Bolton, Barbara. "The TofuTown Decision: What does dairy's monopoly on words mean for plant-based businesses in the UK?." Accessed March 14, 2021. https://www.lexology.com/library/detail.aspx?g=5229937c-2a93-4308-8ee6-b71c5ebbb0a9.

Canselier, Sonia. "Les grands progrès de la protection animale en droit français et européen." *Histoire de la recherche contemporaine* IV, no. 1 (2015): 54–57. https://doi.org/10.4000/hrc.977.

Charte pour l'environnement. Translated by *Conseil Constitutionnel* from: *JORF* no. 0051, March 2, 2005, 3697. https://www.conseil-constitutionnel.fr/sites/default/files/as/root/bank_mm/anglais/charter_environnement.pdf.

Charter of Fundamental Rights of the European Union. *OJ C 326*, 26.10.2012, 391–407, ELI: http://data.europa.eu/eli/treaty/char_2012/oj.

Chevrier, Francis. *Notre gastronomie est une culture: le repas gastronomique des Français au patrimoine de l'humanité*. Paris: F. Bourin, 2011.

Code civil. Article 515-14. Version into force since February 18, 2015.

Code de la consommation. Article L120-1. Version into force since August 6, 2008.

Code rural et de la pêche maritime. Article D230-25. Version into force since August 10, 2017.

Code rural et de la pêche maritime. Article L214-1. Version into force since May 8, 2010.

Conseil constitutionnel. Décision no. 2018-771 DC du 25 octobre 2018, *Loi pour l'équilibre des relations commerciales dans le secteur agricole et alimentaire et une alimentation saine, durable et accessible à tous*. *JORF* no. 0253, November 1, 2018, text no. 2, NOR: CSCL1829418S.

Conseil constitutionnel. Décision no. 71-44 DC du 16 juillet 1971, *Loi complétant les dispositions des articles 5 et 7 de la loi du 1er juillet 1901 relative au contrat d'association*. *JORF* of July 18, 1971. Rec., 29, ECLI : FR:CC:1971:71.44.DC.

Constitution française of October 4, 1958. Last modified December 1, 2009. Article 45. https://www.legifrance.gouv.fr/loda/id/LEGITEXT000006071194/.

Constitution française of 1946. Preamble. Translated by *Conseil Constitutionnel*. Accessed March 14, 2021. https://www.conseil-constitutionnel.fr/sites/default/files/as/root/bank_mm/anglais/cst3.pdf.

Convention for the Protection of Human Rights and Fundamental International Freedoms. Council of Europe. Entered into force September 3, 1953. Council of Europe. ETS no. 005. As amended.

Council Directive 98/58/EC of 20 July 1998 concerning the protection of animals kept for farming purposes. *OJ L 221*, 8.8.1998, 23–27. Consolidated version.

Council Regulation (EEC) no. 1898/87 of 2 July 1987 on the protection of designations used in marketing of milk and milk products. *OJ L 182*, 03/07/1987, 36–38. No longer in force.

Declaration of Cambridge on Consciousness proclaimed on 7 July 2012. Cambridge, United Kingdom. Accessed March 14, 2021. https://fcmconference.org/img/CambridgeDeclarationOnConsciousness.pdf.

Declaration of Human and Civil Rights of 26 August 1789. Translated by *Conseil Constitutionnel*. Accessed March 14, 2021. https://www.conseil-constitutionnel.fr/sites/default/files/as/root/bank_mm/anglais/cst2.pdf.

Décret no. 2012-141 du 30 janvier 2012 relatif à la qualité nutritionnelle des repas servis dans le cadre de la restauration universitaire. *JORF* no. 0026 of January 31, 2012, text no. 49, NOR : AGRG1134513D.

Décret no. 2011–1227 du 30 septembre 2011 relatif à la qualité nutritionnelle des repas servis dans le cadre de la restauration scolaire. *JORF* no. 0229 of October 2, 2011, text no. 29, NOR: AGRG1032342D.

Défenseur des droits, "Un droit à la cantine pour tous. Intérêt supérieur de l'enfant, égalité des droits et non-discrimination." June 19, 2019. https://www.defenseurdesdroits.fr/sites/default/files/atoms/files/rapport-cantine-num-19.06.19.pdf.

Directive (EU) 2015/1535 of the European Parliament and of the Council of 9 September 2015 laying down a procedure for the provision of information in the field of technical regulations and of rules on Information Society services. *OJ L 241*, 17.9.2015, p. 1–15.

European Citizen Initiative. "Mandatory food labelling Non-Vegetarian / Vegetarian / Vegan." ECI(2018)000007. Last modified 2019, November 12. https://europa.eu/citizens-initiative/initiatives/details/2018/000007_en.

European Commission. Act on thc transparency of information on agricultural and food products. 2020/338/F (France). Date received June 5, 2020. https://ec.europa.eu/growth/tools-databases/tris/en/search/?trisaction=search.detail&year=2020&num=338.

European Court of Justice. Judgment of 14 June 2017, *Verband Sozialer Wettbewerb eV v TofuTown.com GmbH*, Case C-422/16, ECLI:EU:C:2017:458.

European Court of Justice. Judgment of 16 July 2015, *UNIC and Uni.co.pel*, C-95/14, EU:C:2015:492.

European Parliament. Common agricultural policy—amendment of the CMO and other Regulations. Texts adopted, October 23, 2020, P9_TA(2020)0289. Last modified February 3, 2021. https://www.europarl.europa.eu/doceo/document/TA-9-2020-0289_EN.html.

Ferguson, Priscilla. "Identité et culture: La gastronomie en France." *Revue De La BNF* 49, no. 1 (2015): 12–17. https://doi-org.ezpum.biu-montpellier.fr/10.3917/rbnf.049.0012.

Ferry, Matthieu. "Le foie gras sous la mitraille." Review of *Contested Tastes: Foie Gras and the Politics of Food*, by Michaela DeSoucey, *La Vie des idées*, October 16, 2017, https://laviedesidees.fr/Le-foie-gras-sous-la-mitraille.html.

Fondation Droit Animal. "Le mot sentience entre dans le Larousse 2020." Accessed March 14, 2021. https://www.fondation-droit-animal.org/102-le-mot-sentience-entre-dans-le-larousse-2020/.

Francione, Gary. *Introduction to Animal Rights: Your Child or the Dog?* Philadelphia: Temple University Press, 2010.

Ifop/Caniprof. "Référendum sur la cause animale Les Français soutiennent les animaux." Accessed March 14, 2021. https://www.ifop.com/publication/les-francais-soutiennent-ils-le-projet-de-referendum-pour-les-animaux/.

Ifop. "La sensibilité des Français à la cause animale à la veille de la séquence électorale." *JF/PC* no. 116072. Accessed March 14, 2021. https://www.ifop.com/wp-content/uploads/2019/02/116072-R%C3%A9sultats-Collectif-AnimalPolitique.pdf.

Ifop/Lesieur. "Le végétal dans l'alimentation des français." *Observatoire des cuisines populaires*. Accessed March 14, 2021. https://www.restauration21.fr/files/Etude%20IFOP-LESIEUR%20pour%20l%27OCPop%20-%20Le%20v%C3%A9g%C3%A9tal%20dans%20l%27alimentation%20des%20Fran%C3%A7ais.pdf.

International Covenant on Economic, Social and Cultural Rights. Adopted December 16, 1966. Entered into force January 3, 1971. United Nations General Assembly, Res. 2200 A (XXI).

International Covenant on Civil and Political Rights. Adopted December 16, 1966. Entered into force March 23, 1976. United Nations General Assembly, Res. 2200 A (XXI).

Julien De Normandie (@J_Denormandie). "Arrêtons de mettre de l'idéologie dans l'assiette de nos enfants ! Donnons-leur simplement ce dont ils ont besoin pour bien grandir. La viande en fait partie. J'ai saisi le Préfet du Rhône." Quote Tweet, February 21, 2021. https://twitter.com/J_Denormandie/status/1363432191888416769.

Laffineur-Pauchet, Marie. "First Animal Code in France: A Response to a Dissonant Animal Law." *dA. Derecho Animal (Forum of Animal Law Studies)* 10, no. 2 (2019): 83–106. https://doi.org/10.5565/rev/da.359.

Laffineur-Pauchet, Marie. "New Food & Agricultural Law in France: Progress for Animals and Plant-Based Food?" *The Vegan's Society Research News*. Accessed March 14, 2021. https://

www.vegansociety.com/about-us/research/research-news/new-food-agricultural-law-france-progress-animals-and-plant-based-food.

Ligue des Droits de l'Homme. "L214, avec le soutien de la ligue des droits de l'homme, attaque la Cellule Demeter en justice." Accessed March 14, 2021. https://www.ldh-france.org/l214-avec-le-soutien-de-la-ligue-des-droits-de-lhomme-attaque-la-cellule-demeter-en-justice/.

Loi no. 2020-699 du 10 juin 2020 relative à la transparence de l'information sur les produits agricoles et alimentaires, *JORF* no. 0142 of June 11, 2020, text no. 1, NOR: AGRX1935395L.

Loi no. 2018-938 du 30 octobre 2018 pour l'équilibre des relations commerciales dans le secteur agricole et alimentaire et une alimentation saine, durable et accessible à tous, *JORF* no. 0253 of November 1, 2018, text no.1, NOR: AGRX1736303L.

Loi no. 76-629 du 10 juillet 1976 relative à la protection de la nature. Article 9. *JORF* of July 13, 1976. Rectified November 28, 1976.

L214 Ethique & Animaux. "L214 ÉTHIQUE & ANIMAUX : PRESENTATION." Accessed March 14, 2021. https://www.l214.com/L214-french-vegan-animal-protection-NGO.L214 Ethique & Animaux. "Foie gras. Le gavage interdit (presque) partout." Accessed March 14, 2021. https://www.l214.com/stop-foie-gras/le-gavage-interdit-a-travers-le-monde/.

L214 Ethique & Animaux. "Cellule Demeter: Stop à la répression des lanceurs d'alerte!" Accessed March 14, 2021. https://www.l214.com/lettres-infos/2020/07/31-recours-justice-cellule-demeter-ligue-droits-homme/.

Marguénaud, Jean-Pierre. "Les militants de l'association L 214 devant le tribunal correctionnel." *Revue Semestrielle de Droit Animalier—RSDA*, no. 1 (2017): 15–24. https://idedh.edu.umontpellier.fr/files/2017/12/RSDA_1_2017-1.pdf.

Marguénaud, Jean-Pierre. "Une révolution théorique: l'extraction masquée des animaux de la catégorie des biens," *Recueil Dalloz*, *JCP G*, no. 305 (2015): 495–501. https://hal.archives-ouvertes.fr/hal-01872337.

Marguénaud, Jean-Pierre, and Leroy, Jacques (dir.) and e. *Code de l'animal*. Paris: LexisNexis, 1st ed., 2018.

Ministère de l'agriculture et de l'alimentation. "Les mesures de la loi EGalim concernant la restauration collective." Accessed March 14, 2021. https://agriculture.gouv.fr/les-mesures-de-la-loi-egalim-concernant-la-restauration-collective.

Ministère de la culture. "La législation sur le patrimoine culturel immatériel en France." Accessed March 14, 2021. https://www.culture.gouv.fr/Sites-thematiques/Patrimoine-culturel-immateriel/Politique-du-PCI/La-legislation-sur-le-PCI-dans-le-monde/La-legislation-sur-le-patrimoine-culturel-immateriel-en-France#NORMES.

Ministère de l'économie, des finances et de la relance, Direction générale de la concurrence, de la consommation et de la répression des fraudes (DGCCRF). "Programme national d'enquêtes 2020." Accessed March 14, 2021. https://www.economie.gouv.fr/files/files/directions_services/dgccrf/dgccrf/pne/2020/pne-2020.pdf.

Ministère de l'économie, des finances et de la relance, Direction générale de la concurrence, de la consommation et de la répression des fraudes (DGCCRF). "Résultats 2018 de la DGCCRF." Accessed March 14, 2021. https://www.economie.gouv.fr/files/files/directions_services/dgccrf/dgccrf/rapports_activite/2018/resultats-dgccrf-2018.pdf.

Ministère de l'économie, des finances et de la relance, Direction générale de la concurrence, de la consommation et de la répression des fraudes (DGCCRF). "Rapport annuel 2018 du plan national de contrôles officiels pluriannuels (PNCOPA) 2016-2020." Accessed March 14, 2021. https://www.economie.gouv.fr/files/files/directions_services/dgccrf/securite/produits_alimentaires/rapport-annuel_2018.pdf.

Ministère de l'intérieur. "Présentation de DEMETER, la cellule nationale de suivi des atteintes au monde agricole." Accessed March 14, 2021. https://www.interieur.gouv.fr/Archives/Archives-ministres-de-l-Interieur/Archives-Christophe-Castaner/Dossiers-de-presse/Presentation-de-DEMETER-la-cellule-nationale-de-suivi-des-atteintes-au-monde-agricole.

Référendum pour les animaux. Accessed March 14, 2021. https://referendumpourlesanimaux.fr/.

Regulation (EU) No. 1308/2013 of the European Parliament and of the Council of 17 December 2013 establishing a common organization of the markets in agricultural products. Consolidated version. *OJ L 347*, 20.12.2013, 671–854, ELI: http://data.europa.eu/eli/reg/2013/1308/oj.

Regulation (EU) No. 1169/2011 of the European Parliament and of the Council of 25 October 2011 on the provision of food information to consumers, amending Regulations (EC) No 1924/2006 and (EC) No 1925/2006 of the European Parliament and of the Council, and repealing Commission Directive 87/250/EEC, Council Directive 90/496/EEC, Commission Directive 1999/10/EC, Directive 2000/13/EC of the European Parliament and of the Council, Commission Directives 2002/67/EC and 2008/5/EC and Commission Regulation (EC) No 608/2004 *OJ L 304*, 22.11.2011, p. 18–63.

Regulation (EC) No. 853/2004 of the European Parliament and of the Council of 29 April 2004 laying down specific hygiene rules for food of animal origin. *OJ L 139*, 30.4.2004, 55–205.

Renan, Ernest. "What Is a Nation?." Translated by Ehan Rundell from: Renan,Ernest. "Qu'est-ce qu'une nation?" Conference delivered at the Sorbonne, March 11, 1882, Paris: Presses-Pocket, 1992, http://ucparis.fr/files/9313/6549/9943/What_is_a_Nation.pdf.

Reus, Estiva. "Sentience!" *Cahiers antispécistes*, no. 26, November, 2005, https://www.cahiers-antispecistes.org/sentience/.

Riot, Cédric. "Legal Personhood of Animals (I): The case for the legal personhood of companion animals," *dA. Derecho Animal (Forum of Animal Law Studies)* 9, no. 2 (2018): 56–60, https://doi.org/10.5565/rev/da.341.

Rowley, Jeanette. *Towards a Vegan Jurisprudence: The Need for a Reorientation of Human Rights*. London: Lexington, 2020.

Standing Committee of the European Convention for the protection of animals kept for farming purposes (T-AP). Recommendation concerning domestic geese (*anser anser f.domesticus, anser cygnoides f.domesticus*) and their crossbreds. Adopted June 22, 1999. Entered into force December 22, 1999.

The Vegan Society. "What rights do vegans have?" Accessed March 14, 2021. https://www.vegansociety.com/get-involved/international-rights-network/what-rights-do-vegans-have#european-law.

Treaty on the Functioning of the European Union. Consolidated version. *OJ C 326*, 26.10.2012, 47–390, ELI: http://data.europa.eu/eli/treaty/tfeu_2012/oj.

Tribunal Administratif de Lille. "Le Calais Vegan Festival aura bien lieu." Accessed March 14, 2021. http://lille.tribunal-administratif.fr/Actualites/Communiques/Le-Calais-Vegan-Festival-aura-bien-lieu.

Tribunal Administratif de Lille. "Ordonnance du 4 septembre 2018, *Association L214 et autres*, no. 1807923." Accessed March 14, 2021. http://lille.tribunal-administratif.fr/content/download/151875/1538369/version/2/file/1807923.pdf.

UNESCO. "Periodic reporting on the Convention for the Safeguarding of the Intangible Cultural Heritage." No. 00824/France, 2014.https://ich.unesco.org/en/state/france-FR?info=periodic-reporting&cp=FR&topic=fr-etat.

UNESCO. "Convention for the safeguarding of the intangible cultural heritage." Decision of the Intergovernmental Committee: 5.COM 6.14. Fifth session Nairobi, Kenya, November 15 to 19, 2010. https://ich.unesco.org/en/decisions/5.COM/6.14.

Universal Declaration of Human Rights. Adopted December 10, 1948. United Nations General Assembly, Res. 217 A. https://www.un.org/en/universal-declaration-human-rights/.

V-label. "Les steaks végétaux: une véritable saga." Accessed March 14, 2021. https://v-label.fr/2018/11/06/les-steaks-vegetaux-une-veritable-saga/.

Van Overstraeten, Benoit. "Le marché végétarien et végan a augmenté de 24% en 2018, selon une étude." Ed. Jean-Michel Bélot. *Capital*. January 8, 2019. https://www.capital.fr/economie-politique/le-marche-vegetarien-et-vegan-a-augmente-de-24-en-2018-selon-un-etude-1322408.

Yougov/L214. "Etude élevage et climat." Accessed March 14, 2021. https://visuels.l214.com/sites/www.l214.com/2015/12-communique-presse/Sondage-Youogov-viande-climat-nov2015.jpg.

Chapter Nine

Veganism as a Protected Belief under United Kingdom Human Rights and Equality Law

Matthew Overton

1. INTRODUCTION

In January 2020, an employment tribunal in England ruled that vegans have a 'protected characteristic' for the application of section 10 of the Equality Act 2010 (EA 2010). Section 10 of the EA 2010 looks to Article 9 of the European Convention on Human Rights (ECHR, the Convention)[1] to define the protected characteristic of religion or religious or philosophical belief. This chapter evaluates this element of human rights law which protects individuals' 'freedom of thought, conscience and religion' ('freedom of conscience'). It examines the legal test and identifies various non-religious beliefs currently deemed to be within the scope of legal protection in the United Kingdom (UK) and Great Britain (GB).

The Equality Act 2010 applies in Great Britain only, while the UK Human Rights Act 1998 gives access to the rights contained in the ECHR in the UK as a whole. European Court of Human Rights jurisprudence is relevant to both Great Britain and Northern Ireland, but it is important to note that Northern Ireland has devolved power to develop and implement its own equality law. In doing so, it aims to align with Great Britain, which is important with regard to the protection of vegans. While Northern Ireland is not obliged to under the Equality Act 2010, it does have similar provisions that can be invoked to protect vegans.[2]

The chapter's scope is limited to assessing protection for 'belief' in the UK and primarily examines the legal test used to decide cases under the Equality Act 2010. It cites the relevant case law of the European Court of

Human Rights (ECtHR) that developed under the Equality Act 2010 for comparison and critique.

The non-religious belief in veganism is used as a focused case study; a belief treated differently across various jurisdictions,[3] but one that is increasingly regarded to be fundamental to a more ethical system of justice. Section two examines the principles for protection in general, the legal test used to assess applicants' beliefs and explains the lack of clarity around what constitutes a qualifying 'belief' in law. Section three explains how veganism meets the legal test but also questions the security of current protection given the power of the judiciary to (re)interpret the scope of the applicable test. Section four looks at the principles of legal protection and their relevance to the manifestation of vegan convictions, with reference to practical situations in employment, medical care and parental rights. The chapter concludes that more clarity is needed about what constitutes a 'belief' in law and that sincerely held non-religious convictions must be given more weight in the UK for their effective protection. It confirms that in the current climate of confusion and insecurity around the protection of 'belief' the work of vegan rights advocates is critical to ensuring that those who wish to defend their right to live without exploiting other animals remain free to do so.

2. THE BOUNDARY OF BELIEF

Article 9(1) of the European Convention on Human Rights outlines the content of the right to freedom of thought, conscience, and religion. Article 9(2) explains the grounds for permissible interference (author's emphasis added):

> 1. Everyone has the right to freedom of thought, conscience and religion; this right includes freedom to change his religion *or belief* and freedom, either alone or in community with others and in public or private, to manifest his religion *or belief*, in worship, teaching, practice and observance.
>
> 2. Freedom to manifest one's religion *or beliefs* shall be subject only to such limitations as are prescribed by law and are necessary in a democratic society in the interests of public safety, for the protection of public order, health or morals, or for the protection of the rights and freedoms of others.[4]

While much focus has been directed towards the religious element of Article 9 at the ECtHR,[5] the non-religious element has, arguably, been given less consideration.[6] However, as Simler, J.[7] said in the case of *General Municipal and Boilermakers Union v Henderson*:

> The law does not accord special protection for one category of belief and less protection for another. All qualifying beliefs are equally protected. Philosophical beliefs may be just as fundamental or integral to a person's individuality and daily life as are religious beliefs.[8]

Indeed, on an international level, the non-religious counterpart is considered equal by the Special Rapporteur for this right[9] and by the Human Rights Committee; as indicated in General Comment 22.[10] While specific lists of what can be deemed legitimate beliefs have not been attempted, a general test, drawn in large part from the case law of the ECtHR has been created and subsequently refined in the case law of Great Britain, can been found in *Grainger v Nicholson.*[11]

The difficult task of defining the right to freedom of thought, conscience and religion was not attempted by the drafters of the European Convention on Human Rights but was left as a flexible notion which could evolve over time, determinable by the courts.[12] An example of evolution in action is the change from Scientology, effectively being considered *not* a religion by the House of Lords,[13] to the Supreme Court ruling recently that Scientology *is* a religion.[14] In this respect, the higher court took a more 'activist' and 'modern approach' to the question:[15] 'what amounts to a religious belief?' Notwithstanding, the question of Scientology's status as a religion is still contested under Strasbourg jurisprudence.[16]

In theory, this ought to have no effect on the individual's right, but as the application of the test in *Grainger* arguably demonstrates, if the individual's belief is more readily assignable to a religion, then the individual's right is more easily secured than if it is considered non-religious. This will become particularly evident in the case of beliefs straddling the political/philosophical borderline.

2.1. The Test in *Grainger:* What Amounts to a Belief?

In the years preceding *Grainger*, confusion arose regarding what amounted to 'philosophical' beliefs in Great Britain, due to the inclusion of the word 'similar' in equality legislation.[17] The domestic legislation was thought to include only philosophical beliefs which were 'similar' to religious beliefs, but to exclude political beliefs (for example, allegiances to political parties, as in the case of *Baggs*).[18] Consequently, 'nationalist beliefs'[19] and far right political beliefs[20] would not be protected. However, following the removal of the word 'similar' in 2006,[21] the courts could re-examine what amounted to a non-religious belief.

As the courts evaluated the law in *Grainger*, the test for non-religious 'philosophical' beliefs was summarized from the case law of the ECtHR and held to be that:

> 1. The belief must be genuinely held.
> 2. It must be a belief and not . . . an opinion or viewpoint based on the present state of information available.
> 3. It must be a belief as to a weighty and substantial aspect of human life and behaviour.

4. It must attain a certain level of cogency, seriousness, cohesion, and importance.
5. It must be worthy of respect in a democratic society, be not incompatible with human dignity and not conflict with the fundamental rights of others.[22]

Under this elastic test, a belief in question 'does not need to constitute . . . a fully-fledged system of thought.'[23] While the test has been praised for offering clarity,[24] this summary of the Strasbourg jurisprudence has conversely been criticized as 'suspect'; Sandberg, for example, notes that the scope of protection remains unclear,[25] the approach of the court being to 'consider all claims, determining their success on their merits.'[26] Case law at the ECtHR has complicated the picture and there exists no 'watertight definition of belief' the only line drawn is that the belief must not be a reflection of mere 'opinions.'[27]

The test is said to be applied arbitrarily both expansively and restrictively,[28] and led to the protection of a wide range of non-religious beliefs including: pacifism;[29] atheism;[30] environmentalism;[31] Spiritualism;[32] beliefs around the immorality of fox hunting,[33] and, among others,[34] beliefs in the virtue of public service broadcasting.[35] Some examples of insufficient 'beliefs' include: beliefs in conspiracy theories regarding 9/11;[36] a belief that Poppies should be worn prior to Remembrance Sunday;[37] and beliefs that one must always be polite and truthful.[38] In the latter decision, the tribunal held that beliefs should not be confused with an individual's 'personal conscience,' stating, 'ethical beliefs were not the same as religious or philosophical beliefs.'[39] An arguably controversial ECtHR case was *Pretty v UK*, which implicitly decided that a belief in the virtue of assisted suicide was insufficient for Article 9 protection.[40]

A series of cases confused the stance on the status of non-religious political beliefs. *Maistry v BBC* implied that even political beliefs may be protectable,[41] which placed doubt on the validity of a prior employment tribunal case (*Kelly v Unison*) which argued the opposite.[42] *Kelly* went on appeal[43] and the beliefs in question (Marxism/Trotskyism) were considered not to be 'philosophical' beliefs. Instead of following the previous *Baggs* case which simply excluded political beliefs from protection,[44] the court in *Kelly* distinguished between 'political beliefs which involve . . . the creation of a legally binding structure by power or government regulating others,' which are not protected, and political beliefs which 'are expressed by his own practice but where he has no ambition to impose his scheme on others,' which may be protected.'[45] Commentators observed the Claimants' 'objectionable,'[46] 'extreme'[47] views 'conflicted with the fundamental rights of others and the dignity of the individual and, as such, are not worthy of respect in a democratic society';[48] particularly considering the 'revolution' element of the beliefs, which operated 'outside of a structured democratic process.'[49] This is further complicated by the fact the European Commission has suggested that communist beliefs came under Article 9's scope[50] as a political ideology.[51] Conversely, in *Redfearn v UK*,[52] after a BNP member alleged he was discriminatorily dismissed 'due to BNP's overt and racist/fascist agenda,'[53] the ECtHR found his Article 9 claims to be 'manifestly ill-founded'; making it 'unclear whether political beliefs were protected under the Equality Act 2010.'[54]

The *Henderson* case,[55] heard in an English Employment tribunal, arguably even 'further mudd[ies] [an] already . . . messy area . . .'[56] The beliefs contested were Marxism and 'left wing democratic socialism.'[57] Following an arguably unsubstantial application of the *Grainger* belief test to the facts,[58] the tribunal 'accepted that beliefs in a political philosophy can be protected even where they are aligned to membership of a political party.'[59] Full discussion of this judgment's validity, and the relevance of *Kelly*, was not given attention on appeal as the respondents conceded the belief point. Thus, 'decisions in discrimination law cases may hinge upon whether or not it is conceded that a claimant has a belief'—a 'clearly unsatisfactory'[60] development with 'the reason for change' unclear.[61]

Thus, the law relating to freedom of thought, conscience and belief became ambiguous regarding whether political beliefs will be protected, leading Sandberg to observe, in relation to equality law in Great Britain:

> It is unclear whether an employer is required to provide equal treatment to requests made to change working hours from employees who are Evangelical Christians, humanists, Marxists, members of the Green party, and those who believe in the value of a lie-in.[62]

He suggests instead, including political beliefs under Article 10 or 11 (rights to freedom of expression and assembly respectively) 'making it clear that they are protected in their own right rather than by stretching the right to religious freedom to provide a misleading and ultimately unsatisfactory impression that political beliefs are religious now.'[63]

These circumstances are clearly worrisome for those seeking protection of their non-religious beliefs, at a time when:

> legal uncertainty makes it all the more desirable . . . for national authorities competent in their respective areas to be as consistent as possible in granting recognition to legitimate religious [and non-religious belief] claims, without thereby privileging some over others, and to admit an interpretation of equal treatment that is not opposed to diversity but rather is one of its constituent parts.[64]

The courts of Great Britain are not solely culpable for uncertainties surrounding belief protection: Evans[65] has criticized the ECtHR's approach in this area for its lack of consistency.[66] He argues that the court refuses to meaningfully engage with analysis of a belief's worthiness of Article 9 protection, stating that the court instead sometimes hides 'behind a façade of inclusivity and non-evaluation.'[67] He sympathizes with the court, 'since denying a belief . . . protection . . . is tantamount to saying . . . it is not "cogent, serious, cohesive or important"'—however, 'there is also a danger that by not doing so it encourages frivolous claims, or extends a mantle of legitimacy over views which are potentially problematic.'

Having examined the law surrounding the complicated and confused protection of non-religious beliefs, this chapter now turns to examine protection for the non-religious belief of veganism.

3. VEGANISM: A CASE STUDY

3.1 The Belief Itself

The Vegan Society definition of veganism, used widely and by international vegan organizations,[68] is as follows:

> A philosophy and way of living which seeks to exclude—as far as is possible and practicable—all forms of exploitation of, and cruelty to, animals for food, clothing or any other purpose; and by extension, promotes the development and use of animal-free alternatives for the benefit of humans, animals and the environment. In dietary terms it denotes the practice of dispensing with all products derived wholly or partly from animals.[69]

Largely associated with abstaining from eating animal products, veganism extends to choices made in other areas of a vegan's life. For example, decisions about clothing, medicine and what entertainment is acceptable. While the primary driver behind veganism is arguably a stance against the harm caused to other sentient beings,[70] another motivator for vegans includes the damaging effects society's use of animals has on the environment via animal agriculture.[71] In addition, some vegans note the positive effect of a vegan or 100% 'plant-based' diet on human health.[72]

3.2. Why Examine Veganism?

The vegan philosophy exemplifies deep convictions concerning the universality of suffering, opposing established dominant majority beliefs and cultural practices. Vegan convictions regarding animal products have previously been considered and accepted as within the scope of Article 9 of the ECHR,[73] and is reportedly labelled as one of the 'fastest growing lifestyle movements' in the UK.[74] Stylized by some as a 'social justice movement,'[75] the number of vegans increased 360% between 2006-2016; reaching an estimated 542,000 vegans in Great Britain.[76] While clearly a minority belief, there is an increasing amount of studies surrounding veganism in recent years.[77] In a study conducted by Mehl,[78] the strength of a growing 'vegan identity' was examined, in a paper which 'investigates the ways . . . vegans negotiate their identities as members of a movement that challenges the normative meanings associated with food and animals in the context of a society that does not hold those same meanings.'[79] Mehl's study demonstrates the risk posed to such minority beliefs in a society holding opposing majority beliefs, consequently necessitating legal protection of these non-religious beliefs in at least a strong a fashion as religious beliefs.

MacInnis and Hodson recently 'empirically tested whether bias exists toward vegetarians and vegans.'[80] Their results demonstrate a particularly negative evaluation of vegans (especially males) overall. Their work 'empirically confirms vegetarians and vegans as targets of bias. Unlike other forms of bias (e.g., racism, sexism), negativity toward vegetarians and vegans is not widely considered a societal problem; rather, negativity toward vegetarians and vegans is commonplace and largely accepted.' This study adds to a 'growing literature finding bias toward benign yet social norm-challenging others,' perhaps unsurprising after uncovering that '73.4% of references to vegans in the UK news media in 2007 were negative.'[81]

In doing less harm in the domains of animals and the environment, 'vegans are perceived as doing harm in another: they undermine the integrity of prevailing social values and traditions that exploit animals.'[82]

This study and other examples in the news[83] 'illustrate how a small segment of society that holds sincere beliefs regarding the ethical and equal treatment for all creatures is often sorely mistreated because of those very beliefs.'[84] While discrimination against vegans may not be considered 'earth-shattering news,' and at times 'trivial,'[85] Soifer notes: 'there is value, however, in exploring the capacity of our legal system to marginalize, or protect, those who do not hold orthodox, mainstream beliefs.'[86]

3.3. Veganism and the security of the 'Belief' Test?

In *R (Williamson) v Secretary of State*[87]—referenced in *Grainger*[88]—vegetarianism was regarded (obiter) as an example of a belief that uncontroversially meets the test for what qualifies as a belief in law. In a recent English employment tribunal case (discussed below)[89] it was held that vegetarianism did not meet the 'belief' test and did not, therefore, qualify for protection in law.

Although deemed within the scope of the human right to freedom of conscience in a European Commission case in 1993, and recently confirmed to be protected under the equality law of Great Britain, judges in future may decide that there is a need to review and verify the current legal status of veganism.[90] Firstly, in view of the confusion discussed above surrounding the political/philosophical belief borderline, clearly the threshold for achieving 'belief' status has evolved in Great Britain. This has engendered ambiguity, and protection for beliefs perhaps, ought not to be taken for granted: communism too was previously arguably accepted under Article 9.[91] Furthermore, following *Redfearn* and *Kelly*, the status of political beliefs/philosophies is ambiguously seated.

Secondly, it may be noted that—as in *Henderson*—in *H v UK* (in which veganism was deemed protected) the UK government had not contested, and therefore, arguably, already conceded that veganism was a 'belief' within the meaning of Article 9 of the ECHR.[92] Consequently, the members of the European Commission did not spend time evaluating the belief status of veganism prior to giving their judgment.[93] As such, as discussed above, while the courts saw it fit to re-evaluate the appropriateness of the protection of Marxist/communist ideologies,[94] regardless of their previously decided status, then a re-evaluation of veganism could, in theory, take place in future discrimination cases, especially given that the 2020 tribunal ruling that veganism meets the test for protection is not binding.

Thirdly, a re-evaluation could be deemed necessary, as veganism is arguably moving from being a philosophical belief to becoming a political issue. Some vegans consider themselves to be 'abolitionists,' referencing opposition to the 18–19th century slave-trade, or 'animal liberationists'—both opposed to the commodification of sentient beings for unnecessary purposes.[95] More recent developments add credence to the politicization of veganism, such as the backlash surrounding the removal of a clause declaring animal sentience in law;[96] consistently high public opposition to fox hunting where its illegality was considered contestable in Parliament by a recent prime minister;[97] and an increasing number of vegetarian and vegan politicians.[98] Regarding the latter, across Europe vegan and animal protection political parties are emerging, with parliamentary seats gained in Portugal and the Netherlands.[99]

3.4. Veganism Assessed

As indicated above, to qualify for protection under the ECHR and under *Grainger*, vegans must show that their convictions meet the threshold of possessing a 'certain level of cogency, seriousness, cohesion and importance.'[100] Arguably veganism is cogent, in that it is clear and logical—refraining from the use of animal products where 'practicable and possible' is an argument based on the fundamental economic principle of supply and demand.[101] In seeking an end to animal exploitation, vegans hope to remove the demand for products which are the result of said exploitation, in the hope the supply would then decrease over time to such a level for the practice to diminish. The belief fundamentally concerns itself with the relationship between humans and non-human animals.

The belief's seriousness concerns a view by vegans that the harm caused to animals (largely through regular, legal practices in the animal agricultural industry) in the UK and internationally is of such a gross level that it is immoral.[102] Vegans argue that farms bearing welfare assurances have been shown to nonetheless sanction great harm to farm animals.[103] Additionally, notwithstanding purportedly 'higher' welfare conditions, vegans object to unnecessary killing of animals, if it is possible to be healthy without.[104] Additionally, a vegan motivated by environmental concerns considers it worse for the environment to have the same quantities of animals eaten today kept in a 'free-range' environment, due to level of resources required for this.[105]

Viewing the extensive literature available on the vegan philosophy, some of which is summarized on The Vegan Society website, the belief arguably possesses a certain level of cohesion.[106] The vegan philosophy's importance, or at least its espoused practices, is observable worldwide in politics and law; particularly in the UK and the European Union (EU).[107] Damaging the environment pertaining to wildlife is regulated in the European Union and internationally,[108] and animal welfare is of sufficient importance to receive a UK national animal welfare act.[109]

In Great Britain, part (i) of the test in *Grainger*, that the view is 'genuinely held,' does not pertain to the validity of veganism itself. Part (ii), that it 'must be a belief and not . . . an opinion or viewpoint based on the present state of information available' is a somewhat ambiguous requirement. However, 'if a person can establish . . . he holds a philosophical belief which is based on science, as opposed . . . to religion, then there is no reason to disqualify it from protection.'[110] Thus, even though the belief is centered around scientific consensus of animals' ability to feel pain and other emotions, according to *Grainger* this ought not defeat its belief status. More widely, arguably, veganism is a belief in the recognition of universal suffering of both human and non-human animals, incorporating emancipatory justice for all animals.[111]

The relevance of the belief to everyday life[112] and the deeply held moral aspect of the belief arguably meets the test in part (iii), which states 'It must be a belief as to a weighty and substantial aspect of human life and behavior.' Observable practices of vegans demonstrate the belief is 'life-directing' with their beliefs surrounding the inclusion of animals in considerations of universal suffering affecting decisions on a plethora of life's activities.[113] Covered above is (iv), that the belief 'must attain a certain level of cogency, seriousness, cohesion and importance,' in its relation to its aim for an emancipation from suffering and regarding climate change, and arguably veganism meets (v) uncontroversially.

This discussion is interesting when considering the recent English employment tribunal case, *Conisbee v Crossley Farms Ltd* (2019),[114] in which the tribunal determined that vegetarianism would not be a sufficient belief to meet the test under the Equality Act 2010, arguably concluding it lacked a sufficient level of cogency and cohesion. The tribunal took issue with the reasoning behind vegetarianism being inconsistent among vegetarians, directly comparing it to veganism which they acknowledge largely comes from the same source and principles, as discussed above:

> The reason for being a vegetarian differs greatly among themselves, unlike veganism where the reasons for being a vegan appear to be largely the same. Vegetarians adopt the practice for many different reasons; lifestyle, health, diet, concern about the way animals are reared for food and personal taste. Vegans simply do not accept the practice under any circumstances of eating meat, fish or dairy products, and have distinct concerns about the way animals are reared, the clear belief that killing and eating animals is contrary to a civilised society and also against climate control. There you can see a clear cogency and cohesion in vegan belief, which appears contrary to vegetarianism, i.e., having numerous, differing and wide varying reasons for adopting vegetarianism.[115]

This assessment illustrates the evolution and importance of legal thinking with regard to potentially offering protection to those who wish to manifest their deep convictions concerning animal welfare. Evidence for the prior dismissal of the importance of such convictions is arguably observable in the ECtHR case of *Herrmann v Germany*.[116] In this case the court refused to consider Herrmann's Article 9 right to freedom of conscience claim,[117] but instead ruled in favor of the applicant under Article 1 of Protocol No.1 (property rights). This resulted in an arguably unsubstantial evaluation of the legitimacy of the applicant's 'belief' by the majority, harking back to Evan's criticism—addressed previously—concerning reluctance of the ECtHR to meaningfully engage in evaluation of a belief to avoid affirming or denying its status as 'cogent, serious, cohesive or important.'[118] To those who hold veganism as a core life-directing belief, it essential that a pattern such as this—of relegating the protection of non-religious beliefs such as veganism, thus threatening their protected status—does not take place.

The debate surrounding the protection of veganism in equality law has recently had a certain amount of attention in Great Britain, in the employment tribunal case of *Casamitjana v The League Against Cruel Sports* (2020).[119] This case involved a claimant who alleged they were dismissed as a result of their vegan beliefs. In brief, the claimant objected to policies whereby the respondent invested portions of its pension funds into companies undertaking animal testing. The claimant was subsequently dismissed. The claimant alleged this was as a result of their vegan belief. In a preliminary hearing, after examining the belief in the context of equality law of Great Britain, the tribunal concluded that there was 'overwhelming evidence . . . that ethical veganism is capable of being a philosophical belief and thus a protected characteristic.' While the employment tribunal's decision does not bind the higher courts, and such an interpretation may be reconsidered in future decisions, there is clearly now increasing legal support for the protection of veganism under the equality law of Great Britain.

4. PRACTICAL EXAMPLES OF VEGANISM'S INTERACTION WITH THE LAW

H v UK[120] and other cases[121] demonstrate that while a belief may qualify for Article 9 protection, not all actions flowing from the belief will be equally protected; the right is primarily limited to private actions and may restrict public expression of beliefs.[122] Consequently, the ECHR does not permit a refusal to abide by legislation, applying neutrally and generally in relation to the freedom of conscience in the public sphere.[123] When facing an opposing majority culture, this may raise issues for minority non-religious beliefs such as veganism, particularly when considering legitimate aim and proportionality assessments relating to the accommodation of vegans. A proportionality assessment can render interference with the Article 9 right justified if the interference is pursuant and rationally connected to a legitimate aim (listed in Article 9(2) above) and utilizes the least intrusive means possible to achieve said aim.[124] This leads to discussion of how vegan beliefs would be protected in concrete examples, which at times displays the difficulty in identifying '*exactly* which practices resulting from a belief are entitled to Article 9 ECHR's guarantee and which are not.'[125]

What follows will be a brief outline of how veganism may interact or has interacted with the law in different contexts.

4.1. Veganism in Employment Law

Vickers notes 'two major reasons' why an individual's beliefs should be protected in the workplace.[126] Firstly, she argues that if freedom of belief is to be 'given practical protection, it must be operable in common areas of daily life, including professional life'; otherwise we risk relegating the right to the 'private sphere.'[127] Secondly, she argues that some (often minority groups) will be less able to access 'the financial and other benefits of work' if their beliefs have rules or practices which can 'interfere with . . . usual rules of the workplace.'[128]

In navigating a society not sharing the vegan belief, vegan employees may find their Article 9 right limited when required to perform acts contravening their beliefs. Examples may include being required to use products tested on animals[129] or mandatory animal skins uniforms.[130] Equally, they may face discrimination *because* of their beliefs. For example, in the UK, the NHS explicitly excluded vegans from applying for a job because the vegan diet was conflated with 'restrictive diets.'[131] In Switzerland, 'a soldier was not allowed to join the army' as his veganism was an 'unsuitable ethical orientation.'[132] In *Hashman*,[133] a vegan employee was dismissed due to anti-fox-hunting beliefs. His beliefs were deemed within Article 9's scope,[134] however, and he was successful in his unfair dismissal claim.[135] As noted above, the English employment tribunal case of *Casamitjana* clearly demonstrates an instance whereby a vegan employee could be dismissed directly as a result of their vegan beliefs.

4.2. Veganism in Medical Law

In one medical law report, providing a vegan diet for those in one's care was arguably conflated with abuse.[136] This conclusion is refuted by reputable health organizations.[137] Additionally, a lack of respect and understanding for the non-religious vegan philosophy may arguably be a concern for elderly vegans, for whom guidance surrounding the Power of Attorney procedure has been provided by advocacy groups.[138]

An additional medical law issue relating to veganism arises in the instance of animal-derived vaccinations.[139] For example, in cases involving immunization of children, the courts of Great Britain have ordered such vaccinations to be administered against vegan parents' wishes.[140] Regarding respecting vegan practices, a reassuring Clinical Ethics Committee report is observable in relation to the pig-derived medicine heparin.[141] The Committee considered whether it was important to inform patients if their medicine contained animal products—they concluded: 'our view is that we . . . have a moral obligation to disclose the derivation of heparin . . . to all patients to allow them to come to [an] . . . informed choice.'[142] The Committee struggled, however, when asked if they would then recommend the purchase of non-animal-derived synthetic alternatives for those with beliefs objecting to animal-derived medicine.[143] A principle concerned was that if alternatives were more expensive, budgetary limitations may factor in.

4.3. Parental Rights and Veganism

Finally, 'parental rights,' engaging Article 2 of Protocol No.1 (ECHR), encompass a right for parents to raise their children according to their religious/philosophical beliefs, often entering the realm of education.[144] This right may affect both vegan teachers and vegan parents. An ECtHR case relevant to the former may include *Dahlab v Switzerland*,[145] where a primary school teacher who had recently converted to Islam was required to remove her headscarf when teaching. It was decided the headscarf was a 'powerful external symbol' liable to 'influence' young children. This thinking could extend to a similarly placed vegan teacher who wished to wear symbols/clothing representative of the vegan philosophy, or who held discussions with children on the topic of animal rights. Following *Dahlab*, these actions may be justifiably limited in the eyes of the ECtHR.

Alternatively, an arguably restrictive approach was given to parental rights as it concerned freedom of belief in the ECtHR cases of *Valsamis*[146] and *Efstratiou v. Greece.*[147] Due to their pacifist philosophy (springing from the parents' Jehovah's Witness religion), two children were disciplined for not attending a school parade commemorating the anniversary of a war.[148] The ECtHR ruled that 'the parade could [not] have offended either girls' pacifist convictions, and that such commemorations . . . served . . . both pacifist objectives and the public interest.'[149] Arguably the ECtHR imposed its interpretation of a pacifist's opinion over the holder of the belief themselves—'interpreting' the belief which consequently removed any interference. Debatably, as pacifists themselves, the applicants would be better suited to determine what offended their philosophy. Thus, debatably, due to confusion over what constitutes veganism's particularities by some, as observed above, a court considering Article 9 of the ECHR may utilise their own view of what would contravene the philosophy of a vegan child, potentially overruling vegans' parental rights.[150]

5. CONCLUSION

To conclude, the aim of this chapter was to examine the test for categorizing which non-religious beliefs may attain protection under the Equality Act 2010, as related to the jurisprudence of the ECtHR, and examine the strength of this right in practice.

United Kingdom law is currently ambiguous and uncertain concerning the boundary between 'philosophical' and 'political' beliefs and whether protection ought to be granted to both. This could become relevant in cases concerning vegans. While attempting to add clarity in the equality law of Great Britain, the *Grainger* test has been confused by cases raising the political/philosophical distinction[151]—arguably further complicated by the ECtHR's reluctance to engage in substantial evaluation of individual beliefs' worthiness of protection.[152] The existence of this confusion surrounding non-religious beliefs serves to leave those wishing to vindicate their rights uncertain, a concern not faced by religious believers.

At an institutional level, there is arguably a certain level of relegation of non-religious beliefs from consideration. Regarding veganism, advocacy organizations have amassed multiple reports of discrimination against vegans,[153] with Rowley observing, 'it is fairly common to see a religious need being met more readily than those . . . who have non-religious beliefs.'[154] It is due to this dismissal of non-religious beliefs, in comparison to religious beliefs, that there has arisen a need for advocacy groups to articulate vegan convictions in light of the principles for protection under the right to freedom of conscience, challenge objections and advocate for compliance with the legal principles of equality law, ameliorating the lack of attention given to them institutionally.

While previously deemed within the scope of Article 9, and reaffirmed in a recent English employment tribunal case, upon assessment veganism clearly meets the *Grainger* test. As such, vegans have the right to be treated equally in various social and employment contexts and manifest their convictions free from interference, but in an absence of institutional support, vegan lawyers have felt the need to propose specific legal changes to better accommodate vegans in daily life.[155] This is, arguably, a manifestation of the legal uncertainty around protection for non-religious belief under the right to freedom of thought, conscience and religion and an indication of the struggle those with life-directing non-religious convictions face.

These circumstances highlight that the primacy given to the equality of protection for belief in international human rights documents[156] contrasts the inadequate protection afforded to non-religious beliefs due to their confused categorization. Freedom to express one's belief serves an integral part of many people's lives and 'without respect for . . . freedom in the area of religious or philosophical convictions the concept of human rights would remain a torso.'[157] As such, sincerely held non-religious convictions must be given more weight for their effective protection under human rights law. However, it is, for now, seemingly more promising for the protection of the non-religious philosophical belief of veganism under equality law of Great Britain, in large part due to the support of vegan advocacy groups ensuring that those who are discriminated against are aware of their rights to manifest their vegan beliefs.

6. NOTES

1. Formally the Convention for the Protection of Human Rights and Fundamental Freedoms (European Convention on Human Rights, as amended) (ECHR).
2. See Equality Commission for Northern Ireland: https://www.equalityni.org/Individuals/I-have-a-work-related-problem/Religious-belief-Political-opinion.
3. Sarah Soifer, "Vegan Discrimination: An emerging and difficult dilemma." *Loyola of LA Law Review* 36 (2003): 1709; Nina Palmstorfer, "Austrian Constitutional Court: Vegan Landowner Must Tolerate Hunting on His Property." *Vienna Journal on International Consti-*

tutional Law 11(1) (2017): 129; Marcus, E., C. Wasserstein Fassberg, J. Namestnik, D. Guedj, Y. Caine, "Strict Vegan, Low-Calorie Diet Administered by Care-Giving Daughter to Elderly Mother—Is This Elder Abuse?" *Med. & L.* 24 (2005): 279–96; Melanie Cole, "Is It Really Vegan or Vegetarian? A Comparative Analysis of the Regulatory Frameworks for Food." *Australian Animal Protection Law Journal* 9 (2013): 44–71; David Rosengard, "Three Hots and a Cot and a lot of talk: Discussing Federal Rights-based Avenues for prisoner access to vegan meals." *Animal Law* 23 (2017): 355–404; Donna Page, "Veganism and Sincerely Held Religious Beliefs in the Workplace: No Protection without Definition." *U. Pa. J. Lab. & Emp. L.* 7 (2005): 363–408; Anita Krajnc, "Bearing Witness: Is Giving Thirsty Pigs Water Criminal Mischief or a Duty." *Animal L.* 23 (2017): 479–98.

4. ECHR, Article 9 (author's emphasis added); domestically in the United Kingdom: the Human Rights Act 1998, Article 9.

5. *Eweida v United Kingdom* [2013] ECHR 37; *Lautsi v Italy* [2011] ECHR 2412; *Sahin v Turkey* [2006] E.L.R. 73; *SAS v France* [2014] ECHR 695; *Osmanoğlu and Kocabaş v. Switzerland* [2017] ECHR 14.

6. Jim Murdoch, "Freedom of thought, conscience and religion—A guide to the implementation of Article 9 of the European Convention on Human Rights." *Human rights handbooks*, No. 9, accessed August 16, 2020, https://rm.coe.int/168007ff4f; hardly any attention in the preparatory notes for Article 9 was paid to the non-religious element of the right: European Commission for Human Rights (1956), 'European Commission of Human Rights Preparatory Work on Article 9 of the European Convention on Human Rights'; Jeanette Rowley, 'Vegan Rights: Questions and Answers,' accessed August 16, 2020, https://web.archive.org/web/20170321074323/http://www.theivra.com/Documents/Vegan%20Rights.pdf.

7. The present UK Employment Appeals Tribunal President—Unknown. "Mrs Justice Simler," accessed August 16, 2020, https://www.judiciary.gov.uk/publications/mrs-justice-simler/.

8. *General Municipal and Boilermakers Union v Henderson* [2015] UKEAT/0073/14/DM (13 March 2015), [62].

9. Heiner Bielefeldt, "Protecting and Implementing the Right to Freedom of Religion or Belief: Interview with Heiner Bielefeldt." *Journal of Human Rights Practice* 3:3 (2011) 229, https://doi.org/10.1093/jhuman/hur021; Heiner Bielefeldt, "Misperceptions of Freedom of Religion or Belief." *Human Rights Quarterly* 35(1) (2013): 33–68.

10. UN Human Rights Committee (HRC), "CCPR General Comment No. 22: Article 18 (Freedom of Thought, Conscience or Religion)," 30 July 1993, CCPR/C/21/Rev.1/Add.4, accessed August 16, 2020, http://www.refworld.org/docid/453883fb22.html.

11. [2010] IRLR 4 (EAT).

12. Council of Europe, "Guide to Article 9," accessed August 16, 2020, https://www.echr.coe.int/Documents/Guide_Art_9_ENG.pdf.

13. *R v Registrar General, ex parte Segerdal* [1970] 2 QB 697.

14. *R (Hodkin) v Registrar General of Births, Deaths and Marriages* [2013] UKSC 77; Brice Dickson, "Activism and Restraint within the UK Supreme Court." *European Journal of Current Legal Issues* 21(1) (2015): 3.

15. *Ibid* Dickson, 3.

16. *Supra* Council of Europe, "Guide to Article 9," (2015), 8; Malcolm Evans, "The Freedom of Religion or Belief in the ECHR since Kokkinakis. Or 'Quoting Kokkinakis'." *Religion & Human Rights* 12(2-3) (2017) 89-90.

17. Employment Equality (Religion or Belief) Regulations 2003, Reg 2(1); Russell Sandberg, "Are political beliefs religious now?" *Law & Just.—Christian L. Rev.* 175 (2015): 180; Laura Ford and Mark Levine, "Do you believe in fairies?" *Employment Law Journal* 121 (2011): 4.

18. *Ibid* Sandberg, "Are political beliefs religious now?" (2015); *Baggs v Fudge* [2005] ET 1400114/2005 (23 March 2005); Ruth Buchanan, "Protecting philosophical beliefs—has the law gone too far?" *T.E.L.L.* 16:12 (2011): 93.

19. *Williams v South Central Limited* [2004] ET 2306989/2003 (16 June 2004); *Finnon v Asda Stores Ltd* ET/2402142/05.

20. *Baggs v Fudge* [2005] ET 1400114/2005 (23 March 2005).

21. Nicholas Fry and Shah Qureshi, "Protecting philosophical beliefs." *E.L.A. Briefing* 17(2) (2010): 4; Equality Act 2006.
22. [2009] UKEAT 0219/09/ZT (3 November 2009), [24].
23. *Supra* Sandberg, "Are political beliefs religious now?" (2015), 183; *ibid,* [28].
24. *Supra* Fry and Qureshi, "Protecting philosophical beliefs," (2010), 5.
25. *Campbell and Cosans v United Kingdom* (1982) 4 EHRR 29; *Supra* Sandberg, "Are political beliefs religious now?," (2015), 182-183.
26. *Ibid* Sandberg.
27. *Ibid* Sandberg.
28. *Supra* Sandberg, "Are political beliefs religious now?," (2015), 184.
29. *Arrowsmith v UK* (1978) 3 EHRR 218, 7050/75.
30. *Kokkinakis v Greece* [1993] 17 EHRR 397.
31. *Grainger v Nicholson plc* [2009] UKEAT 0219/09/ZT (3 November 2009).
32. *Greater Manchester Police Authority v Power* [2009] EAT 0434/09/DA (12 November 2009).
33. *Hashman v Milton Park (Dorset) Ltd* [2011] ET 3105555/2009 (31 January 2011).
34. Humanist beliefs: *Streatfield v London Philharmonic Orchestra Ltd* [2012] 2390772/2011 (22 May 2012).
35. *Maistry v The BBC* [2011] ET1213142/2010 (14 February 2011).
36. *Farrell v South Yorkshire Police Authority* [2011] ET 2803805/2010 (24 May 2011).
37. *Lisk v Shield Guardian Co Lid & Others* [2011] ET 3300873/2011 (14 September 2011).
38. *Moore v Hartlepool Borough Council* (EOR 199); Sandra Wallace, "Religion or belief: the limits of 'philosophical belief'." *E.O.R.* 211 (April 2011): 20; *Devine v Home Office (Immigration and Nationality Directorate)* ET/2302061/04.
39. *Ibid* Wallace, "Religion or belief," (2011).
40. *Pretty v United Kingdom* (2002) 35 E.H.R.R. 1, [82].
41. *Maistry v The BBC* [2011] ET1213142/2010 (14 February 2011), [19]; *supra* Ford and Levine, "Do you believe in fairies?," (2011), 5.
42. *Ibid Maistry v The BBC*, [19].
43. [2009] ET 2203854/08 (22 December 2009).
44. *Baggs v Fudge* [2005] ET 1400114/2005 (23 March 2005).
45. [2009] ET 2203854/08 (22 December 2009), para114; *supra* Sandberg, "Are political beliefs religious now?," (2015), 185.
46. *Kelly v Unison* [2009] ET 2203854/08 (22 December 2009), [102].
47. *Supra* Buchanan, "Protecting philosophical beliefs," (2011), 93.
48. *Supra* Wallace, "Religion or belief," (2011), 20.
49. *Supra* Buchanan, "Protecting philosophical beliefs," (2011), 93.
50. ECmHR, 11 Oct. 1991, *Hazar and Others v. Turkey*, DR 72/200, Application Nos. 16311/90, 16312/90 and 16313/90; Jean-François Renucci, "Introduction to the European Convention on Human Rights," accessed August 16, 2020, http://echr.coe.int/Documents/Pub_coe_HFfiles_2005_01_ENG.pdf.
51. *Supra* Murdoch, "Freedom of thought, conscience and religion," (2007), 12.
52. [2013] IRLR 51, [60].
53. *Supra* Sandberg, "Are political beliefs religious now?," (2015), 186.
54. *Ibid*, 187.
55. *General Municipal and Boilermakers Union v Henderson* [2013] ET 33016908/2012 (30 September 2013).
56. *Supra* Sandberg, "Are political beliefs religious now?," (2015), 193.
57. *Ibid,* 192; *General Municipal and Boilermakers Union v Henderson* [2013] ET 33016908/2012 (30 September 2013), [48].
58. *General Municipal and Boilermakers Union v Henderson* [2013] ET 33016908/2012 (30 September 2013), [25] and [48]; *supra* Sandberg, "Are political beliefs religious now?," (2015).
59. *Ibid* Sandberg.
60. *Ibid,* 195.
61. *Ibid,* 192.

62. *Ibid,* 195–96.
63. *Ibid*, 197.
64. Marie-Claire Foblets, "Freedom of religion and belief in the European workplace: Which way forward and what role for the European Union?" *International Journal of Discrimination and the Law* 13(2-3) (2013): 254–55.
65. Evans, "The Freedom of Religion or Belief in the ECHR since Kokkinakis," 83.
66. *Ibid*, 89-90.
67. *Ibid*, 90–91.
68. Go Vegan World, "What is veganism?" accessed August 16, 2020, https://goveganworld.com/what-is-veganism/; Czech Vegan Society, "What is veganism?" accessed August 16, 2020, https://web.archive.org/web/20171002022500/http://veganskaspolecnost.cz/basic-information/what-is-veganism/. The author accepts that there are discussions within the animal rights and vegan movements about the definition of veganism. See for example an alternative definition that includes 'a moral duty to actively oppose animal exploitation': https://veganflag.org/veganism/, and see Karp, and Roussel and Labchuk in this volume. The definition of The Vegan Society has been cited as helpful in recent case law and is thus, relevant for the present discussion.
69. The Vegan Society, "Definition of veganism," accessed August 16, 2020, https://www.vegansociety.com/go-vegan/definition-veganism.
70. European Union, *Consolidated version of the Treaty on the Functioning of the European Union*, 13 December 2007, 2008/C 115/01, Title II, Article 13; Phillip Low, *The Cambridge Declaration on Consciousness* (2012), edited by Jaak Panksepp, Diana Reiss, David Edelman, Bruno Van Swinderen, Philip Low and Christof Koch, accessed August 16, 2020, http://fcmconference.org/img/CambridgeDeclarationOnConsciousness.pdf; Marc Bekoff, "Animals are conscious and should be treated as such." *New Scientist*, September 19, 2012, accessed August 16, 2020, https://www.newscientist.com/article/mg21528836-200-animals-are-conscious-and-should-be-treated-as-such/.
71. Pierre Gerber et al., "Tackling climate change through livestock—a global assessment of emissions and mitigation opportunities." Rome: FAO (2013): 115; Henning Steinfeld et al., "Livestock's Long Shadow: Environmental Issues and Options," Rome: FAO (2006); The Vegan Society, "Environment," accessed August 16, 2020, https://www.vegansociety.com/go-vegan/environment; Felicity Carus, "UN urges global move to meat and dairy-free diet," accessed August 16, 2020, https://www.theguardian.com/environment/2010/jun/02/un-report-meat-free-diet; Damian Carrington, "Eating less meat essential to curb climate change, says report." *The Guardian*, June 2, 2010, accessed August 16, 2020, https://www.theguardian.com/environment/2014/dec/03/eating-less-meat-curb-climate-change; Laura Wellesey, "Can eating less meat help reduce climate change?" *BBC News*, November 24, 2015, accessed August 16, 2020, http://www.bbc.com/news/science-environment-34899066; Bobbu Magill, "Studies Show Link Between Red Meat and Climate Change," accessed August 16, 2020, https://www.climatecentral.org/news/studies-link-red-meat-and-climate-change-20264; Laurent Cousineau, "The Meat Industry," accessed August 16, 2020, http://www.climate-change-guide.com/meat-industry.html; The Vegan Society, "Ripened by human determination: 70 years of The Vegan Society," accessed August 16, 2020, https://www.vegansociety.com/sites/default/files/uploads/Ripened%20by%20human%20determination.pdf.
72. *Ibid.* The Vegan Society, "Ripened by human determination," 8; Craig Winston, "Health effects of vegan diets." *The American Journal of Clinical Nutrition* 89(5) (May 2009): 1627S–1633S, https://doi.org/10.3945/ajcn.2009.26736N; Kristina Pepelko, "Vegan Strongman Patrik Baboumian Breaks World Record," accessed August 16, 2020, https://www.onegreenplanet.org/news/vegan-strongman-patrik-babaoumain-breaks-world-record/; The Vegan Society, "Health," accessed August 16, 2020, https://www.vegansociety.com/go-vegan/health; Jamie Berger, "Veganism raises your game. Just ask Jermain Defoe." *The Guardian*, March 29, 2017, accessed August 16, 2020, https://www.theguardian.com/commentisfree/2017/mar/29/veganism-jermain-defoe-plant-diet.
73. *H v United Kingdom* (1993) 16 EHRR (CD) 44.
74. Caroline Lowbridge. "Veganism: How a maligned movement went mainstream." *BBC News*, December 30, 2017, accessed August 16, 2020, http://www.bbc.co.uk/news/uk-england-

leicestershire-40722965; Jasmijn de Boo, "How Many Vegans? One of the Fastest Growing Lifestyle Movement." *Huffington Post*, May 19, 2016, accessed August 16, 2020, http://www.huffingtonpost.co.uk/jasmijn-de-boo/how-many-vegans_b_10002562.html; Sue Quinn, "Number of vegans in Britain rises by 360% in 10 years." *The Telegraph,* May 18, 2016, accessed August 16, 2020, http://www.telegraph.co.uk/food-and-drink/news/number-of-vegans-in-britain-rises-by-360-in-10-years/; The Vegan Society, "Find out how many vegans are in Great Britain," accessed August 16, 2020, https://www.vegansociety.com/whats-new/news/find-out-how-many-vegans-are-great-britain.

75. See for example, Jeanette Rowley, *Towards a Vegan Jurisprudence: The Need for a Reorientation of Human Rights* (Lexington, 2020); Hope Ferdowsian, "Why Justice for Animals Is the Social Movement of Our Time," accessed August 16, 2020, https://www.psychologytoday.com/gb/blog/animal-emotions/201603/why-justice-animals-is-the-social-movement-our-time; Gary Smith, "Veganism Is a Social Justice Movement," accessed August 16, 2020, http://thethinkingvegan.com/veganism-is-a-social-justice-movement/.

76. *Supra*, The Vegan Society, "Find out how many vegans are in Great Britain," (2016).

77. *Supra* Palmstorfer, "Austrian Constitutional Court," (2017), 129; *supra* Rosengard, "Three Hots and a Cot and a lot of talk," (2017), 355; Ainsley Newson, "Clinical Ethics Committee Case 9: Should we inform our patient about animal products in his medicine?" *Clinical Ethics* 5:1 (2010): 7; Cara MacInnis and Godron Hodson, "It ain't easy eating greens: Evidence of bias toward vegetarians and vegans from both source and target." *Group Processes & Intergroup Relations* 20(6) (2017): 721–24; Jeanette Rowley, "Towards a Vegan Jurisprudence: The Need for a Reorientation of Human Rights." (PhD thesis, Lancaster University, 2017. Now published: London, Lexington 2020).

78. Sian Mehl, "Hailing seitan silently: Negotiating vegan identities in a non-vegan world" (Thesis, Northern Arizona University, 2017).

79. *Ibid*, ii.

80. *Supra*, MacInnis and Hodson, "It ain't easy eating greens," (2017), 721.

81. Matthew Cole and Karen Morgan, "Vegaphobia: Derogatory discourses of veganism and the reproduction of speciesism in UK national newspaper." *British Journal of Sociology* 62 (March 2011): 134, doi:10.1111/j.1468-4446.2010.01348.x.

82. *Supra* MacInnis and Hodson, "It ain't easy eating greens," (2017), 739.

83. BBC, "Shropshire chef said she 'spiked' vegan meal." *BBC News*, January 2, 2018, accessed August 16, 2020, http://www.bbc.co.uk/news/uk-england-shropshire-42543108; ABC, "Vegan teacher loses job over Facebook post," ABC, December 13, 2014, accessed August 16, 2020, http://abc13.com/news/vegan-teacher-loses-job-over-facebook-post/435278/; Maria Chiorando, "Major Survey Reveals Extent Of Discrimination Against Vegans," accessed August 16, 2020, https://www.plantbasednews.org/post/major-survey-reveals-extent-of-discrimination-against-vegans?utm_source=Plant+Based+News+Subscribers+Combined&utm_campaign=bda5a1e880-Weekly+News+Updates&utm_medium=email&utm_term=0_5651a57357-bda5a1e880-192767081; Go Vegan Scotland, "Results of Survey on Vegan Provision in Scotland," accessed August 16, 2020, https://docs.wixstatic.com/ugd/d95b36_f4bccc9845854533ba8aea3cf8e590b2.pdf; BBC, "Italy proposal to jail vegans who impose diet on children," August 10, 2016, accessed August 16, 2020, https://www.bbc.co.uk/news/world-europe-37034619.

84. *Supra*, Soifer, "Vegan Discrimination," (2003), 1710.

85. *Ibid*; *supra* Page, "Veganism and Sincerely Held Religious Beliefs in the Workplace," (2005), 391; *supra* Rowley, "Vegan Rights," (2014), 3.

86. *Ibid,* Soifer.

87. *R (Williamson) v Secretary of State for Education and Employment* [2005] 2 AC 246, [55].

88. *Grainger plc v Nicolson* [2010] I.C.R. 360, [20].

89. *Conisbee v Crossley Farms Ltd & Ors* [2019] UKET 3335357/2018 (6 September 2019).

90. *Casamitjana v The League Against Cruel Sports* [2020] UKET 3331129/2018 (21 January 2020).

91. ECmHR, 11 Oct. 1991, *Hazar and Others v. Turkey*, DR 72/200.

92. *H v United Kingdom* (1993) 16 EHRR (CD) 44.

93. *Ibid.*

94. *Kelly v Unison* [2009] ET 2203854/08 (22 December 2009).

95. Garry Francione and Robert Garner, *The Animal Rights Debate: Abolition Or Regulation?* (New York City: Columbia University Press, 2010); Garry Francione and Anna Charlton, "The Six Principles of the Abolitionist Approach to Animal Rights," accessed August 16, 2020, http://www.abolitionistapproach.com/about/the-six-principles-of-the-abolitionist-approach-to-animal-rights/#.U6KEkkCSjIU.

96. Department for Environment, Food & Rural Affairs, Animal and Plant Health Agency and the Rt Hon Michael Gove MP, "Environment Secretary confirms sentience of animals will continue to be recognised and protections strengthened when we leave the EU," accessed August 16, 2020, https://www.gov.uk/government/news/environment-secretary-confirms-sentience-of-animals-will-continue-to-be-recognised-and-protections-strengthened-when-we-leave-the-eu; Martin Belam, "MPs hog social media as they deny voting animals are not sentient." *The Guardian*, November 22, 2017, accessed August 16, 2020, https://www.theguardian.com/politics/2017/nov/22/mps-social-media-deny-vote-animals-are-not-sentient-protocol-uk-law; BBC, "Gove attacks 'distorting' social media after animal sentience row." *BBC News*, September 24, 2017, accessed August 16, 2020, http://www.bbc.com/news/uk-politics-42108236.

97. Ashley Cowburn, "85% of the British public are opposed to repealing fox hunting ban, poll reveals." *The Independent*, December 26, 2017, accessed August 16, 2020, http://www.independent.co.uk/news/uk/politics/fox-hunting-poll-boxing-day-league-against-cruel-sports-ban-theresa-may-election-a8127851.html.

98. Richard Warry, "Jeremy Corbyn and other famous vegetarian politicians." *BBC News*, September 5, 2017, accessed August 16, 2020, http://www.bbc.co.uk/news/uk-politics-40058342; Viva, "Vegan Politicians," accessed August 16, 2020, https://www.viva.org.uk/vegan-vegetarian-politicians; Ian McD, "UK now has 4 vegan MPs," accessed August 16, 2020, https://theveganoption.org/2017/06/08/uk-ge2017-election-night-guide/.

99. Party for the Animals, "International movement," accessed August 16, 2020, https://www.partyfortheanimals.nl/international-movement/; James Badock, "Portugal's 'animal party' could be kingmaker with policy of lower taxes on pet food." *The Telegraph*, October 6, 2019, accessed August 16, 2020, https://www.telegraph.co.uk/news/2019/10/06/portugals-animal-party-could-kingmaker-policy-lower-taxes-pet/.

100. *Campbell and Cosans v United Kingdom* [1982] ECHR 1, [36]; *supra* Cranmer, "Employment, religion or belief, the Equality and Human Rights Commission and the Daily Mail."

101. Investopedia Staff, "Law of Supply and Demand," accessed August 16, 2020, https://www.investopedia.com/university/economics/economics3.asp.

102. US: Nation Earth, "Earthlings," accessed August 16, 2020, http://www.nationearth.com/; UK: Ed Winters and Luna Woods, "Land of Hope and Glory," accessed August 16, 2020, https://www.landofhopeandglory.org/.

103. Viva, "RSPCA Assured (Previously Freedom Foods)," accessed August 16, 2020, https://www.viva.org.uk/pig-farming-report/RSPCA-Assured; Ed Winters, "Land of Hope and Glory: An Open Letter from the Filmmakers to the RSPCA," accessed 16th Aug 2020, https://www.plantbasednews.org/post/land-of-hope-and-glory-an-open-letter-from-the-filmmakers-to-the-rspca; RSPCA, "Land of Hope and Glory film," accessed August 16, 2020, https://www.rspcaassured.org.uk/land-of-hope-and-glory-film.

104. British Dietetic Association, "British Dietetic Association confirms well-planned vegan diets can support healthy living in people of all ages," accessed August 16, 2020, https://www.bda.uk.com/news/view?id=179; Vesanto Melina, Winston Craig and Susan Levin, "Position of the Academy of Nutrition and Dietetics: Vegetarian Diets." *J Acad Nutr Diet.* 116(12) (2016): 1970-1980, doi: 10.1016/j.jand.2016.09.025; NHS, "The vegan diet," accessed August 16, 2020, https://www.nhs.uk/Livewell/Vegetarianhealth/Pages/Vegandiets.aspx.

105. L. Harper, O. Denmead, J. Freney, and F. Byers, "Direct measurements of methane emissions from grazing and feedlot cattle." *J Anim Sci.* 77(6) (1999): 1392–401; Michael Mosley, "Can eating meat be eco-friendly?" *BBC News*, August 20, 2014, accessed August 16, 2020, http://www.bbc.co.uk/news/science-environment-28858289; George Monbiot, "*Good-*

bye—and good riddance—to livestock farming." *The Guardian,* October 4, 2017, accessed August 16, 2020, https://www.theguardian.com/commentisfree/2017/oct/04/livestock-farming-artificial-meat-industry-animals; Cat DiStasio, "Leading environmentalist says free-range meat is worse for the environment than airplane travel," accessed August 16, 2020, https://inhabitat.com/leading-environmentalist-says-free-range-meat-is-worse-for-the-environment-than-airplane-travel/; Amy Westervelt, "Ethical farming dilemma: should we be helping the chicken or fixing the egg?" *The Guardian,* March 7, 2014, accessed August 16, 2020, https://www.theguardian.com/sustainable-business/eggs-environment-farming-health-cage-free; Sara Farr, "Here's Why Grass-Fed Beef is Just as Bad for the Environment as Grain-Fed," accessed August 16, 2020, https://www.onegreenplanet.org/environment/grass-fed-beef-is-just-as-bad-for-the-environment-as-grain-fed/.

106. The Vegan Society, "Why go vegan?," accessed August 16, 2020, https://www.vegansociety.com/go-vegan/why-go-vegan.

107. European Union, *Consolidated version of the Treaty on the Functioning of the European Union,* 13 December 2007, 2008/C 115/01, Title II, Article 13; United Kingdom Environmental Law Association, "European Protection of Nature and Wildlife," accessed August 16, 2020, http://www.environmentlaw.org.uk/rte.asp?id=211; International Fund for Animal Welfare, "Protecting animals with international law and policy," accessed August 16, 2020, http://www.ifaw.org/united-states/our-work/political-advocacy/protecting-animals-international-law-and-policy.

108. *Ibid.*

109. Animal Welfare Act 2006.

110. *Grainger v Nicholson* [2009] UKEAT 0219/09/ZT (3 November 2009), [30].

111. For a comprehensive discussion about veganism as a fundamental matter of human conscience and of human rights, see Jeanette Rowley, *Towards a Vegan Jurisprudence: The Need for a Reorientation of Human Rights* (New York: Lexington Book, 2020).

112. Supra Page, "Veganism and Sincerely Held Religious Beliefs in the Workplace," (2005), 389–390.

113. The Vegan Society, "Definition of veganism," accessed August 16, 2020, https://www.vegansociety.com/go-vegan/definition-veganism; The Vegan Society, "Lifestyle," accessed August 16, 2020, https://www.vegansociety.com/go-vegan/definition-veganism.

114. *Conisbee v Crossley Farms Ltd & Ors* [2019] UKET 3335357/2018 (6 September 2019).

115. *Ibid,* [41].

116. *Herrmann v Germany* App No 9300/07 (ECtHR, 26th June 2012).

117. *Ibid,* [87].

118. Supra Evans, "The Freedom of Religion or Belief in the ECHR since Kokkinakis," 83; Katherine Barnes and Mark Hill, "Limitations on Freedom of Religion and Belief in the Jurisprudence of the European Court of Human Rights in the Quarter Century since Its Judgment in *Kokkinakis v. Greece.*" *Religion & Human Rights* 12(2–3) (2017): 196–97.

119. *Casamitjana v The League Against Cruel Sports* [2020] UKET 3331129/2018 (21 January 2020).

120. *H v United Kingdom* (1993) 16 EHRR (CD) 44.

121. *X v Germany* (1970) application no. 4445/70; *Pichon and Sajous v. France* (2001) application no. 49853/99.

122. Luc Gonin, 'Freedom of Thought, Conscience and Religion in the ECHR: The scope of Article 9 ECHR, Terminological distinctions and current legal difficulties.' *Fides et libertas* 1940-6924 (2013): 66.

123. *C v UK* (1983) DR 142 (Application no. 10358/83).

124. *Bank Mellat* [2013] UKSC 39, [74].

125. *Supra* Gonin (2013), 66.

126. Lucy Vickers, "Freedom of Religion or Belief and Employment Law." *Religion and Human Rights* 12 (2017): 165–66.

127. *Ibid.*

128. *Ibid.*

129. *H v United Kingdom* (1993) 16 EHRR (CD) 44.

130. *Supra* Rowley, "Vegan Rights," (2014), 15 and 25–37.

131. Monidipa Fouzder, "Vegan challenges discriminatory job ad," *The Law Society Gazette*, 3rd July 2017, accessed August 16, 2020, https://web.archive.org/web/20181004012111/https://www.lawgazette.co.uk/lawyer-in-the-news/vegan-challenges-discriminatory-job-ad/5061773.article; Barbra Bolton, "In the courts: vegan rights in the UK." *The Lawyer*, accessed August 16, 2020, https://l2b.thelawyer.com/vegan-rights-uk/. The NHS removed and amended this discriminatory advert following correspondence from Jeanette Rowley of the International Vegan Rights Alliance (personal correspondence on file with author).

132. *Supra* Rowley, "Towards a Vegan Jurisprudence, (2017), 19; Christoper Harres, 'Vegan Soldier Rejected by Swiss Army for Failing to Wear Leather Boots,' *International Business Times*, 26th January 2016, accessed August 16, 2020, http://www.ibtimes.com/vegan-soldier-rejected-swiss-army-refusing-wear-leather-boots-2280206.

133. *Hashman v Milton Park (Dorset) Ltd t/a Orchard Park* ET 310555/2009.

134. *Supra* Wallace, "Religion or belief," (2011), 19; *supra* Buchanan, "Protecting philosophical beliefs," (2011), 93.

135. Clarks Legal. "Decision that Anti-fox hunting stance is a "philosophical belief" upheld," accessed August 16, 2020, http://www.clarkslegal.com/Blog/Post/Decision_that_Antifox_hunting_stance_is_a_philosophical_belief_upheld.

136. *Supra*, Marcus et al, "Strict Vegan, Low-Calorie Diet Administered by Care-Giving Daughter to Elderly Mother, (2005); see also: *Melville v Muller* 2006 BCSC 895 (CanLII).

137. *Supra* British Dietetic Association, "British Dietetic Association confirms well-planned vegan diets can support healthy living in people of all ages," (2017); *supra* Melina, Craig and Levin, "Position of the Academy of Nutrition and Dietetics: Vegetarian Diets," (2016); *supra* NHS "The vegan diet," (2018).

138. Barbra Bolton, "Ensuring your veganism is protected if you lose capacity to manage your affairs," accessed August 16, 2020, https://web.archive.org/web/2017*/http://www.theivra.com/Documents/Power%20of%20Attorney.pdf.

139. *Supra* Rowley, "Vegan Rights," (2014), 28–29; The Vegan Society, "Definition of veganism," accessed August 16, 2020, https://www.vegansociety.com/go-vegan/definition-veganism.

140. *F v F (Welfare of Children: Immunisation)* [2013] EWHC 2683 (Fam); *BC v EF (Parental Responsibility: Immunisation)* [2016] EWFC 69 (05 December 2016); *supra* Rowley, "Towards a Vegan Jurisprudence, (2017), 18.

141. *Supra* Newson, "Clinical Ethics Committee Case 9," (2010), 7–12.

142. *Ibid*, 9.

143. *Ibid*, 10.

144. *Supra* Council of Europe, "Guide to Article 9," (2015), 5.

145. *Dahlab v Switzerland* (dec.), no. 42393/98, ECHR 2001-V.

146. *Valsamis v Greece*, no. 21787/93, 18 December 1996, *Reports of Judgments and Decisions* 1996-VI.

147. *Efstratiou v. Greece*, no. 24095/94, 18 December 1996, Reports of Judgments and Decisions 1996-VI.

148. *Supra* Council of Europe, "Guide to Article 9," (2015), 21.

149. *Efstratiou v. Greece*, no. 24095/94, 18 December 1996, Reports of Judgments and Decisions 1996-VI, [32]; *Valsamis v Greece*, no. 21787/93, 18 December 1996, *Reports of Judgments and Decisions* 1996-VI, [31]; *supra* Council of Europe, "Guide to Article 9," (2015), 21.

150. For a more extensive discussion on vegans in education see Rowley and Bowles, in this volume.

151. *Kelly v Unison* [2009] ET 2203854/08 (22 December 2009); *General Municipal and Boilermakers Union v Henderson* [2013] ET 33016908/2012 (30 September 2013); *Maistry v The BBC* [2011] ET1213142/2010 (14 February 2011); ECmHR, 11 Oct. 1991, *Hazar and Others v. Turkey*, DR 72/200, Application Nos. 16311/90, 16312/90 and 16313/90; *Redfearn v United Kingdom* [2013] IRLR 51.

152. *Supra* Evans, "The Freedom of Religion or Belief in the ECHR since Kokkinakis," 90-91.

153. IVRA, "Our challenges," accessed August 16, 2020, https://web.archive.org/web/20180708064428/https://www.theivra.com/challenges.html.

154. *Supra* Rowley, "Vegan Rights," (2014), 33.

155. IVRA, "Concluding Declaration of the 1st International Law Symposium on Vegan Rights," accessed August 16, 2020, https://web.archive.org/web/20190223183008/https://www.theivra.com/Documents/Concluding%20Declaration%20of%20the%201st%20International%20Law%20Symposium%20on%20Vegan%20Rights.pdf.

156. Michael Kirby, "Law, Human Rights, and Religion—of Genocide, Sexuality, and Apostasy," *Macquarie Law Journal* 9 (2009): 3-60; Universal Declaration of Human Rights (adopted 10 December 1948 UNGA Res 217 A(III) (UDHR), Article 18; Convention for the Protection of Human Rights and Fundamental Freedoms (European Convention on Human Rights, as amended) (ECHR), Article 9.

157. *Supra* Bielefeldt, "Misperceptions of Freedom of Religion or Belief," (2013), 34.

7. REFERENCES

ABC. "*Vegan Teacher Loses Job Over Facebook Post.*" *ABC*, December 13, 2014. Accessed August 16, 202., http://abc13.com/news/vegan-teacher-loses-job-over-facebook-post/435278/

Animal Welfare Act 2006.

Arrowsmith v UK (1978) 3 EHRR 218, 7050/75.

Badock, James. "Portugal's 'Animal Party' Could be Kingmaker with Policy of Lower Taxes on Pet Food." *The Telegraph,* October 6, 2019. Accessed August 16, 2020. https://www.telegraph.co.uk/news/2019/10/06/portugals-animal-party-could-kingmaker-policy-lower-taxes-pet/.

Baggs v Fudge [2005] ET 1400114/2005 (23 March 2005).

Bank Mellat [2013] UKSC 39.

Barnes, Katherine and Mark Hill. "Limitations on Freedom of Religion and Belief in the Jurisprudence of the European Court of Human Rights in the Quarter Century Since its Judgment in *Kokkinakis* v. *Greece.*" *Religion & Human Rights* 12(2–3) (2017): 174–97.

BBC. "Gove Attacks 'Distorting' Social Media After Animal Sentience Row." *BBC News,* September 24, 2017. Accessed August 16, 2020. http://www.bbc.com/news/uk-politics-42108236.

BBC. "Italy Proposal to Jail Vegans Who Impose Diet on Children." August 10, 2016. Accessed August 16, 2020. https://www.bbc.co.uk/news/world-europe-37034619.

BBC. "Shropshire Chef Said She 'Spiked' Vegan Meal." *BBC News*, January 2, 2018. Accessed August 16, 2020. http://www.bbc.co.uk/news/uk-england-shropshire-42543108.

BC v EF (Parental Responsibility: Immunisation) [2016] EWFC 69 (05 December 2016).

Bekoff, Marc. "Animals are Conscious and Should be Treated as Such." *New Scientist*, September 19, 2012. Accessed August 16, 2020. https://www.newscientist.com/article/mg21528836-200-animals-are-conscious-and-should-be-treated-as-such/.

Belam, Martin. "MPs Hog Social Media as They Deny Voting Animals are Not Sentient." *The Guardian*, November 22, 2017. Accessed August 16, 2020. https://www.theguardian.com/politics/2017/nov/22/mps-social-media-deny-vote-animals-are-not-sentient-protocol-uk-law.

Berger, Jamie. "Veganism Raises Your Game. Just Ask Jermain Defoe." *The Guardian*, March 29, 2017. Accessed August 16, 2020. https://www.theguardian.com/commentisfree/2017/mar/29/veganism-jermain-defoe-plant-diet.

Bielefeldt, Heiner. "Misperceptions of Freedom of Religion or Belief." *Human Rights Quarterly* 35(1) (2013): 33–68.

Bielefeldt, Heiner. "Protecting and Implementing the Right to Freedom of Religion or Belief: Interview with Heiner Bielefeldt." *Journal of Human Rights Practice* 3:3 (2011) 229–44. https://doi.org/10.1093/jhuman/hur021.

Bolton, Barbra. "Ensuring Your Veganism is Protected if You Lose Capacity to Manage Your Affairs." Accessed August 16, 2020. https://web.archive.org/web/2017*/http://www.theivra.com/Documents/Power%20of%20Attorney.pdf.

Bolton, Barbra. "In the Courts: Vegan Rights in the UK." *The Lawyer*. Accessed August 16, 2020. https://l2b.thelawyer.com/vegan-rights-uk/.

British Dietetic Association. "British Dietetic Association Confirms Well-Planned Vegan Diets Can Support Healthy Living in People of All Ages." Accessed August 16, 2020. https://www.bda.uk.com/news/view?id=179.

Buchanan, Ruth. "Protecting Philosophical Beliefs—Has the Law Gone Too Far?" *T.E.L.L.* 16:12 (2011): 91–93.

C v UK (1983) DR 142 (Application no. 10358/83).

Campbell and Cosans v United Kingdom (1982) 4 EHRR 29, [1982] ECHR 1.

Carrington, Damian. "Eating Less Meat Essential to Curb Climate Change, Says Report." *The Guardian*, June 2, 2010. Accessed August 16, 2020. https://www.theguardian.com/environment/2014/dec/03/eating-less-meat-curb-climate-change.

Carus, Felicity. "UN Urges Global Move to Meat and Dairy-Free Diet." Accessed August 16, 2020. https://www.theguardian.com/environment/2010/jun/02/un-report-meat-free-diet.

Casamitjana v The League Against Cruel Sports [2020] UKET 3331129/2018 (21 January 2020)

Cha'are Shalom Ve Tsedek v. France [GC], no. 27417/95, ECHR 2000-VII.

Chiorando, Maria. "Major Survey Reveals Extent Of Discrimination Against Vegans." Accessed August 16, 2020. https://www.plantbasednews.org/post/major-survey-reveals-extent-of-discrimination-against-vegans?utm_source=Plant+Based+News+Subscribers+Combined&utm_campaign=bda5a1e880-Weekly+News+Updates&utm_medium=email&utm_term=0_5651a57357-bda5a1e880-192767081.

Clarks Legal. "Decision That Anti-fox Hunting Stance Is a "Philosophical Belief" Upheld." Accessed August 16, 2020.Vhttp://www.clarkslegal.com/Blog/Post/Decision_that_Antifox_hunting_stance_is_a_philosophical_belief_upheld.

Cole, Matthew and Karen Morgan. "Vegaphobia: Derogatory discourses of veganism and the Reproduction of Speciesism in UK National Newspaper." *British Journal of Sociology* 62 (March 2011): 134-153, doi:10.1111/j.1468-4446.2010.01348.x.

Cole, Melanie. "Is It Really Vegan or Vegetarian? A Comparative Analysis of the Regulatory Frameworks for Food." *Australian Animal Protection Law Journal* 9 (2013): 44-71.

Conisbee v Crossley Farms Ltd & Ors [2019] UKET 3335357/2018 (6 September 2019)

Convention for the Protection of Human Rights and Fundamental Freedoms (European Convention on Human Rights, as amended) (ECHR).

Council of Europe Committee of Ministers Recommendation Rec (2006)2 of the Committee of Ministers to member states of the European Prison Rules (*Adopted by the Committee of Minister on 11 January 2006 at the 952nd meeting of the Ministers' Deputies*)

Council of Europe. "Framework Convention for the Protection of National Minorities and Explanatory Report." (Strasbourg, February, 1995) H (95) 10.

Council of Europe. *Framework Convention for the Protection of National Minorities* (FCNM), adopted 10 November 1994, open for signatures 1 February 1995 and in force February 1998. ETS no. 157.

Council of Europe. "Guide to Article 9." Accessed August 16, 2020. https://www.echr.coe.int/Documents/Guide_Art_9_ENG.pdf.

Cousineau, Laurent. "The Meat Industry." Accessed August 16, 2020. http://www.climate-change-guide.com/meat-industry.html.

Cowburn, Ashley. "85% of the British Public are Opposed to Repealing Fox Hunting Ban, Poll Reveals." *The Independent*, December 26, 2017. Accessed August 16, 2020. http://www.independent.co.uk/news/uk/politics/fox-hunting-poll-boxing-day-league-against-cruel-sports-ban-theresa-may-election-a8127851.html.

Craig, Winston. "Health Effects of Vegan Diets." *The American Journal of Clinical Nutrition* 89(5) (May 2009): 1627S–1633S, https://doi.org/10.3945/ajcn.2009.26736N.

Cranmer, Frank. "Employment, Religion or Belief, the Equality and Human Rights Commission and the Daily Mail." Accessed August 16, 2020. http://www.lawandreligionuk.com/

2013/04/09/employment-religion-or-belief-the-equality-and-human-rights-commission-and-the-daily-mail/.

Czech Vegan Society. "What Is Veganism?" Accessed August 16, 2020. https://web.archive.org/web/20171002022500/http://veganskaspolecnost.cz/basic-information/what-is-veganism/.

Dahlab v Switzerland (dec.), no. 42393/98, ECHR 2001-V.

de Boo, Jasmijn. "How Many Vegans? One of the Fastest Growing Lifestyle Movement." *Huffington Post*, May 19, 2016. Accessed August 16, 2020. http://www.huffingtonpost.co.uk/jasmijn-de-boo/how-many-vegans_b_10002562.html.

Department for Environment, Food & Rural Affairs, Animal and Plant Health Agency, and the Rt Hon Michael Gove MP. "Environment Secretary Confirms Sentience of Animals will Continue to be Recognised and Protections Strengthened When we Leave the EU." Accessed August 16, 2020. https://web.archive.org/web/20200127051002/https://www.gov.uk/government/news/environment-secretary-confirms-sentience-of-animals-will-continue-to-be-recognised-and-protections-strengthened-when-we-leave-the-eu.

Devine v Home Office (Immigration and Nationality Directorate) ET/2302061/04.

Dickson, Brice. "Activism and Restraint within the UK Supreme Court." *European Journal of Current Legal Issues* 21(1) (2015).

DiStasio, Cat. "Leading Environmentalist Says Free-Range Meat is Worse for the Environment than Airplane Travel." Accessed August 16, 2020. https://inhabitat.com/leading-environmentalist-says-free-range-meat-is-worse-for-the-environment-than-airplane-travel/.

ECmHR, 11 Oct. 1991, *Hazar and Others v. Turkey*, DR 72/200, Application Nos. 16311/90, 16312/90 and 16313/90.

Efstratiou v. Greece, no. 24095/94, 18 December 1996, *Reports of Judgments and Decisions* 1996-VI.

Employment Equality (Religion or Belief) Regulations 2003.

Equality Act 2006.

Equality Act 2010.

Equality and Human Rights Commission (2009) "Employment Statutory Code of Practice (Draft for Consultation)." Available: https://www.elaweb.org.uk/sites/default/files/docs/Draft%20Employment%20Code%20of%20Practice%201109798532.pdf. Accessed Aug 16, 2020.

Equality and Human Rights Commission. "Employment Statutory Code of Practice (Draft for Consultation)." Accessed August 16, 2020. https://www.elaweb.org.uk/sites/default/files/docs/Draft%20Employment%20Code%20of%20Practice%201109798532.pdf.

Equality and Human Rights Commission. "Article 9: Freedom of Thought, Belief and Religion." Accessed August 16, 2020. https://www.equalityhumanrights.com/en/human-rights-act/article-9-freedom-thought-belief-and-religion.

Equality and Human Rights Commission. "Employment: Statutory Code of Practice" Accessed August 16, 2020. https://www.equalityhumanrights.com/sites/default/files/employercode.pdf.

Equality and Human Rights Commission. "The Equality Act Codes of Practice Post Consultation Report." Accessed August 16, 2020. https://www.equalityhumanrights.com/sites/default/files/post_consultation_cop_report.pdf.

European Union, Consolidated version of the Treaty on the Functioning of the European Union, 13 December 2007, 2008/C 115/01.

European Union: Council of the European Union. "Council Directive 2000/78/EC of 27 November 2000 Establishing a General Framework for Equal Treatment in Employment and Occupation." 27 November 2000. OJ L 303, 02/12/2000 P. 0016-0022.

Evans, Malcolm. "The Freedom of Religion or Belief in the ECHR Since Kokkinakis. Or 'Quoting Kokkinakis'." *Religion & Human Rights* 12(2–3) (2017): 83–98.

Eweida v United Kingdom [2013] ECHR 37.

F v F (Welfare of Children: Immunisation) [2013] EWHC 2683 (Fam).

Farr, Sara. "Here's Why Grass-Fed Beef is Just as Bad for the Environment as Grain-Fed." Accessed August 16, 2020. https://www.onegreenplanet.org/environment/grass-fed-beef-is-just-as-bad-for-the-environment-as-grain-fed/.

Farrell v South Yorkshire Police Authority [2011] ET 2803805/2010 (24 May 2011).

Ferdowsian, Hope. "Why Justice for Animals Is the Social Movement of Our Time." Accessed August 16, 2020. https://www.psychologytoday.com/gb/blog/animal-emotions/201603/why-justice-animals-is-the-social-movement-our-time.

Finnon v Asda Stores Ltd ET/2402142/05.

Foblets, Marie-Claire. "Freedom of Religion and Belief in the European Workplace: Which Way Forward and What Role for the European Union?" *International Journal of Discrimination and the Law* 13(2–3) (2013): 240–55.

Ford, Laura and Mark Levine. "Do You Believe in Fairies?" *Employment Law Journal* 121 (2011): 2–5.

Fouzder, Monidipa. "Vegan Challenges Discriminatory Job Ad." *The Law Society Gazette*, 3rd July 2017. Accessed August 16, 2020. https://web.archive.org/web/20181004012111/https://www.lawgazette.co.uk/lawyer-in-the-news/vegan-challenges-discriminatory-job-ad/5061773.article.

Francione, Garry, and Anna Charlton. "The Six Principles of the Abolitionist Approach to Animal Rights." Accessed August 16, 2020. http://www.abolitionistapproach.com/about/the-six-principles-of-the-abolitionist-approach-to-animal-rights/#.U6KEkkCSjIU.

Francione, Garry and Robert Garner. *The Animal Rights Debate: Abolition or Regulation?* New York City: Columbia University Press, 2010.

Fry, Nicholas and Shah Qureshi. "Protecting Philosophical Beliefs." *E.L.A. Briefing* 17(2) (2010): 4–5.

General Municipal and Boilermakers Union v Henderson [2013] ET 33016908/2012 (30 September 2013).

General Municipal and Boilermakers Union v Henderson [2015] UKEAT/0073/14/DM (13 March 2015).

Gerber, Pierre, Henning Steinfeld, Benjamin Henderson , Anne Mottet, Carolyn Opio, Jeroen Dijkman, Alessandra Falcucci and Giuseppe Tempio. "Tackling Climate Change Through Livestock—A Global Assessment of Emissions and Mitigation Opportunities." Rome: FAO (2013).

Go Vegan Scotland. "Results of Survey on Vegan Provision in Scotland." Accessed August 16, 2020. https://docs.wixstatic.com/ugd/d95b36_f4bccc9845854533ba8aea3cf8e590b2.pdf.

Go Vegan World. "What Is Veganism?" Accessed Aug 16, 2020. https://goveganworld.com/what-is-veganism/.

Gonin, Luc. (2013) 'Freedom of Thought, Conscience and Religion in the ECHR: The Scope of Article 9 ECHR, Terminological Distinctions and Current Legal Difficulties.' *Fides et libertas* 1940–6924 (2013): 59–87.

Grainger plc v Nicholson [2010] IRLR 4 (EAT), [2009] UKEAT 0219/09/ZT (3 November 2009).

Greater Manchester Police Authority v Power [2009] EAT 0434/09/DA (12 November 2009)

H v United Kingdom (1993) 16 EHRR (CD) 44.

Harper, L., O. Denmead, J. Freney, and F. Byers. 'Direct Measurements of Methane Emissions from Grazing and Feedlot Cattle.' *J Anim Sci.* 77(6) (1999): 1392–401.

Harres, Christoper. 'Vegan Soldier Rejected by Swiss Army for Failing to Wear Leather Boots.' *International Business Times*, January 26, 2016. Accessed August 16, 2020. http://www.ibtimes.com/vegan-soldier-rejected-swiss-army-refusing-wear-leather-boots-2280206.

Hashman v Milton Park (Dorset) Ltd [2011] ET 3105555/2009 (31 January 2011).

Henson, Philip. 'Beyond belief' *S.J.* 154(10) 2010: 8–11.

Herrmann v Germany App No 9300/07 (ECtHR, 26th June 2012).

Human Rights Act 1998.

International Fund for Animal Welfare. "Protecting animals with international law and policy." Accessed August 16, 2020. http://www.ifaw.org/united-states/our-work/political-advocacy/protecting-animals-international-law-and-policy.

Investopedia Staff. "Law of Supply and Demand." Accessed August 16, 2020. https://www.investopedia.com/university/economics/economics3.asp.

International Vegan Rights Alliance. "Concluding Declaration of the 1st International Law Symposium on Vegan Rights." Accessed August 16, 2020. https://web.archive.org/web/20190223183008/https://www.theivra.com/Documents/Concluding%20Declaration%20of%20the%201st%20International%20Law%20Symposium%20on%20Vegan%20Rights.pdf.

International Vegan Rights Alliance. "Our challenges." Accessed August 16, 2020. https://web.archive.org/web/20180708064428/https://www.theivra.com/challenges.html.

Jakóbski v. Poland no. 18429/06, 7 December 2010.

Kelly v Unison [2009] ET 2203854/08 (22 December 2009).

Kirby, Michael. "Law, Human Rights, and Religion—of Genocide, Sexuality, and Apostasy." *Macquarie Law Journal* 9 (2009): 3–60.

Kokkinakis v Greece [1993] 17 EHRR 397.

Krajnc, Anita. "Bearing Witness: Is Giving Thirsty Pigs Water Criminal Mischief or a Duty." *Animal L.* 23 (2017): 479-498.

Lautsi v Italy [2011] ECHR 2412

Lisk v Shield Guardian Co Lid & Others [2011] ET 3300873/2011 (14 September 2011).

Low, Phillip. *The Cambridge Declaration on Consciousness* (2012), edited by Jaak Panksepp, Diana Reiss, David Edelman, Bruno Van Swinderen, Philip Low and Christof Koch. Accessed 16th August 16, 2020. http://fcmconference.org/img/CambridgeDeclarationOnConsciousness.pdf.

Lowbridge, Caroline. "Veganism: How a Maligned Movement Went Mainstream," *BBC News*, December 30, 2017. Accessed August 16, 2020. http://www.bbc.co.uk/news/uk-england-leicestershire-40722965.

MacInnis, Cara and Godron Hodson. "It Ain't Easy Eating Greens: Evidence of Bias Toward Vegetarians and Vegans From Both Source and Target." *Group Processes & Intergroup Relations* 20(6) (2017): 721–24.

Magill, Bobby. "Studies Show Link Between Red Meat and Climate Change." Accessed August 16, 2020. https://www.climatecentral.org/news/studies-link-red-meat-and-climate-change-20264.

Maistry v The BBC [2011] ET1213142/2010 (14 February 2011).

Marcus, E., C. Wasserstein Fassberg, J. Namestnik, D. Guedj, Y. Caine. "Strict Vegan, Low-Calorie Diet Administered by Care-Giving Daughter to Elderly Mother—Is This Elder Abuse." *Med. & L.* 24 (2005): 279–96.

McD, Ian. "UK Now Has 4 Vegan MPs." Accessed August 16, 2020. https://theveganoption.org/2017/06/08/uk-ge2017-election-night-guide/.

Mehl, Sian. "Hailing Seitan Silently: Negotiating Vegan Identities in a Non-Vegan World" (Thesis, Northern Arizona University, 2017).

Melina, Vesanto, Winston Craig and Susan Levin. "Position of the Academy of Nutrition and Dietetics: Vegetarian Diets." *J Acad Nutr Diet.* 116(12) (2016): 1970-1980. doi: 10.1016/j.jand.2016.09.025.

Melville v Muller 2006 BCSC 895 (CanLII).

Monbiot, George. "Goodbye—and Good Riddance—to Livestock Farming." *The Guardian,* 4th October 2017. Accessed August 16, 2020. https://www.theguardian.com/commentisfree/2017/oct/04/livestock-farming-artificial-meat-industry-animals.

Moore v Hartlepool Borough Council (EOR 199).

Mosley, Michael. "Can Eating Meat be Eco-Friendly?" *BBC News,* August 20, 2014, Accessed August 16, 2020. http://www.bbc.co.uk/news/science-environment-28858289.

Murdoch, Jim. "Freedom of thought, Conscience and religion—A Guide to the Implementation of Article 9 of The European Convention on Human Rights." *Human rights handbooks*, No. 9. Accessed August 16, 202., https://rm.coe.int/168007ff4f.

Nation Earth. "Earthlings." Accessed August 16, 2020. http://www.nationearth.com/.

Newson, Ainsley. "Clinical Ethics Committee Case 9: Should we Inform our Patient about Animal Products in his Medicine?" *Clinical Ethics* 5:1 (2010): 7–12.

NHS. "The Vegan Diet." Accessed August 16, 2020. https://www.nhs.uk/Livewell/Vegetarianhealth/Pages/Vegandiets.aspx.

Osmanoğlu and Kocabaş v. Switzerland [2017] ECHR 14.

Page, Donna. "Veganism and Sincerely Held Religious Beliefs in the Workplace: No Protection without Definition," *U. Pa. J. Lab. & Emp. L.* 7 (2005): 363-408.

Palmstorfer, Nina. "Austrian Constitutional Court: Vegan Landowner Must Tolerate Hunting on His Property." *Vienna Journal on International Constitutional Law* 11(1) (2017): 129.

Party for the Animals. "International Movement." Accessed August 16, 2020. https://www.partyfortheanimals.nl/international-movement/.

Pepelko, Kristina. "Vegan Strongman Patrik Baboumian Breaks World Record." Accessed August 16, 2020. https://www.onegreenplanet.org/news/vegan-strongman-patrik-babaoumain-breaks-world-record/.

Pichon and Sajous v. France (2001) application no. 49853/99.

Pretty v United Kingdom (2002) 35 E.H.R.R. 1.

Quinn, Sue. "Number of Vegans in Britain Rises by 360% in 10 years" *The Telegraph,* May 18, 2016. Accessed August16, 2020. http://www.telegraph.co.uk/food-and-drink/news/number-of-vegans-in-britain-rises-by-360-in-10-years/.

R (Hodkin) v Registrar General of Births, Deaths and Marriages [2013] UKSC 77

R v Registrar General, ex parte Segerdal [1970] 2 QB 697.

Redfearn v United Kingdom [2013] IRLR 51.

Renucci, Jean-François. "Introduction to the European Convention on Human Rights" Accessed August 16, 2020. http://echr.coe.int/Documents/Pub_coe_HFfiles_2005_01_ENG.pdf.

Roberts, I., West, R., Ogilvie, D. and Dillon, M. "Malnutrition in Infants Receiving Cult Diets: a Form of Child Abuse." *British Medical Journal* 1(6159) (1979): 296.

Rosengard, David. "Three Hots and a Cot and a lot of talk: Discussing Federal Rights-Based Avenues for Prisoner Access to Vegan Meals." *Animal Law* 23 (2017): 355–404.

Rowley, Jeanette. "Vegan Rights: Questions and Answers." 2014. Accessed August 16, 2020. https://web.archive.org/web/20170321074323/http://www.theivra.com/Documents/Vegan%20Rights.pdf.

Rowley, Jeanette. *Towards a Vegan Jurisprudence: The Need for a Reorientation of Human Rights*. London: Lexington Books, 2020.

RSPCA. "Land of Hope and Glory film." Accessed August 16, 2020. https://www.rspcaassured.org.uk/land-of-hope-and-glory-film.

Sahin v Turkey [2006] E.L.R. 73.

Sandberg, Russell. "Are Political Beliefs Religious Now?" *Law & Just.—Christian L. Rev.* 175 (2015): 180–97.

SAS v France [2014] ECHR 695.

Smith, Gary. "Veganism Is A Social Justice Movement." Accessed August 16, 2020. http://thethinkingvegan.com/veganism-is-a-social-justice-movement/.

Soifer, Sarah. "Vegan Discrimination: An Emerging and Difficult Dilemma." *Loyola of LA Law Review* 36 (2003): 1709.

Steinfeld, Henning, Pierre Gerber, Tom Wassenaar, Vincent Castel, Mauricio Rosales, Cees de Haan. "Livestock's Long Shadow: Environmental Issues and Options," Rome: FAO (2006).

Streatfield v London Philharmonic Orchestra Ltd [2012] 2390772/2011 (22 May 2012).

The Vegan Society. "Definition of veganism," Accessed 16th August 2020, https://www.vegansociety.com/go-vegan/definition-veganism.

The Vegan Society. "Environment." Accessed August 16, 2020. https://www.vegansociety.com/go-vegan/environment.

The Vegan Society. "Find Out How Many Vegans are in Great Britain." Accessed August 16, 2020. https://www.vegansociety.com/whats-new/news/find-out-how-many-vegans-are-great-britain.

The Vegan Society. "Health." Accessed August 16, 2020. https://www.vegansociety.com/go-vegan/health.

The Vegan Society. "Lifestyle." Accessed August 16, 2020. https://www.vegansociety.com/go-vegan/definition-veganism.

The Vegan Society. "Ripened by Human Determination: 70 Years of The Vegan Society." Accessed August 16, 2020. https://www.vegansociety.com/sites/default/files/uploads/Ripened%20by%20human%20determination.pdf.

The Vegan Society. "Why go vegan?" Accessed August 16, 2020. https://www.vegansociety.com/go-vegan/why-go-vegan.

UN Human Rights Committee (HRC). "CCPR General Comment No. 22: Article 18 (Freedom of Thought, Conscience or Religion)," 30 July 1993, CCPR/C/21/Rev.1/Add.4. Accessed August 16, 2020. http://www.refworld.org/docid/453883fb22.html.

United Kingdom Environmental Law Association (2020). "European Protection of Nature and Wildlife." Accessed August 16, 2020. http://www.environmentlaw.org.uk/rte.asp?id=211.

Universal Declaration of Human Rights (adopted 10 December 1948 UNGA Res 217 A(III) (UDHR).

Unknown. "Herrmann v. Germany (GC): the importance of precedent and Strasbourg 'micro-management'." Accessed August 16, 2020. https://strasbourgobservers.com/2012/07/12/herrmann-v-germany-gc-the-importance-of-precedent-and-strasbourg-micromanagement/.

Unknown. "Mrs Justice Simler." Accessed August 16, 2020. https://www.judiciary.gov.uk/publications/mrs-justice-simler/.

Valsamis v Greece, no. 21787/93, 18 December 1996, *Reports of Judgments and Decisions* 1996-VI.

Vartic v Romania (no. 2) no. 14150/08, 17 December 2013.

Vickers, Lucy. "Freedom of Religion or Belief and Employment Law." *Religion and Human Rights* 12 (2017); 164–73.

Viva. "RSPCA Assured (Previously Freedom Foods)." Accessed August 16, 2020. https://www.viva.org.uk/pig-farming-report/RSPCA-Assured.

Viva. "Vegan Politicians." Accessed August 16, 2020. https://www.viva.org.uk/vegan-vegetarian-politicians.

Wallace, Sandra. "Religion or Belief: The Limits of 'Philosophical Belief'." *E.O.R.* 211 (April 2011): 19-20.

Warry, Richard. "Jeremy Corbyn and Other Famous Vegetarian Politicians" *BBC News,* 5tj September 2017. Accessed August 16, 2020. http://www.bbc.co.uk/news/uk-politics-40058342.

Wellesey, Laura. "Can Eating Less Meat Help Reduce Climate Change?" *BBC News*, November 24, 2015. Accessed August 16, 2020. http://www.bbc.com/news/science-environment-34899066.

Westervelt, Amy. "Ethical farming dilemma: should we be helping the chicken or fixing the egg?" *The Guardian*, March 7, 2014. Accessed August 16, 2020. https://www.theguardian.com/sustainable-business/eggs-environment-farming-health-cage-free.

Williams v South Central Limited [2004] ET 2306989/2003 (16 June 2004).

Winters, Ed. "Land of Hope And Glory: An Open Letter From The Filmmakers To The RSPCA." Accessed Aug 16, 2020. https://www.plantbasednews.org/post/land-of-hope-and-glory-an-open-letter-from-the-filmmakers-to-the-rspca.

Winters, Ed, and Woods, Luna. "Land of Hope and Glory." Accessed August 16, 2020. https://www.landofhopeandglory.org/.

X v Germany (1970) application no. 4445/70.

Chapter Ten

Veganism, Law and Education in the United Kingdom

Jeanette Rowley and Edie Bowles

1. INTRODUCTION

This chapter explores veganism and the law applicable to the provision of education in the United Kingdom (UK). It recognizes that the moral convictions of vegans are within the scope of the legal meaning of the primary human right to freedom of thought, conscience and religion (commonly referred to as freedom of conscience, or freedom of belief), and that, therefore, vegans should not experience unlawful interference with the manifestation of their convictions, should be respected, and should have due regard given to their needs in the provision of education.

The definition of veganism adopted by The Vegan Society has been helpful in case law.[1] The Vegan Society defines veganism as:

> A philosophy and way of living which seeks to exclude—as far as is possible and practicable—all forms of exploitation of, and cruelty to, animals for food, clothing or any other purpose; and by extension, promotes the development and use of animal-free alternatives for the benefit of animals, humans and the environment. In dietary terms it denotes the practice of dispensing with all products derived wholly or partly from animals.[2]

Given that nonhuman animals are used in a variety of ways in the provision of education—for example, as food, in reading and practical resources, and entertainment—the chapter examines the needs of vegan pupils in relation to the human right to freedom of conscience, and the related legal requirement that the state must 'respect the right of parents to ensure such education and teaching that aligns with their own religious and philosophical convictions,' as provided by Article 2 of Protocol No. 1 of the Convention for the Protection of Human Rights and Fundamental Freedoms.[3]

The discussion in this chapter first explains complaints made by some vegan parents and pupils, and relevant law in the UK, before explaining Article 2, Protocol 1 and its background and function. It then explains the practical application of legal principles and how they can be applied in the event of a violation.

The chapter concludes with the assertion that to comply with the law, the philosophy of veganism and vegans' way of life should feature in teaching, learning resources, and the wider range of activities related to the provision of education.

2. ISSUES FACED AND COMPLAINTS MADE BY VEGANS IN THE EDUCATION SYSTEM

On the face of it, it is probably hard to imagine how a vegan could be adversely affected within the education system. In fact, when the topic of vegans having enforceable rights in education is brought up to a lay person, it is often greeted with an eye roll and confusion as to what the complaint could be. Surely education is neutral and serves to inform, not impose? Unfortunately, however, there are aspects of education that are far from neutral. Bias in education is one of the most common areas for complaints, with some serious consequences if left unaddressed. After all, what we are taught in school influences the way we see the world.

The most visible issue is of course the school menu, which quite often does not cater for vegans, and direct bullying of vegans,[4] allegedly by both teachers and pupils. However, there are many more insidious issues that are harder for non-vegans to spot and therefore more of a challenge to find a solution.

Some complaints raised by vegan parents and pupils about issues in education,[5] referred to on social media and news reports, include: dissection of animals,[6] chick-hatching,[7] raising animals for slaughter,[8] lack of provision of vegan food,[9] and state subsidies for the provision of only dairy milk in schools.[10] In addition, some vegans have requested advocacy support[11] for less publicized issues such as how to submit requests for their vegan children to be exempt from excursions to zoos and aquariums, from handling and preparing meat and dairy products in food technology classes, and from other uses of nonhuman animals such as deboning animal bodies for the purposes of assessment, the use of leather and wool products in art classes, the use of sports equipment made of animal skin, and participation in the care and feeding of captive animals. Some vegan parents have complained that their vegan children were given biased developmental reading material that presented a sanitized version of animal suffering in the process of dairy milk and meat production. Parents have also complained that advisory letters about school uniform indicate a preference for leather shoes, that their vegan children have been silenced in class discussions about meat-eating and dairy production, and humiliated and ridiculed by both teachers and other pupils when giving presentations on veganism.

Further, vegan parents, pupils and teachers have been unfairly drawn into the language of terrorism, some inappropriately accused and investigated under counter-extremism strategies for potentially radicalizing vulnerable people.

These complaints and subsequent demands made by vegans invoke human and equality rights on the grounds that they concern an individual's right to freedom to live according to their beliefs and practice their sincerely held moral convictions free from unlawful interference. The human right to freedom of conscience is one of our most important human rights; therefore, whilst these claims are important for vegans themselves, their appeals to human rights also challenge entrenched prejudice towards other animals in the education system, demanding compassion—and, moreover, honesty—in education.

3. INTERSECTING ISSUES IN EDUCATION: ANIMAL EXPLOITATION AND ACCOMMODATING VEGANS

In her article on dissection in schools, Ingrid Newkirk reiterates the commonly held view that dissection 'desensitizes' pupils and reproduces the harmful message that living beings are 'disposable tools.' Newkirk promotes the use of information technology and indicates that humane teaching methods are as effective, if not better, than dissection. She also points to studies showing that students prefer using humane methods and that a requirement to attend classes in dissection is a factor in some young female students' decisions to reject furthering their careers in science-related fields. Newkirk notes how, historically, pupils have felt unable to object to a requirement to participate in dissection classes.[12]

Complaints about schools raising animals for slaughter and classes involving chick-hatching revolve around the lack of compassion in education and raise the issue of hidden facts about the reality of life for farmed animals and chicks in the egg and chicken industry.[13] They also refer to the damaging message conveyed that animals are—and can unquestionably be—used as commodities and resources.[14]

Ed Winter, who launched a petition asking one UK state school not to send the pigs it had raised to slaughter, stated 'the school has made students and parents uncomfortable, by discriminating against their beliefs by condemning these pigs to death.' He also made the point that the pupils 'never had a say in the matter' and claimed they were not being given 'an objective education with both sides of the story.'[15]

Allegations of biased educational curricula, coercion and discrimination are common to the range of complaints raised by vegan parents and school pupils. For example, where pupils have been successful in their requests to be exempt from participating in school-organized excursions to zoos or aquariums, some have reported that the exemption would be marked as 'unauthorized absence,' even where the parents have arranged an alternative educational experience for their vegan child. In these cases, parents complain that not only is the school curriculum biased but that they feel pressure to comply because if they don't, they will suffer the disadvantage that their child will be marked as absent, without authorization, from school. They subsequently feel such circumstances to be discriminatory because, they argue, their ability to live according to their moral convictions as vegans is unreasonably frustrated.

The same feelings are expressed by vegan parents and pupils in complaints about assessed coursework that requires their participation in practices that they are uncomfortable with. Vegans experience bias in teaching, and feel pressure to comply with requirements, for example, to debone a chicken in food technology assessments, or to work with wool, silk or rabbit glue in art and textile assessments, because failure to do so will result in a low overall grade in a subject for which they show great promise and in which they wish to undertake further study. These assessments may not only concern the school curriculum but can also originate from external assessment bodies.[16]

Complaints from vegans about bias, coercion and discrimination in the teaching and learning environment relate, therefore, both to what is taught, the teaching resources used, and what can be described as the normalized context for education: one that is fundamentally oppositional to veganism. On a daily basis, vegan pupils and parents raise a range of issues, from being given what they regard as inappropriate reading material (for example, stories about how happy cows in the dairy industry are, which vegans know is not the case) to having no option but to provide their own milk and packed lunches for their vegan children because vegan food and milk are not provided as it is for non-vegan children: when it is requested, vegan parents sometimes face opposition from the authorities.[17]

The dietary practice of vegans is a significant issue in the context of standard school catering. Default catering in the vast majority of schools is a meat-based diet, and despite the official school food standards observing that there are alternative recognized sources of nutrition, and that plant-based milk is highly nutritious,[18] schools receive state subsidies for the provision of cows' milk only.

In addition to the issue of biased education and its normalization of animal exploitation in its use of resources and its food culture, some vegan parents and pupils have also reported experiencing a negative and prejudiced attitude towards veganism and themselves because they are vegan. For example, during a class discussion on the dairy industry and the benefits of dairy milk, one vegan parent reported that when her child participated by offering information about the true reality for cows and the benefits of plant-based milk, the teacher instructed the pupil to refrain from participating in the discussion because what she was saying was irrelevant, emphasizing that the discussion was about the benefits of dairy milk. In another situation, during a class in which each pupil was required to give a presentation on a subject of their choice, a pre-teenage pupil was jeered at by his classmates throughout his talk on veganism. The pupil's teacher apparently did little to stem the tirade of insults and instead brought the pupil's presentation to a premature close.

Recently, vegans in educational contexts have also reported being unreasonably and unfairly investigated under the UK's 'Prevent' strategy, which is a government program designed to prevent people from being drawn into terrorism.[19] On one occasion, a vegan parent was barred from future school fundraising events following complaints from parents that he had been discussing with the schoolchildren who approached his stall how products of animal origin are obtained and used and the benefits of plant-based products. The school's investigation was grounded by the Prevent strategy, and the outcome was that he was barred on the grounds of 'radicalizing' the school pupils. In another case, a very experienced and highly regarded teacher who discussed veganism was suspended pending an investigation into 'extremism' following complaints from parents. The teacher had not inappropriately taught vegan values in the classroom but was reprimanded for speaking publicly about the need for and value of discussion of veganism within the school curriculum.[20]

The examples highlighted above show how aspects of the teaching and learning environment require some vegan pupils to either stand against, or participate in, practices that are contrary to their ethical convictions.

Animal exploitation and its manifestations are entrenched in the education system, and in these circumstances, vegans report a historical fear of objecting to certain practices and requirements in education, a lack of democracy, and feeling silenced and pressured to comply and assimilate into an opposing mainstream culture. They report dismissive attitudes to their needs, requests and complaints, allege unfair treatment and discrimination against their beliefs, and, in some cases, experience prejudice against themselves as vegans. Some have become fearful of expressing their veganism.

School curricula and wider activities and policies implemented in the course of providing education must, therefore, be examined in the context of an unaddressed culture of animal exploitation in which some individual vegan pupils struggle to practice their sincerely held convictions and deal with their alleged detriment and disadvantage. In the absence of a much-needed paradigm shift in education, vegans alleging unfairness or discrimination in education can seek redress by invoking human rights and equality provisions. The legal measures available to vegans will now be explored.

4. THE LEGAL PROTECTION OF VEGANS IN THE UK

Vegans in the UK can be protected by the Human Rights Act 1998[21] (the HRA) and the Equality Act 2010[22] (EA 2010). The HRA gives effect to the rights contained in the European Convention on Human Rights[23] (the Convention) and explicitly obliges public authorities not to contravene the rights it contains.[24] Under Article 9 of the Convention, the right to freedom of thought, conscience and religion, vegans have an absolute right to believe in veganism and a qualified right to manifest their beliefs, free from unlawful interference, in their daily practice.[25] Lawful interference with the right of vegans to practice their beliefs is strictly limited, permissible only if there is a law that is required in a democracy for a very a good reason; such as for the protection of public morals, public order, health, or safety, or to protect the fundamental rights and freedoms of other people.[26]

In terms of British equality law, veganism (in its 'ethical' form as distinct from the mere practice of its dietary norms[27]) meets the legal test to qualify as a philosophical, non-religious 'belief' under the protected characteristic 'religion or belief' of the Equality Act 2010 (EA 2010). This was confirmed in the case of *Casamitjana* in January 2020;[28] although such was the strength of existing evidence that vegans came within the scope of protection that vegans in Britain have successfully (and with the support of the authors of this chapter) grounded their claims on the Equality Act 2010 for some years prior to the recent tribunal ruling.[29]

Vegans are within the scope of the protected characteristic 'religion or belief' of the EA 2010 because its application is broad to align with the European Court of Human Right's interpretation of Article 9 of the Convention (the right to freedom of thought, conscience, and religion). Although equality case law in Britain has developed independently, the legal test used is broadly similar to that used at the European Court of Human Rights (ECtHR) to decide Article 9 (freedom of conscience) cases. The legal test for protection for a belief under the Equality Act 2010 requires that:

1. The belief must be genuinely held.
2. It must be a belief and not an opinion or viewpoint based on the present state of information available.

> 3. It must be a belief as to a weighty and substantial aspect of human life and behavior.
> 4. It must attain a certain level of cogency, seriousness, cohesion and importance.
> 5. It must be worthy of respect in a democratic society, be not incompatible with human dignity and not conflict with the fundamental rights of others.[30]

Under UK equality law, both public and private sector entities are under a duty not to discriminate against vegans. The EA 2010 prohibits two types of discrimination, 'direct' and 'indirect,' and prohibits 'harassment' and 'victimization.' Generally, direct discrimination is unfavorable treatment because an individual has a protected characteristic; indirect discrimination can be a consequence of an apparently neutral policy, practice, or arrangement if its application has the effect of causing an individual with a protected characteristic a disadvantage; harassment is a broad category that takes into account the complainant's subjective feelings. It involves unwanted conduct which is related to a relevant characteristic and has the purpose or effect of creating an intimidating, hostile, degrading, humiliating or offensive environment. Harassment can be caused in several ways including spoken or written words, gestures, comments on social media, and drawings.[31] Victimization is a category of protection that can be invoked in situations where an individual has raised an issue relevant to their protection under the EA 2010 and as a result is subsequently treated badly for doing so. Vegan pupils must not be treated less favorably than non-vegan pupils and schools must be able to show that policies and practices serve a legitimate aim and can be objectively justified.

The protections afforded to vegans in the UK under the right to freedom of conscience and equality law (Great Britain) are relevant to education. Schools are either public bodies or private bodies performing a public function. They are therefore under a duty not to contravene Convention rights and are equally under a duty not to discriminate against those with protected characteristics. In addition, the Public Sector Equality Duty (PSED) introduced by section 149 of the Equality Act 2010 requires education providers to monitor, record and publish data on the measures they take to eliminate discrimination, promote equality, and foster good relations between those with protected characteristics and those who share a protected characteristic and those who do not. The objective is to remove disadvantages experienced by those with protected characteristics because of those characteristics and to take all reasonable steps to meet their needs.[32]

These statutory provisions supporting a vegan's rights to practice veganism are grounded by Article 2 of Protocol No. 1 of the Convention for the Protection of Human Rights and Fundamental Freedoms, which obliges the state to 'respect the right of parents to ensure that education and teaching conform with their own religious and philosophical convictions.'

5. THE RIGHT TO EDUCATION AND RESPECT FOR PHILOSOPHICAL CONVICTIONS

Article 2 of Protocol No. 1 of the Convention for the Protection of Human Rights and Fundamental Freedoms provides that:

> No person shall be denied the right to education. In the exercise of any functions which it assumes in relation to education and to teaching, the State shall respect the right of parents to ensure such education and teaching in conformity with their own religious and philosophical convictions.

This provision entrenches the principle of inclusivity in education. It requires that individuals are not subjected to an education that is contrary to their beliefs. The international commitment to these principles can be traced back to Article 26 of the Universal Declaration on Human Rights,[33] which includes provisions stating that education shall promote understanding, tolerance and friendship among different groups and that parents have a prior right to choose the kind of education that shall be given to their children.

The working documents (*Travaux préparatoires*) to the development of the Protocol to the European Convention on Human Rights show that there were extensive, thorough and comprehensive discussions about both the inclusion of such a right and its content and meaning, and that the discussion involved several groups of specialists, including a consultative assembly, a committee of experts, a committee of ministers and a legal and administrative committee. It is clear from the discussions held that the right to education was intended to honor and give expression to the human right to freedom of religion or belief.[34]

The records also show that discussions were held regarding the nature of religious and non-religious beliefs and the type of beliefs to be protected. There were discussions around the meaning of 'philosophical convictions' and the merits of descriptive concepts such as 'creed': a concept which was, ultimately, rejected. The final wording of the Protocol treats religious and philosophical convictions equally to ensure that education would be aligned with European liberal values.

These principles underpinning the right to education enjoy wider international agreement, as evidenced by Article 18 of the International Covenant on Civil and Political Rights.[35] Under this provision, respect for the liberty of parents and, when applicable, legal guardians to ensure the religious and moral education of their children in conformity with their own convictions is intrinsic to the right to freedom of thought, conscience and religion. Article 18—the right to freedom of thought, conscience and religion—provides that:

1. Everyone shall have the right to freedom of thought, conscience and religion. This right shall include freedom to have or to adopt a religion or belief of his choice, and freedom, either individually or in community with others and in public or private, to manifest his religion or belief in worship, observance, practice and teaching.
2. No one shall be subject to coercion which would impair his freedom to have or to adopt a religion or belief of his choice.
3. Freedom to manifest one's religion or beliefs may be subject only to such limitations as are prescribed by law and are necessary to protect public safety, order, health, or morals or the fundamental rights and freedoms of others.
4. The States Parties to the present Covenant undertake to have respect for the liberty of parents and, when applicable, legal guardians to ensure the religious and moral education of their children in conformity with their own convictions.

The relationship of the right to freedom of conscience to the right to education is reflected in the current guidance on Article 2 of Protocol No. 1, published by the Council of Europe:

> The two sentences of Article 2 of Protocol No. 1 must be read not only in the light of each other but also, in particular, of Articles 8, 9 and 10 of the Convention, which proclaim the right of everyone, including parents and children, "to respect for his private and family life," to "freedom of thought, conscience and religion," and to "freedom . . . to receive and impart information and ideas." (*Kjeldsen, Busk Madsen and Pedersen v Denmark*, §52).[36]

The guidance also explains that Article 2 of Protocol No. 1 is closely linked to the prohibition of discrimination under Article 14. With reference to relevant case law, the guidance explains that '[f]or a difference in treatment not to be regarded as discriminatory, it must pursue a legitimate aim,' but 'in order to comply with Article 14, the existence of a legitimate aim is insufficient. The difference in treatment must also be proportionate.'[37]

The requirement to give due regard to the philosophical convictions of parents in the provision of education was discussed in the 1976 case of *Kjeldsen, Busk Madsen and Pedersen v Denmark*,[38] in which it was explained that Article 2 of Protocol No. 1, 'requires the state to respect parents' convictions, be they religious or philosophical, throughout the entire State education programme,' and that a useful way to interpret Article 2 of Protocol 1 is to understand that compliant education systems will be grounded by, and built upon, the principle that information disseminated in the teaching and learning environment will be *objective, critical and plural*. In fulfilling its functions, the state

> must take care that information or knowledge included in the curriculum is conveyed in an objective, critical and pluralistic manner. The State is forbidden to pursue an aim of indoctrination that might be considered as not respecting parents' religious and philosophical convictions. That is the limit that must not be exceeded.
>
> Such an interpretation is consistent at one and the same time with the first sentence of Article 2 of the Protocol (P1-2), with Articles 8 to 10 (art. 8, art. 9, art. 10) of the Convention and with the general spirit of the Convention itself, an instrument designed to maintain and promote the ideals and values of a democratic society.

In addition, the European Court of Human Rights has considered the meaning of the word 'respect' in the context of Article 2 of Protocol 1 in the 1982 case of *Campbell and Cosans v the United Kingdom* when it stated that 'respect' means more than merely 'acknowledge' or 'take into account.' The word 'respect' means that there is a positive obligation on the part of the state that cannot necessarily be overridden by striking a balance between the conflicting views involved.[39]

Regarding the meaning of 'convictions,' in *Cosans,* the court stated that its ordinary meaning is not synonymous with 'opinions' or 'ideas,' but that its use is more akin to 'beliefs' that attain a certain level of cogency, seriousness, cohesion and importance.[40] The expression 'philosophical convictions' means convictions worthy of respect in a democracy and not incompatible with human dignity.

Additionally, *Cosans* clarified the meaning of 'functions' in the protocol, confirming that the duty was not limited to teaching the curriculum only:

> The education of children is the whole process whereby, in any society, adults endeavour to transmit their beliefs, culture and other values to the young, whereas teaching or instruction refers in particular to the transmission of knowledge and to intellectual development.

In the 1996 case of *Valsamis v Greece*, the court reiterated this principle:

> Article 2 of Protocol No. 1 (P1-2) enjoins the State to respect parents' convictions, be they religious or philosophical, throughout the entire State education programme. . . . That duty is broad in its extent as it applies not only to the content of education and the manner of its provision but also to the performance of all the "functions" assumed by the State.[41]

Valsamis also confirmed an additional existing principle that

> although individual interests must on occasion be subordinated to those of a group, democracy does not simply mean that the views of a majority must always prevail: a balance must be achieved which ensures the fair and proper treatment of minorities and avoids any abuse of a dominant position . . .

The jurisprudence of the ECtHR on the meaning of Article 2 of Protocol No. 1 clearly supports vegan parents and pupils. Their convictions should be respected and considered in all aspects of education. The requirement that information or knowledge that is included in the curriculum must be disseminated in an *objective, critical and pluralistic* manner is of great significance because it points to the need to include a critical assessment of animal exploitation and vegan perspectives as a matter of diversity in education.

The British Equality and Human Rights Commission has a statutory duty to monitor and oversee the legal measures implemented by government and has published its interpretation of duty under Article 2 of Protocol No, 1: the right to education:

> The right to education does not give you the right to learn whatever you want, wherever you want. The courts have ruled that the right to education relates to the education system that already exists. It does not require the government to provide or subsidise any specific type of education.
>
> The government is allowed to regulate the way education is delivered. For example, it can pass laws making education compulsory or imposing health and safety requirements on schools. Schools are allowed to use admission policies so long as they are objective and reasonable.
>
> Although parents have a right to ensure their religious or philosophical beliefs are respected during their children's education, this is not an absolute right. As long as these beliefs are properly considered, an education authority can depart from them provided there are good reasons and it is done objectively, critically and caters for a diversity of beliefs and world views.

From the above account of responsibilities in education, it is clear that in the provision of education, the state is 'forbidden to pursue an aim of indoctrination that might be considered as not respecting parents' religious and philosophical convictions.' This is highly relevant to the elements of teaching that reinforce the entrenched resource status of nonhuman animals, and the provision of education to vegan pupils. To achieve balance in the teaching and learning environment, the duty placed on education providers is to observe 'the limit that must not be exceeded' in all functions related to the provision of education. Intrinsic to this duty is the obligation to pay careful attention to what measures are required to achieve the necessary balance.

The principles that underpin the rights of vegans in education have now been explored in detail. The next section will explore what those principles look like in practice and how they can be applied in the event of a violation.

6. VEGAN RIGHTS AND EDUCATION IN PRACTICE

6.1. The Law Relating to Issues Faced by Vegans in the Education System

As noted in section 2 above, issues faced by vegan parents and pupils in education and raised as complaints have related to the use of animal products in class, on-site animal farming and husbandry, and impartiality issues with teaching and the national curriculum.

Not all adverse consequences experienced by vegans in education will be unlawful. The lawfulness of any detriment suffered will depend on the facts in question, and will mostly be centered around whether the detriment was proportionate to what was trying to be achieved.

To help clarify the position, we will examine the relevant law on some specific examples of issues vegans experience in the education system. As mentioned above, the relevant law includes the Human Rights Act, which gives effect to the Convention rights, in this case Article 9 (freedom of belief) and Article 2 of Protocol No 1 (the right for a parent to have their child taught in accordance with their beliefs). It also includes the Equality Act, which makes it unlawful to discriminate against (directly and indirectly), harass or victimize vegans on the basis that veganism is a protected belief. There is also a vast body of case law under the Human Rights Act and the Equality Act.

6.1.2. Participating in Non-Vegan Lessons

The likelihood of vegans experiencing discomfort in school is high. As noted earlier, it can be caused by a requirement to use animal products in cooking classes, textiles in arts and crafts, dead animals for dissection in science or being taught about animal farming and husbandry, possibly with practical exercises involving live animals. There are several legal issues these classes bring up for vegans.

A vegan child or vegan parent is unlikely to want to take part or have their child take part in any of the above activities. They may feel like the lesson or activity is going against their belief, as not only would it be teaching something they believe is inherently cruel and unnecessary, but it may also involve doing something directly to an animal or with an animal product which they may view as involving cruelty.

In terms of whether a parent or child is able to insist that they do not take part, there is a series of decisions from the European Court of Human Rights that make it clear that it is sometimes necessary to grant an exemption from certain classes and activities. This is on the basis that an individual's Article 9 right (freedom of belief) and/or a parent's Article 2 of Protocol 1 (parents' right to have their children taught in accordance with their beliefs), which applies to both teaching and activities, have been infringed. The decisions of the European Court of Human Rights in Strasbourg must be taken into account when judges in England have to consider human rights law; it is therefore a good indicator for how a UK court would decide.

In the case of *Mansur Yalçın and Others v Turkey*,[42] the court found that an exemption from certain classes could be granted if the parents found that the 'religious culture and ethical knowledge' were taught in such a way that might cause a conflict between what is taught in the school and the values of the family. This would be very apparent in the case of non-vegan practical lessons if a child was required to use an animal product or participate in an activity involving an animal that would not be acceptable at home and would go against the values of the family.

In the case of *Folgerø and Others v Norway*,[43] a distinction was made between knowledge transmitted and an activity, with an exemption only being granted for the latter. The rationale presumably being that transmitting knowledge serves the purpose of education, whereas an activity would force a person to practice something they do not believe in. In terms of veganism, this could mean that teaching someone about animal industries and produce is acceptable, but a vegan can be exempted from participating in activities such as using an animal product or interacting with an animal in an exploitative setting (e.g., farming).

It is clear from above that a vegan will most likely be able to opt out of a lesson that is not consistent with veganism. Opting out, however, may not be satisfactory; the vegan pupil will be missing out on a lesson. Ideally the vegan pupil would be given an alternative lesson using vegan-friendly alternatives, for example vegan baking or cooking, using synthetic material in textiles, learning anatomy from a book or dissecting artificial animals, being taught about plant-based farming techniques, etc. The next section will look at whether a school must provide these alternatives.

6.1.3. Are Vegans Able to Insist on Vegan-Friendly Alternative Lessons?

It is arguable that a vegan is legally entitled to a vegan-friendly lesson or activity as an alternative to the non-vegan counterpart. The reasons for this are:

1. The requirement for fair and proper treatment of minority beliefs under human rights legislation.
2. The right not to be discriminated against under equality legislation.
3. The requirement for balance in education.

Fair and Proper Treatment of Minority Beliefs Under Human Rights Legislation. At the heart of the European Court of Justice's case law on

Article 9 and Protocol 1 Article 2 is the principle 'safeguarding pluralism in education which . . . is essential for the preservation of the "democratic society."'[44] The idea behind this principle is that everyone should be free to practice their religion or belief. In recognizing the importance of this principle, the Convention and the Court have been clear that the majority cannot oppress the minority and instead a careful balance must be struck to ensure 'the fair and proper treatment of minorities.'[45]

In terms of providing plural education, it is difficult to know how this balance will be struck in schools. The setting of the curriculum falls on the member state; however, as made clear in the case of *Kjeldsen, Busk Madsen and Pedersen v Denmark*, 'the curriculum [must be] conveyed in an objective, critical and pluralistic manner. The State is forbidden to pursue an aim of indoctrination that might be considered as not respecting parents' religious and philosophical convictions. That is the limit that must not be exceeded.' Yet understandably a school cannot be expected to dedicate resources to ensure every protected belief in its student body will be covered by it. In *Mansur Yalçın*, mentioned above, the court felt that just because the school curriculum favored the dominant religion, it did not mean it had failed on objectivity and pluralism. In this case, an exemption from the lesson for the pupil was sufficient.

Further, in the case of *Osmanoğlu et Kocabaş v Switzerland*,[46] it was made clear that compliance with the Convention does not require the state to teach certain lessons.

What seems to be apparent from the case law is that minority views must be respected, and indoctrination and abuse are not allowed. However, it is not the case that a minority belief must be taught under human rights legislation, and instead, an opt-out may be sufficient.

The facts of the cases presented above, however, must be examined alongside Article 14 (prohibition on discrimination) of the Convention. If it could be shown that the absence of vegan-friendly lessons occurred as a result of discrimination, then this would not be permitted. Proving that such discrimination is taking place will turn on the facts, but evidence might include the fact that a similar-sized protected group has had representation on the curriculum.

Furthermore, due to the nature of the non-vegan position and the way that it permeates so many aspects of a person's education and life, it cannot be clearly categorized and compartmentalized in the same way that religious education can be. Therefore, the case could be made that it is not possible to separate out indoctrination of the dominant non-vegan position onto vegans. You could argue that for this reason an opt-out is not sufficient, as the vegan in question is still likely to experience routine discrimination, which can only be avoided if a vegan-friendly alternative is made available.

The Right Not to be Discriminated Against Under Equality Legislation. As explained earlier, discrimination under the Equality Act comes in two different forms—direct and indirect. Direct discrimination is where someone is treated unfairly due to a protected characteristic. Indirect discrimination is where a practice in place applies to everyone, but it negatively affects someone due to their protected characteristic. Ethical veganism is a protected characteristic by virtue of it being a cogent belief system.

The fact that non-vegan lessons and activities are intrinsic to the school curriculum is not directly discriminatory; the school is not singling out vegans and preventing them from taking part in classes or activities that reinforce the normalization of animal exploitation. The issue is, instead, that elements of the curriculum are indirectly discriminatory; a vegan would not want to take part in certain elements and would therefore be put at a disadvantage due to their protected belief.

The test of whether the school has acted unlawfully and is obliged to provide a vegan alternative will depend on whether the discrimination was proportionate in order to achieve a legitimate aim. The UK guidance on the Equality Act and Schools explained this as meaning that 'both that the reason for the rule or practice is legitimate, and that it could not reasonably be achieved in a different way which did not discriminate.'

The school would need to prove that the non-vegan lesson or activity was legitimate and that it could not reasonably be achieved in a way that did not discriminate against vegans. Each case would turn on the facts at hand. In the case of *R (Elias) v Secretary of State for Defence*,[47] it was said that a legitimate aim 'must correspond to a real need and the means used must be appropriate with a view to achieving the objective and be necessary to that end.'

In the case of non-vegan lessons, such arguments may include that the legitimate aim was cooking, sewing, science, etc. and that a lack of teaching resources and suitable alternatives meant the school could not reasonably provide a vegan-friendly alternative. There is significant case law that states that saving money will not be considered a legitimate aim to justify discrimination; however, a distinction is made between saving money and the 'fair distribution of limited resources,' which may be applicable in schools.

A vegan parent, on the other hand, would make the case that cooking, sewing, science, etc. could all be achieved with vegan-friendly replacements and that the discrimination could reasonably be avoided by providing such alternatives to a vegan child.

Under section 85(2) of the Equality Act, a school is required not to discriminate in several ways, including in the way it provides education for the pupil; such discrimination could be by not affording the pupil access to a benefit, facility or service or by subjecting the pupil to any other detriment. This section, however, does not apply to anything done in connection with the content of the curriculum. It has therefore been interpreted as meaning that the prohibition of discrimination is in relation to the delivery of the curriculum, not the curriculum itself. In the case of the curricular activities that affect vegans, such as cooking, science, farming, etc., the case could possibly be made that if these can be delivered in a non-discriminatory way, they should be.

Under section 149 of the Equality Act, there is also a public sector duty placed on publicly run or funded schools. These include maintained schools, academies and free schools. This duty requires that the schools it applies to must have due regard to the need to:

1. eliminate discrimination, harassment, victimization and any other conduct that is prohibited by or under this Act;
2. advance equality of opportunity between persons who share a relevant protected characteristic and persons who do not share it; and
3. foster good relations between persons who share a relevant protected characteristic and persons who do not share it.

The Equality and Human Rights Commission explains:

> How much regard is "due" will depend on the circumstances and in particular on the relevance of the needs in the general equality duty to the decision or function in question in relation to any particular group. The greater the relevance and potential impact for any group, the greater the regard required by the duty.

The Public Sector Equality Duty Guidance for Schools in England issued by the Equality and Human Rights Commission[48] goes on to explain that the meaning of 'due regard' for schools is as follows:

- When making a decision or taking an action a school must assess whether it may have implications for people with particular protected characteristics.
- It should consider equality implications before and at the time that it develops policy and takes decisions; not as an afterthought, and it needs to keep them under review.
- It should consciously consider each aspect of the duty (having due regard to the need to eliminate discrimination is not the same thing as having due regard to the need to advance equality of opportunity).
- It should assess the risk and extent of any adverse impact that might result from a policy or decision and the ways in which the risk may be eliminated before the adoption of a proposed policy.
- The equality duty has to be integrated into the carrying out of a school's functions.

- The analysis necessary to comply with the duty should be carried out rigorously and with an open mind—it is not a question of just ticking boxes.
- Schools need to do this themselves and cannot delegate responsibility for carrying out the duty to anyone else. The steps they have taken to meet the duty must be recorded.

What is clear is that under the equality duty, schools should be carefully considering the needs of vegans, including when determining the curriculum and keep their policies under permanent review.[49]

The Requirement for Balance in Education. In the event that a school is permitted to discriminate against an ethical vegan, perhaps because the specific activity falls within its margin of appreciation under human rights law or because it is a proportionate means of achieving a legitimate aim, it is still possible that it will be breaching its duty to provide a balanced education.

As mentioned above, under human rights law there is a requirement to provide education in an 'objective, critical and pluralistic manner.' Whilst this does not mean that a vegan pupil or their parent can insist on a specific lesson being taught, it does mean that teaching must be done objectively and without indoctrination.

In the case of *Hasan and Eylem Zengin v Turkey*,[50] the court agreed that whilst the curriculum falls within the competence of the country, it was unlawful that the syllabus was not taught objectively and that textbooks were biased.

This legal reasoning is supported by education law. Maintained schools and academies are bound by section 78 Education Act 2002, which requires that the curriculum be 'balanced and broadly based curriculum which [. . .] promotes the spiritual, moral, cultural, mental and physical development of pupils at the school and of society.' Section 5 of Schedule 1 of the Education (Independent School Standards) Regulations 2014 applies to independent schools and requires that:

> the spiritual, moral, social and cultural development of pupils at the school [. . .] promotes the fundamental British values of democracy, the rule of law, individual liberty, and mutual respect and tolerance of those with different faiths and beliefs [. . .] paying particular regard to the protected characteristics set out in the 2010 Act.

Section 5 of Schedule 1 also requires that political beliefs are provided by a 'balanced presentation of opposing views.'

This requirement for balance and respect is very relevant to vegans, because whilst it may not be possible to insist that veganism features explicitly on the curriculum, it should mean that when a non-vegan lesson is being taught, this should be done in an objective manner; for example, by providing or permitting alternatives to teaching animal welfare through farming classes or by ensuring that baking and cooking can be done without animal produce.

In 2015, a judicial review was brought in the UK by members of the British Humanist Association.[51] The claim was against the Secretary of State for Education's statement, which said that the content of the religious studies program prescribed by the Secretary of State was 'consistent with the requirement for the provision of religious education in current legislation.' The applicants argued this was an error in law because the prescribed content failed to treat religious and non-religious views on an equal footing, and in a non-partisan way, which was not permitted, for all the reasons discussed above. The High Court agreed that the statement was misleading, because whilst 'it *could* be enough to meet the State's [. . .] obligations [. . .] it will not necessarily be so' and that as such, the statement could lead to those responsible for the syllabus in schools acting unlawfully by not considering the rights of the parents and pupils.

This case is by no means a clear-cut victory for balance and pluralism in education, but it does show that those devising the curriculum and syllabus must stay ever mindful of ensuring that their duties under human rights, equality and education law are met.

6.2. Case Study: Farming and Animal Husbandry

A growing trend in education seems to be including lessons in animal farming and/or animal husbandry. Examples range from hamsters and chicks featuring in classroom activities, through to pig farming taking place on school property. The argument for such practices is to show pupils how to take care of animals and where their food comes from. Vegan parents, however, would argue that an animal that is frequently handled by children in a class will not have a good quality of life, and that farming on school property will present a sanitized version of animal farming; children will not be exposed to the reality of industrial farming or slaughter. It also normalizes animal consumption without also highlighting vegan farming as an alternative.

Many of the same arguments mentioned above will apply in these situations. It would likely be contrary to a pupil's and their parents' Convention Rights if they were forced to participate in an activity that required them to suspend their ethical practice. It may also be possible for the pupil or parent to insist on an alternative (vegan-friendly version) of the lesson under the Equality Act. Teaching animal farming and husbandry in school is not direct discrimination, as the school is not saying the pupil cannot be involved, but rather the vegan pupil will be at a disadvantage when either opting out of a class or being exposed to an activity which is not in accordance with their beliefs. Provision of such an activity will be indirectly discriminatory if it cannot be shown that the disadvantage caused was a proportionate means to achieve a legitimate aim. The legitimate aim may be teaching children about animals and where food comes from. Questions as to whether or not the disadvantage caused to vegan pupils is proportionate or not may be whether real animals were needed to achieve that aim and whether vegan farming could have been offered instead of or in addition to the activity.

Furthermore, there is an argument that teaching only sanitized animal farming while failing to show the reality that animals face in the food system and failing to show veganism as an alternative is contrary to the requirement for objectivity and pluralism under human rights legislation and the requirement for balance under the Education Act.

7. CONCLUSION

This chapter has raised the issue of entrenched bias in education and has considered the relationship of veganism to the law applicable to the provision of education in the UK. It is clear that the goal of the legal provisions discussed is to deal with disadvantage and foster inclusion in education, and these provisions must be accepted as relevant to inclusive education for those who reject animal exploitation.

It is unknown whether a court would be sympathetic to the arguments made in support of inclusive vegan education, but the judicial review mentioned above showed that schools will need to consider carefully whether they are meeting all their legal duties to safeguard the rights of pupils and parents. These duties, clearly documented in international treaties, domestic legislation, case law and legal guidance apply equally to the needs of vegans in school and call for objectivity and balance in teaching, learning resources, and the wider range of activities related to the provision of education.

8. NOTES

1. See *Casamitjana* below. The authors accept the many debates on the meaning and definition of veganism. For the purposes of this chapter, we acknowledge the important of the definition of The Vegan Society in case law. For further comment see Roussel and Labchuk, Casamitjana, and Karp in this volume.

2. The Vegan Society, 'History,' accessed January 14, 2021, https://www.vegansociety.com/go-vegan/definition-veganism.

3. Convention for the Protection of Human Rights and Fundamental Freedoms (European Convention on Human Rights, as amended) (ECHR) Protocol 1. https://www.echr.coe.int/Documents/Convention_ENG.pdf.

4. Sebastian Murphey-Bates, "The Schoolboy Bullied for Being VEGAN: 'Cruel' Pupils Told 11-Year-Old to 'Eat GRASS' and 'Shoved Tuna Melt in His Face' Due to his Meat-Free

Stance," *Mail Online*, December 23, 2019, accessed January 22, 2021. https://www.dailymail.co.uk/news/article-7821093/Cruel-pupils-shoved-tuna-melt-vegan-pupils-face-Birmingham-school.html.

5. Early research on vegan equality advised that more research should be undertaken in this area following the comments of a very limited number of vegans who participated in a small-scale research project conducted in 2013-2014. See Jeanette Rowley, "Veganism and Equality Research: An Investigation into the Experiences of UK Vegans in the Context of Human Rights and Equality Provisions," accessed February 2, 2021. https://eprints.lancs.ac.uk/id/eprint/74384/1/Vegan_Equality_Survey.pdf.

6. Ingrid Newkirk, "Cutting Dissection Out of the Curriculum," *PeTA Prime*, August 19, 2019, accessed January 30, 2021, https://prime.peta.org/2019/08/cutting-dissection-out-of-the-curriculum/.

7. Suzanne, "How One Inspirational Vegan Mum Educated Her Child's School Over Chick Hatching," *The Plantway.com,* accessed January 22, 2021. https://www.theplantway.com/inspirational-vegan-mum-educated-childs-school-chick-hatching/.

8. BBC, "Vegan Parent Complains about Lymington School's Pigs," *BBC News*. January 23, 2018, accessed January 22, 2021, https://www.bbc.co.uk/news/uk-england-hampshire-42782437.

9. BBC, "Vegan School Meal Options Promised After Mother's Campaign," *BBC News*, November 5, 2019, accessed January 22, 2021, https://www.bbc.co.uk/news/uk-scotland-50249679.

10. The Vegan Society, "Play Fair with Plant Milk: Calls to Include Vegan Milk in Schools on a Par with Cow's Milk." *The Vegan Society*, September 24, 2019, accessed January 22, 2021, https://www.vegansociety.com/whats-new/news/play-fair-plant-milk-calls-include-vegan-milk-schools-par-cow%E2%80%99s-milk. The provision of milk in school is likely to change very soon. At the time of preparing this draft chapter for publication, 05-03-2021, after making full use of law to bring about equality for vegans in schools, the Scottish Government announced that it will now fund plant-based milk for nursery children. In its children's rights assessment, it observed the view that the new scheme would be inclusive for vegans. The Milk and Healthy Snack Scheme (Scotland) Regulations 2021 (legislation.gov.uk).

11. Anonymized cases and materials formerly published on the website of the International Vegan Rights Alliance, and personal communication between the authors and individual vegans.

12. Ingrid Newkirk, "Cutting Dissection Out of the Curriculum," *PeTA Prime*, August 19, 2019, accessed January 30, 2021, https://prime.peta.org/2019/08/cutting-dissection-out-of-the-curriculum/.

13. See for example, Heather Saul, "Hatched, Discarded, Gassed: What Happens to Male Chicks in the UK," *Independent*, March 5, 2015, accessed January 22, 2021. https://www.independent.co.uk/life-style/food-and-drink/hatched-discarded-gassed-what-happens-to-male-chicks-in-the-uk-10088509.html.

14. Suzanne, "How One Inspirational Vegan Mum Educated Her Child's School Over Chick Hatching," *The Plantway.com,* accessed January 22, 2021. https://www.theplantway.com/inspirational-vegan-mum-educated-childs-school-chick-hatching/.

15. BBC, "Vegan Parent Complains About Lymington School's Pigs." *BBC News*, January 23, 2018, accessed January 22, 2021, https://www.bbc.co.uk/news/uk-england-hampshire-42782437.

16. For example, to pass the AQA GCSE examination paper on 'food and nutrition' a pupil must answer all questions, including how to safely store fresh prawns and reheat cooked chicken. They must also assess the nutrient content of a fish pie and a meat pie dish to assess the suitability of each meal for an elderly person, and evaluate which meal is the healthier choice. There are no alternative questions for vegans to evaluate the dietary element of vegan practice. See AQA past paper 2018, GCSE Food Preparation and Nutrition: Paper 1 Food Preparation: https://www.aqa.org.uk/subjects/food/gcse/food-preparation-and-nutrition-8585/assessment-resources.

17. In some cases, vegan parents have been disallowed to self-supply. See BBC, "Vegan School Meal Options Promised After Mother's Campaign," *BBC News*, November 5, 2019, accessed January 22, 2021, https://www.bbc.co.uk/news/uk-scotland-50249679.

18. UK Government. "School Food Standards: A Practical Guide for Schools their Cooks and Caterers," January 5, 2015, accessed January 22, 2021, https://assets.publishing.service.gov.uk/government/uploads/system/uploads/attachment_data/file/847621/School-Food-Standards-Guidance-FINAL-V3.pdf.

19. The UK Prevent Strategy includes the use of terms such as 'extremism' and 'radicalization' and has been the subject of much criticism for including non-violent groups in training guides. See Vikram Dodd and Jamie Greierson, "Greenpeace Included with Neo-Nazis on UK Counter-Terror List," *The Guardian*, January 17, 2020, accessed January 22, 2021, https://www.theguardian.com/uk-news/2020/jan/17/greenpeace-included-with-neo-nazis-on-uk-counter-terror-list

20. It should be emphasized that there is widespread controversy and political and social confusion about the relationship of the Prevent Strategy to non-violent practitioners of various lawful and peaceful campaign groups. See Dodd and Greierson, noted above. However, also note that animal rights activists are mentioned in the current counter terrorism strategy. See HM Government, "Contest the United Kingdom's Strategy for Countering Terrorism June 2018," https://assets.publishing.service.gov.uk/government/uploads/system/uploads/attachment_data/file/716907/140618_CCS207_CCS0218929798-1_CONTEST_3.0_WEB.pdf. For more information on how vegans have been drawn into the language and policy of terrorism see Jeanette Rowley, "How Veganism Came to be Associated with 'Extremism,' 'Radicalisation' and 'Counter Terrorism'," Conference Presentation, *The Vegan Society* 2019 https://www.vegansociety.com/jeanette-rowley.

21. H.M. Government, https://www.legislation.gov.uk/ukpga/1998/42/contents.

22. H.M Government, https://www.legislation.gov.uk/ukpga/2010/15/contents.

23. Council of Europe. https://www.echr.coe.int/Documents/Convention_ENG.pdf.

24. Article 6(1) HRA: 'It is unlawful for a public authority to act in a way which is incompatible with a Convention right.' (Under art.1. the ECHR obliges contracting parties to secure the rights and freedoms it contains to everyone within the state, and under art. 14. rights and freedoms granted by the Convention shall be secured without discrimination on any ground.)

25. *H v United Kingdom* (1993) 16 EHRR.

26. As set out in Article 9 ECHR.

27. We do imply that the separate practice of eating a plant-based diet would not fall within the scope of equality law.

28. *Mr J Casamitjana Costa v The League Against Cruel Sports*: 3331129/2018—Preliminary.

29. Existing evidence included cases referring to the protection of vegetarianism, statements about the legal meaning and scope of protection for 'philosophical belief,' including the protection of the vegan belief in anti-foxhunting, and legal guidance from the Equality and Human Rights Commission.

30. *Grainger plc and others v Nicholson* EAT/0219/09.

31. The legal definition of harassment does not apply to matter of religion or belief in the context of education: schools must be free to explore religions and beliefs free from the threat of claims of harassment. However, harassment remains unlawful and cases could be brought on the grounds of direct discrimination.

32. For links to information see H.M. Government, https://www.gov.uk/government/publications/public-sector-equality-duty.

33. Adopted December 10, 1948, by the United Nations General Assembly.

34. Though the preparatory discussions have no legal force, they are persuasive when considering legal meaning.

35. The European Convention on Human Rights is influenced by wider international developments on matters of the same: Vienna Convention on the Law of Treaties (adopted 23 May 1969) 1155 UNTS 331.

36. Council of Europe/European Court of Human Rights, 'Guide on Article 2 of Protocol No. 1 to the European Convention on Human Rights,' accessed January 7, 2021, https://www.

right-to-education.org/sites/right-to-education.org/files/resource-attachments/ECHR_Guide_Art_2_Protocol_1_ENG_0.pdf, p. 2.

37. Council of Europe/European Court of Human Rights, 'Guide on Article 2 of Protocol No. 1 to the European Convention on Human Rights' accessed January 7, 2021https://www.right-to-education.org/sites/right-to-education.org/files/resource-attachments/ECHR_Guide_Art_2_Protocol_1_ENG_0.pdf, p. 7. Article 14 provides that, '[t]he enjoyment of the rights and freedoms set forth in this European Convention on Human Rights shall be secured without discrimination on any ground such as sex, race, colour, language, religion, political or other opinion, national or social origin, association with a national minority, property, birth or other status.'

38. *Kjeldsen, Busk Madsen and Pedersen v. Denmark*, 7 December 1976, Series A no. 23.

39. *Campbell and Cosans v. the United Kingdom*, 25 February 1982, Series A no. 48. See full quote at paragraph 37a.

40. *Campbell and Cosans v. the United Kingdom*, 25 February 1982, Series A no. 48.

41. *Valsamis v. Greece*, 18 December 1996, Reports of Judgments and Decisions 1996-VI.

42. Application no 21163/11: European Court of Human Rights.

43. Application no 15472/02: European Court of Human Rights.

44. *Kjeldsen, Busk Madsen and Pedersen v Denmark.*

45. *Young, James and Webster v. the United Kingdom.*

46. Application no 29086/12: European Court of Human Rights.

47. [2006] EWCA Civ 1293, 1 WLR 3213.

48. https://www.equalityhumanrights.com/sites/default/files/psed_guide_for_schools_in_england.pdf.

49. https://webarchive.nationalarchives.gov.uk/20130104123602/ and https://www.education.gov.uk/schools/teachingandlearning/curriculum/b00199686/inclusion.

50. App. No. 1448/04 (ECtHR 9 February 2007).

51. *R* (Fox and others) v Secretary of State for Education [2015] EWHC 3404 (Admin); [2015] WLR (D) 481.

9. BIBLIOGRAPHY

AQA. Past Paper 201, GCSE Food Preparation and Nutrition: Paper 1 Food Preparation. https://www.aqa.org.uk/subjects/food/gcse/food-preparation-and-nutrition-8585/assessment-resources. Accessed February 26, 2021.

BBC. "Vegan Parent Complains about Lymington School's Pigs." BBC News, January 23, 2018. Accessed January 22, 2021. https://www.bbc.co.uk/news/uk-england-hampshire-42782437.

BBC. "Vegan School Meal Options Promised After Mother's Campaign." BBC News, November 5, 2019. Accessed January 22, 2021. https://www.bbc.co.uk/news/uk-scotland-50249679.

Campbell and Cosans v. the United Kingdom. 25 February 1982, Series A no. 48.

Convention for the Protection of Human Rights and Fundamental Freedoms (European Convention on Human Rights, as amended) (ECHR) Protocol 1. https://www.echr.coe.int/Documents/Convention_ENG.pdf.

Council of Europe. https://www.echr.coe.int/Documents/Convention_ENG.pdf.

Council of Europe/European Court of Human Rights, 'Guide on Article 2 of Protocol No. 1 to the European Convention on Human Rights.' Accessed January 7, 2021. https://www.right-to-education.org/sites/right-to-education.org/files/resource-attachments/ECHR_Guide_Art_2_Protocol_1_ENG_0.pdf, p. 2.

Dodd, Vikram and Greierson, Jamie. "Greenpeace Included with Neo-Nazis on UK Counter-Terror List." *Guardian*, January 17, 2020. Accessed January 22, 2021. https://www.theguardian.com/uk-news/2020/jan/17/greenpeace-included-with-neo-nazis-on-uk-counter-terror-list.

Folgerø and Others v. Norway. Application no 15472/02: European Court of Human Rights *R* (Fox and others) v Secretary of State for Education [2015] EWHC 3404 (Admin); [2015] WLR (D) 481.

Grainger plc and others v Nicholson EAT/0219/09.

H v United Kingdom. (1993) 16 EHRR.

Hasan and Eylem Zengin V. Turkey. Application no. 1448/04: European Court of Human Rights.

HM Government. "Contest the United Kingdom's Strategy for Countering Terrorism June 2018." https://assets.publishing.service.gov.uk/government/uploads/system/uploads/attachment_data/file/716907/140618_CCS207_CCS0218929798-1_CONTEST_3.0_WEB.pdf.

Kjeldsen, Busk Madsen and Pedersen v. Denmark. 7 December 1976, Series A no. 23: European Court of Human Rights.

Mansur Yalçın and Others v. Turkey. Application no. 21163/11: European Court of Human Rights.

Mr J. Casamitjana Costa v The League Against Cruel Sports: 3331129/2018—Preliminary.

Murphey-Bates, Sebastian. "The Schoolboy Bullied for Being VEGAN: 'Cruel' Pupils Told 11-Year-Old to 'Eat GRASS' and 'Shoved Tuna Melt in His Face' Due to his Meat-Free Stance." Mail Online, December 23, 2019. Accessed January 22, 2021. https://www.dailymail.co.uk/news/article-7821093/Cruel-pupils-shoved-tuna-melt-vegan-pupils-face-Birmingham-school.html.

Newkirk, Ingrid. "Cutting Dissection Out of the Curriculum," PeTA Prime, August 19, 2019. Accessed January 30, 2021, https://prime.peta.org/2019/08/cutting-dissection-out-of-the-curriculum/.

Osmanoğlu et Kocabaş v. Switzerland. Application no. 29086/12: European Court of Human Rights.

Rowley Jeanette. "How Veganism Came to be Associated with 'Extremism,' 'Radicalisation' and 'Counter Terrorism'," Conference Presentation, *The Vegan Society* 2019, Accessed March 14, 2021. https://www.vegansociety.com/jeanette-rowley.

Rowley, Jeanette. "Veganism and Equality Research: An Investigation into the Experiences of UK Vegans in the Context of Human Rights and Equality Provisions," Accessed February 2, 2021. https://eprints.lancs.ac.uk/id/eprint/74384/1/Vegan_Equality_Survey.pdf.

Saul, Heather. "Hatched, Discarded, Gassed: What Happens to Male Chicks in the UK." *Independent*, March 5, 2015. Accessed January 22, 2021. https://www.independent.co.uk/life-style/food-and-drink/hatched-discarded-gassed-what-happens-to-male-chicks-in-the-uk-10088509.html.

Suzanne. "How One Inspirational Vegan Mum Educated Her Child's School Over Chick Hatching." The Plantway.com. Accessed January 22, 2021. https://www.theplantway.com/inspirational-vegan-mum-educated-childs-school-chick-hatching/.

The Milk and Healthy Snack Scheme (Scotland) Regulations 2021 (legislation.gov.uk).

The Vegan Society. 'History.' Accessed January 14, 2021, https://www.vegansociety.com/go-vegan/definition-veganism.

The Vegan Society. "Play Fair with Plant Milk: Calls to Include Vegan Milk in Schools on a Par with Cow's Milk." The Vegan Society, September 24, 2019. Accessed January 22, 2021. https://www.vegansociety.com/whats-new/news/play-fair-plant-milk-calls-include-vegan-milk-schools-par-cow%E2%80%99s-milk.

UK Government. "School Food Standards: A Practical Guide for Schools their Cooks and Caterers." January 5, 2015. Accessed January 22, 2021. https://assets.publishing.service.gov.uk/government/uploads/system/uploads/attachment_data/file/847621/School-Food-Standards-Guidance-FINAL-V3.pdf.

Valsamis v. Greece. 18 December 1996, Reports of Judgments and Decisions 1996-VI: European Court of Human Rights.

Vienna Convention on the Law of Treaties (adopted 23 May 1969) 1155 UNTS 331.

Young, James and Webster v. the United Kingdom. Application no. 7601/76; 7806/77 European Court of Human Rights.

Chapter Eleven

Treatment for Disordered Eating in England

Balancing Vegan Rights and Treatment Requirements

Jade Elliott-Archer

1. INTRODUCTION

This chapter explores the treatment of vegans with eating disorder. It gives an overview of eating disorder and clinical treatment, explains the specific practical difficulties for clinicians treating vegans with eating disorder, and how the rights of vegans, issues regarding consent, negligence, and capacity, along with mental health law all feature in this sensitive and complex area of clinical practice.

According to the eating disorder support charity BEAT, approximately 1.25 million people in the United Kingdom (UK) have an eating disorder.[1] Eating disorders vary substantially in symptomology and severity, and the term 'eating disorder' includes anorexia nervosa, bulimia nervosa, binge eating disorder, and other non-specified feeding and eating disorders.[2]

The root causes for the development of eating disorders are wide-ranging, and an individual with disordered eating may be underweight, a normal weight, or overweight. Recommended treatment is varied. However, most treatment regimens will include encouragement of healthy eating, learning about nutrition and monitoring of dietary intake.[3]

Historical studies suggest that there could be a link between eating disorders and vegetarian diets,[4] and that vegetarianism can be used as a method of covert dietary restriction.[5] Other studies, however, have been unable to identify any increased incidence of body image issues or health-based reasons for dietary choices by vegetarians versus non-vegetarians.[6] While no substantive research confirms that there is a link between disordered eating and veganism, anecdotal evidence reported by the Royal College of Psychiatrists (RCPsych) in 2019 seems to indicate that a high number of patients with eating disorders had been following a vegan diet on admission. It is important to note that this is simply an observation; the RCPsych are keen to point out that veganism should not be regarded as a causal factor in eating disorders.[7]

Eating disorders are most frequently treated in outpatient community settings. However, where a sufferer's physical health is so severely compromised that their life is at risk and/or outpatient treatment has been unsuccessful, inpatient treatment may be indicated.[8] Inpatient treatment may include an element of refeeding, and such treatment may be provided voluntarily or involuntarily.

During any medical treatment, the rights of the patient must be balanced carefully with their treatment needs, taking into account their capacity to consent to or refuse treatment. Given that vegans have the protection of law, there will be specific factors in relation to rights which will need to be taken into account where a patient follows an ethical vegan lifestyle, i.e. 'a way of living which seeks to exclude, as far as is possible and practicable, all forms of exploitation of, and cruelty to, animals for food, clothing or any other purpose.'[9]

1.1. General Principles Involved in Treating Vegans with Eating Disorder

Given that vegans do not consume products of animal origin, some aspects of standardized treatment may need to be individualized to meet the needs of vegan patients, and treatment centers must be aware of the practical adjustments which may be required to ensure legal compliance when treating vegan patients.

Public bodies are under a specific duty not to act in a way that undermines the rights of individuals and should take reasonable steps to ensure that vegan diets can be catered for within healthcare settings. In the case of treatment for eating disorders, this may be more complex, as veganism could potentially be seen as a method of dietary restriction and therefore a manifestation of the disorder. To ensure legal compliance, healthcare providers will need to be aware that the patient's veganism may represent a cogently held and therefore protected philosophical belief. This can be a complex judgment, and where there is any doubt as to whether veganism is a cogently held philosophical belief, healthcare providers who intend to provide non-vegan treatment would be advised to refer to the Court of Protection for a determination of the issue or otherwise face the potential prospect of being held negligent or in breach of the patient's human rights. In addition, a vegan patient's right to express their philosophical belief must be balanced against other rights, and against treatment needs where the patient lacks capacity or is admitted involuntarily. The remainder of this chapter explores the issues in this complex area of clinical practice in more detail, starting with the practical difficulties involved in treating vegan patients with eating disorder.

2. PRACTICAL DIFFICULTIES IN RESPECT OF TREATMENT FOR VEGAN PATIENTS WITH DISORDERED EATING

If a vegan patient's body weight is so low that medical refeeding is required, there is unfortunately no Advisory Committee on Borderline Substances (ACBS)-approved refeeding formulation. Most formulations and supplements include milk and/or vitamin D from animal sources.[10] The British Dietetic Association has published a consensus statement, in conjunction with the Royal College of Psychiatrists and the eating disorder charity Beat, calling for more vegan-friendly treatments for eating disorder patients.[11] In the meantime, there are various vegan options for nutritional support which can be considered. However, as these options are not ACBS-approved, in life-threatening situations a non-vegan product may be deemed to be necessary by the treating team. Vegan foods tend to be less calorie-dense than animal products, and this can mean that more food is required to reach a satisfactory calorie intake. This can not only present psychological difficulties for the patient, but also has the potential to cause physical issues such as delayed gastric emptying.[12]

In addition, it may be difficult for both the vegan patient and clinician to determine the extent to which the patient's veganism does in fact represent a cogent philosophical and ethical belief, and the extent to which it is a symptom of or contributing factor to the eating disorder itself.

These concerns may lead a vegan eating disorder patient to conclude that whilst undergoing initial treatment and recovery from their eating disorder, it is not possible or practicable for them to exclude any or all animal products from their diet. In these circumstances, the patient could continue their vegan lifestyle in respect of clothing and toiletries with a view to resuming the vegan diet when they are able to do so.

However, there may be some circumstances where a vegan patient does not wish to engage with therapeutic intervention which would compromise their beliefs.

A comprehensive survey of eating disorder patients, caregivers and their health professionals identified that a holistic and client-centered approach was most beneficial when treating eating disorders.[13] Respecting a vegan patient's philosophical belief may therefore represent a positive way for them to re-engage with food. Conversely, of course, a vegan diet may not represent a genuinely held philosophical belief but rather a way to restrict food intake. Assessing the distinction between a genuinely held vegan belief and an attempt to use a vegan diet to restrict food intake may not be straightforward. There may well be crossover between the two—for example, a patient suffering from an eating disorder may, despite having a clear belief in living a vegan lifestyle, find that the label-checking often required to identify vegan products exacerbates the symptoms of eating disorder. An individual may lack insight into the extent of their illness, resulting in their feeling that their commitment to veganism is a strongly held philosophical belief when in fact it does represent a symptom of the mental disorder.

The above challenges may result in a situation where the vegan patient refuses treatment. This may put their life at risk, causing a tension between the applicable rights to their freedom of conscience and their healthcare providers' legal duty to protect their right to life.

3. VEGAN RIGHTS

3.1. Freedom of Thought

The right to 'freedom of thought, conscience and religion' is protected by Article 9 of the European Convention on Human Rights (ECHR).[14] This is subject to such limitations 'as are prescribed by law and are necessary in a democratic society in the interests of public safety, for the protection of public order, health or morals or for the protection of the rights and freedoms of others.'

Dietary choices as an observance of religious belief have been accepted by the European Court of Human Rights (ECtHR) to fall squarely within the scope of Article 9 ECHR.[15] The ECtHR held in *Jakobski*[16] that the failure of a prison service to provide a vegetarian diet did not strike a fair balance between the interests of authorities and the applicant's right to manifest his Buddhist religious beliefs. The position of a prisoner is likely to be considered analogous to that of a hospital inpatient (particularly a non-voluntary admission), and failing to provide an adequate diet which aligns with a patient's religious or philosophical beliefs in many circumstances is therefore likely to be a breach of their Article 9 rights.

The Human Rights Act 1998 (HRA) reflects the rights set out in the ECHR, and Article 9 HRA brings the right to express religion and philosophical belief directly into English law. The HRA provides a remedy against public authorities acting in a way which is incompatible with Convention rights. Many of these rights are reflected in the Equality Act 2010, which also applies to the private sector. The Equality Act guidance confirms that the right to express a religious or philosophical belief is directly linked to Article 9 ECHR.[17]

The United Kingdom Equality and Human Rights Commission has published guidance which cites veganism as an example of a philosophical belief.[18]

The concept of veganism as a philosophical belief has also been considered on a number of occasions by UK courts and tribunals. Although the determinations in many of these cases do not directly apply to healthcare settings, they nonetheless provide insight into the approach of the English courts when considering veganism as a protected belief under the applicable legislation.

The legal test for consideration of philosophical beliefs is helpfully summarized in the employment case of *Grainger v Nicholson.*[19] Mr Grainger claimed unfair dismissal on the basis of his belief in man-made climate change. Reference was made to the following criteria for consideration of philosophical beliefs under the Equality Act 2010, which reflect the Statutory Code of Practice:[20]

- The belief must be genuinely held,
- It must be a belief and not an opinion/viewpoint,
- It must relate to a weighty and substantial aspect of human life and behavior,
- It must attain a certain level of cogency, seriousness, cohesion and importance,
- It must be compatible with human dignity and must not conflict with the rights of others.

In the case of *Conisbee*,[21] the Employment Tribunal (ET) found that the Appellant's vegetarianism fell short of a 'belief.' It was considered that the claimant's vegetarianism amounted to an opinion or viewpoint, rather than a belief. It was indicated that veganism could be considered differently, as there was a clear 'cogency and cohesion.' This indicates that the approach to whether veganism is considered as a philosophical belief to engage Article 9 will be dependent on the facts of each individual case, and the extent to which the individual's belief affects their life.

In the ET case of *Casamitjana*, the Judge concluded that there was overwhelming evidence that ethical veganism was within the scope of the legal meaning of philosophical belief, and was therefore protected under the Equality Act 2010. It was confirmed that the question of whether a particular individual's veganism would meet the criteria would be fact-specific. Notably, in *Casamitjana* the Judge confirmed at paragraph 12 of the Judgment that '*ethical veganism is not just about choices of diet, but about choices relating to what a person wears, what personal care products he or she uses, their hobbies and the job he or she does.*'[22] The extent to which the patient's veganism extends to issues outside of dietary choice is therefore likely to be a key factor in assessment of the cogency of any vegan belief expressed by a patient with an eating disorder.

Other key factors to be considered in assessing whether Article 9 ECHR is engaged have been summarized in guidelines published by the British Dietetic Association in relation to veganism and eating disorders.[23] These include:

- whether there is a religious reason for the vegan diet,
- whether the family are also vegan/supportive of the patient's veganism (although the patient will also need to establish that they are not being unduly influenced by other parties),[24]
- whether the patient's veganism pre-dated the eating disorder symptoms,
- whether the patient's reason for following a vegan lifestyle is predominantly health-based or ethics-based,
- whether the patient's veganism reaches to non-food aspects of life (e.g. clothing, makeup, household products etc.).

The Human Rights Act 1998 (section 6) provides that a public body must not act in a way which is incompatible with a Convention right. Based on judgments from both the English courts and the ECtHR, this should include ensuring that a philosophical belief in veganism is respected by public bodies providing medical care.

The rights explored above mean that a vegan patient, provided that their veganism is a cogent and clearly held belief, should not be discriminated against on the grounds of that belief when treatment is being provided by public bodies. Discrimination in the provision of medical treatment could be 'direct' or 'indirect.'

Direct discrimination takes place where, contrary to section 13 of the Equality Act 2010, certain groups/people are treated differently because they hold a protected characteristic. An example of direct discrimination could be a blanket refusal to provide vegan meal plans or a refusal to accept vegans with eating disorders into services.

Indirect discrimination can take place where, contrary to section 19 of the Equality Act 2010, there is an apparently neutral policy which applies to all but which has the effect of disadvantaging certain groups/people (e.g. those expressing their philosophical belief in veganism). This could be a refusal to discharge any eating disorder patient from services until they have demonstrated that they can consume dairy milk. Healthcare providers have a potential defense to a claim of indirect discrimination if they can establish that the policy represents a proportionate means of achieving a legitimate aim,[25] commonly referred to as the 'objective justification.'

In order to ensure legal compliance and prevent claims of discrimination, healthcare providers should, as far as is possible, provide adequate vegan catering and specialized meal plans for ethical vegan patients in all settings, including when providing treatment for disordered eating.

3.2. Right Not to Be Subject to Degrading Treatment

Patients also have the right under Article 3 ECHR not to be subject to degrading or inhumane treatment. The ECtHR has considered this in the context of enforced psychiatric treatment, including the forcible provision of food and medications.[26] The ECtHR held that medical treatment would not be inhumane or degrading, provided it was medically necessary. Being force-fed to treat disordered eating may constitute lifesaving and justifiable treatment. It is also, however, an invasive, unpleasant and potentially psychologically damaging experience, which has the potential to constitute interference with Article 3 rights. If the feed which is forcibly provided is also non-vegan, and therefore also undermines a strongly held philosophical belief in veganism, it is arguably even more degrading.

In order to prevent any claims under Article 3, public bodies providing treatment for patients with disordered eating who claim to have a philosophical belief in veganism would be advised to carefully consider the issue of medical necessity and whether a less invasive or suitable vegan option can be identified. If this is not possible, clinicians will need to assess the cogency of the belief and the capacity of the individual to determine whether any refusal should be upheld. If there is any doubt, healthcare providers would be wise to apply to the court for a declaration to support the approach to be taken.

3.3. Right to Life

Medical units are also under an active duty, prescribed by Article 2 ECHR, to protect their patients' right to life. This is an 'operational duty' which has the effect of enforcing a positive obligation on public authorities to protect the right to life.[27] If a patient who lacks capacity to make decisions in relation to their own mental healthcare is, for example, able to end their own life whilst they are an inpatient, then it may be determined that their right to life has been violated.[28] In the context of treatment for disordered eating, this may mean that an inpatient unit which fails to commence an adequate refeeding regime for a patient suffering with an eating disorder because the patient does not wish to consume non-vegan nutritional supplements could be at risk of being found to have breached the patient's right to life if the patient does not survive as a result.

The mortality in relation to anorexia nervosa is historically significant.[29] Increased mortality risk arises not only from the physical consequences of the disorder itself, but also from the increased suicide risk arising from psychological factors. Mortality in respect of other eating disorders, such as bulimia nervosa and eating disorders not otherwise specified, has also been reported to be elevated to a similar level to those found in patients suffering with anorexia nervosa.[30] The mortality risk is a factor which the courts will clearly therefore take into account when considering best-interests decisions or rights interference in respect of eating disordered patients. This mortality risk, and the potential for Article 2 rights to be violated, will therefore need to be carefully balanced with a vegan patient's right to express their philosophical belief against consuming animal products.

4. ISSUES OF CONSENT AND NEGLIGENCE

The basic starting point in respect of an adult with capacity to make decisions in relation to their medical treatment is that treatment cannot be provided without their consent. This would include a vegan eating disorder patient refusing to consume non-vegan foods as part of their treatment. To provide treatment without consent or other legal justification represents a potentially criminal act.[31] When providing treatment where consent has been given (or is not required), clinicians must act in accordance with practices accepted as proper by a responsible and reasonable body of clinicians.[32]

In respect of psychological therapies and refeeding regimes, provided the clinician has offered the appropriate treatment in a reasonable manner and in accordance with the National Institute of Care and Excellence (NICE) guidelines, it is likely to be extremely difficult to establish negligence in providing non-vegan treatment options.

If a vegan patient was provided with a non-vegan tube feed or meal replacement, it is likely that, if challenged in negligence, a clinician would be able to identify a responsible body to support the provision of non-vegan feed, particularly as there is presently no ACBS-approved vegan tube feed.

The patient may be able to argue that they were not given sufficient information to enable them to provide informed consent and that in view of their philosophical belief in ethical veganism advice regarding non-vegan ingredients in the proposed intervention should have formed part of consent process. If the patient has capacity to make decisions about their medical treatment and is not admitted under the MHA, then this may have some force.[33]

However, for a claim to succeed in negligence, the patient must also be able to show that the identified failure has caused a loss which can be remedied by compensatory damages. Such treatment is likely to improve, rather than worsen, the patient's physical condition, and such is unlikely to be actionable. The patient may feel that the incident has caused deterioration in their psychological state. However, establishing that providing non-vegan treatment without appropriate consent has caused a psychological injury capable of compensation and distinct from the pre-existing eating disorder is likely to be extremely difficult. In any event, such an injury will in most cases only result in *de minimis* damages such that it would be disproportionate to pursue. A claim in negligence is, therefore, unlikely to represent an appropriate remedy, although this would not preclude a separate action for breach of applicable rights.

5. ASSESSING MENTAL CAPACITY

5.1. General Principles

As a general principle (albeit subject to some exclusions), adult patients who have capacity to make decisions about their medical treatment should only be treated in accordance with consent that they have provided.

The principles and assessment of capacity in adults are governed by the Mental Capacity Act 2005 (MCA). The MCA provides that patients, including those who are diagnosed as suffering from a mental illness such as an eating disorder, must be assumed to have capacity unless it is established that capacity is lacking.[34]

The MCA provides that *'a person is not to be treated as unable to make a decision merely because he makes an unwise decision.'*[35] If an individual does lack capacity, any decisions made should be in their best interests.[36]

An individual may be deemed to lack capacity if, because of *'an impairment of or disturbance in the functioning of the mind or brain,'* they are unable to:

- understand the information relevant to the decision,
- retain that information,
- use or weigh that information,
- communicate the decision.[37]

It is well established in law that a mentally competent patient has the absolute right to refuse treatment. Refusal can be provided for any reason, whether this is rational, irrational or no reason is given at all. This is the case even where the patient's decision may lead to death.[38]

The position in respect of capacity can be more complex in relation to treatment for mental health conditions. An individual with a mental health condition may lack capacity to make certain decisions, but retain capacity to make other decisions. It is also possible for a patient's capacity to fluctuate over time.

Capacity is decision-specific, and a particular patient's capacity to make a decision will need to be considered at the point when the decision is to be made. Types of decisions which an eating disorder patient may need to make could include:

- which psychological therapies are to be undertaken and whether to engage with the same,
- whether—and what—food, fluids, supplements are to be consumed,
- whether to undertake nasogastric feeding if recommended,
- whether to agree to be admitted as an inpatient.

Given that the primary symptomology of all eating disorders includes pathological views in relation to food, the impact of the illness on the patient's capacity to consent to refeeding regimes is likely to be an issue of great importance in the management of eating disorders, particularly in the inpatient setting.

Only a small proportion of patients receiving inpatient treatment for an eating disorder receive nasogastric feeding (an average of 1.5%, according to a 2012 review[39]). If a vegan patient wishes to refuse potentially lifesaving non-vegan nasogastric food products, it will be important for the treating clinicians to consider whether they have capacity to make such a refusal.

Most patients will receive treatment on an outpatient basis and therefore will, in many respects, remain in control of their own dietary intake, based on guidance provided by their treating team.

A patient with capacity is entitled to refuse to comply with any element of the treatment plan or refeeding plan with which they are uncomfortable. If a patient has capacity and is an ethical vegan, then refusal by their treatment provider to continue with treatment unless the patient consumes animal products, or refusal to offer an alternative vegan plan, is likely to constitute discrimination and an interference with their human rights. The British Dietetic Association has provided guidance to clinicians treating vegans with eating disorders, and this includes an example high-calorie vegan meal plan.[40]

5.2. Patients Who Lack Capacity

The MCA provides that where an individual is deemed to lack capacity, their *'past and present wishes and feelings'* should be taken into account when determining their best interests.[41] This means that even if a patient is deemed to lack capacity to make decisions regarding consumption of food by virtue of their eating disorder, their beliefs surrounding the importance of a vegan diet can and should be one of the factors taken into account when determining their best interests.

This will need to be balanced against the risk to the patient in not proceeding with treatment, the suffering this may entail, and the positive obligation of the medical provider to support the patient's right to life.[42] There may be vegan patients who have a strong ethical belief in veganism but would still be prepared to accept non-vegan treatment if their life was in danger and there was no vegan alternative. This approach would remain in line with the Vegan Society definition of veganism as excluding animal products as far as practicable.[43] If a vegan patient is considered to lack capacity, the treating team would therefore need to consider whether the vegan belief is likely to have extended to a refusal of life-saving treatment when assessing best interests.

The Court of Protection has previously held that *'there is a strong presumption in favour of taking all steps which would prolong life.'*[44] It has also been held that, although a patient had stated that she did not want to be kept alive and would want to be allowed to die, in the absence of an advance directive clearly amounting to a direction that she preferred to be deprived of food and drink until she died, it was in her best interests to reinsert a feeding tube.[45] This finding was not in relation to treatment for an eating disorder, and the courts may therefore be more likely to make a best interests decision to provide forcible treatment when assessing a decision to refuse food and drink in a patient who may have a pathological reason for denying the same.

One approach to assist vegan patients in ensuring clarity would be for them to prepare an advance directive to confirm any refusal of life-sustaining non-vegan treatment. However, complexities can remain even when advance directives are made, as it must be established that the patient had capacity at the time of making the directive. This can be difficult, given that the need to prepare such a directive may well only be identified following the onset of the eating disorder. This was demonstrated in the 2012 case of *Re E*,[46] where a 32-year-old patient with a diagnosis of anorexia refused to eat and refused medical intervention. The patient had signed two separate advance directives the year before, confirming that she did not want to be given medical intervention to prolong her life. The court held that the patient's obsessive fear of weight gain made her incapable of weighing the advantages and disadvantages of eating in any meaningful way. The court held that it had insufficient evidence that the patient had capacity at the time of making either of the advance directives. It was held that interference with the patient's rights, namely Article 8 (right to private and family life) and Article 3 (right not to be subject to degrading treatment) were justified to protect her Article 2 right to life.

Historically, therefore, the courts appear to have taken a relatively paternalistic approach to the consideration of wishes and feelings when assessing the issue of life-saving treatment for patients lacking capacity. However, more recent decisions have emphasised the need for clinicians to take into account the patient's wishes and feelings when considering best interest decisions in respect of life-sustaining treatment. Recent judgments have confirmed that life-sustaining treatment can be ceased where to continue the same would be contrary to the patient's wishes.[47] A Supreme Court decision confirmed that life-sustaining treatment in the form of hydration and nutrition could be withdrawn when deemed to be in the best interests of a patient who lacks capacity without an application to the court being required.

These cases focused on wishes by patients not to be kept alive in circumstances they considered to be intolerable, rather than as a result of any philosophical belief such as veganism. The addition of the potential pathological cause for a denial of nutrition by a vegan eating disorder patient would add an additional layer of complexity. A court declaration may therefore remain the safest approach if it is considered that non-vegan life-saving nutritional support should be withheld due to the wishes and beliefs of a vegan patient who lacks capacity.

5.3. Assessing Capacity in Children

Although the onset of eating disorders can occur at any age, many eating disorders develop during adolescence.[48] The legal framework for assessment of mental capacity varies when considering children and adolescents.

Although only technically applicable in private proceedings, the requirements of the Children Act 1989 are of assistance when considering the likely approach of the courts when making best interests decisions regarding children. The Act provides that when a court determines questions in respect of a child's upbringing, 'the child's welfare shall be the paramount consideration.'[49] The Act goes on to set out a number of circumstances which the court will take into account. These are as follows:

- the ascertainable wishes and feelings of the child concerned (considered in light of his age and understanding),
- his physical, emotional and educational needs,
- the likely effect on him of any change in his circumstances,
- his age, sex, background and any characteristics of his which the court considers relevant,
- any harm which he has suffered or is at risk of suffering,
- how capable each of his parents, and any other person in relation to whom the court considers the question to be relevant, is of meeting his needs,
- the range of powers available to the court under this Act in the proceedings in question.[50]

The courts have demonstrated that when assessing treatment refusal by minors, the question of harm takes precedence over the minor's wishes, feelings and relevant characteristics.

5.4. Minors under the Age of 16

A child under the age of 16 has the legal capacity to consent to medical examination and treatment if they have sufficient maturity and intelligence to understand the nature and implications of the same (otherwise known as '*Gillick* competency').[51] This is akin to the requirements of the MCA in assessing capacity in adult patients.

The courts require a demonstration of understanding of not just the procedure itself and the reasons for refusal, but the wider context of the decision. For example, when assessing decisions by minor patients refusing blood products on religious grounds, the courts have held that the children lacked sufficient understanding of the full implications of the decision,[52] as, for example, they were not aware of the likely gruesome nature of death following refusal.[53]

Irrespective of competence, the courts retain jurisdiction to override a competent minor's decision using its inherent wardship powers.[54]

The courts have considered the issue of treatment refusal in the context of vegan beliefs in family proceedings regarding immunizations.[55] Children of ages 11 and 15 refused an MMR vaccine as, amongst other reasons, one of the children was a vegan and the vaccine contained animal products. The court ordered that it was in both of the children's best interests to be immunized. The court found that the children had a lack of understanding, demonstrated by the over focus on the non-vegan ingredients of the vaccine itself to the exclusion of other issues such as the non-vegan ingredients of medications which would be required if the children were to contract the diseases that the vaccine was to protect against. This case did not consider the issue of the child's veganism as a philosophical belief in any detail or with regard to her Article 9 rights, although the case law referenced above in respect of religious refusals provides an indication that the same decision is likely to have been made had those issues been considered by the court in further detail.

5.5. Minors over the Age of 16

There is a presumption that a child over the age of 16 can provide or refuse consent to surgical, medical or dental treatment without parental input.[56] This presumption is rebuttable if the patient is shown to lack capacity by reference to the criteria of the MCA, as considered above. Even if the child patient is deemed to have capacity, the court is still able to override this in the child's best interests.

An example of this can be seen in *An NHS Foundation Hospital v P*,[57] where a 17-year-old refused treatment following a drug overdose. The court was not satisfied that she lacked capacity, but nonetheless found that it could overrule the decision of a minor using its inherent jurisdiction. The court found that in imposing treatment, the claimant's Article 8 Right to privacy and family life was interfered with; however, it concluded that this was justified to protect her Article 2 right to life.

Even where a patient's beliefs constitute the reason for the treatment refusal, this has been overridden by the courts. For example, a court overrode the decision of a patient who was just under 17 years of age to refuse blood products on religious grounds, as it determined this was in the patient's best interests.[58] The court did note that there would be some circumstances in which a 16- or 17-year-old's refusal would be determinative—for example, if treatment was only likely to prolong life for a few months.

However, the examples given are unlikely to be applicable to a refusal of treatment from a patient with an eating disorder. This was demonstrated in a case concerning a 16-year-old patient who refused a transfer to a specialized eating disorder unit to be treated for anorexia.[59] The court held that, although the patient had sufficient intelligence and understanding to make informed decisions, the transfer was in her best interests. The court commented upon the 'unique characteristic' of anorexia nervosa that the patient desires not to be cured. A further consideration was the possibility that adhering to the minor's wishes could result in severe permanent injury or death.

In respect of treatment for a minor of any age suffering with an eating disorder, any refusal of non-vegan medical treatment is likely to be overridden by the courts on the basis that the minor's welfare and right to life must be the primary consideration—even where the Article 9 right to express a philosophical belief in veganism has been engaged, and even if the child is deemed to have capacity to make a refusal.

6. MENTAL HEALTH ACT

Some admissions to inpatient units in respect of both adults and children will be governed by the Mental Health Act 1983 (MHA) rather than the MCA. The patient may choose to be admitted voluntarily, in which case the principles of consent and capacity will apply as considered above and as regulated by the MCA/*Gillick*. However, the MCA does not authorize medical providers to give medical treatment for a mental disorder if the patient is detained under the MHA.[60] Therefore, for patients involuntarily detained under the MHA, different provisions apply in respect of consent.

Under the MHA, patients can be compulsorily admitted for assessment[61] or treatment[62] of their mental disorder. Although different rules apply for assessment or short-term stays, the average stay for a patient admitted due to anorexia nervosa was, in a 2008 survey, estimated at 18.2 weeks.[63] The law is therefore considered here only as it applies to admission and treatment, rather than to assessment or very short term MHA admissions.

In respect of treatment for disordered eating, primary treatment will ordinarily be undertaken in the community. However, where the patient's physical health is severely compromised such that refeeding and stabilization cannot take place within an outpatient setting, inpatient admission may be indicated.[64]

For admission under the MHA, appropriate treatment must be available. Treatment modalities for disordered eating are varied. There is a range of evidence-based psychological therapies available, including Eating Disorder Focused Cognitive Behavioral Therapy, Maudsley Anorexia Nervosa Treatment for Adults, Specialist Supportive Clinical Management, Eating Disorder Focused Focal Psychodynamic Therapy, and specialist treatments for children and adolescents.[65] As well as psychological therapy, physical health assessment and monitoring, nutritional support and meal plans are likely to be provided. The appropriate therapy will of course be dependent on the individual's circumstances. Given the wide range of treatment and support which can be provided, any argument that a vegan patient cannot be admitted under the MHA on the basis that there is no ACBS-approved refeeding formula and therefore no 'appropriate treatment' is unlikely to be successful.

If a patient is admitted under the MHA, then consent is not required for medical treatment given to address the mental disorder (subject to some exclusions, which are unlikely to be relevant when considering eating disorder patients).[66]

'Medical treatment' is defined under the MHA as including nursing, psychological intervention, specialist mental health habilitation, rehabilitation and care. 'Treatment for medical disorder' is defined widely, as any treatment *'the purpose of which is to alleviate, or prevent a worsening of, the disorder or one or more of its symptoms or manifestations.'*[67] The court's determination of what constitutes a symptom or manifestation of a disorder is not always straightforward, although a refusal to eat has been held to constitute a manifestation of a number of mental illnesses and is not confined to eating disorders.[68] For example, the court was required to assess whether forcible feeding of a prisoner on hunger strike could be carried out under the MHA. The patient was diagnosed with Narcissistic Personality Disorder rather than with an eating disorder, but nonetheless the court found that the decision to undertake the hunger strike was in fact a manifestation of the mental disorder.[69] Clinically indicated forcible feeding of a vegan eating disorder patient admitted under MHA is therefore likely to be deemed to meet the criteria for 'medical treatment.' This would include both non-vegan ACBS-approved or vegan non-ACBS-approved refeeding formulations.

The MHA itself is focused on treatment for mental disorders and therefore does not directly address the position where the patient has a belief protected by Article 9 ECHR which conflicts with the treatment which can be forcibly provided under the MHA.

This interplay between MHA treatment and belief was considered in *Nottinghamshire Healthcare NHS Trust v RC*.[70] A Jehovah's Witness with a history of self-harming behaviors and a diagnosis of Antisocial and Emotionally Unstable Personality Disorder made an advance decision refusing blood products. It was determined by the court that the provision of blood products to treat the effects of a lacerated artery would constitute treatment under the MHA. Although technically treatment could therefore have been forcibly provided under the MHA, the court considered that, as the advance decision made by the patient was valid, forcible treatment under the MHA would be inappropriate. The court considered that to impose a transfusion would be to deny the patient *'a most basic freedom,'* i.e. the right to express their religious belief.

If an issue was to be brought in front of a court where a detained patient was refusing nasogastric feeding on the basis that no vegan option was available, then, in line with the case law considered above in the context of religious belief, the court would need to consider whether the refusal is a manifestation of the illness or a true expression of vegan philosophical belief. If it is determined that the patient does not have a genuine philosophical belief in veganism but rather their dietary restriction of animal products is a manifestation of an eating disorder, clinically indicated forcible nasogastric feeding (even with a non-vegan nutritional supplement) is likely to be permitted under the MHA. However, if the patient's veganism does constitute a philosophical belief, then forcible treatment under the MHA with a non-vegan food product would arguably represent an interference with the patient's Article 9 rights, even where this course of action is permitted by the MHA. The appropriate course of action in these delicate circumstances is likely to be for a declaration to be sought from the court to confirm the proposed course of action.

7. REMEDIES

The first step for a vegan patient is likely to be to ensure that the treating team is notified of their vegan diet, and the extent of their vegan beliefs. If a vegan patient is concerned that their human rights have been or are going to be breached as a result of a refusal by their treating teams to support their vegan beliefs, and/or if non-vegan forcible feeding is being contemplated, there are various steps which can be taken. The patient can request a review by their treating team to raise any concerns. If this does not assist in resolving the situation, a formal complaint can be made. If NHS care is being provided, a complaint is likely to be dealt with initially by the Patient Advice and Liaison Service (PALS).

If a patient remains dissatisfied with the outcome of any internal complaints scheme, they may be able to raise the issue through the courts. If a patient is admitted under the MHA, an application can be made for review by an MHA tribunal or for judicial review.

Judicial review challenges in respect of the issues considered here are likely to be made on one or more of the following bases:[71]

- the medical provider has misdirected itself in law,
- the decision is unreasonable, fails to adequately take relevant matters into account, or is made in bad faith,
- the medical provider has made the decision incorrectly, with bias and without good reason.

Legal challenges can be brought against a hospital's decision whilst the patient is in hospital. If there is an urgent dispute which arises at a critical point during treatment, there may be insufficient time to await the outcome of any internal complaints procedure, in which case an application to court may be the preferred approach.

Where the position in relation to capacity is unclear, contentious and/or has lifesaving or life-threatening implications, the hospital trust may choose to make an application to the Court of Protection for a declaration that the proposed action or inaction is appropriate. This will provide protection in the event that the patient or their family subsequently claims that the treatment provided was inappropriate. The patient and their family are similarly able to make an application to the Court of Protection in order to challenge the capacity decision and/or best interests decisions being made on behalf of a person who has been assessed as lacking capacity.

Where an individual or institution wishes to challenge a decision in which the MCA is engaged, the Court of Protection is the appropriate body to rule on the issue, and judicial review in the civil courts is therefore not an appropriate remedy.[72]

It is important for patients to be aware of the time limits applicable to court challenges. Applications for judicial review (which can include claims for human rights breaches) must be brought within three months from when the grounds to make a claim arises.[73] Standalone claims for human rights breaches must be brought within one year from the date when the act took place.[74]

In respect of a claim for breach of human rights, there is no formal upper limit for the amount of compensation which can be awarded. However, in practice, the awards for damages in respect of breaches of human rights are limited.[75]

8. SUMMARY

When considering medical treatment for eating disorder patients who follow a vegan diet, there are various legal frameworks in place which are sometimes contradictory and sometimes complementary.

If the patient has a strongly held and cogent belief in veganism as a lifestyle, then it may be appropriate for a vegan diet to be accommodated in treatment and dietary plans—whether or not the patient is deemed to have capacity. Failing to support the patient in doing so may well represent a breach of their right to express their philosophical belief without discrimination.

An individual has the right to refuse any treatment, provided they have capacity and are not detained under the MHA. Any such treatment must be provided reasonably and responsibly. To treat such a patient outside of these requirements is likely to constitute a breach of the patient's ECHR rights and is potentially negligent.

The position is more complex, however, when considering life-sustaining treatment, and in particular the provision of nasogastric feeding. In individuals who lack capacity, there is a strong presumption in favor of the preservation of life, and treatment could be provided forcibly, notwithstanding evidence of any philosophical belief, if it is deemed to be in the patient's best interests. In respect of minors, the court is likely to override any refusal to protect the child's right to life. Providing forceable non-vegan feeding to a patient who lacks capacity or is a minor but who has a cogent philosophical belief in veganism is likely to be a breach of the patient's ECHR right to express their philosophical belief, although the court may conclude that this is justified to protect their right to life.

Where a patient is detained involuntarily, treatment to address the mental disorder can be provided even in the absence of consent, and this is likely to extend to forcible feeding in patients where this is determined to be clinically indicated. However, if the patient has a cogent philosophical belief in veganism, then a decision to provide forcible non-vegan nasogastric feeding is likely to interfere with their right to express that belief, representing a direct conflict between two applicable legal principles. If the patient has capacity or has a valid advance decision expressing their wishes, then the safest course of action would be for the treatment provider to apply to the court for a declaration as to the validity of the proposed course of action.

When seeking to challenge a decision made or action taken by a public body which relates to medical care, various legal remedies are available. These include a civil claim in negligence or by way of human rights legislation which may result in compensatory damages being awarded. In respect of decisions regarding the MHA, an application can be made to a tribunal, or to the court for judicial review of decisions. This may result in decisions being reviewed and can also result in payments of compensation. In respect of unwelcome or uncertain MCA decisions, an application can be made either by the patient, the treatment provider, or the patient's family to the Court of Protection.

An effective remedy in many circumstances is perhaps best obtained through practical rather than legal means, with the patient and their treating team considering how the approach can be individualized to ensure that the patient is supported in engaging in treatment in a way which also enables them to express their beliefs. Collaborative and voluntary outpatient treatment is generally preferred, and in many cases it will be possible to reach an agreement as to the approach to be taken without recourse to the courts. If there is a dispute between a treatment centre and a patient/family in respect of the relevance of vegan beliefs, then the most effective remedy may well be an application to the court to decide the issue and protect all parties involved.

9. NOTES

1. Beat, "Statistics for Journalists," accessed May 10, 2020, https://www.beateatingdisorders.org.uk/media-centre/eating-disorder-statistics

2. National Institute for Health and Care Excellence (NICE), "Eating Disorders: Recognition and Treatment NICE Guideline [NG69]," 23 May 2017, accessed November 14, 2020, https://www.nice.org.uk/guidance/ng69

3. National Institute for Health and Care Excellence (NICE), "Eating Disorders: Recognition and Treatment NICE Guideline [NG69]," 23 May 2017, accessed November 14, 2020, https://www.nice.org.uk/guidance/ng69

4. Anna M. Bardone-Cone, Ellen E. Fitzsimmons-Craft, Megan B. Harney, Christine R. Maldonado, Melissa A. Lawson, Roma Smith, D. Paul Robinson, "The Inter-Relationships between Vegetarianism and Eating Disorders among Females," *Journal of the Academy of Nutrition and Dietetics* (2012) 112(8), 1247–52; Kelly Zuromski, Tracy Witte, April Smith, Natalie Goodwin, Lindsay Bodell, Mary Bartlett, Nicole Sigfried, "Increased Prevalence of Vegetarianism among Women with Eating Pathology," *Eating Behaviours* vol. 19 (2015), 24–27; Murat Baş, Efsun Karabudak, Gül Kiziltan, "Vegetarianism and Eating Disorders: Association Between Eating Attitudes and Other Psychological Factors Among Turkish Adolescents," *Appetite*, (2015) 44(3), 309–15.

5. Victoria Sullivan and Sadhana Damani, "Vegetarianism and Eating Disorders—Partners in Crime?" *European Eating Disorders Review*, (2000), 8, 263–266; Simon M. Gilbody, Sara F. L. Kirk , Andrew J. Hill, "Vegetarianism in Young Women: Another Means of Weight Control?" *International Journal of Eating Disorders,* (1999), 26(1), 87–90; M. O'Connor, S. Touyz, S. Dunn and P. Beaumont, "Vegetarianism in Anorexia Nervosa? A Review of 116 Consecutive Cases," *The Medical Journal of Australia*, (1987) 147(11–12), 540–42.

6. Brian Fisak, R.D. Peterson, S. Tantleff-Dunn, J.M. Molnar, "Challenging Previous Conceptions of Vegetarianism and Eating Disorders," *Eating Weight Disorders* (2006) Vol 11, 195–200.

7. Royal College of Psychiatrists (RCPsych), British Dietetic Association and BEAT, "Consensus Statement on Considerations for Treating Vegan Patients with Eating Disorders," 2019, accessed October 30, 2020, https://www.rcpsych.ac.uk/docs/default-source/members/faculties/eating-disorders/vegan-patients-eating-disorders-mar19.pdf?sfvrsn=be96d428_2.

8. NICE, "Eating Disorders: Recognition and Treatment NICE Guideline [NG69]," para. 1.11, 23 May 2017.

9. Vegan Society, "Definition of Veganism," accessed May 10, 2020, https://www.vegansociety.com/go-vegan/definition-veganism

10. The Association of UK Dietitians, "Practice Guidance: Veganism and Eating Disorders," July 2019.

11. Royal College of Psychiatrists (RCPsych), British Dietetic Association and BEAT, "Consensus Statement on Considerations for Treating Vegan Patients with Eating Disorders," 2019, accessed October 30, 2020, https://www.rcpsych.ac.uk/docs/default-source/members/faculties/eating-disorders/vegan-patients-eating-disorders-mar19.pdf?sfvrsn=be96d428_2

12. The Association of UK Dietitians, "Practice Guidance: Veganism and Eating Disorders."

13. Tatiana Escobar-Koch, Judith D. Banker, Scott J Crow, Jan Cullis, Susan Ringwood, Gráinne Smith, Eric Van Furth, Kitty Westin, Ulrike Schmidt, "Service Users' Views of Eating Disorder Services: An International Comparison," *Int J Eat Disord* (2010) 43: 539–59.

14. Council of Europe, *European Convention for the Protection of Human Rights and Fundamental Freedoms, as amended by Protocols Nos. 11 and 14*, 4 November 1950, ETS 5.

15. *Jewish Liturgical Association Cha'are Shalom Ve Tsedek v France* (27417/95) 9 B.H.R.C.

16. *Jakobski v Poland* [2010] ECHR 1974.

17. "Equality Act 2010 Explanatory Notes," Section 10, accessed May 10, 2020, http://www.legislation.gov.uk/ukpga/2010/15/notes/division/3/2/1/7

18. Equality and Human Rights Commission, "Religion or Belief, a Guide to the Law" (December 2016).

19. *Grainger v Nicholson* [2010] IRLR 4 (EAT).

20. Equality and Human Rights Commission, "Equality Act 2010 Code of Practice" (2011).

21. *Consibee –v- Crossley Farms Limited* 3335357/2018.

22. *Casamitjana v The League Against Cruel Sports* [2020] UKET 3331129/2018.

23. The Association of UK Dietitians, "Practice Guidance: Veganism and Eating Disorders."

24. *T* (adult: refusal of treatment) [1992] 4 All ER 649, CA.

25. Equality Act 2010, s19(2)(d).

26. *Herczegfalvy v Austria* (Applications 10533/83) (1992) 15 EHRR 437.

27. *Osman v UK* (1998) 29 EHRR 245, [1999] 1 FLR 193; *Rabone v Pennine Care NHS Foundation Trust* [UKSC 2], *A NHS Trust v Dr A* [2013] EWHC 2273 (Fam).

28. *Reynolds v UK* 2694/08 [2012] ECHR 437.

29. Fotios C. Papadopoulos, Anders Ekbom, Lena Brandt and Lisa Ekselius, "Excess Mortality, Causes of Death and Prognostic Factors in Anorexia Nervosa," *Br J Psychiatry* (Jan 2009) 94(1): 10–17.

30. Scott J. Crow, Carol B. Peterson, Sonja A. Swanson, Nancy C. Raymond, Sheila Specker, Elke D. Eckert James E. Mitchell, "Increased Mortality in Bulimia Nervosa and other Eating Disorders," *American Journal of Psychiatry* (Dec 2009), 166(12): 1342–46.

31. Re MB (Medical Treatment) [1997] EWCA Civ 3093; *Airdale NHS Trust v Bland* [1993] AC 789.

32. *Bolam v Friern Hospital Management Committee* [1957] 1 WLR 583; *Bolitho v City and Hackney Health Authority* [1996] 4 All ER 771.

33. *Montgomery v Lanarkshire Health Board* [2015] UKSC 11.

34. Mental Capacity Act 2005, Part 1 (2).

35. Mental Capacity Act 2005, Part 1 (4).

36. Mental Capacity Act 2005, Part 1 (5).

37. Mental Capacity Act 2005 section 3(1).

38. *Re MB* (Medical Treatment); PC (by her litigation friend the Official Solicitor) v A Local Authority [2013] All ER (D) 71 (May); Re B (adult: refusal of medical treatment) [2002] 2 All ER 449.

39. Royal College of Psychiatrists, "Eating Disorders in the UK: Service, Distribution, Service Development and Training," CR170 March 2012.

40. The Association of UK Dietitians, "Practice Guidance: Veganism and Eating Disorders."

41. Mental Capacity Act 2005 s4(6).
42. *Re H* (adult patient) (medical treatment) [2006] All ER (D) 372 (May).
43. Vegan Society (2019), "Definition of Veganism," accessed November 14, 2020, https://www.vegansociety.com/go-vegan/definition-veganism. The author accepts that there are discussion and debates about the definition of veganism. The definition of the Vegan Society was helpful in *Casamitjana*, above. For further comment see Roussel and Labchuk and Karp in this volume.
44. *A NHS Trust v Dr A* [2013] EWCH 2442 (COP).
45. *W Healthcare NHS Trust v H* [2004] EWCA Civ 1324, (2004) Times, 9 December.
46. *Re E* (Medical Treatment Anorexia) [2012] EWHC 1639.
47. A Clinical Commissioning Group v P (withdrawal of CANH) [2019], EWCOP 18.
48. Umberto Volpe, Alfonso Tortorella, Mirko Manchia, Alessio M. Monteleone, Umberto Albert, Palmiero Monteleone, "Eating Disorders: What Age at Onset?" *Psychiatry Research* vol 238 30 April 2016, 225–27.
49. Children Act 1989 s1.
50. Children Act 1989 s1(3).
51. *Gillick v West Norfolk and Wisbech Area Health Authority* [1985] 3 All ER 402, HL.
52. *Re E* (a minor) (Wardship: medical treatment) [1993] 1 F.L.R. 386.
53. *L* (medical treatment: Gillick competency), Re [1999] 2 FCR 524 [1998], 2 FLR 81.
54. *R* (a minor), Re [1992], Fam 11 [1991], 4 All ER 177, CA.
55. *F v F* (Welfare of Children: Immunization)—[2013] All ER (D) 149 (Oct).
56. Family Law Reform Act 1969 s8(1).
57. An NHS Foundation Hospital v P [2014] EWHC 1650 (Fam) (Transcript).
58. *Re P* (Medical Treatment: Best Interests) [2003] EWHC 2327 (Fam).
59. *Re W* (A Minor) (Medical Treatment) [1992] All ELR.
60. Mental Capacity Act 2005, s28 (1) (a).
61. Mental Health Act (1983) s2.
62. Mental Health Act (1983) s3.
63. Royal College of Psychiatrists, "Eating Disorders in the UK: Service, Distribution, Service Development and Training."
64. NICE, "Eating Disorders: Recognition and Treatment NICE Guideline [NG69]," Para. 1.11.1.
65. NICE, "Eating Disorders: Recognition and Treatment NICE Guideline [NG69]," Para. 1.3–1.6.
66. Mental Health Act (1983), s63.
67. Mental Health Act (1983), s145(4).
68. B v Croydon [1995] 2 WLR 294 CA; Thameside & Glossop nHS Trust v CH [1996] 1 FLR 762.
69. *R v Collins ex p Ian Steward Brady* [2000] Lloyd's Rep Med 355.
70. Nottinghamshire Healthcare NHS Trust v RC [2014] EWCOP 1317.
71. Halsbury's Laws of England, 2018, 61A, 2.
72. *DO v LBH* [2012] EWHC 4044 (Admin) EC.
73. Civil Procedure Rules 54.5.
74. Human Rights Act 1998 s7 (5).
75. *Savage v South Essex Partnership NHS Foundation Trust* [2010] EWHC 865 (QB); *Rabone v Pennine Care NHS Foundation Trust [2012] UKSC 2.*

10. REFERENCES

A Clinical Commissioning Group v P (Withdrawal of CANH) [2019] EWCOP 18.
A NHS Trust v Dr A [2013] EWHC 2273 (Fam).
Airdale NHS Trust v Bland [1993] A.C 789.
An NHS Foundation Hospital v P [2014] EWHC 1650 (Fam) (Transcript).
B v Croydon [1995] 2 WLR 294 CA.

Bardone-Cone, Anna M. Fitzsimmons-Craft, Ellen E., Harney, Megan B., Maldonado, Christine R., Lawson, Melissa A. Smith, Roma, and Robinson, D. Paul. "The Inter-Relationships Between Vegetarianism and Eating Disorders among Females." *Journal of the Academy of Nutrition and Dietetics* (2012) 112(8), 1247–52.

Bas, Murat, Efsun Karabudak, and Gül Kiziltan. "Vegetarianism and Eating Disorders: Association Between Eating Attitudes and Other Psychological Factors among Turkish Adolescents." *Appetite*, (2015) 44(3), 309–15.

Beat, "Statistics for Journalists." Accessed November 15, 2020, https://www.beateatingdisorders.org.uk/media-centre/eating-disorder-statistics.

Bolam v Friern Hospital Management Committee [1957] 1 WLR 583.

Bolitho v City and Hackney Health Authority [1996] 4 All ER 771.

Casamitjana v The League Against Cruel Sports [2020] UKET 3331129/2018.

Children Act 1989.

Civil Procedure Rules.

Consibee v Crossley Farms Limited ET 3335357/2018.

Council of Europe. European Convention for the Protection of Human Rights and Fundamental Freedoms as amended by Protocols Nos. 11 and 14, 4 November 1950, ETS 5.

Crow S. J., Peterson C. B., Swanson S. A., Raymond N.C., Specker S., Elke D. Eckert E.D., Mitchell J.E. "Increased Mortality in Bulimia Nervosa and Other Eating Disorders." *American Journal of Psychiatry* (Dec 2009), 166(12): 1342–46.

DO v LBH [2012] EWHC 4044 (Admin) EC.

Equality Act 2010.

Equality Act 2010. "Explanatory Notes," s10. http://www.legislation.gov.uk/ukpga/2010/15/notes/division/3/2/1/7.

Equality and Human Rights Commission. "Equality Act 2010 Code of Practice" (2011).

Equality and Human Rights Commission. "Religion or Belief, a Guide to the Law" (December 2016).

Escobar-Koch, Tatiana, Banker, Judith D., Crow, Scott J., Cullis, Jan, Ringwood, Susan, Smith, Gráinne, Van Furth, Eric, Westin, Kitty and Schmidt, Ulrike. "Service Users' Views of Eating Disorder Services: An International Comparison." *Int J Eat Disord* (2010) 43: 539–59.

F v F (Welfare of Children: Immunisation)—[2013] All ER (D) 149 (Oct).

Family Law Reform Act.

Fisak, Brian, Peterson, R.D., Tantleff-Dunn, S. and Molnar, J.M. "Challenging Previous Conceptions of Vegetarianism and Eating Disorders." *Eating Weight Disorders* (2006), Vol. 11, 195–200;

Gilbody Simon M., Kirk Sara F.L. and Hill Andrew J. "Vegetarianism in Young Women: Another Means of Weight Control?" *International Journal of Eating Disorders,* (1999), 26(1), 87–90.

Gillick v West Norfolk and Wisbech Area Health Authority [1985], 3 All ER 402, HL.

Grainger v Nicholson [2010] IRLR 4 (EAT).

Halsbury's Laws of England (2018) London: Lexis Nexis.

Herczegfalvy v Austria (Applications 10533/83) (1992) 15 EHRR 437.

Human Rights Act (1998).

Jakobski v Poland [2010] ECHR 1974.

Kings College NHS Foundation Trust v C & V [2015] EWCOP 59.

L (medical treatment: Gillick competency), Re[1999] 2 FCR 524, [1998] 2 FLR 81.

Mental Capacity Act (2005).

Mental Health Act (1983).

Montgomery v Lanarkshire Health Board [2015] UKSC 11.

National Institute for Health and Care Excellence (NICE). "Eating Disorders: Recognition and Treatment NICE Guideline [NG69]" 23 May 2017. Accessed November 14, 2020, https://www.nice.org.uk/guidance/ng69.

Nottinghamshire Healthcare NHS Trust v RC—138 BMLR 147.

O'Connor, M., Touyz, S., Dunn, S. and Beaumont, P. "Vegetarianism in Anorexia Nervosa? A Review of 116 Consecutive Cases." *The Medical Journal of Australia*, (1987) 147(11–12), 540–42.

Osman v UK (1998) 29 EHRR 245.

Papadopoulos, Fotios C., Ekbom, Anders, Brandt, Lena and Ekselius, Lisa. "Excess Mortality, Causes of Death and Prognostic Factors in Anorexia Nervosa." *Br J Psychiatry* (Jan 2009) 94(1): 10–17.

PC (by her litigation friend the Official Solicitor) v A Local Authority [2013], All ER (D) 71 (May).

Rabone v Pennine Care NHS Foundation Trust [UKSC 2].

R (a minor), Re [1991], 4 All ER 177, CA.

Re B (adult: refusal of medical treatment) [2002] 2 All ER 449.

Re E (Medical Treatment Anorexia) [2012] EWHC 1639.

Re E (a minor) (Wardship: medical treatment) [1993] 1 F.L.R. 386

Re H (adult patient) (medical treatment)[2006] All ER (D) 372 (May).

Re MB (Medical Treatment) [1997] EWCA Civ 3093.

Re P (Medical Treatment: Best Interests) [2003] EWHC 2327 (Fam).

R v, Collins ex p Ian Steward Brady [2000] Lloyd's Rep Med 355.

Re W (A Minor) (Medical Treatment) [1992] All ELR.

Reynolds v UK 2694/08 [2012] ECHR 437.

Royal College of Psychiatrists. "Consensus Statement on Considerations for Treating Vegan Patients with Eating Disorders," 2019, https://www.rcpsych.ac.uk/docs/default-source/members/faculties/eating-disorders/vegan-patients-eating-disorders-mar19.pdf?sfvrsn=be96d428_2.

Royal College of Psychiatrists. "Eating Disorders in the UK: Service, Distribution, Service Development and Training," CR170 March 2012.

Savage v South Essex Partnership NHS Foundation Trust [2010] EWHC 865 (QB).

Sullivan, Victoria, and Damani, Sadhana. "Vegetarianism and Eating Disorders—Partners in Crime?" *European Eating Disorders Review*, (2000), 8, 263–66.

T (adult: refusal of treatment) [1992] 4 All ER 649, CA.

Thameside & Glossop NHS Trust v CH [1996] 1 FLR 762.

The Association of UK Dietitians. "Practice Guidance: Veganism and Eating Disorders," published July 2019.

Vegan Society. (2019) Definition of Veganism. Accessed November 14, 2020, https://www.vegansociety.com/go-vegan/definition-veganism

Volpe, Umberto, Tortorella, Alfonso, Manchia, Mirko, Monteleone, Alessio M., Albert, Umberto and Monteleone, Palmiero. "Eating Disorders: What Age at Onset?" *Psychiatry Research*, vol. 238, 30 April 2016: 225–27.

W Healthcare NHS Trust v H [2004] EWCA Civ 1324, (2004) Times, 9 December.

Zuromski, Kelly, Witte, Tracy, Smith, April, Goodwin, Natalie, Bodell, Lindsay, Bartlett, Mary and Sigfried, Nicole. "Increased Prevalence of Vegetarianism among Women with Eating Pathology." *Eating Behaviours*, vol. 19, 2015, 24–27.

Chapter Twelve

The Confirmation of Ethical Veganism as a Protected Philosophical Belief in Great Britain

A Personal Account of Triumph

Jordi Casamitjana

1. INTRODUCTION

My name is Jordi Casamitjana, I am a zoologist who works in animal protection and have been an ethical vegan since 2002. I am known for having helped to confirm the legal protection of ethical vegans in Great Britain due to litigation I initiated in 2018, which led to an employment tribunal judge officially confirming that ethical veganism is a protected philosophical belief under the Equality Act 2010.

A case concerning veganism was first heard at the European Court of Human Rights in 1993. The case was about a vegan prisoner in the United Kingdom (UK) who did not want to work with dyes in a prison print facility because they were likely to have been tested on non-human animals. The vegan involved claimed that his right to freedom of belief, under Article 9 of the European Convention on Human Rights, had been breached. The court found that veganism was within the scope of protection under the Convention, but that working in the print facility was required under the Prison Rules and necessary for good order in the prison. The Court decided, therefore, that any interference with the applicant's right to freedom of belief was lawful. The UK authorities did not contest that vegan convictions were within the scope of human rights law, and this case confirmed that the beliefs of vegans in the care or control of state authorities must be given due consideration.

This case was later used as the basis for the strategy of the International Vegan Rights Alliance (IVRA[1]) to campaign for vegans around the world to be beneficiaries of protective rights.

While this case showed that vegans could benefit from human rights law when in conflict with public bodies, a case under the Equality Act 2010 (the UK domestic equality legislation that deals with discrimination in the workplace, and in the provision of goods and services) had yet to be heard. This chapter explains my journey to veganism and how I contributed to changing the legal landscape for vegans in Great Britain through the first successful employment tribunal claim under the Equality Act 2010 involving discrimination against a vegan.

2. MY JOURNEY TO VEGANISM

My journey to veganism was a long one. When I was growing up in my native Catalonia in the 1960s, the country was under the fascist regime of General Francisco Franco. This regime oppressed the Catalan nation for over forty years and isolated it from many social and political advances.[2] I never met any vegans in Catalonia or even heard the term mentioned. This feeling of oppression during my childhood made me want to be closer to animals than to humans, who seemed very dangerous to me. It also made me more sympathetic to other oppressed victims and, naturally, this included all animals exploited by people.

In my teenage years, I graduated as a zoologist and began my PhD studies on animal behavior. The subject I chose to study was the behavior of social wasps of the genus *Polistes*.[3] The first encounter with one of these wasps' nest is what awoke the animal protectionist within me. A wasp that was taking the role of 'guard' at the entrance of the nest clearly spotted me, and for a few seconds assessed whether I was dangerous enough for it to raise the alarm. It appeared to me that the wasp decided that I was not dangerous and thus did not try to prevent me from observing. The experience of having been correctly judged by a one-inch individual that would most likely be killed by most humans at the first opportunity had a profound effect on me. The more I studied them, the more I realized how much they (and all animals) are much more similar to us than we realize, and also how much they suffer unfairly because of human ignorance.

I decided that, in addition to being a zoologist, I wanted to dedicate my life to helping animals in need. At the time, the prospect of being able to do both these things whilst living in Catalonia was slim, so before I finished my PhD studies I left and moved to the UK, where I knew animal protection was already an established profession.

In 1995, I was appointed as a Research and Rehabilitation Coordinator at the Monkey Sanctuary (now called Wild Futures) in Looe, Cornwall, which kept a colony of woolly monkeys. Since then, I have worked only in animal protection; I have worked in a variety of roles, both freelance and salaried, for reputable animal protection organizations. The Sanctuary operated as a community where staff worked and lived in the same house. Most of the staff were either vegetarian or vegan, so the communal meals were either vegan or had a vegetarian option. Although I was still a meat-eater at the time, I only ate meat when I was outside the sanctuary grounds.

The Sanctuary was anti-captivity. Although it was reliant on funds provided by visitors coming to see the monkeys, the focus was on trying to return the animals to the wild, where possible, and that was the primary purpose of my job role. Whilst working at the Sanctuary, I developed several non-invasive research projects[4] with the monkeys, which were then scrutinized by my work colleagues to ascertain if they were ethically sound. It was through my conversations with my colleagues that I began to be introduced further into the concept of ethical veganism, which, as I understood it at the time, was based on trying to do as little harm as practically possible to sentient beings.

Although I was drawn to veganism, I resisted becoming vegan for some years through a fear that it would be too difficult to keep up when I was outside the Sanctuary. In 2000, I left the Monkey Sanctuary, but I soon found employment as the Zoo Check Coordinator for the Born Free Foundation that led a campaign against keeping wild animals in zoos. At Born Free, I met other committed vegans, and this made me wonder whether my fears over how difficult veganism may be were unfounded.

There were many ethical issues in my mind that I wanted to explore, so I decided to take a break to write a novel that I felt would help me explore them. I spent twenty-three days in isolation over the 2001/02 Christmas period in a cottage on a Scottish island, during which I wrote the novel (titled *The Demon's Trial*).[5] The isolation that I experienced on this break, as well as the careful examination of all my rationalizations, operated as some sort of 'epiphany' and made me realize how wrong I had been in justifying the consumption of some animal products, and how I could and should do better in putting my ethical views into practice. It was during that process that I became an ethical vegan, and my novel represents an account of what my thoughts were during this transformation.

The set of beliefs that I developed on the island were that I should live my life in a way that causes as little exploitation to animals as I could realistically manage. When I returned from the island, I went straight to following a complete vegan lifestyle (from meat-eater to vegan without any vegetarian transition). I stopped consuming animal products (no meat of any kind, including fish, and no milk, eggs, honey, etc.). I gradually got rid of any clothes I had that contained animal products and stopped supporting any company or organization that directly contributed to the exploitation of animals. My previous fears had been unfounded; I learnt that my new lifestyle was far easier than I had thought it would be, and I felt healthier than ever.

My transition to following a 100% vegan diet happened instantly after returning from the island, but the process of getting rid of all animal products in my house took longer. After a couple of months, the only remaining animal-derived objects I possessed were some woolen clothes and leather belts and shoes. I intended to use them until they were worn out and then replace them with vegan alternatives. However, feeling guilty, perhaps a year or so after returning from the island, I decided to throw them away or give them to charities, even if they were still in good condition. Finding suitable vegan-friendly suppliers for financial products or commodities took much longer.

I started to educate myself more on ethical veganism and soon realized that there was also a strong political component to it. I realized that if it were only a personal lifestyle choice, the number of animals that I would not be hurting by becoming vegan would still be a very small percentage of the total numbers being harmed. Society remained inundated with animal exploitation, and veganism remained a minority social movement. I knew that in order to make a substantial contribution to animal protection and the environment, it was necessary for me to help other people become vegan too.

I realized that part of being an ethical vegan was to promote veganism and to try to persuade as many people as possible to adopt a vegan lifestyle. This became increasingly easy over the years as the false stigma of veganism being unhealthy went away and scientists and authorities began to publicly recognize that not only was it perfectly healthy but that in most cases it was also healthier than meat-eating.[6]

I became a very outspoken vegan, and I improved my veganism every year by becoming better at avoiding products and services with links to any form of animal exploitation. I continued working in animal protection for other organizations until, in 2018, I was dismissed from one of them. This led to the litigation mentioned earlier that confirmed the protection of all ethical vegans in Great Britain.

3. WHAT VEGANISM MEANS TO ME

I am an ethical vegan, and what I mean by this is that I am a person who holds the belief of veganism as originally defined by The Vegan Society. It therefore affects all aspects of my life—not only my diet. I use the adjective 'ethical' to emphasize that my veganism is not just a diet, but a serious and cogent philosophical belief. The adjective has become necessary in recent times due to the uptake of the word 'vegan' to describe those who follow only the dietary element of vegan practice. There are other adjectives that could be used instead ('true vegan,' 'full vegan,' 'original vegan,' etc.), although 'ethical' is the most commonly used.

Veganism itself is not a religion. It is a philosophical belief based on facts and sincere convictions that affect my daily life. My view is that certainty in religious beliefs is grounded by faith, the trust of religious leaders or scriptures, or in culturally supported superstitions, whereas non-religious beliefs, such as ethical veganism, are based on logic, the analysis of evidence and philosophical speculation.

As with any set of beliefs, I would expect that within the ethical vegan community there are nuances regarding the finer points of individual beliefs held.[7] The term 'vegan' was first coined by Donald Watson, who founded The Vegan Society in the UK in 1944.[8] However, vegans have existed for many centuries in different parts of the world, and vegan lifestyles have been followed by both individuals and members of religious and social groups.

Philosophically, the concept of veganism is rooted in the ancient concept of 'ahimsa,' which is one of the main premises of the Indian religion of Jainism. Ahimsa means 'not to injure,' and is also referred to as "non-violence."[9] Although I am an atheist and, therefore, do not follow any religion, I am a firm believer that people should live their lives following the principles of ahimsa as much as possible.

When The Vegan Society became a registered charity in 1979, the Memorandum and Articles of Association updated the definition of 'veganism' as:

> A philosophy and way of living which seeks to exclude—as far as is possible and practicable—all forms of exploitation of, and cruelty to, animals for food, clothing or any other purpose; and by extension, promotes the development and use of animal-free alternatives for the benefit of humans, animals and the environment. [10]

This philosophy, so defined by the Vegan Society, is the one that I ascribe to and that constitutes the basis of my philosophical belief, which acts as my creed and moral framework.

These days, there are many different types of vegans, and the type is defined by a person's lifestyle and the main reason they adopted veganism.[11] These can be broadly divided into two types; ethical vegans, and health vegans (who are sometimes called dietary vegans or strict vegetarians). The former chooses veganism for ethical reasons and, normally, veganism affects every aspect of their lives, not just their diet. The latter choose veganism for health reasons and, therefore, it normally only affects their diet. People belonging to this category of 'vegans' are sometimes referred to as 'following a plant-based diet' rather than as 'vegans.'

In turn, ethical vegans could be sub-classified into two groups: those for whom the main ethical reason stems from the exploitation and abuse of animals (commonly referred to as ethical vegans for the Animals, or just 'ethical vegans,' and these are the ones who follow literally the definition of veganism by the Vegan Society), and those for whom the main ethical reason is the destruction of the environment due to animal agriculture. Those who are vegan for environmental reasons hardly ever describe themselves as 'ethical vegans,' but rather as 'vegans for the environment.'[12] Many ethical vegans consider themselves to come within both sub-divisions. I am one of them, as I am now an ethical vegan for the environment as well (so the term 'ethical vegan' fully fits my identity), although my personal philosophical belief is in ethical veganism for the Animals (and this was my primary reason to become vegan in the first place).

Some religious vegans attach a particular metaphysical explanation to their belief. Some Judeo-Christian vegans may use the story of Adam and Eve to support their veganism, as it is said that before the original sin they lived a vegan lifestyle in the Garden of Eden.[13] Other vegans that follow Eastern religions may refer to some of their Gods as vegan and to a vegan lifestyle as an attempt to become 'purer.' Some may believe in reincarnation and, therefore, they believe that animals that are eaten possess souls that could have been in a human before. Many vegans also follow what can be broadly labelled as 'New Age' philosophies in which concepts such as 'energy' or 'the universe' are used almost as a substitute for a deity.

I am an atheist and a Neo-Darwinist scientist, meaning that I take a rational approach to Nature. I don't believe in any single metaphysical explanation of veganism, but I do draw common themes from all of them, and I see no conflict between them and the fundamental aspects of ethical veganism that I follow—in particular the desire to end suffering for all individual animals across the range of species (ethical vegans do not discriminate against particular animal species and, therefore, they are anti-speciesist[14]). However, I believe that there is a basic quasi-metaphysical principle of ethical veganism in the ecological and biological kinship we share with all sentient beings.

4. THE NEED TO USE LAWS TO PROTECT VEGANS

When a person becomes an ethical vegan, they join a community of people sharing their belief. They, therefore, incorporate their belief as a new constantly reinforced 'identity' that defines them and the members of that community. Although not all ethical vegans actively embrace this new community, non-vegans may nevertheless see vegans as 'outsiders'; as no longer part of their group. I believe that this is when the problem begins.

Since I became vegan, I have experienced all types of prejudice and discrimination. Most of the time, I just 'take it on the chin,' tolerate it and do nothing. My experiences range from mild mockery, which 'crossed the line' to a point where it would not have been seen to be justified if it had happened on the basis of sexual orientation or religion, to having to work hungry because I was not provided with subsistence when the rest of my colleagues were. Certainly, the most common form of discrimination tends to be around catering scenarios, where vegan food options are not provided at events or meetings, or those options provided are clearly insufficient and tokenistic. Similar types of discrimination are experienced by other vegans. For example, vegan children are not provided with vegan options in schools, vegan patients are not provided with vegan food in hospitals, and vegans in the service industries are not provided with vegan-friendly uniforms. There are anecdotal reports alleging that an application to become a foster parent was denied on account of the applicant being vegan. There are reports of a pub that had a sign at the door stating 'vegans not welcome.'

There have been surveys in the UK showing that such incidents of discrimination against vegans are not isolated. The first survey, conducted at Lancaster University in 2013, analyzed the experience of seventy-four vegans. It found that most of the participants endured a range of unpleasant, unfair and discriminatory experiences.[15] At that time, the vegan community was not familiar with the idea of vegan discrimination or using law to protect vegans. The IVRA's publicity campaign generated support for vegan rights and produced the first short guide on veganism and law, 'Vegan Rights: Questions and Answers' (now superseded). Following the growth of awareness that vegans could use law to protect themselves from discrimination, a second survey was conducted in 2017 by Go Vegan Scotland. This survey attracted views from 483 Scottish vegans, and concluded that vegans were routinely ignored, dismissed, marginalized and made to feel as though they did not count.[16] In 2019, the UK law firm Crossland Employment Solicitors conducted a further survey of 1,000 vegans, concluding that a staggering 45% of them felt discriminated against by their employers. A further 31% said they felt harassed at work or unfairly treated due to their veganism. The survey also polled 1,000 employers. It found that 48% did nothing to accommodate the needs of their vegan staff, and that 3% would not hire someone if they knew they were vegan.[17]

The number of people subscribing to a vegan lifestyle is greatly increasing, and the latest poll from The Vegan Society estimated that there were around 600,000 vegans in the UK in 2018. This suggests that since 2014, the number of vegans in the UK is doubling every two years or so.[18] I believe that the growth of veganism and the fact that it has become more mainstream means that legal protection of vegans is imperative. This is because more people will interact with vegans without knowing enough about their needs and how to accommodate them.

In my view, every time a new minority group appears in society, 'ignorance' about this group will initiate a chain reaction that goes from ignorance to prejudgment, from prejudgment to prejudice, from prejudice to discrimination and from discrimination to hate. And when it gets to the 'hate' stage, violence may occur and there may be a need to deal with 'veganphobia' as a hate crime. But if legal protection is granted at the prejudice and discrimination stages before the social 'hate' has developed, this sequence can be stopped in its tracks.

This is what I hope will happen as a result of my legal case, which confirmed ethical veganism as a protected philosophical belief under the Equality Act 2010. Vegans already had protection under human rights law in the UK: public bodies, such as the police, prisons, the health service and, schools, etc. were already under a duty not to unlawfully interfere with a vegan's ethical practice. It is now formally confirmed that under British equality law it is unlawful to discriminate against (directly or indirectly), harass or victimise ethical vegans in both the public and private sector (including private sector employment and in the provision of goods and services).

5. MY LEGAL CASE

It all started with an issue over workplace pension arrangements. In 2016, I was employed by an animal protection organization in the UK as their Head of Policy and Research and, as is required by law, I was auto-enrolled in my employer's default pension fund. But, being an ethical vegan, I always read all labels of all the products I consider buying and try to find out about any connections or associations that manufacturers and service providers might have with animal exploitation.

When I researched where the money of the pension fund was invested, I discovered that it was invested in pharmaceutical and tobacco companies that conduct tests on animals. These practices are clearly incompatible with my beliefs.

I considered the auto-enrolment an act of indirect discrimination, as the pension fund that the organization had chosen as their default fund was incompatible with the beliefs of all ethical vegans in the organization—not just mine. After raising my concerns with the management, they agreed to change it. I asked for my contributions to pause until the change took place. However, a year later the change that was promised had not been implemented and my contributions had not been paused, despite my request. At that point, I felt directly discriminated against.

When, in 2018, I informed my colleagues about what I had found out regarding the pension fund issue, I was dismissed on the grounds of failing to follow a reasonable management instruction and serious insubordination (which I considered direct discrimination and victimization). During my disciplinary process, I was told that my ethical principles clouded my judgement and made me biased. I considered this to be harassment.

On the basis of the facts, I decided to make a complaint against my former employer to the Employment Tribunal with a claim of discrimination. However, there had never been a case where veganism was presented to court as a protected philosophical belief under the Equality Act 2010, and, though there were prior indications in case law that vegans would be protected, there was no direct precedent for my case. A pre-hearing was, therefore, arranged for a judge to assess if ethical veganism falls within the scope of the relevant protected characteristic.

I had become aware that the Equality Act 2010 imposes a duty not to discriminate and protects individuals under nine 'protected characteristics.' A few of these protected characteristics are sex, age, race, and disability. My case sought protection under the protected characteristic 'religion or belief.' This category recognizes that not only religious beliefs deserve protection and uses the term 'philosophical belief,' which provides protection for 'non-religious' beliefs. Not all non-religious beliefs will deserve the protection of law: my case would determine whether or not veganism qualifies.

The Employment Appeals Tribunal uses a set of criteria that a belief needs to fulfil to qualify for protection. This legal test was set in a previous case brought under the Equality Act 2010[19] and reflects that used by judges at the European Court of Human Rights when it considers whether an applicant's belief can qualify for protection under the human right to freedom of belief. The criteria are: the belief must be genuinely held; it must be a belief and not an opinion based on present available information; it must be a weighty or substantial aspect of human life and behavior; it must have a level of cogency, seriousness, cohesion and importance; and it must be worthy of respect in a democratic society as well as being not incompatible with human dignity or in conflict with the rights of others.

5.1 The Court Hearing

On the 3rd of January 2020, a judge in the Norwich Employment Tribunal ruled that I had presented overwhelming evidence that ethical veganism (as following the definition of veganism of The Vegan Society) was indeed a protected philosophical belief and that it met all the criteria.[20] My discrimination case continued in February and it was eventually settled in my favor.

The success of my case means that from that moment on, it is recognized in Great Britain (as the Equality Act 2010 does not apply directly to Northern

Ireland), in both the public and private sector, that it is unlawful to discriminate against ethical vegans. Importantly, the application of the legal test—as influenced by that of the European Court of Human Rights—to my case in order to determine whether ethical vegans hold beliefs that qualify for protection shows that the protection is real, effective and grounded in strong legal principles and law.

6. CONSEQUENCES OF ETHICAL VEGANISM BEING CONFIRMED AS A PROTECTED CHARACTERISTIC

The news of my landmark case spread all over the world, with more than 1,400 websites in more than sixty countries talking about it. This is important because effective protection for vegans cannot be achieved if the general public does not become aware of such protection (as my case proves, litigation is costly and long, so it is always better if discrimination is prevented rather than punished).

Due to my case and the publicity it generated, the work of the IVRA and The Vegan Society over the years and its publication of a useful guide for employers,[21] most employers in the UK are now likely to understand more about veganism and what they need to do to prevent discrimination against their vegan employees. Positive changes in the approach to and consideration of vegans in workplaces can already be seen.

As the Equality Act 2010 covers discrimination in the workplace and the provision of services (both public and private), there are many potential benefits for vegans subsequent to my case. I expect that one of the clearest effects will be in schools and hospitals (The Vegan Society has already achieved very good results in these areas by using the principles of human rights and equality law), but also in the canteens of all public bodies.

My case may also lead to an improvement in food labelling for its suitability for vegans, to a vegan-friendlier approach in the design of office kitchens (for example, designated shelves in fridges exclusively for vegan food), and to changes in companies' team-building events and social gatherings (no longer team-bonding trips to the zoo or the races). And it may also have an effect in financial services, promoting the development of vegan-friendly pension funds and banks.

Already I have received information from parents of vegan children informing me that after a long time asking their school to provide them with suitable vegan meals, finally, apparently because of my case, they will now do so. I also received photos of workplace kitchens that now provide separate microwave ovens for vegans. Other vegan workers have told me that their employer now provides plant-based milk, while before it was refused despite numerous requests. I am also aware that due to the outcome of my case, the

UK fire service is now automatically issuing vegan Personal Protective Equipment such as boots and gloves (no longer leather or suede) to all vegan firefighters and are even trying to find a suitable alternative to the current helmets, which have a leather chin strap.

One of the most interesting indirect consequences of my case is that many vegans who were afraid to express their beliefs in public may feel more confident to do so knowing that they are now better protected. As my case has proved, part of the manifestation of the ethical veganism belief is to be able to communicate to others which products and services are suitable for vegans and which are not. We vegans strongly rely on the vegan community to share this sort of information, as otherwise we would not be able to choose the option that is compatible with our beliefs in each and every choice we need to make. If employers punish their employees who share such information, or employees feel intimidated by the possible consequences they may face if they share this information, more people will be unwillingly contributing to animal exploitation. Therefore, my case may help vegans become more effective in avoiding animal-related products, which may help them become more vocal about their veganism, and this is likely to increase the number of people who adopt veganism. And it is undoubtedly better for the animals and the environment.

Another indirect consequence of my case is the inspiration it offers to other jurisdictions in other countries to follow suit and aspire to develop legal measures to protect ethical vegans. Over one thousand pages of evidence which I produced for my pre-hearing, are now public[22] and I am aware that campaigners from many countries may be using them in order to try to achieve the same protection in their countries, either via litigation or by lobbying for a change in legislation. Countries with similar Common Law systems as in the UK, which already have equality legislation, may be able to achieve this sooner. In some countries, they may not have 'philosophical beliefs' as one of the already established, protected characteristics, but they may have concepts such as 'creed,' which could perhaps be used instead.

In some countries, protection for vegans may take longer to achieve, as they may not even have general equality laws or, even if they do, only one religion, or only established religions, may be explicitly protected. But it should be easier in any country that has signed the European Convention on Human Rights and Fundamental Freedoms, as it sets out in its Article 9 the right to freedom of thought, conscience and belief. There have already been court cases at European level, and out-of-court settlements in the UK, when it has been recognized that non-religious beliefs, including veganism, are included in the protection offered.[23]

I am also aware that in Spain there is now a campaign from the group ESVECO[24] aimed at changing the official definition of 'vegan' by the Spanish Royal Academy of Language, as it currently does not use the definition of

The Vegan Society, but one that only describes veganism as an 'attitude.' My case has inspired these campaigners, who have been campaigning for vegan food options to be added in schools, hoping that such change in the definition may eventually lead to recognition of veganism as a protected belief, as it is now in the UK.

I believe we are entering a new phase in the vegan movement: the policy phase. From the conceptual phase we moved to the outreach phase, but it is possible that now, with my case and others, we are entering a new era where policies, rules, regulations and laws are developed not only to protect the 'messenger,' but also to promote the message as well. There are now enough vegans in the general population to be able to find vegans in the political population too. There has been at least one vegan MP in the UK Parliament since 2005, and, currently, there are five. There is also an All-party Parliamentary Group of Veganism and Vegetarianism in the UK Parliament. The increasing recognition among politicians of all parties of the negative effects of animal agriculture on the environment will help too. Last but not least, publications like the one you are reading right now are very useful in order for vegans to begin advancing in this new phase—they can help to foster expertise in the field of vegan rights at the international level and enable the sharing of strategic and tactical advances in the policy side of the vegan movement.

7. NOTES

1. The International Vegan Rights Alliance was established in 2012 to disseminate information about the human right to freedom of conscience and its applicability to vegans. It merged with The Vegan Society in 2019.
2. Caitlin O'Connor, "How Catalan Culture and Identity Survived the Franco Regime," (2000), URC Student Scholarship, accessed March 13, 2020, https://scholar.oxy.edu/handle/20.500.12711/984.
3. Jordi Casamitjana i Costa, "Aspectes Ecoetòlogics de les Vespes del Gènere Polistes de Catalunya (I): Estudi de la Nidificació d'una Població Semiurbana de Polistes ominulus Christ, 1791 (Hymenoptera: Vespidae)," *Sessió Conjunta d'Entomologia* 6, no.1 (March 1989): 87–96.
4. Jordi Casamitjana, "The Vocal Repertoire of the Woolly Monkey Lagothrix Lagothricha," *Bioacoustics* 13 (2002): 1–19.
5. J.C. Costa, *The Demon's Trial* (Victoria: Trafford Publishing, 2006).
6. British Association of UK Dietitians, "British Dietetic Association Confirms Well-planned Vegan Diets Can Support Healthy Living in People of All Ages," 2017, accessed May 4, 2020, https://www.bda.uk.com/resource/british-dietetic-association-confirms-well-planned-vegan-diets-can-support-healthy-living-in-people-of-all-ages.html.
7. Xavier Cohen, "How Should Vegans Live?" *Journal of Practical Ethics* 3, no 2 (December 2015): 61–65.
8. The Vegan Society, "Ripened by Human Determination, 70 years of the Vegan Society," Birmingham, accessed June 1, 2020, https://www.vegansociety.com/sites/default/files/uploads/Ripened%20by%20human%20determination.pdf.
9. D.M. Mayton, and C.A. Burrows, "Psychology of Nonviolence," *The Encyclopedia of Peace Psychology* 1 (2012): 713–716 and 720–723.

10. The Vegan Society, "Memorandum and Articles of Association," Birmingham, accessed March 13, 2020, https://www.vegansociety.com/about-us/further-information/memorandum-and-articles-association. The author is aware that there are discussions about the definition of veganism. The Vegan Society definition was useful in this particular case.

11. Jordi Casamitjana. *Ethical Vegan. A Personal and Political Journey to Change the World* (Tunbridge Wells: September Publishing, 2020).

12. Tristram McPherson, "A Case for Ethical Veganism: Intuitive and methodological consideration," *Journal of Moral Philosophy* 11, no 6 (November 2014): 677–703.

13. Akiva Gersh, "Adam and Eve Were Vegan (and a Whole Bunch of Israelis Are Too)," *The Times of Israel*, 2016, accessed March 13, 2020, https://blogs.timesofisrael.com/adam-and-eve-were-vegan-and-a-whole-bunch-of-israelis-are-too/.

14. Cédric Sueur, "Speciesism, Anti-Speciesism and Animal Rights," Strasbourg, 2019, accessed March 13, 2020, https://www.researchgate.net/publication/333904160_Speciesism_anti-speciesism_and_animal_rights.

15. Jeanette Rowley, "Veganism and Equality Research. An Investigation into the Experiences of Vegans in the Context of Human Rights and Equality Provisions" (Lancaster: Lancaster University, 2013), accessed March 13, 2020, https://eprints.lancs.ac.uk/id/eprint/74384/1/Vegan_Equality_Survey.pdf.

16. "Results of a Survey of Vegan Provision in Scotland," Go Vegan World, (2017), accessed March 13, 2020, https://docs.wixstatic.com/ugd/d95b36_f4bccc9845854533ba8aea3cf8e590b2.pdf. This survey was initiated by Go Vegan Scotland.

17. Crossland Employment Solicitors, "Nearly Half of Vegans Feel Discriminated Against at Work," May 2019, accessed March 13, 2020, https://www.crosslandsolicitors.com/site/hr-hub/nearly-half-of-vegans-feel-discriminated-against-at-work.

18. "Statistics," The Vegan Society, accessed March 13, 2020, https://www.vegansociety.com/news/media/statistics#vegandietintheuk.

19. Grainger Plc v Nicholson [2010] ICR 360.

20. "Mr J Casamitjana Costa v The League Against Cruel Sports: 3331129/2018," Employment Tribunal, January 2020, accessed March 13, 2020, https://www.gov.uk/employment-tribunal-decisions/mr-j-casamitjana-costa-v-the-league-against-cruel-sports-3331129-2018.

21. "Supporting Veganism in the Workplace: A guide for Employers," Birmingham, The Vegan Society, 2020, accessed March 13, 2020, https://www.vegansociety.com/sites/default/files/uploads/downloads/TVS%20Employer%20Booklet.pdf.

22. Slater and Gordon, "Ethical Veganism as a Protected Philosophical Belief—Jordi Casamitjana Costa," London, Slater and Gordon, 2020, accessed March 13, 2020, https://www.slatergordon.co.uk/media-centre/blog/2019/12/ethical-veganism/.

23. Jeanette Rowley, "My Personal Support for Jordi Casamitjana in his Presentation of Veganism to Norwich Employment Tribunal," Birmingham, The Vegan Society, 2019, accessed March 13, 2020, https://www.vegansociety.com/get-involved/international-rights-network/international-rights-network-blog/my-personal-support-jordi-casamitjana-his-presentation-veganism-norwich-employment-tribunal.

24. "Plataforma por una Educación Sostenible, Vegana y Ecológica," ESVECO, accessed March 13, 2020, https://plataformaesveco.wordpress.com/.

8. REFERENCES

British Association of UK Dietitians. "British Dietetic Association Confirms Well-Planned Vegan Diets Can Support Healthy Living in People of All Ages." *British Association of UK Dietitians*, 2017. Accessed May 4, 2020. https://www.bda.uk.com/resource/british-dietetic-association-confirms-well-planned-vegan-diets-can-support-healthy-living-in-people-of-all-ages.html.

Casamitjana, Jordi. *Ethical Vegan. A Personal and Political Journey to Change the World.* Tunbridge Wells: September Publishing, 2020.

Casamitjana, Jordi. "The Vocal Repertoire of the Woolly Monkey Lagothrix lagothricha." *Bioacoustics* 13 (2002): 1–19.

Casamitjana i Costa, Jordi. "Aspectes ecoetòlogics de les vespes del gènere Polistes de Catalunya (I): Estudi de la nidificació d'una població semiurbana de Polistes Dominulus Christ, 1791 (Hymenoptera: Vespidae)." *Sessió Conjunta d'Entomologia* 6, no 1 (March 1989): 87–96.

Cohen, Xavier. "How Should Vegans Live?." *Journal of Practical Ethics* 3, No. 2 (December 2015): 61–65.

Costa, J.C. *The Demon's Trial.* Victoria: Trafford Publishing, 2006.

Crossland Employment Solicitors. "Nearly Half of Vegans Feel Discriminated Against at Work." *Crossland Employment Solicitors,* May 2019. Accessed March 13, 2020. https://www.crosslandsolicitors.com/site/hr-hub/nearly-half-of-vegans-feel-discriminated-against-at-work.

Crown. Grainger Plc v Nicholson [2010] ICR 360.

Employment Tribunal. "Mr J Casamitjana Costa v The League Against Cruel Sports: 3331129/2018." *Crown,* January 2020. Accessed March 13, 2020. https://www.gov.uk/employment-tribunal-decisions/mr-j-casamitjana-costa-v-the-league-against-cruel-sports-3331129-2018.

ESVECO. "Plataforma por una Educación Sostenible, Vegana y Ecológica." *ESVECO.* Accessed March 13, 2020. https://plataformaesveco.wordpress.com/.

Gersh, Akiva. "Adam and Eve Were Vegan (and a Whole Bunch of Israelis Are Too)." *The Times of Israel,* 2016. Accessed March 13, 2020. https://blogs.timesofisrael.com/adam-and-eve-were-vegan-and-a-whole-bunch-of-israelis-are-too/.

Go Vegan World. "Results of a Survey of Vegan Provision in Scotland." *Go Vegan World,* 2017. Accessed March 13, 2020. https://docs.wixstatic.com/ugd/d95b36_f4bccc9845854533ba8aea3cf8e590b2.pdf.

Mayton, D.M., & Burrows, C.A. "Psychology of Nonviolence." *The Encyclopedia of Peace Psychology* 1 (2012): 713–716 and 720–723.

McPherson, Tristram. "A Case for Ethical Veganism: Intuitive and methodological consideration." *Journal of Moral Philosophy* 11, no 6 (November 2014): 677–703.

Rowley, Jeanette. "My Personal Support for Jordi Casamitjana in his Presentation of Veganism to Norwich Employment Tribunal." Birmingham. *The Vegan Society.* 2019. Accessed March 13, 2020. https://www.vegansociety.com/get-involved/international-rights-network/international-rights-network-blog/my-personal-support-jordi-casamitjana-his-presentation-veganism-norwich-employment-tribunal.

Rowley, Jeanette. "Veganism and Equality Research. An Investigation into the Experiences of Vegans in the Context of Human Rights and Equality Provisions." Lancaster: Lancaster University, 2013. Accessed March 13, 2020. https://eprints.lancs.ac.uk/id/eprint/74384/1/Vegan_Equality_Survey.pdf.

Slater and Gordon. "Ethical Veganism as a Protected Philosophical Belief—Jordi Casamitjana Costa." London. *Slater and Gordon,* 2020. Accessed March 13, 2020. https://www.slatergordon.co.uk/media-centre/blog/2019/12/ethical-veganism/.

Sueur, Cédric. "Speciesism, Anti-Speciesism and Animal Rights." Strasbourg: Strasburg University, 2019. Accessed March 13, 2020. https://www.researchgate.net/publication/333904160_Speciesism_anti-speciesism_and_animal_rights.

The Vegan Society. "Memorandum and Articles of Association." *The Vegan Society.* Birmingham. Accessed March 13, 2020. https://www.vegansociety.com/about-us/further-information/memorandum-and-articles-association.

The Vegan Society. "Ripened by Human Determination, 70 years of the Vegan Society." *The Vegan Society.* Accessed June 1, 2020. https://www.vegansociety.com/sites/default/files/uploads/Ripened%20by%20human%20determination.pdf.

The Vegan Society. "Statistics." *The Vegan Society.* Accessed March 13, 2020. https://www.vegansociety.com/news/media/statistics#vegandietintheuk.

The Vegan Society. "Supporting Veganism in the Workplace: A Guide for Employers." Birmingham. *The Vegan Society,* 2020. Accessed March 13, 2020. https://www.vegansociety.com/sites/default/files/uploads/downloads/TVS%20Employer%20Booklet.pdf.

Afterword

A Vegan Citizen's Struggle to Change the Law

Sorin Ionescu

1. INTRODUCTION

The introduction to this volume refers to the complexity of animal liberation in consumerist societies and how consumer conglomerates, government entities and powerful corporations play a role in shaping our life choices and opportunities. I believe that this observation is relevant to the exercise of the human right to freedom of thought and conscience—in particular, the right to *adopt* and *manifest* veganism as belief of choice.

In her book *Towards a Vegan Jurisprudence: The Need for a Reorientation of Human Rights*, Jeanette Rowley argues that our concern for other animals is innate. She believes that it is natural to be compassionate and care about those who suffer, but that human beings are constructed and shaped, at least in part, by a false notion of human rights: one that centres on the primacy of the human individual ego. Arguing that the origin of human rights recognises our concern for the suffering of others, Rowley argues that human rights should orient away from claiming rights that benefit individuals and more towards honoring rights that exercise the duty we feel to protect others, especially with regard to their suffering.[1]

Rowley argues that the legal protection of vegans is uncontentious in the context of the intended scope of the primary human right to be free to live according to conscience, and that we have a duty to include other animals in our system of ethical justice. In this regard, Rowley encourages vegans to appeal to law, to claim their right to manifest vegan practice to help bring about and shape social policies and practices that will help dismantle speciesism and support the transition to a more just and compassionate society.

Regarding the human right to freedom of conscience and the possibility of bringing about the social conditions in which it is easier for people to adopt veganism and sustain plant-based living, the question I will address in this chapter is whether it is possible to change hearts and minds through the use of law, particularly on the subject of the transition to a vegan, plant-based food system. Not having yet found an effective way to achieve this, my answer explains an attempt to appeal to law that did not work for us at Vegan Option Canada or later for us at Animal Rebellion (or rather, that has not worked yet).

I will share some lessons from the research I have undertaken to understand why the use of law did not work. I am a regular citizen, and this chapter generally contains my own reflections and opinions on the lessons I have learned.

Before exploring my experiences and thoughts about our attempt to use law at Vegan Option Canada, I think it is useful to explain my personal context.

About ten years ago, my father's death pushed me into a deep depression. The world views depression as an illness of the individual, but some say that in many cases it is an unconscious sign that something needs to be changed. In my case, it forced me to start thinking critically about myself.

The search for truth is a difficult path. In my experience, our view of truth comes first in the form of belief. After much thought and scientific research, this may become cognitive understanding of what is logical and coherent. Sometimes, cognitive comprehension is not the end. Deep awareness is required to properly comprehend and integrate complex issues. Knowledge may become wisdom through a long process of integration, and even, in extreme cases, neurobiological restructuring of the brain. In my search for truth, I was constantly thinking about the cognitive dissonances and illusions we all live with. My own inconsistencies bothered me a lot, but I did not know how to eliminate them.

On a beautiful summer day in 2013, I was in the passenger seat of a minivan travelling through the forests and plains of the Gaspé Peninsula in Quebec. I was thinking about two cognitive dissonances that made me ask myself two big questions. First, how is it possible that I love my dog so much, but I also like to eat pork chops? Phrased differently, why do I pet an animal with one hand, yet stick my fork into another of equal intelligence and consciousness with the other? Second, how can I buy hot dogs and hamburgers at the supermarket as if they were fruits and vegetables, when they don't grow on trees or plants?

The idea that there was something hidden that I was choosing not to look at and not to face prevailed in my mind. I sought solace from my unsettling thoughts and my eyes were drawn to the greenery that surrounded us. At that moment, they fell upon a magnificent view. Two majestic deer were striding across the field. My peace was disturbed as I realized that they were heading straight for the road. I warned the driver and we managed to avoid a head-on collision. One deer succeeded in fleeing, but the second deer was not so lucky—the tow truck behind us ran its two huge rear wheels over the deer's frail body.

We pulled over to the side of the road. As I got out to investigate, the tow truck driver wrapped his massive hand around the rear legs of the dying deer and dragged him to the side of the road. Showing some compassion, he asked me if I had a hammer—something to smash the deer's head with and put him out of his misery. I do not remember if I had a hammer or not, but I remember that I answered no. I hoped I could save the deer, or that the authorities would. In my mind, completely disconnected from reality, a Bambi ambulance was just waiting to come storming in and rescue the deer. What kind of society would let an innocent being die in agony?

After a useless call to the police and with the tow-truck driver long gone, I found myself alone, staring at the deer, who was looking at me with big, soft eyes. He had blood coming out of his mouth. A little heart-to-mind journey came to an end that day, and although I did not have the compassion and strength to end that being's suffering, I realized intuitively with my heart and logically with my mind that animals suffer, that I didn't think they should suffer, and that I didn't want them to suffer for any reason—including for my own desires, my own tastebuds.

It took me more than a year to gradually integrate this truth into my thoughts and actions. Finally, after watching the movie *Earthlings*, I became vegan in the summer of 2015.

I was overwhelmed by what I discovered in my research on veganism and I needed to tell the world about it. I immediately began to inform all my friends, family and Facebook network of the horrible truth. I told them much more than they desired. This was my first type of activism and, in retrospect, it was the worst type. Looking back, I admit that it was ineffective; I was only concerned with the desire to do something. Soon, I felt lonely. I started to feel like Sisyphus,[2] pushing a rock up a mountain and watching it fall down, only to start all over again. I then tried to join demonstrations and engage in other forms of activism.

Unfortunately, this Sisyphus complex never left me. However, it always pushed me to look for better ways to make a difference.

A final experience of mine is worth mentioning in this context. At the end of 2015, when my vegan journey was just beginning, I found myself hospitalized for about a month. I was surprised to discover fish in the first vegan meal I requested. The hospital had only vegetarian options, and fish was considered vegetarian. The caterers were happy to add a note to my records requesting 'no fish.' To my surprise, my next meal consisted of a dairy cheese omelette. The concept of vegan and plant-based didn't hold water in this hospital, where I almost never saw the busy doctors, and the nurses told me to focus on healing because this was a place of healing. I shouted and screamed, threatened to sue, refused to eat the cruelty-filled dishes, and asked for vegan meals. Nothing helped. A hospital is a serious place that cares about health and matters such as life and death, not petty things like the 'hobby' of veganism.

2. VEGAN OPTION CANADA

2.1. What and Why

When my partner told me about a petition calling for the provision of vegan options in public places in Canada,[3] it reminded me of my days in the hospital. It also struck me as a good 'foot in the door' approach. We were not asking for animal rights, but for human rights—rights that needed to be explicit due to the inconsistency in the provision of plant-based food. It is sometimes possible to obtain vegan food in hospital, but it is provided on request for religious, not ethical, reasons. We wanted to promote this petition as a way to call for a change in the law to validate the choice of a plant-based diet as an ethical decision, rather than just a personal choice. We also wanted to create the social conditions under which it would be possible to adopt veganism as a belief of choice and increase the popularity of veganism so that more people would become vegan, more animals would be saved, and our planet would be preserved.

The concept has been tested in Portugal. The Portuguese Vegetarian Association has been successful in campaigning for the creation of legislation mandating that vegan meals should be made available in all public establishments in the country.[4] This result was achieved mainly thanks to popular demand and to the contribution of more than 15,000 people who signed a petition. We had hoped to gather signatures and submit a petition. In our case, our appeal to politics and law was significantly more difficult.

The first challenge was to get broad public support for the petition in Canada. Unfortunately, there were no associations that supported and promoted it. We had no funds, no resources and no functioning network. Some organizations refused to become partners because they were charitable organizations and working to change the law in Canada could have negatively affected their charitable status. Others partnered, but on a regional basis. Most vegan and vegetarian associations are based in the cities and have only the interests of their cities in mind.

Since there were no such associations willing to support this petition, we had no choice but to create one. Vegan Option Canada was created[5] to support this petition and any further tactics required for this campaign. If we wanted to reach a wider audience, we had to focus on networking, we had to be present at the vegan festivals, and we had to have presence and promotions on social media, such as Facebook.

The assumption that Canada is a united country is false. It is actually separated into two regions: English Canada and Quebec. It is my experience that progressive people and organizations do not want to join as one, even though the federal government responsible for the laws we want to change is resolved and organized in its dominion. This is the first lesson I have learned—how difficult it is to join progressives and citizens together to help bring about change in a broad movement in Canada. The federal and provincial governments pass laws that affect us all, while we, the citizens, are separated into municipalities, and even when we advocate for change, we do so with our voices segregated by region and cause. Municipalities do not have the jurisdiction to implement the required change on a national scale. This personal realization was reinforced later by my experience of the Extinction/Animal Rebellion's failure to unite into a large and strong movement in Canada.

3. CASE STUDY: VEGAN OPTION QUEBEC

Quebec is recognized by some as one of the most progressive provinces in Canada. Its population is about 8 million people, almost equal to the overall population of Portugal (about 10 million people). In Portugal, a similar petition for plant-based food to be provided in public canteens obtained 15,000 signatures. It therefore made sense to us to test the strategy of petitions in Quebec. In three months, we obtained around 1,350 signatures.

After we submitted the petition to the Quebec government via a member of the legislature, we received a vague response,[6] which was not even addressed to us. Disappointed by the response, the initiator of this petition wrote to the minister, directly requesting more concrete action and a possible meeting. On 3 June 2020, the minister replied:

> There is no Quebec or Canadian data available on the proportion of the population that is vegetarian or vegan. Moreover, the orientations of the food reference frameworks currently in effect in health and social services institutions, schools and educational childcare services encourage the inclusion of a variety of healthy foods, including those containing plant-based proteins.
>
> Given these elements, it does not appear justified at this time to create a bill to require the introduction of a variety of vegan options in Quebec's public canteens. We will therefore not follow up on your request for a meeting.[7]

And yet, on 18 July 2018, Canadian television network CTV had announced:

> Vegetarians and vegans now account for nearly 10 per cent of Canada's population, and their increased presence is forcing the restaurant and meat produc-

> tion industries to consider new approaches. According to research from Dalhousie University, there are 2.3 million vegetarians in Canada, up from 900,000 15 years ago. Another 850,000 people consider themselves vegan. Those two numbers add up to 9.4 per cent of the Canadian population.[8]

I expect that in 2021, those numbers have probably increased.

4. WHAT IS WRONG?

During the years we worked for Vegan Option Canada, I made significant efforts to understand politics, democracy and the process by which laws are changed. In the beginning, I knew very little—next to nothing—and I was keen to learn. The following sections explain what I learned through meeting and communicating with various assistants of Canadian Members of Parliament (MPs), befriending government bureaucrats, and reading many articles and books.

4.1. About Petitions and Lobbying

In my experience, Canadian MPs almost never respond to emails or requests for meetings by themselves. They act through their assistants. As I understand it, each MP has four assistants. The assistants are politicians, and politicians are, in my experience (at least regarding our cause) very polite—but unfortunately very unhelpful. They understand the petitioning process and they know which text is good for petitions and which text is bad. An MP has only a few minutes to submit a petition to Parliament and will choose how to represent it and how to try to turn it into a bill. If the MP does not lobby, there is a good chance that the attempt to turn the petition into a bill will be defeated. If the rest of Parliament is against it, the chances of success are not good either.

I have had to befriend some officials who have explained to me a little more about how things work. Public servants, who work for the government and are not elected, are not politicians per se. However, through their work, they gain valuable insights, including understanding the petitioning process. I believe their accounts are truthful because it is not in their interests to lie; their position is not re-electable. I was told, in a rather amused tone, that I was a dreamer. I was told that a petition is only there to give an aspirational segment of the public the impression that something can be done to change the things they care about and that the government is open to listening to its citizens. It was suggested to me that the reality is that the government chooses not to govern in a way that creates the opportunity to listen to its citizens, despite the fact that its job is to represent them. It was also suggested to me that the only way to attempt to change the law that might work is through lobbying. However, lobbying for our cause would require money and it would also compete with the interests of the very rich and powerful agricultural lobbies.

We have never (yet) tried to lobby directly for Vegan Option Canada. However, there is another movement in Canada that is lobbying in an attempt to change the way subsidies to animal agriculture are distributed. Their slow progress, seen from the outside, reminds me of our slow progress, seen from the inside, and has led me to believe that lobbying alone is not enough to change the law either. There are many other activist organizations in the United States (US) that are trying to make progressive changes to laws through lobbying, and my observations show that for every progressive lobbyist, the sectors in opposition send many more. From my observations, it is clear that as large companies have more money, a significant imbalance of power is generated within the lobbying system. It seems that money influences whether laws change or stay the same much more than the efforts and action of concerned citizens.

4.2. Some Shortcomings of Democracy

The following are my opinions on the workings of democracy, based on observations during the past few years as an engaged, concerned citizen.

4.2.1. Jurisdictions

My critical observations on jurisdictions apply to Canada, but I believe other countries may have similar issues.

In Canada, there are three types of politicians: Federal, Provincial, and Municipal.[9] Jurisdiction over changing laws fall into these three categories. It is my understanding that well-intentioned lawyers who want to bring about change, are themselves confused by the complexity of the task. Public servants and administrative employees who work in hospitals or schools, for example, are also confused when it comes to which jurisdiction a change needs to come from. Ordinary, engaged citizens who are concerned with change quickly find they have no chance of making significant progress towards the changes they want to see. Most vegan and vegetarian associations in Canada are associated with their cities, and, therefore, their members are primarily interested in municipal laws. However, for change to occur at the provincial and federal levels, large organizations would have to lobby the provincial and federal governments. In my view, the lack of such large organizations at the federal and provincial levels means that there is a disconnect between the power of the people, politicians, and the processes of changing laws. Vegan Option Canada has not managed to bridge this gap yet, even for a simple change in the law such as adding a mandatory vegan option to public menus. It seems to me that what we need is for city-based associations and progressives in general to unite, collaborate and organize themselves in order for change to happen.

4.2.2. Lack of Proportional Representation

The voting system in Quebec and Canada is called 'first-past-the-post'[10] or 'British ballot.' Under this voting system, citizens have the opportunity to vote for only one person (first-past-the-post) in their electoral district. In a constituency, the person elected is the one who gets the most votes, but not necessarily an absolute majority of the votes (>50% of the votes); they can win by only one vote or with a low percentage of voters. All other votes in the constituency have no further impact.

My understanding of the problem is as follows: we have already seen that in 2018 there were 850,000 vegan Canadians. The population of Canada in 2018 was 37.06 million. Vegans constitute about 2.3% of the population. In theory, if a party represented the interests of vegans, and under the idealistic assumption that all vegans are entitled to vote and would prioritize their veganism over any other issue, under a system of proportional representation it would win 2.3% of the vote. Again, this means that 2.3% of the 338 MPs should represent the interests of vegans. Therefore, we should have seven or eight MPs introducing bills that represent the interests of vegans. This is far from being the case in Canada. When we repeat this exercise with almost 9% of the population being vegetarian or vegan (Dalhousie University research, cited above), we realize how much more effectively the voice of vegetarians and vegans would be heard.

Under the current system, citizens are forced to vote for the party, or rather the representative, who has the best chance of winning against the dominant party. This often means strongly compromising on their values. In many cases, it is almost a vote against, instead of a vote for.[11] In reality, there are only two parties left in Canada with a chance of winning—the Conservatives and the Liberals. Both have neo-capitalist tendencies, and there is almost no difference if one or the other wins, because both represent primarily economic interests.

Furthermore, there are those who believe that the parties in power are trying to maintain the status quo and their monopoly. In the 2015 election, the Liberals promised an 'electoral system that better reflects the concerns and voices of Canadians from coast to coast and gives us a better level of governance.'[12] Justin Trudeau, who ran for the leadership of the Liberal Party in 2013, said that he preferred proportional representation. It is 2021 at the time of writing, and no changes have been made.

4.2.3. Propaganda and Manufacturing of Consent

Even in the best democracies, which are free of corruption and in which the voices of the citizens are properly represented, there are still some shortcomings. Not least among them is that most citizens who will determine the winning party do not have the time to do adequate research and understand the issues that concern them. They rely on the media for their education and awareness of important issues. Perhaps there was a time when journalism was free of outside influence and manipulation, but I personally do not think that is the case today.

In the times of kings and nobles, power was concentrated in the hands of a few, and it was no secret. Over time, with the advent of the industrial revolution, the aristocracy lost its power to the bourgeoisie. Finally, with the advent of democracy, power was supposed to belong to everyone. In democracy, universal rights to vote and receive education should ensure that all common people rule. The people would cede their power by election to a government that would govern with their well-being and best interests at heart. There was a problem in that regard. The interests of the people were in the hands of the most wealthy. There is some evidence to suggest that those in power soon realised that with enough money, ordinary people's perceptions of their own interests could be manufactured.

Nowhere is this better illustrated than in the life story of Edward Bernays,[13] who was the nephew of Sigmund Freud and considered to be the father of public relations in America. The term 'public relations' (PR) is used nowadays because the word 'propaganda' acquired a bad reputation after World War Two.[14] Bernays is responsible for many things that pervade society even today, such as the concept and popularity of bacon and eggs for breakfast, the popularity of beer, and anecdotally the establishment of corrupt governments in Guatemala and other Central American countries.

Delving deeper into the subject of the influence of Edward Bernays would require an entire book, and in fact a four-hour BBC documentary is available, titled *Century of the Self*. However, I will mention here one of the most famous stories about him; the one that built his reputation. In Bernays' time, cigarettes were not very popular with women, and were considered inappropriate and even dirty. Bernays was hired by the president of a tobacco company to change that. While talking about convincing women to smoke, the president said, 'It will be like opening a gold mine in front of our house.' After consulting with his uncle, Bernays came up with a strategy. He hired women to march in the 1929 Easter Sunday parade and light cigarettes in front of the cameras, making cigarettes the symbol of emancipation and equality in the first wave of feminism. Cigarettes became 'torches of freedom.'[15] Of course, at that time the health issues would not have been known.

Although the concept of propaganda has negative connotations, it is arguable that positive PR can exist. When PR is used to spread lies in order to manipulate for personal gain, it is negative. When PR is used to share the truth for the benefit of all, it is positive.

But it is without doubt that there is a very dark side to propaganda; it is a way to manufacture consent and interest, and it is a process that is still used today. I can't say it better than through the following quote from Bernays himself:

> The conscious and intelligent manipulation of the organized habits and opinions of the masses is an important element in democratic society. Those who manipulate this unseen mechanism of society constitute an invisible government which is the true ruling power of our country. [16]

4.2.4. Psychological Operations

Mohammad Mosaddeq is considered by many Iranians as the main defender of secular democracy in his country, having introduced a series of social measures, such as social security. In 1951, he nationalized Iranian oil, which provoked the anger of the United Kingdom (UK). In 1953, the US Central Intelligence Agency (CIA), along with the UK's MI6, orchestrated Operation AJAX, the Iranian coup that ousted him from power. [17] This is one of the first stories of economic hitmen that was recognized by the CIA.

The 'United States Senate Select Committee to Study Governmental Operations with Respect to Intelligence Activities,' commonly referred to as the 'Church Committee,' was established in 1975 with a mandate to study classified information and the activities of the CIA, the National Security Agency (NSA), the Federal Bureau of Investigation (FBI) and the Internal Revenue Service (IRS) in order to investigate abuses of authority. [18] What it discovered was extremely disturbing. The full Church Committee report is available, but in summary, the agencies turned their power on ordinary citizens. In particular, social change activists and left-wing movements were targeted, placed under surveillance and harassed. Martin Luther King received letters of intimidation from the FBI, and there were multiple attempts to discredit him. There were some horrific, yet successful, attempts to disrupt social movements such as the Black Panthers and the Students for a Democratic Society, which were seen as threats to order. In many instances, officials, up to and including the president, were not even informed of these activities.

What is worrying is that it seems to me that almost nothing has changed since then. I believe that this is not a past reality, but our present reality. The outcome of the Church Committee report[19] was that the Foreign Intelligence Surveillance Act (FISA) was put in place in order to control the activities of these agencies. Only 0.33% of the requests for monitoring were denied by the court. But after 9/11, the Bush administration simply bypassed the court.[20]

As an example of abuse of power, let us look at a very well-known and terribly tragic case. COINTELPRO (COunter INTELligence PROgram) was a series of secret and illegal projects conducted by the FBI between 1956 and 1971. The program targeted the KKK, but also the feminist, anti–Vietnam War, civil rights, environmental and animal rights movements, among others. In 1969, the FBI conspired with Chicago police to murder 21-year-old Fred Hampton, along with Mark Clark, another member of the Black Panthers. The police and the FBI fired about 99 shots, while the Panthers' only shot was probably fired by Mark Clark after he was fatally wounded. Evidence shows that Hampton was sedated by the FBI and killed while unconscious. Hampton's lawyer, Jeffrey Haas, describes it in detail in his book, *The Assassination of Fred Hampton: How the FBI and the Chicago Police Murdered a Black Panther.*[21]

The Five Eyes[22] is the alliance of the intelligence services of the US, Australia, New Zealand, the UK and Canada. In 2013, the global surveillance of the NSA and three of its Five Eyes partners (Australia, the UK and Canada) was revealed by Edward Snowden. Several books, a film and many articles have been written about it, so it is perhaps not necessary to go into detail. It is not uncommon to learn from media reports, however, that domestic surveillance is ongoing, that Google and Yahoo accounts are frequently breached, that the results are not only used for national security, but also for industrial espionage, and that everything can be and is being tracked. According to the leaks, there is a working agreement between 14 nations, officially known as SIGINT Seniors Europe (SSEUR). These are the same members of Nine Eyes (Five Eyes and Denmark, France, the Netherlands and Norway), plus Belgium, Germany, Italy, Spain and Sweden.

4.2.5. Neoliberalism and the Limited Voting Choice

It seems that governance and democracy in the West are strongly linked to financial interests, and it is impossible not to mention this when seriously discussing policy change.

After the fall of communism, the idea that there is no alternative to the free market has become unchallenged. All those who criticize capitalism try to remedy its shortcomings, but do not consider any other economic alternative, because it is believed that no other economic system can work. Some say that even if the state had all the capital, it would not know what to do with it outside the competitive scenario of supply and demand. From my point of view, communism, as a government or collective altruistic economic system, has never existed except as a dream in Marx's conceptual world. Lenin used it to seize power from the tsar in Russia because it was a popular idea, and the cruel Stalin and the vanguard Communist Party followed his autocratic rule, setting an example for most Eastern European countries.[23] Communism was an idea for a collective cooperative world; this idea could not compete with competitive capitalism from the outside and human corruption from the inside. In my opinion, the alternative to capitalism cannot be just a governmental idea, but must be an economic system of cooperatives in the service of the public interest. The economy must be at the service of the public, just as the state must be at the service of the public.

The free market is not so free from intervention either. Public funds were used in 2008 to bail out the greed and bankruptcy of American conglomerates such as Fannie Mae and Freddie Mac.[24] The government reserves most of its interventions for those who are too big to fail whilst letting others struggle to meet their needs. Meritocracy and the idea that 'hard work pays' ignore the privilege with which many are born. The idea that no man is an island is not understood and is underestimated. The bailouts and the austerity that followed (where 'the 99%' had to bear the brunt of the failure resulting from the greed of the 1%) created such a low standard of living worldwide that they may be responsible for the Arab Spring revolutions and the Wall Street Occupy movements.[25]

In the US, as well as in Canada, there are only two parties that have exchanged power over the last few decades.[26] Both have strong neoliberalism and neo-capitalist tendencies. It is not even possible for a party to have non-liberal ideas. Only economic growth matters, and both powerful parties are committed to it.

5. CORPORATOCRACY AND THE MONEY PRIMARY

In the previous sections, I have discussed the difficulties of changing the law using the citizens' petition system or through lobbying by citizens and NGOs, the problem of proportional representation, the habits and manipulations made using propaganda, the control and abuse of power by governments, and, finally, neo-capitalism. What does all this represent? The image of a world where power and money are closely linked, interconnected and concentrated in the hands of very few people at the top of a pyramid system. This system, corporatocracy, is best described by former economic hitman John Perkins, in the following quote:

> Members of the corporatocracy are not part of a conspiracy, but they are characterized by an obsession with winning. They will invest vast amounts of money to get their way. They also share a common goal: to maximize profits regardless of environmental and social costs. In seeking that goal, they have created an extremely unstable, unjust, and dangerous world.[27]

Let's go into a little more detail. 'Boss' Tweed, a 19th-century American politician, stated: *'I don't care who makes the election, as long as I make the nomination.'*[28] Once again, it might seem that this is an outdated concept that is no longer relevant today. Let us first look at an example whose pertinence is obvious to most. In March 2019, demonstrations broke out in Hong Kong. The 3.8 million voters can elect district councilors, but only 1,200 of them can vote for the chief executive of the city. This 1,200-person nominating committee represents mainly business interests and is a clear example of the failure of democracy.[29]

Another, less obvious but well-known, example is what is known in the US as 'money primary.' During this process, candidates compete for campaign funds. They learn to 'lean towards green.' What is the result? The study 'Testing Theories of American Politics: Elites, Interest Groups, and Average Citizens' finds that the average citizens' preference for policy change has no effect on its probability of being adopted, whereas the economic elite's preference is more likely to be adopted.[30]

6. IDEAS FOR A BETTER FUTURE

The previous sections present a sad picture—one of a world in which the primary human right to live according to anti-speciesist moral values is subject to a range of socio-political complexities. A world in which progressive policy changes towards a more just society are almost doomed to failure. Although it probably contains no new information for the informed, and I have not gone into detail for each observation, I think it is a model that is an accurate representation of reality. How can we remedy this? Unfortunately, I cannot pretend to know the answer to this question (and I don't think anyone does). I know what is not working, and I have personally tested other theories of change. I believe that I have learned valuable lessons that I gladly share with others in the hope that they will be useful.

6.1. Mass Non-Violent Civil Disobedience and the Rebellion

Extinction Rebellion (XR) was launched in May 2018.[31] Disappointed by a system that refuses to accept any change, I was immediately seduced by another way of requesting change. I joined as soon as I could and attended the first meeting of the Ottawa XR Chapter. I have understood The Intergovernmental Panel on Climate Change (IPCC) report[32] and I have become aware of the seriousness of the climate situation. I have listened to and read Jem Bendell's widely distributed paper, *Deep Adaptation*,[33] and I have realised that the situation is even worse than that which the IPCC portrays. I admire Roger Hallam and have listened to almost all of his videos and read his recent book. My only problem with XR was that, as a vegan, I wanted us to discuss further the potential of a complete transition to a plant-based food system as a crucial step to avoid the impending collapse. On the other hand, as an anti-speciesist, I understood the importance of political change over individual change, so I took this approach. Of course, when Animal Rebellion was launched in July 2019, I took the opportunity to follow this path. In fact, in September 2019, I left my full-time job to follow my heart and mind into rebellion as deeply as possible. My partner and I even left our apartment, bought a recreational vehicle, and began a North American tour to spread the seeds of rebellion as far and wide as possible. The next section explains some lessons I have learned. Some are obvious, some are not.

7. THE REBELLION THEORY OF CHANGE

Past successful examples show that if the population contributes to sustained peaceful mass civil disobedience, change is possible.[34] My view is that as it reacts to non-violent civil resistance, the government is faced with a difficult choice: it could become completely authoritarian in broad daylight and risk a total uprising or give in to the demands of the citizens. '*This is an Uprising*' is the most popular book of the Rebellion (when I say 'the Rebellion,' I mean XR, Animal Rebellion, and any other allied forces from the Rebel Alliance), and many other activist movements have adopted it. However, as I understand it, even when the perfect conditions are in place, only about 54% of the uprisings are successful. Consequently, it may be that movements must learn to master 'whirlwind moments,' or special conditions that motivate the masses to rise up and no longer accept the status quo.

The Rebellion has other assets. It promotes non-violence, not only because compassion and love cannot be built on hatred, but also because earlier studies by Erica Chenoweth show that non-violent movements are more likely to succeed.[35] It accepts that citizens are traumatized by a broken system and promotes a regenerative culture in which the principles of no blame and no shame play an important role. No one is turned away or accused of being hypocritical because they have not made enough individual change, because it is widely recognised that individual change in a broken system is very difficult to achieve and that inclusive participation is important for legitimate social change. In addition, it promotes a system of self-organization of the distributed authority that should enable everyone to feel empowered.

The citizens' assembly requested by the movement is another interesting request. As far as I understand, this entails an additional element to current governmental decision-making processes by introducing judicial decision-making concepts. Ordinary citizens would be selected at random, would be provided with expert input and would discuss and deliberate targeted issues.

Government decision-making would be guided by citizen recommendations. This logic can give maximum weight to rational arguments and science, and it would be difficult to corrupt a large number of citizens. In my view this is a system that would respect current power structures and ensure the transition from what is now deeply flawed (i.e., voting-based only) form to a much more participatory form of democracy.[36]

7.1 Shortcomings

Perhaps we have to accept that no movement is perfect. I have observed certain shortcomings, which I share in the hope that future movements or the present one will remedy them. The following opinions are mine alone, so I will only share them in the hope that my troubled thoughts will do more good than harm.

Regenerative culture and the self-organizing system are the blood and cells of the body, but they take a long time to integrate for most people, myself included. Most of us have habits that we have acquired and that we cannot get rid of so easily in order to adapt to these new ways of operating. Power is not being distributed effectively. Communication can be painful and sometimes ineffective.

The worst flaw I have observed is the lack of cooperation. Similar observations to those above suggest that most active and engaged citizens abhor power and centralization. This translates into an uneven movement. The world's powerful, as we have seen, are fairly united in their monopoly of the world. The left, the opposition, is not. We separate first into organizations, in which political identity and ego come into play, and then into regions, in which, again, the local ego comes into play. A particular example that has troubled me personally is the October 2019 Rebellion in Eastern Canada. Montreal, Ottawa and Toronto could have united in a single action, but this did not occur, despite the attempt by some to join forces. Each one stood alone, and I watched with great pain, in a particular place at an event, where there were more police officers than participants, and the few brave people standing up for change were slowly being arrested and taken away. Had we all joined forces in one place, such as the capital Ottawa, halfway between Toronto and Montreal, things might have been different.

Another shortcoming in my view is the lack of global cooperation. There is currently no discussion of a global citizens' assembly. Global cooperation with the Rebellion is at best weak, and the UK still has a dominant role in the movement, despite the fact that much of the power is still concentrated in the US. And yet, based on my understanding of the works of acclaimed professor Yuval Noah Harari,[37] the question raised is this: how are we going to address important issues at the local level, such as climate change, that affect the whole world? A localist approach is probably adopted to avoid colonialism, which has already done much harm to the world, but the world's powerful do not have these noble desires as they participate in extracting resources and exploiting the world in a very globalised way.

8. PEOPLE POWER: HOPE PERSISTS

Despite the shortcomings described above, I remain firmly convinced that this or a similar movement can bring about change in this way. Frederick Douglass famously said: 'Power concedes nothing without a request. It never has and never will.'[38] The demand must be present and it must be strong and clear.

8.1. People Power

The biggest illusion most people are under is that they have no power. Despite all the talk of the world's elite, despite the surveillance and abuse of power, despite the propaganda, the 99% have all the power. The problem is that attempting to change the system as individuals can seem like a losing battle for each one of us. To have power, the 99% must be united, and that is where the difficulty lies. The good news is that we don't really need 99%; Erica Chenoweth's studies[39] show that 3.5% of citizens who are sufficiently aware of the seriousness of the situation and of the theory of change, and who are ready to unite and take back their power by no longer listening to corrupt powers, might succeed.[40] Gandhi's Salt March[41] gave us a powerful lesson that should not be forgotten: that every ruler, every corporation, every system of oppression depends on the cooperation of its people.

8.1. Support from Lawyers

This text may be read by those who know and practice law. It is a plea to them. I call for support for ordinary citizens who are trying to implement change, who choose to put their freedom on the line. It is, in my humble opinion, one of the best ways lawyers can help the system change. Ordinary citizens must be educated and helped. They must not be left to fend for themselves or pay incredible defence costs. Unfortunately, that is the case today in some instances.

8.2. On Individual Change

We sometimes forget, when we talk about system and policy change, that individual change and system change go hand in hand.[42] With respect to veganism, many activist organizations advocate for individual change. In fact, veganism is a way of life and a lifestyle where individual change is somehow required by definition. I strongly believe that individual change is necessary to achieve lasting change.

There's a big difference between guilt and regret. We have to understand this when it comes to raising awareness. Guilt is a negative feeling that is associated with feelings of being a bad person, and it leads to feelings of powerlessness. If people feel guilty about not making enough individual changes, they will simply protect their own well-being by refusing to accept that change is necessary. It can also be argued that free will is an illusion. Because we don't choose our birthplace, our genetics, our environment and many other details of our journey, we often make choices, but we don't choose how we do so. Regret, on the other hand, can be acceptable if it does not generate negative feelings (which are always pointless), as it can help us learn from our mistakes, do better in the future and, if possible, to repair the harm done.[43]

Another important aspect to understand is that individuals do not implement change or even understand theories without stories. We tell each other a lot of stories and myths in order to understand reality. This text often tells personal stories, interwoven with observations of the world. Yuval Noah Harari describes in his best-selling books how the enormous collaborative power of humans comes from our ability to share common myths and stories. To implement individual change, we must therefore change our stories.

9. CONCLUSION

I have explained how Vegan Option Canada's appeal to law failed and explored my personal thoughts on achieving policy and legal changes by sharing personal stories, experiences and lessons learned along the way.

Some readers might think I have gone into too much detail about US policy and have gone off on a tangent. There are countless examples of abuse of power in the US, so why mention an incident with the 1969 Black Panthers in a chapter on the use of legal channels to promote veganism in Canada and elsewhere? I am talking about financial interests, and I mention alternative economic systems. Why did I do that?

I wanted to illustrate, from my experience and past, that it is very difficult to rely on international human rights provision to bring about positive policy change for vegans in North America. This is probably true in other countries as well. There is corruption and there are shortcomings in our democracies. There are manufactured habits and desires. The socio-political system is interconnected and very complex. It seems to me that it might be pointless to try to discuss one aspect of changing the law without examining the big picture: by way of an analogy, this is like changing the window of a house without foundations, with rotten walls and with a falling roof. Perhaps we need to build the foundations of a new house and examine the utility of legal principles and provisions in this context.

I argue that we need an ecosystem of change that supports the implementation of new anti-speciesist policies. We must adapt quickly. We need to collaborate and cooperate much more than before, in different ways. We need to get away from competition. We need to understand that we are all interconnected, and that what affects one of us affects us all. We have very little time to do so, and I hope we will.

On the other hand, there are many change agents who claim to understand what is wrong with the world today. For example, most people in my network clearly believe that there is a corrupt power that controls the media, and that people are misinformed. But no one, including me, understands how to remove or participate in that power, how to free the media, so that everyone is properly informed and can make better choices. Some people talk about mass disruption. We cannot have mass disturbances without the masses. Others mention individual changes. We cannot have individual changes of the necessary magnitude in a corrupt system of ill-informed individuals. I believe that reality is very difficult to understand, that understanding it is made deliberately more difficult by self-interest, and that most of us have lost the ability to pay attention and make the effort to be informed. Reality is simply too complex for one mind. Humans are social animals and need to think together. To be saved from our own ignorance, we need super intelligence—and I am not talking about artificial intelligence. With respect to those advocating for legal change from within the current system, and the positive developments achieved, I believe we need to combine our efforts to create a truly selfless and well-organized 'think and do' tank, a collective benevolent wisdom with a collaborative capacity for effective action, concerned with the well-being of all sentient beings, present and future.

10. NOTES

1. Jeanette Rowley, *Towards a Vegan Jurisprudence: The Need for a Reorientation of Human Rights* (New York: Lexington Book, 2020).
2. SparkNotes, "The Myth of Sisyphus," SparkNotes, accessed March 19, 2021, https://www.sparknotes.com/philosophy/sisyphus/section11/.
3. Vegan Option Canada, "Federal Petition," Vegan Option Canada, February 18, 2019, accessed March 19, 2021, https://veganoptioncanada.org/en/federal-petition/.
4. Ashitha Nagesh, "It Is Now Illegal Not to Offer Vegan Food at Prisons, Hospitals and Schools in Portugal," Metro.co.uk, March 10, 2017, accessed March 19, 2021, https://metro.co.uk/2017/03/10/it-is-now-illegal-not-to-offer-vegan-food-at-prisons-hospitals-and-schools-in-portugal-6501872/. See also, Nuno Alvim in this volume.
5. Lauren Wills, "Vegan Options Urged to Become Mandatory in Public Sector by Canadian Lobby Group," Livekindly, December 15, 2018, accessed March 19, 2021, https://www.livekindly.co/lobby-group-vegan-option-canada/#:~:text=to%20Public%20Sector-,New%20Lobby%20Group%20'Vegan%20Option%20Canada'%20to%20Bring%20More%20Plant,Based%20Food%20to%20Public%20Sector&

text=A%20group%20of%20Canadian%20citizens,mandatory%20in%20the%20public%20sector.

6. Vegan Option Canada, "Quebec Petition: MAPAQ Response," Vegan Option Canada, March 25, 2020, accessed March 19, 2021, https://veganoptioncanada.org/en/news/quebec-petition-mapaq-response/.

7. Vegan Option Canada, "Petiton OVC QC Reponse Horacio Arruda," Vegan Option Canada, September 29, 2020, accessed March 19, 2021, https://veganoptioncanada.org/en/news/petiton-ovc-qc-reponse-horacio-arruda/.

8. Ryan Flanagan, "More Than 3 Million Canadians Vegetarian or Vegan: Study," CTV News, July 25, 2018, accessed March 19, 2021, https://www.ctvnews.ca/canada/more-than-3-million-canadians-vegetarian-or-vegan-study-1.4027606#:~:text=Vegetarians%20and%20vegans%20now%20account,from%20900%2C000%2015%20years%20ago.

9. Parliament of Canada, "Our Country, Our Parliament: An Introduction to How Canada's Parliament Works," Parliament of Canada, 2020, accessed March 19, 2021, https://lop.parl.ca/about/parliament/education/ourcountryourparliament/html_booklet/three-levels-government-e.html.

10. Elections Canada, "The Electoral System of Canada," Elections Canada. Elections Canada, May 12, 2020, accessed March 19, 2021, https://www.elections.ca/content.aspx?section=res&dir=ces&document=part1&lang=e.

11. Fair Vote Canada, "First-Past-the-Post Must Go," Fair Vote Canada, 2020, accessed March 19, 2021, https://www.fairvote.ca/first-past-the-post-must-go/.

12. Aaron Wherry, "Trudeau's Promise of Electoral Reform: From 'We Can Do Better' to Accusations of Betrayal," CBC news February 5, 2017, accessed March 19, 2021, https://www.cbc.ca/news/politics/wherry-trudeau-electoral-reform-promise-betrayal-1.3962386.

13. Iris Mostegel, "The Original Influencer," *History Today*, February 6, 2019, accessed March 19, 2021, https://www.historytoday.com/miscellanies/original-influencer.

14. Richard Gunderman, "The Manipulation of the American Mind: Edward Bernays and the Birth of Public Relations," *The Conversation*, July 9, 2015, accessed March 19, 2021, https://theconversation.com/the-manipulation-of-the-american-mind-edward-bernays-and-the-birth-of-public-relations-44393.

15. Rakhi Chakraborty, "Torches of Freedom: How the World's First PR Campaign Came to Be," YourStory.com, August 6, 2014, accessed March 19, 2021, https://yourstory.com/2014/08/torches-of-freedom.

16. Edward Bernays, "Propaganda (1928) by Edward Bernays," History Is a Weapon, 2020, http://www.historyisaweapon.com/defcon1/bernprop.html.

17. Bethany Allen-Ebrahimian, "64 Years Later, CIA Finally Releases Details of Iranian Coup," *Foreign Policy*, June 20, 2017, accessed March 19, 2021, https://foreignpolicy.com/2017/06/20/64-years-later-cia-finally-releases-details-of-iranian-coup-iran-tehran-oil/

18. Stuart Taylor, "The Big Snoop: Life, Liberty, and the Pursuit of Terrorists," The Brookings Institution, April 29, 2014, accessed March 19, 2021, http://csweb.brookings.edu/content/research/essays/2014/big-snoop.html.

19. United States. Congress. Senate. Select Committee to Study Governmental Operations with Respect to Intelligence Activities, "Final Report of the Select Committee to Study Governmental Operations with Respect to Intelligence Activities, United States Senate: Together with Additional, Supplemental, and Separate Views," January 1, 1976, accessed March 19, 2021, https://archive.org/details/finalreportofsel01unit.

20. Nina Totenberg, "Why the FISA Court Is Not What It Used to Be," NPR, June 18, 2013, accessed March 19, 2021, https://www.npr.org/2013/06/18/191715681/why-the-fisa-court-is-not-what-it-used-to-be.

21. Jeffrey Haas, *The Assassination of Fred Hampton: How the FBI and the Chicago Police Murdered a Black Panther* (Chicago, Illinois: Lawrence Hill Books, 2011).

22. Privacy International, "Five Eyes: Privacy International," Five Eyes Privacy International, 2020, accessed March 19, 2021, https://privacyinternational.org/learn/five-eyes.

23. Cris Shore, "Lenin and the Crisis of Communism: The View from Inside," *Government and Opposition* 26, no. 1 (1991): 86-100, accessed January 30, 2021. http://www.jstor.org/stable/44482557.

24. Marc Davis, "US Government Financial Bailouts," Investopedia January 29, 2021, accessed March 19, 2021, https://www.investopedia.com/articles/economics/08/government-financial-bailout.asp#bank-rescue-of-2008-or-the-great-recession.

25. Roula Khalaf, Heba Saleh, and Abeer Allam, "The Economics of the Arab Spring," *Financial Times*, October 9, 2011, accessed March 19, 2021, https://www.ft.com/content/9565ebac-f0d0-11e0-aec8-00144feab49a.

26. J.J. McCullough, "Canada's Repressive Political Parties," *The Washington Post*, April 1, 2019, accessed March 19, 2021, https://www.washingtonpost.com/news/global-opinions/wp/2018/08/29/canadas-repressive-political-parties/.

27. John Perkins, *Hoodwinked: An Economic Hit Man Reveals Why the Global Economy Imploded—and How to Fix It* (New York: Crown, 2011).

28. Evan Andrews, "Boss Tweed's Flight from Justice," History.com, December 3, 2015, accessed March 19, 2021, https://www.history.com/news/boss-tweeds-flight-from-justice.

29. Tania Branigan and Lily Kuo, "How Hong Kong Caught Fire: The Story of a Radical Uprising," *The Guardian*, June 9, 2020, accessed March 19, 2021, https://www.theguardian.com/world/2020/jun/09/how-hong-kong-caught-fire-radical-uprising-protest-china.

30. Martin Gilens and Benjamin I. Page, "Testing Theories of American Politics: Elites, Interest Groups, and Average Citizens," *Perspectives on Politics* 12, no. 3 (2014): 564–81. doi:10.1017/S1537592714001595.

31. Matthew Taylor, "The Evolution of Extinction Rebellion," *The Guardian*, August 4, 2020, accessed March 19, 2021, https://www.theguardian.com/environment/2020/aug/04/evolution-of-extinction-rebellion-climate-emergency-protest-coronavirus-pandemic.

32. See United Nations Body for Assessing the Science Related to Climate Change (IPCC): https://www.ipcc.ch/reports/.

33. Professor Jem Bendell, "The Study on Collapse They Thought You Should Not Read—Yet," July 26, 2018, accessed March 19, 2021, https://jembendell.com/2018/07/26/the-study-on-collapse-they-thought-you-should-not-read-yet/.

34. Michelle Nicholasen, "Why Nonviolent Resistance Beats Violent Force in Effecting Social, Political Change," *Harvard Gazette*, April 22, 2019, https://news.harvard.edu/gazette/story/2019/02/why-nonviolent-resistance-beats-violent-force-in-effecting-social-political-change/.

35. Erica Chenoweth and Maria J. Stephan, *Why Civil Resistance Works: The Strategic Logic of Nonviolent Conflict* (New York: Columbia University Press, 2012).

36. Irish Citizens' Assembly, "The Irish Citizens' Assembly Project," 2020, accessed March 19, 2020, http://www.citizenassembly.ie/.

37. For publications see: https://www.ynharari.com/about/#

38. Black Past, "(1857) Frederick Douglass, 'If There Is No Struggle, There Is No Progress'," *Black Past*, August 8, 2019, accessed March 19, 2021, https://www.blackpast.org/. https://www.blackpast.org/african-american-history/1857-frederick-douglass-if-there-no-struggle-there-no-progress/.

39. International Center on Nonviolent Conflict, "The Success of Nonviolent Civil Resistance," International Center on Nonviolent Conflict, August 31, 2020, accessed March 19, 2021, https://www.nonviolent-conflict.org/resource/success-nonviolent-civil-resistance/.

40. David Robson, "The '3.5% Rule': How a Small Minority Can Change the World," BBC Future, May 13, 2019, accessed March 19, 2021, https://www.bbc.com/future/article/20190513-it-only-takes-35-of-people-to-change-the-world.

41. See Sky history, https://www.history.co.uk/article/gandhis-salt-march-the-tax-protest-that-changed-indian-history.

42. Ayni Institute, "Movement Ecology," Ayni Institute, 2020, accessed March 19, 2021, https://ayni.institute/movementecology/.

43. Matthieu Ricard, "What to Do When I Have Been the Cause of Misery to Others?" Matthieu Ricard, May 25, 2011, https://www.matthieuricard.org/en/blog/posts/what-to-do-when-i-have-been-the-cause-of-misery-to-others.

11. REFERENCES

Allen-Ebrahimian, Bethany. "64 Years Later, CIA Finally Releases Details of Iranian Coup." *Foreign Policy*, June 20, 2017. Accessed March 19, 2021. https://foreignpolicy.com/2017/06/20/64-years-later-cia-finally-releases-details-of-iranian-coup-iran-tehran-oil/.

Andrews, Evan. "Boss Tweed's Flight from Justice." History.com, December 3, 2015. Accessed March 19, 2021. https://www.history.com/news/boss-tweeds-flight-from-justice.

Ayni Institute. "Movement Ecology." 2020. Accessed March 19, 2021. https://ayni.institute/movementecology/.

Bendell, Jem. "The Study on Collapse They Thought You Should Not Read—Yet." July 26, 2018. Accessed March 19, 2021. https://jembendell.com/2018/07/26/the-study-on-collapse-they-thought-you-should-not-read-yet/.

Bernays, Edward. "Propaganda (1928) by Edward Bernays." *History Is a Weapon*, 2020. Accessed March 19, 2021. http://www.historyisaweapon.com/defcon1/bernprop.html.

Black Past. "Frederick Douglass, 'If There Is No Struggle, There Is No Progress' (1857)." *Black Past*, August 8, 2019. Accessed March 19, 2021. https://www.blackpast.org/african-american-history/1857-frederick-douglass-if-there-no-struggle-there-no-progress/.

Branigan, Tania, and Kuo, Lily. "How Hong Kong Caught Fire: The Story of a Radical Uprising." *The Guardian*, June 9, 2020. Accessed March 19, 2021. https://www.theguardian.com/world/2020/jun/09/how-hong-kong-caught-fire-radical-uprising-protest-china.

Chakraborty, Rakhi. "Torches of Freedom: How the World's First PR Campaign Came to Be." YourStory.com, August 6, 2014. Accessed March 19, 2021. https://yourstory.com/2014/08/torches-of-freedom.

Chenoweth, Erica, and Stephan, Maria, J. *Why Civil Resistance Works: The Strategic Logic of Nonviolent Conflict* (New York, New York: Columbia University Press, 2012).

Davis, Marc. "US Government Financial Bailouts." Investopedia, January 29, 2021. Accessed March 19, 2021. https://www.investopedia.com/articles/economics/08/government-financial-bailout.asp#bank-rescue-of-2008-or-the-great-recession.

Elections Canada. "The Electoral System of Canada." May 12, 2020. Accessed March 19, 2021. https://www.elections.ca/content.aspx?section=res&dir=ces&document=part1&lang=e.

Fair Vote Canada. "First Past-the-Post Must Go." 2020. Accessed March 19, 2021. https://www.fairvote.ca/first-past-the-post-must-go/.

Flanagan, Ryan. "More Than 3 Million Canadians Vegetarian or Vegan: Study." CTV News, July 25, 2018. Accessed March 19, 2021. https://www.ctvnews.ca/canada/more-than-3-million-canadians-vegetarian-or-vegan-study-1.4027606#:~:text=Vegetarians%20and%20vegans%20now%20account,from%20900%2C000%2015%20years%20ago.

Gilens, Martin, and Page, Benjamin, I. "Testing Theories of American Politics: Elites, Interest Groups, and Average Citizens." *Perspectives on Politics* 12, no. 3 (2014): 564–81. doi:10.1017/S1537592714001595.

Gunderman, Richard. "The Manipulation of the American Mind: Edward Bernays and the Birth of Public Relations." *The Conversation*, July 9, 2015. Accessed March 19, 2021. https://theconversation.com/the-manipulation-of-the-american-mind-edward-bernays-and-the-birth-of-public-relations-44393.

Haas, Jeffrey. *The Assassination of Fred Hampton: How the FBI and the Chicago Police Murdered a Black Panther*" (Chicago, Illinois: Lawrence Hill Books, 2011).

International Center on Nonviolent Conflict. "The Success of Nonviolent Civil Resistance." International Center on Nonviolent Conflict, August 31, 2020. Accessed March 19, 2021. https://www.nonviolent-conflict.org/resource/success-nonviolent-civil-resistance/.

Irish Citizens' Assembly. "The Irish Citizens' Assembly Project." 2020, Accessed March 19, 2020. http://www.citizenassembly.ie/.

Khalaf, Roula, Saleh, Heba, and Allam, Abeer. "The Economics of the Arab Spring." *Financial Times*, October 9, 2011. Accessed March 19, 2021. https://www.ft.com/content/9565ebac-f0d0-11e0-aec8-00144feab49a.

McCullough, J.J. "Canada's Repressive Political Parties." *The Washington Post*, April 1, 2019. Accessed March 19, 2021. https://www.washingtonpost.com/news/global-opinions/wp/2018/08/29/canadas-repressive-political-parties/.

Mostegel, Iris. "The Original Influencer." *History Today*, February 6, 2019. Accessed March 19, 2021. https://www.historytoday.com/miscellanies/original-influencer.

Nagesh, Ashitha. "It Is Now Illegal Not to Offer Vegan Food at Prisons, Hospitals and Schools in Portugal." Metro.co.uk, March 10, 2017. Accessed March 19, 2021. https://metro.co.uk/2017/03/10/it-is-now-illegal-not-to-offer-vegan-food-at-prisons-hospitals-and-schools-in-portugal-6501872/.

Nicholasen, Michelle. "Why Nonviolent Resistance Beats Violent Force in Effecting Social, Political Change." *Harvard Gazette*, April 22, 2019. https://news.harvard.edu/gazette/story/2019/02/why-nonviolent-resistance-beats-violent-force-in-effecting-social-political-change/.

Parliament of Canada. "Our Country, Our Parliament: An Introduction to How Canada's Parliament Works." 2020. Accessed March 19, 2021. https://lop.parl.ca/about/parliament/education/ourcountryourparliament/html_booklet/three-levels-government-e.html.

Perkins, John. *Hoodwinked: An Economic Hit Man Reveals Why the Global Economy Imploded—and How to Fix It* (New York, New York: Crown, 2011).

Privacy International. "Five Eyes: Privacy International." 2020. Accessed March 19, 2021. https://privacyinternational.org/learn/five-eyes.

Ricard, Matthew. "What to Do When I Have Been the Cause of Misery to Others?" May 25, 2011. Accessed March 19, 2021. https://www.matthieuricard.org/en/blog/posts/what-to-do-when-i-have-been-the-cause-of-misery-to-others.

Robson, David. "The '3.5% Rule': How a Small Minority Can Change the World." BBC Future, May 13, 2019. Accessed March 19, 2021. https://www.bbc.com/future/article/20190513-it-only-takes-35-of-people-to-change-the-world.

Rowley, Jeanette. *Towards a Vegan Jurisprudence: The Need for a Reorientation of Human Rights* (New York: Lexington Book, 2020).

Shore, Cris. "Lenin and the Crisis of Communism: The View from Inside." *Government and Opposition* 26, no. 1 (1991): 86–100. Accessed January 30, 2021. http://www.jstor.org/stable/44482557.

SparkNotes. "The Myth of Sisyphus." Accessed March 19, 2021. https://www.sparknotes.com/philosophy/sisyphus/section11/.

Taylor, Matthew. "The Evolution of Extinction Rebellion." *The Guardian*, August 4, 2020. Accessed March 19, 2021. https://www.theguardian.com/environment/2020/aug/04/evolution-of-extinction-rebellion-climate-emergency-protest-coronavirus-pandemic.

Taylor, Stuart. "The Big Snoop: Life, Liberty, and the Pursuit of Terrorists." The Brookings Institution, April 29, 2014. Accessed March 19, 2021. http://csweb.brookings.edu/content/research/essays/2014/big-snoop.html.

Totenberg, Nina. "Why the FISA Court Is Not What It Used to Be." NPR, June 18, 2013. Accessed March 19, 2021. https://www.npr.org/2013/06/18/191715681/why-the-fisa-court-is-not-what-it-used-to-be.

United Nations Body for Assessing the Science Related to Climate Change (IPCC). https://www.ipcc.ch/reports/.

United States Senate. Select Committee to Study Governmental Operations with Respect to Intelligence Activities. "Final Report of the Select Committee to Study Governmental Operations with Respect to Intelligence Activities, United States Senate: Together with Additional, Supplemental, and Separate Views." January 1, 1976. Accessed March 19, 2021. https://archive.org/details/finalreportofsel01unit.

Vegan Option Canada. "Federal Petition." Vegan Option Canada, February 18, 2019. Accessed March 19, 2021.https://veganoptioncanada.org/en/federal-petition/.

Vegan Option Canada. "Petiton OVC QC Reponse Horacio Arruda." September 29, 2020. Accessed March 19, 2021. https://veganoptioncanada.org/en/news/petiton-ovc-qc-reponse-horacio-arruda/.

Vegan Option Canada. "Quebec Petition: MAPAQ Response." March 25, 2020. Accessed March 19, 2021. https://veganoptioncanada.org/en/news/quebec-petition-mapaq-response/.

Wherry, Aaron. "Trudeau's Promise of Electoral Reform: From 'We Can Do Better' to Accusations of Betrayal." CBC News, February 5, 2017. Accessed March 19, 2021. https://www.cbc.ca/news/politics/wherry-trudeau-electoral-reform-promise-betrayal-1.3962386.

Wills, Lauren. "Vegan Options Urged to Become Mandatory in Public Sector by Canadian Lobby Group." Livekindly, December 15, 2018. Accessed March 19, 2021. https://www.livekindly.co/lobby-group-vegan-option-canada/#:~:text=to%20Public%20Sector-,New%20Lobby%20Group%20'Vegan%20Option%20Canada'%20to%20Bring%20More%20Plant,Based%20Food%20to%20Public%20Sector&text=A%20group%20of%20Canadian%20citizens,mandatory%20in%20the%20public%20sector.

Yuval Noah Harari. Accessed 13-03-2021. https://www.ynharari.com/book/sapiens-2/.

About the Editors and Contributors

Nuno Alvim has a master's degree in law and criminology and is the board director of the Portuguese Vegetarian Association. He in known for actively lobbying and campaigning for the right to plant-based meals in public facilities. His petitioning work has resulted in the approval of ground-breaking legislation for the provision of strict vegetarian food in public canteens.

Edie Bowles is a solicitor specializing in animal protection law. She has advised many animal protection organizations and individuals on a wide range of issues, including all aspects of the Animal Welfare Act and regulations made under it, the Zoo Licensing Act, Animals (Scientific Procedures) Act and more. She is a trustee of The Humane League and a former trustee of the UK Centre for Animal Law, where she set up and managed the nationwide student group. She often speaks on animal protection issues and has done so in the UK Parliament, the French Senat and the East African Legislative Assembly.

Jordi Casamitjana is originally from Catalonia but has resided in the UK for several decades. He is a vegan zoologist specializing in animal behavior and has been involved in different aspects of animal protection for many years. In addition to undertaking scientific research, he has worked mostly as an undercover investigator, animal welfare consultant, and animal protection campaigner. Jordi's most notable work achievements have been his involvement with the first successful prosecutions under the Hunting Act 2004, the exposé of trail hunting as a false alibi for illegal hunters and his participation in the campaign that led to the ban of bullfighting in Catalonia. Jordi has been an ethical vegan for over 18 years and, in 2020, he became known for securing the legal protection of ethical vegans in Great Britain from discrimination in a landmark employment tribunal case that was discussed all over the world. Under the pen name J.C. Costa, Jordi has published the novel *The Demon's Trial,* in which he explores many of the dilemmas animal protectionists face. He is also the author of the book *Ethical Vegan: A Personal and Political Journey to Change the World,* published in 2020.

Jade Elliott-Archer is a specialist medical negligence lawyer working with national law firm Irwin Mitchell LLP. Jade acts exclusively for patients who have suffered significant injuries to investigate the standard of care they have received, provide answers as to how their injuries came about and ensure that they have access to therapies and equipment they need to improve their quality of life. Jade is passionate about ensuring that all patients, including vegans, have access to appropriate medical care. Jade is also committed to helping vegans ensure that their right to live a lifestyle in line with their ethical beliefs is supported, by considering both legal and practical avenues to address any barriers. Jade has a particular interest in the law as applicable to vegans in healthcare settings.

Sorin Ionescu is a co-founding member of Vegan Option Canada (VOC), a registered pan-Canadian non-profit organization and a citizen-based political activist organization with the mission to secure the right to access vegan options. He believes vegan rights are important because they support vegans and those who wish to adopt veganism. Sorin is also a founding member of Animal Rebellion Turtle Island, member of the Organisation for the Prevention of Intense Suffering (OPIS), ally of the Algosphere Alliance, and on the Organizing Committee of the newly formed Plant Based Transition Coalition, a collaborative nationwide effort that uses a combined theory of change to bring about a transition to a just and sustainable plant-based food system. The goal of this coalition is to organize food system reform by converging maximum human potential towards this objective. Sorin believes that compassion and rationality are important engines in the pursuit of alleviating suffering, and he strives to create bridges and partnerships between social change groups with diverse approaches. He believes better governance systems are essential to solving the complex problems of our modern society. Sorin holds a master's degree in software engineering from Concordia University in Montreal and has a background in artificial intelligence.

Adam P. Karp, a Martindale-Hubbell AV preeminent-rated and AVVO 10.0 superb-rated 'superlawyer' and fellow of the American Bar Foundation practices animal law throughout Washington, Oregon, and Idaho. Adam graduated from Gonzaga University (BA Honors) and University of Washington (JD and MS statistics) and has practiced law for twenty-three years. Adam founded the Washington and Idaho State Bar Associations' Animal Law

Sections, has been a vice chair of the American Bar Association's Animal Law Committee since 2004, and taught animal law at the universities of Washington and Seattle. Adam has been quoted in TIME, the National Law Journal, the ABA Journal, and other periodicals. He has published practice-based articles, multiple animal law related articles and treatises for Thomson Reuters's legal encyclopedias, and authored *Understanding Animal Law* (Carolina Academic Press, 2016). Adam received the Excellence in the Advancement of Animal Law Award (2012) and the SEEDS Award from the International Society for Animal Rights (2019). Adam has evaluated over 7500 animal law cases to date, and argued before various appellate courts, achieving decisions in animal law that many regard as seminal. Collectively vegan for nearly half a century, Adam and his wife are animal rights activists and volunteers in vegan outreach.

Camille Labchuk is an animal rights lawyer and executive director of Animal Justice—Canada's only animal law advocacy organization. Under her leadership, Animal Justice fights legal cases in courtrooms across the country, works to pass groundbreaking new laws, and ensures industries are held accountable for illegal animal cruelty. Camille has litigated to advance animals' legal interests at all levels of court, including before the Supreme Court of Canada. She regularly testifies before legislative committees and was instrumental in passing a precedent-setting national ban on whale and dolphin captivity in 2019. She has filed false advertising complaints against companies making misleading humane claims, documented Canada's commercial seal slaughter, and exposed hidden suffering behind the closed doors of farms and zoos through undercover exposés. Camille was previously a founding board member of Mercy for Animals Canada, press secretary to the leader of a federal Canadian political party, and is a former two-time candidate for Parliament. Camille is a frequent lecturer on animal law, co-host of the Paw & Order podcast, and a regular contributor to national publications like the *Globe and Mail* and the *Toronto Star*. She is a fellow at the Oxford Centre for Animal Ethics.

Marie Laffineur-Pauchet is a PhD candidate in public law on sustainable food at the University of Montpellier (France) for the research lab Institute of European Law of Human Rights (IDEDH), under the direction of Professor Claire Vial. She is an alumni of the master's degree in animal law and society (UAB) and of the Sorbonne University (law and philosophy degrees) and has been a legal trainee in EU Institutions (European Food Safety Authority, November 2019 to April 2021; European Commission, March to July 2019). Marie has written articles on French animal and food law and participated in conferences on plant-based food labeling and international wildlife protection. She was involved in the creation of the Prix de l'Animalisme Francophone, an award that symbolically acknowledges francophone initiatives that aim to provide long-term protection for non-human animals.

Ralf Müller-Amenitsch is a German lawyer and pioneer in vegan law. He published *Vegan im Recht* [Vegan Rights] (2016), co-authored the Austrian edition, and published the collection of international and German national court decisions on plant based food issues *Urteilssammlung Veggie-Food* (2020). Ralf co-founded the first International symposium on vegan law and represented Germany at the conferences of the International Vegan Rights Alliance (IVRA) held in Berlin, Milan and Glasgow. Ralf is a member of the Vegan Society's International Rights Network for Germany since its merger with the IVRA in 2019. Ralf represents PETA-Germany in conferences on vegan topics and edits its blog and podcast on vegan law. Since 2018 Ralf has lectured on vegan consumer law and animal rights at the University of Applied Science FHM. Since 2019 he is the expert member of the ISO committee for implementation of an international standard (ISO WD 23662) for vegan and vegetarian food products and is the vice chairman for the corresponding DIN Norm commitee (NA 057-08-03AA) for plant-based food. Ralf edits news articles on vegan law for *Vegconomist* and is currently drafting a legal opinion on ISO WD 23662, which is due for publication in 2021.

Matthew Overton has been a vegan since spring 2017 and is a University of Bristol Law graduate. He was awarded the British Council's Hong Kong 'Scholarship for Excellence' and studied animal law and human rights law at the University of Hong Kong. Matthew has a great interest in international human rights law and received a first-class grade for his final year dissertation which concerned the protection of vegan belief under British antidiscrimination law. He has presented at two international vegan law conferences: Glasgow, Scotland (2018), and Milan, Italy (2019). During his undergraduate years he was treasurer for the University of Bristol Animal law society and engaged in *pro bono* legal volunteer work as a member of the University of Bristol Law Clinic. Matthew currently works as an alternative dispute resolution (ADR) adjudicator in Bristol, United Kingdom.

Carlo Prisco is a lawyer and holds a PhD in philosophy of law. He is an assistant professor at the State University of Milan in philosophy of law and bioethics. Carlo is the creator and founder of the moral philosophy Eusebism and author of *Eusebism: Moral and Right.* He has also authored *The Duty of Vegetarianism* and *The Right to Vegetarianism,* published in Italy and the U.S. (Hamilton, 2016). He is also the Italian translator of *Animals as Persons* by Gary L. Francione.

Angela Radich holds a BA in applied ethics and a Bachelor of Laws, and she is a senior associate in the international dispute resolution team at a global law firm. She graduated with First Class Honors in law and was an associate to a Justice of the High Court of Australia. Angela has been vegan since 2003 and she was chair of the New South Wales (NSW) Young Lawyers Animal Law Committee (part of the NSW Law Society). In that role she organized and chaired Australia's first animal law conference and undertook numerous other projects. She later helped establish a pro bono animal law service at the NSW Public Interest Law Clearing House (PALS@PILCH), a legal referral service connecting animal protection advocates with pro bono lawyers. While at PALS@PILCH Angela also worked to identify and pursue opportunities for strategic litigation to promote animal interests. Angela is the author of the article "Appearing Amicus Curiae in Proceedings Involving Animal Interests" published in the *Australian Animal Protection Law Journal*.

Krystal-Anne Roussel recently graduated from the University of Ottawa, Faculty of Law, where she pursued her research interests in animal law, environmental law, and Indigenous laws and legal traditions. While completing her studies, Krystal-Anne was awarded the Newton Rowell Scholarship for academic excellence and interest in public service. Krystal-Anne also has an undergraduate degree in criminology and anthropology from St. Thomas University and a Certificate in humane education and advanced animal legal issues from Thompson Rivers University. Krystal-Anne worked as a summer student with Animal Justice in 2018 and East Coast Environmental Law in 2019. She is currently completing her articling placement at the Canadian Environmental Law Association. In law school, Krystal-Anne was founder and president of the Student Animal Justice Association and co-president of the Environmental Law Students' Association. She has written academically on vegan rights, enforcement of criminal animal cruelty laws, interspecies justice, and the environmental impacts of animal agriculture. Krystal-Anne also gave a presentation about vegan rights at the International Vegan Rights Alliance Conference alongside Animal Justice Executive Director Camille Labchuk in 2019. Krystal-Anne lives in Toronto, Ontario, with her two adopted cats—Simba and Bagheera.

Jeanette Rowley is known for explaining veganism as a qualifying belief within the scope of the human right to freedom of conscience. She founded the International Vegan Rights Alliance in 2012 to form a network of vegan legal professionals to protect vegans and advance veganism. The alliance merged with the Vegan Society in 2019, and Jeanette now works as an advisor to the society, where she also manages its 'vegan rights' service and continues to chair what is now the Vegan Society's International Rights Network. Jeanette has helped bring about important policy changes in the provision of goods and services, employment and education, and achieved out of court settlements for vegans in the UK who have suffered discrimination. Jeanette was awarded a Master of Laws with distinction and holds a PhD in human rights and veganism. She has published widely and presented globally since 2012 on how legal protection for those who do not wish to participate in the exploitation of other animals supports the animal rights cause. She is a fellow of the Higher Education Academy, member of the Vegan Society's Academic Research Committee and supports students with independent research projects on vegan legal issues.

Richard Twine, PhD, is a senior lecturer in social sciences and co-director of the Centre for Human-Animal Studies at Edge Hill University, UK. He is author of *Animals as Biotechnology—Ethics, Sustainability and Critical Animal Studies* (Routledge, 2010) and co-editor of *The Rise of Critical Animal Studies—From the Margins to the Centre* (Routledge, 2014). His website can be found at http://www.richardtwine.com.

Joe Wills is a lecturer in law at the University of Leicester, where he was awarded a PhD in 2013. He is a fellow of the Higher Education Academy with research interests primarily in human rights, animal rights and moral and political philosophy. Joe has published numerous articles in the field of animal and human rights in well-established and respected journals including in the *Global Journal of Animal Law* and has received numerous invitations to speak on human and animal rights issues at high profile human and animal rights conferences. Joe is a member of multiple professional bodies, including Economic and Social Rights Academic Network UK and Ireland, Global Animal Law, the International Expert Group in Animal Law and the UK Centre for Animal Law, Working Group on Animal Personhood.

www.ingramcontent.com/pod-product-compliance
Lightning Source LLC
LaVergne TN
LVHW091533200926
848483LV00002B/385